S0-EIT-264

Five Latin American Nations

A Comparative Political Study

Five Latin American Nations
A Comparative Political Study

PETER RANIS *York College, City University of New York*

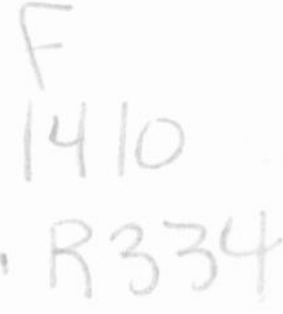

The Macmillan Company, New York · Collier-Macmillan Limited, London

Printed in the United States of America

The Macmillan Company
866 Third Avenue, New York, New York 10022

Collier-Macmillan Canada, Ltd., Toronto, Ontario

Library of Congress catalog card number: 70–123453

First Printing

To Gloria, Maria, and Paul

Preface

This book involves a study of political change in Latin America since independence with an examination of contemporary levels of political development, the role of political culture, political systems and political forces, and the social and economic obstacles to modernization. I have tried to be selective in the choice of political phenomena in order to emphasize the crucial patterns of events and acts of leadership that helped to shape institutions and nations. Historical development is analyzed in terms of those factors that have served to substantially influence and shape the contemporary political processes.

This study is comparative, involving five Latin American political systems (those of Mexico, Argentina, Chile, Brazil, and Peru) and focusing on several important factors: the application of the concepts of political development and modernity to the selected Latin American nations, the introduction of a party typology that can assist in the better understanding of Latin American political party systems, and an examination of political culture, social structures, and economic systems as they directly affect politics and the implementation of public policy in Latin America.

The book is intended for students concerned not only with Latin America but more generally interested in comparative politics and the problems of political maturation in developing countries.

In all, six years have transpired during the contemplation, planning, and writing of this book. I have incurred several debts along the way and would like to take this opportunity to thank those individuals and institutions involved. I am particularly grateful to my wife, Gloria, for her valuable editorial assistance and, above all, for her constant good humor and perspective during the preparation of the book.

I would also like to thank Professors Charles W. Anderson, Robert H. Dix, and Samuel P. Huntington for their very helpful comments and suggestions. Each of them read several chapters of the manuscript at varying stages of its development. I appreciate very much the generous assistance of Professor Paul Y. Hammond, whose exhaustive reading of the completed manuscript was of great assistance. In many ways the positive elements in this book have been much strengthened by these people while its weaknesses substantially minimized. It does not seem inappropriate to reiterate the often repeated caveat that these individuals are not responsible for the errors and misjudgments that undoubtedly remain.

Several institutional grants made it possible for me to spend parts of consecutive summers on the research and writing of this book. I thank the Social Science Research Council for a grant in the summer of 1966 while I was at the University of New Mexico, and the State University of New York for grants in the summers of 1967 and 1968 while I was at SUNY at Stony Brook.

P. R.

Contents

PART I

Introduction 1

CHAPTER 1 Modernity and Political Development in Latin America 3

PART II

Political Institutions in Preindependence Latin America 47

CHAPTER 2 Indigenous Period 49
CHAPTER 3 Colonial Period 56

PART III

Political Evolution in Postindependence Latin America 63

CHAPTER 4 The Authoritative Phase 67
CHAPTER 5 The Aggregative Phase 91
CHAPTER 6 The Distributive Phase 110

PART IV

Political Culture 149

CHAPTER 7 Latin American Political Culture 153
CHAPTER 8 Federalism, Legitimacy, and Political Culture 177
CHAPTER 9 Ideologies and Political Culture 202

PART V

Political Forces 223

CHAPTER 10 Executive Power and Administrative Dominance 225
CHAPTER 11 Political Parties 237
CHAPTER 12 Nonparty Political Groups 257

PART VI

Politics, Economics, and the Social System 279

CHAPTER 13 A General Statement on Modernization 281
CHAPTER 14 The Obstacles to Economic Development 286
CHAPTER 15 Politics and the Development Process 300
CHAPTER 16 The Dual Nature of Latin American Society: "Agraria" and "Industria" 304
CHAPTER 17 The Social System and Political Development 315

Index 325

PART I

Introduction

Modernity and political development are important concepts in helping to define the extent and nature of development in the emerging nations. In regard to Latin America, the two concepts or, in many cases, the two terms have been used interchangeably to describe the evolved level of political institutions, economic growth, and overall social well being. Sometimes there is discussion of a particular sector of society, and sometimes a macrosocial approach is applied. Modernity and political development have been employed both in static analyses of a particular nation at a particular point in time or as dynamic measures to categorize a nation's level of progress over a given time span.

In this chapter these methods of approach will be examined and applied to five of the most crucial and significant of the Latin American nations. An effort will be made to distinguish between the two concepts, demonstrating their contribution to analyses and then showing the interconnection between them.

Historically it appears that the association of political development with modernity has almost invariably been made, though there are significant autonomous features about each set of propositions. There is, however, a complementary relationship often cited between political development, with its emphasis on factors such as constitutional longevity, stability, and popular participation—electorally and otherwise—and modernity, with its emphasis on social and economic well being. That is, under normal circumstances, political stability will afford a society the social peace in which to progress industrially and commercially. At the same time rapid economic development and the greater distribution of social welfare gains should preserve a fairly consistent degree of political stability in government and assure a moderate amount of popularity for the governmental leaders.

The concepts are also used in a more dynamic causal relationship. For example, a high Gross National Product increase per annum for several years often has a salutary effect on fostering positive feelings of the people toward their government; high inflationary rates or many months of deep depression may lead to military interventions, mass protests, and, occasionally, revolutionary turmoil; responsive and/or strong governmental structures over long periods of time can explain much about subsequent economic growth in the latter stages of such political phases; and extreme forms of political instability marked with violence, civil unrest, and the loss of political legitimacy may often have a deleterious impact on society and, concomitantly, on the economy.

Using the complementary and causality factors in an historical perspective, it becomes essential in the analysis of modernity and political development to describe the stage of national development in which a particular nation finds itself. At certain periods, political development is an essential ingredient for allowing a continuation of the general modernization process. Political development may allow a society to consolidate recent economic gains and social-welfare achievements. For overall national progress such basic requirements as governmental continuity of a predictable variety, at least a minimum of identification between the government and most constituent groups, and built-in mechanisms for peaceful change are necessary.

Similarly, a given stage of political development may result, in one instance, in a slow process of modernity and, at another time, give rise to more rapid change. The variables that affect the velocity of change are many. Such factors as wars, inflation or depression, droughts and floods, corruption and mismanagement, and entrepreneurial breakthroughs may either help to retard or maximize the modernization process. Thus modernity levels are often a result of partly fortuitous circumstances as well as planned changes by national political-leadership groups. Despite the precision one would like to apply to the development process, there are many changes that, lacking a more comprehensive theoretical framework, still cannot be ascribed to self-conscious and predictable decision making.

CHAPTER 1 Modernity and Political Development in Latin America*

The term *modernity* has been used in many different ways. Most descriptions discuss high levels of consumption and production, general technological specialization, and cultural complexity.[1] The extent of modernity often indicates the pattern of resource allocation by given leadership groups. Modernity can be measured by such factors as doctors and dentists per thousand population, number of television sets, amounts of daily newspaper consumption, and the general availability of cultural and artistic resources.[2]

Industrialization, on the other hand, is usually determined, for example, by a nation's steel production, railroad cars per mile of track, and kilowatt hours of electricity generated. There is usually a direct relationship made between industrialization and modernity. Further, industrialization has been discussed as a particular variety of modernization.[3] Certainly there is a connection between the level of industrialization and the capacity to generate and provide for a comfortable and relatively secure social life. In some nations, however, there exists an unwillingness to do away with certain material and social benefits for the sake of rapid industrialization.

It does not necessarily follow, therefore, that every nation with a low level of industrialization need maintain correspondingly low indices of modernity. Nor is it invariably true that highly industrialized societies must have concentrated on proliferating social benefits and satisfying consumer desires.

* Sections of Chapter 1 were originally published as a monograph, *Modernity and Political Development in Five Latin American Countries* (Rutgers University, Studies in Comparative International Development, 1968–1969).

[1] For some examples of this type of description, see Daniel Lerner, *Passing of Traditional Society* (New York: Free Press, 1958); Max Millikan and Donald Blackmer, *The Emerging Nations* (Boston: Little, Brown, 1961); W. W. Rostow, *The Stages of Economic Growth* (Oxford: Cambridge, 1960); Robert Ward and Dankwart Rustow (eds.), *Political Modernization in Japan and Turkey* (Princeton: Princeton University Press, 1964).

[2] See S. M. Lipset, "Some Social Requisites of Democracy: Economic Development and Political Legitimacy," *American Political Science Review*, vol. 53, no. 1 (March 1959) and Karl Deutsch, "Social Mobilization and Political Development," *American Political Science Review*, vol. 55, no. 3 (September 1961). Both correlate modernity factors with rates of economic development and social mobilization.

[3] David Apter has discussed this problem in terms of relating industrialization to modernization in a descending order, modernization being a particular type of development. *The Politics of Modernization* (Chicago: University of Chicago Press, 1965), p. 67.

I do not contradict the general concept of modernity as a substantial and valid indication of the industrialization level. Rather an attempt will be made to distinguish between the process of modernization and the level of modernity. The processes of modernization involve profound socio-political and economic changes. Modernity levels are usually concerned with those criteria that make for a secure and comfortable society. A dichotomy exists between the many-faceted and broad process of achieving modernity and the more precise claims that can be made regarding a country's general standard of living, well being, and extent and breadth of cultural and technological opportunities, that we may call "civilizing paraphernalia."

In historical perspective modernization appears to be synonymous with general concepts of political, social, and economic development. Some have felt that the phenomena of political and social change are by-products of economical development, specifically of industrialization.[4] Agreement exists only that the terms modernization, political development, economic development, and industrialization have not been fully related to one another. The task remains, in any case, to define the concepts one employs.

Though it is difficult to isolate the concept of political development from general problems of societal change, isolating the concept is of special concern to political science.[5] Political development will be viewed in terms of its contemporary requirements as well as in terms of political evolution in the nineteenth and twentieth centuries.

We can isolate at least three components of political development. First, it appears a nation must set up a viable and self-sustaining government that can elicit support by persuasion or coercion or both and that has the loyalty of the people. A government must have the capacity to maintain a fair amount of social harmony and political stability. The orderly and predictable transfer of leadership is an indication of such durability of political institutions.[6] Perhaps the best word is "penetration," as used by Lucian Pye,

[4] A leading proponent of this view is Reinhard Bendix, *Nation-Building and Citizenship* (New York: John Wiley, 1964).

[5] One student of political development, Samuel Huntington, has suggested that political modernization (i.e., increasing rates of mobilization and participation) may undermine political development (i.e., political institutionalization). See his "Political Development and Political Decay," *World Politics*, vol. 17, no. 3 (April 1965), p. 386. Approaches to the concept of Political development are growing very numerous in the literature of political science. Robert Packenham notes the various conditions for political development that writers on the subject have suggested. "Approaches to the Study of Political Development," *World Politics*, vol. 17, no. 1 (October 1964), pp. 108–120. Lucian Pye in *Aspects of Political Development* (Boston: Little, Brown, 1966), has summarized ten different meanings given to political development in the literature of social science.

[6] Samuel Huntington makes this point as one of his measures adaptability of political institutions, one of four criteria (with complexity, autonomy, and coherence) of political development. Huntington, *World Politics*, pp. 386–430.

to describe the effectiveness of formal institutions in establishing rapport and communication with increasingly large groups of citizens over extended time spans.[7] The result may enhance confidence in the government's powers of survival against external and internal forces; therefore, a basic minimum *strength* in governing institutions is necessary.

Second, it appears a government must accept the responsibility for legislating on behalf of the poorly represented, the disenfranchised, and all parochial and subject individuals not yet integrated politically or mobilized economically. One must measure the willingness of governments to undertake socioeconomic, ameliorative programs and the success of their methods. Such public policymaking again requires a growing politicized citizenry and a growing interaction between the leaders and the led. *Compassion* then seems to be a second ingredient of political development.

Third, it appears the political community must see the government as a fair arbiter on issues of national survival and as a judicious mediator among competing (and usually organized) social groups. The interaction between the private and public sectors of society must be regularized, and the outer perimeter of the arena within which the process of political exchange takes place must be institutionalized. Thus a *just* government is equally important.

In summary, political development appears to require a stable, full-time, dutiful government which assumes an ever more responsible role within society and which, in turn, can expect increasing individual political participation, the free and unfettered organization of a multitude of interests, and properly channelled discontent and opposition.[8]

Since the process of modernization involves not only economic but social and political development as well, a different definition of modernity is needed. In this distinct sense we may view modernity, then, as the amount of civilizing paraphernalia that political leaders are capable of supplying or willing to provide the public, or, said in another way, a particular pattern of political allocation of both economic resources and societal values.

We may, in summary, say that a society is "modern" that has achieved a sufficiently advanced level of political, social, and economic development. Therefore, the combined processes of political, economic, and social development may be classified as the process of modernization.

[7] Lucian Pye, *Aspects of Political Development*, p. 64. Regarding this problem, Richard Fagen suggests that we need more study on the use, content, and effects of communication as indications of political development. *Political Communication* (Boston: Little, Brown, 1966), pp. 134–135.

[8] We accept the definition here of Douglas Chalmers who called development the ". . . capacity of top leadership to undertake and implement, through government, complex programs to stimulate social and economic change." "National-International Linkages: Latin American Polities" (Paper prepared for delivery at the 1966 Annual Meeting of American Political Science Association, New York City, September 6–10, 1966), p. 10.

Among the many criteria of a modern society, the more tangible ones can be quantified. The industrial capacity to produce these tangible components may be present, but whether or not they will be produced or distributed is related to political development levels.

The same extent to which we can classify a country as modern governs the extent to which we may assume that that country has achieved corresponding combined levels of political, social, and economic development. A country may be more politically or more economically developed at any given time, but the combined effect will show up in the modernity indices. Modernity indicates, therefore, a balanced level in the development process and depends upon the political management of the achieved societal economic advances.

Modernity

In the following pages we will attempt to compile various indices of modernity in general and some specific categories involving aspects of what we have defined as political development.[9] The overwhelming majority of these figures were collected for the period 1958 to 1968. Should there be any major aberration in these statistical sources they will be so identified in the following pages.

Modernity levels in Latin America have been compared with those of some other countries. The comparable United States figures have usually been included, and wherever possible we have included a list of five other nations with various historical, geographical, and cultural contexts: West Germany, Italy, Nigeria, India, and Japan. Whenever any of the five Latin American nations are not included, it is because the relevant statistics were not available.

Demography represents perhaps the prime element in comprehending the pattern of life and its manifestations in various countries. On a regional basis Latin America's population was far below Europe's and just a bit more than the entire population of the Soviet Union.

The five countries that interest us here—namely, Mexico, Peru, Brazil, Chile, and Argentina—make up roughly 70 per cent of the total population of Latin America, including the Western European possessions and former Caribbean colonies. Surprisingly as it may seem, though Latin American nations have generally a high birth rate, the density level of population is

[9] Many of these statistics have been compiled from the statistical surveys of Arthur S. Banks and Robert B. Textor, *A Cross-Polity Survey* (Cambridge: M.I.T. Press, 1963), Bruce M. Russett, et al., *World Handbook of Political and Social Indicators* (New Haven: Yale University Press, 1964), *Statistical Abstract of Latin America* (Los Angeles: U.C.L.A., 1969), *United Nations Demographic Yearbook* (New York, 1966 and 1969), and *United Nations Statistical Yearbook* (New York, 1965 and 1970).

TABLE 1-1

Regional Population in Millions	
Asia	1,946
Europe	455
Africa	336
Latin America	267
USSR	238
North America	222
Oceania	19

Source: United Nations Demographic Yearbook (1969), p. 83.

still low compared to other parts of the world. Though this does not take into consideration the resources the countries may tap in providing for their people, we can for the moment assume that the developing nations everywhere have similar difficulties in sustaining their populations without relying somewhat on the need to import foodstuffs.

TABLE 1-2

Ranking Among 133 Nations	*Country*	*Population (1961) in Millions*
2	India	442
4	United States	184
7	Japan	94
8	*Brazil*	73
9	West Germany	54
11	Italy	49
13	*Mexico*	36
14	Nigeria	36
25	*Argentina*	20
42	*Peru*	11
55	*Chile*	8

Source: Bruce M. Russett et al., *World Handbook of Political and Social Indicators*, pp. 18–20.

More recent figures for the Western Hemisphere give us a more contemporary population approximation (Table 1-3).

In terms of the more crucial problem of relative density of population, the Latin American countries are among the very least populated in the world.

It seems, then, that a great proportion of the areas within the confines of the five countries (and Latin America in general) are in many respects underpopulated and that the problem of economic-development retardation and

TABLE 1-3

Country Population (1968)	
United States	201 million
Brazil	88
Mexico	47
Argentina	24
Peru	13
Chile	9

Source: Statistical Abstract of Latin America (1969), p. 57 ff.

TABLE 1-4

Ranking Among 133 Nations	Country	Population per Sq. Kilometer (1961)
11	Japan	254
12	West Germany	217
17	Italy	164
22	India	138
56	Nigeria	39
73	United States	20
93	Chile	11
100	Brazil	9
105	Argentina	8
105	Peru	8

Source: Russett et al., *World Handbook of Political and Social Indicators,* pp. 138–144.

political pressures lies in an uneven distribution of the population rather than in its absolute number. With the development of family planning and the creation of industries in the hinterland, Latin America does not appear to face the more overburdening demographic handicaps among the nations of Africa and Asia. In the unit of measure of the United States we have a further breakdown on density.

TABLE 1-5

Country	Population per Sq. Mile (1967)
Mexico	60
United States	56
Chile	31
Brazil	26
Peru	25
Argentina	22
Latin America	33

Source: Statistical Abstract of Latin America (1969), p. 66.

This again demonstrates that not only is Latin America less densely populated than most parts of Africa, Asia, and Western Europe, but that its comparative position is substantially below the position of the United States.

However, in terms of population-growth indices Latin America proves to be the fastest growing geographical region in the world.

TABLE 1-6

Ranking Among 111 Nations	*Country*	*Population in Millions*	*% Rate of Population Increase (1961–65)*
11	*Brazil*	81	3.6
21	*Mexico*	41	3.1
46	*Chile*	9	2.4
54	India	472	2.2
65	*Peru*	12	2.0
69	Nigeria	56	1.9
77	*Argentina*	22	1.7
77	United States	195	1.7
86	West Germany	56	1.2
93	Japan	97	0.9
106	Italy	51	0.5

Source: Compiled from Russett et al., *World Handbook of Political and Social Indicators*, pp. 42–44.

Argentina stands out in this compilation as maintaining a population growth rate not too dissimilar to birth rates in the United States and Western Europe. Many factors contribute to this situation—among them such phenomena as the Argentina's age distribution, urbanization index, and certain civilizing paraphernalia that moderate large birth rates.

In going further into the urbanization phenomenon it is worth noting Argentina's urbanization advantage. It is then fairly evident that Argentina and Chile do not substantiate the view that the essential demographic character of all Latin America is rural. These percentages, of course, do

TABLE 1-7 Percentage of Population in Cities Over 100,000

Argentina	40%
Chile	30
United States	30
Mexico	21
Brazil	18
Peru	14

Source: Statistical Abstract of Latin America (1966), p. 13.

not tell another story important enough to relate. The urbanization character of many Latin American countries is grossly disproportioned to the extent that normally one major city (usually the capital) comprises the vast segment of those people considered urban. This can be documented by Table 1-8.

TABLE 1-8 Largest City as Percentage of Population (author's approximation)

	In Millions	Percentage
Buenos Aires, Argentina	8.0	33
Santiago, Chile	2.4	29
Mexico City, Mexico	5.0	14
Lima, Peru	2.0	13
Tokyo, Japan	11.0	11
New York, United States	11.5	6
São Paulo, Brazil	5.0	6
Rome, Italy	2.6	5
West Berlin, West Germany	2.1	4
Bombay, India	5.4	1
Lagos, Nigeria	.7	1

Source: Ibid., p. 24, and *United Nations Demographic Yearbook* (1969), pp. 164–189.

This obvious uneven distribution of population in Latin America has a generally harmful effect on industrial potential and economic efficiency. On the other hand it does not seriously matter, in terms of the civilizing paraphernalia of urban centers, whether the cities are over half a million or several million in population. It is still true that a certain modicum of physical, technological, and cultural benefits are more readily available in metropolitan areas than in rural locales. However, from both the political and economic viewpoint, it has been a handicap for any nation to have most of its skills, manpower, finances, and leadership centralized in one or two major metropolises.

To establish an even clearer dichotomy between an essentially urban and rural mode of living, we can assume that large metropolitan centers of 100,000 or more offer the most cultural, commercial, and educational advantages. However, many surveys take urban (with the usually implied facilities) to mean those towns that include 20,000 or more inhabitants. Here one deals with population centers that apparently have all the potentially rudimentary physical requirements of living with few of the cultural and technological amenities of big-city life. Here a slightly different population distribution results.

The move toward urban centers, as one would expect, continues unmiti-

TABLE 1-9 Percentage of Population in Towns Over 20,000

Ranking Among 120 Nations	*Country*	*Percentage*	*Year*
8	West Germany	55	1961
10	United States	52	1955
14	*Argentina*	48	1955
16	*Chile*	46	1959
17	Japan	43	1955
38	Italy	30	1955
42	*Brazil*	28	1960
47	*Mexico*	24	1950
72	*Peru*	14	1955
79	India	12	1951
83	Nigeria	11	1955

Source: Russett et al., *World Handbook of Political and Social Indicators,* pp. 49–53.

gated throughout the world at a consistent level. An incomplete example of which is shown in Table 1-10.

Latin Americans here again demonstrate a higher-than-average propensity toward conglomerating in urban environments. Though reasons for patterns of migrations remain in many instances unclear, in Latin America it has been found that the move toward cities is based on factors heavily influenced by the economic opportunities of the urban environment.[10] One of the more interesting findings that have come to light is the importance of female urbanization rates. The female is going to urban areas in growing numbers seeking work, and statistically she demonstrates a greater likelihood than the male of living there than in her former rural surroundings.

TABLE 1-10 Average Annual Increase of Percentage of Population in Cities Over 20,000

Ranking Among 50 Nations	*Country*	*Percentage*	*Year*
7	West Germany	.7	1945–60
9	Japan	.6	1920–50
11	*Mexico*	.6	1940–50
19	*Brazil*	.5	1920–60
35	Italy	.2	1936–51
37	India	.2	1921–51
39	United States	.2	1920–50

Source: Ibid.

[10] Documentation in Mexico points to a pressure of poverty as being the prime cause of a trend toward urbanization. Wilbert E. Moore, "Utilization of Human Resources Through Industrialization," in *Modernization Programs in Relation to Human Resources and Population Problems* (New York: Millbank Memorial Foundation, 1950), p. 58.

TABLE 1-11 Percentage of Each Sex Living in Urban Area

Country	*Male Urban Percentage*	*Female Urban Percentage*
United States	69	71
Argentina (1947)	60	65
Mexico	49	52
Peru	47	47

Source: Statistical Abstract of Latin America (1966), p. 14.

It is interesting that in countries with a rapidly increasing pattern of internal migration there is also substantial international immigration, both of which correspond to a fairly high level of development.[11]

TABLE 1-12 Immigrants per 1,000 Population

Ranking Among 41 Nations	*Country*	*Number*	*Years*
15	United States	1.68	1957–58
21	*Argentina*	.99	1958
23	*Brazil*	.84	1957–58
25	Italy	.55	1946–57
36	*Mexico*	.16	1957–58

Source: Russett et al., *World Handbook of Political and Social Indicators,* pp. 231–233.

Urbanization is one measure of modernity. Certainly on a comparative basis the five Latin American nations maintain fairly high urbanization indices, implying certain features, particularly in Chile and Argentina, that would appear to give them a good potential for political development. Among these advantages are an increase in social group interaction and a better access to political life.[12]

Interest groups tend to proliferate in an urban environment as do independent political associations. Generally the capacity to make a rational political choice is enhanced by an urban situation, though extreme societal discontent is at least as frequent there as in a rural setting. However, the agents of political organization, the party, neighborhood community project, labor unions, credit unions, and residential cooperatives, are more readily accessible.

[11] Bruce Russett et al., *World Handbook of Political and Social Indicators,* (1964), pp. 231–233.

[12] Certain statistical records state that 2,000 inhabitants is the cutoff point between urban and rural, in which case indices in this sample would be even more skewed toward urbanization. United States 70 per cent, Chile 67 per cent, Argentina 63 per cent, Mexico 51 per cent, Peru 47 per cent, and Brazil 45 per cent.

At the same time public authorities may better assess the requirements of urban groups because these groups are more articulate and can better penetrate the governmental bureaucracy by formal contracts or skillfully applied pressures.[13] An urbanized nation is usually more industrially developed and its bureaucracy more proficient, making it easier for an individual to rise in economic or social status. The urban centers provide the tools, the institutions, and often the stimulation by which a member of the community may pursue some form of self-improvement beneficial not only to himself but also to his society. Cities provide alternative choices. An individual grows to respect the government which provides him with opportunities for advancement. Without such respect, a consensual society would be difficult to achieve.

Urbanization, however, is by no means the prime factor in development; it is, rather, that historically, urbanization has marked the commercial and industrial revolutions, and it is the pattern of change to which sociologists attribute a substantial amount of inevitability. Nevertheless, some analyses may be made of the special importance and preponderance of the largest cities in Latin America. The major cities, like Mexico City, Lima, Buenos Aires, and somewhat later, Santiago, were the centers of colonial governmental and administrative organizations. With the fusion of religious and secular functions under Spain's colonial policy these same cities became the centers of religious life, which often led to their importance as educational and cultural centers.

With the advent of free trade and the beginnings of industrialization these already constructed cities took on the added task of providing the industrial basis for economic development, which required the centralizing of commercial and financial services within these cities. Since these countries had essentially monocultural export economies with limited entrepreneurial and capital resources, the concentration of available investment and skilled labor supply filtered to these centers, drying up development potential in other sections. This type of "multifunctional" city of Latin America can be compared to London or Paris.[14]

[13] In Daniel Goldrich et al., "The Political Integration of Lower Class Urban Settlements in Chile and Peru" (Paper prepared for delivery at the 1966 Annual Meeting of the American Political Science Association, New York City, September, 1966), pp. 17–21. Sample surveys were undertaken in the "Barriadas" of Lima, Peru, and the "Calampas" of Santiago, Chile. It was found that although politicization of new urban groups may be a discontinuous process, their integration and the channeling of their demands depends to a large extent on the competence and flexibility, by way of political penetration and resource allocations, of political parties and public bureaucracies.

[14] An interesting and evocative typology of cities has been treated in Bert F. Hoselitz, *Sociological Aspects of Economic Growth* (New York: Free Press, 1960), especially Ch. 7. Also see his "A History of the Long-Term Development of the City" in Glenn H. Beyer (ed.), *The Urban Explosion in Latin America* (Ithaca, N.Y.: Cornell University Press, 1967), pp. 18–33.

Buenos Aires, Santiago, and Lima still maintain their overriding demographic and economic predominance, though Mexico has made strides to spread at least its industrial base to Torreon, San Luis Potosí, and Monterrey. In Brazil, related to the less centralized Portuguese colonialism, commercial and industrial centers developed in São Paulo and Recife while Rio de Janeiro became the cultural and administrative center. The successful evolution of Brasilia as the new capital was a further attempt to remove the political and administrative apparatus to still another city. The urban functions in the United States have been largely distributed among several cities since the beginnings of the nineteenth century. Today Washington serves as the undisputed administrative and political capital, New York and other cities as commercial and financial centers, and Chicago, Detroit, and many others as important industrial hubs. The early United States settlement pattern between Virginia and Massachusetts can be compared to the type of agro-commercial coastal settlements of colonial Brazil that Richard Morse describes as "modest in size and appearance, generally haphazard or 'natural' in layout."[15] He contrasted these towns to the more thoroughly planned and precisely located Spanish-American communities near the sources of Indian labor.

These developments help to explain the special urbanization syndrome of Latin American nations. And since urbanization appears to be a more persistent process than rapid industrialization, we may expect to see very modern cities evolving in Latin America faster than the rates of industrialization would indicate. Again we return to the original premise that industrializing countries may purposely retard the rate at which modernity occurs or its civilizing paraphernalia become widely distributed. It is a system of priorities among public policy makers which in many respects distinguishes the political systems of developing and developed countries as diverse as China, the Philippines, USSR and the United States.

The following sections deal with the modernity indices of normal natality, mortality, and general health and nutrition levels. These figures represent comparable health standards, age expectancy, and benefits of modern medicine available to these Latin American countries, and they are invariably used by United Nations and other international agencies as significant means of assessing the facilities and conveniences available to the citizenry of individual nations. They give some indication of the general modernity level that has been reached and indicate the established priorities within different nations.

In the first category of infant mortality rates, the Latin American states compare unfavorably to the more economically developed countries (Table 1-13).

[15] Richard Morse, "Recent Research on Latin American Urbanization," in *Latin American Research Review*, vol. 1, no. 1 (Fall, 1965), p. 37.

TABLE 1-13 Number of Deaths of Infants Under 1 Year per 1,000 Live Births: 1964–68

Japan	15
United States	22
West Germany	23
Italy	33
Argentina	58
Peru	62
Mexico	63
Nigeria	68
Chile	100
India	139

Source: United Nations Demographic Yearbook (1969), pp. 366–374.

The much smaller general mortality rates follow essentially a similar pattern. This increases the pressures upon the Latin American societies in the process of modernization. Because of medical and other scientific advances, their death rates have declined considerably more than their birth rates. One of the results of early modernity is its uneven progression and the added burden it places upon economic development. It is essentially a price to be paid when geriatrics, as a branch of medicine, can be more easily applied at a certain level of societal change than can birth control with its widespread social and moral implications.[16]

TABLE 1-14 Number of Deaths per 1,000: 1964–68 (excludes fetal and infant deaths)

Japan	7
Peru	8
Argentina	9
United States	9
Mexico	9
Italy	10
Chile	10
West Germany	12
Brazil	12
India	13
Nigeria	14

Source: United Nations Demographic Yearbook (1969), pp. 375–385.

[16] Life expectancy at birth is steadily increasing in Latin America. Argentina —67 years, Mexico—66, Chile—58, Brazil—55, and Peru—54. See Sixth Annual Report of Inter-American Development Bank's Social Progress Trust Fund (Washington, D.C., 1967), p. 22.

The relative degree of progress made with basically curable diseases is illustrated in Tables 1-15 and 1-16.

The tables point out the lag among the five Latin American countries and India; the statistics for Nigeria and Brazil must be taken with reservations.

Tables 1-17 and 1-18 compare national criteria in the area of medical attention afforded the public.

TABLE 1-15

Country	*Tuberculosis of Respiratory System—Deaths per 100,000 (1962–67)*
United States	3
Italy	10
West Germany	11
Japan	17
Argentina	18
Nigeria	19 (Lagos only)
Mexico	18
Peru	28
Chile	36
India	61
Brazil	78 (State of Guanabara only)

Source: United Nations Demographic Yearbook (1969), pp. 416–427.

TABLE 1-16

Country	*Poliomyelitis—Deaths per 100,000 (1962–67)*
Japan	0.0
United States	0.0
West Germany	0.0
Chile	0.4
Italy	0.5
Mexico	0.5
Peru	0.7
India	0.9
Argentina	1.7

Source: Ibid.

Rudimentary domestic comfort in the Western Hemisphere countries is compared in Table 1-20.

Beyond the basic questions of where and how one lives, literacy rates represent the most valid means of measuring a population's capacity for fully participating in and benefiting from a modern environment. Literacy is, perhaps, the most important mobility ingredient because it is closely related

TABLE 1–17 Inhabitants per Physician (1958–61)

Ranking Among 126 Nations	Country	Inhabitants per Physician
4	Argentina	660
8	Italy	746
10	United States	780
12	West Germany	798
23	Japan	930
42	Chile	1,700
42	Mexico	1,700
47	Brazil	2,100
47	Peru	2,100
71	India	5,200
105	Nigeria	32,000

Source: Russett et al., *World Handbook of Political and Social Indicators* (1964), pp. 202–206.

TABLE 1-18 Inhabitants per Hospital Bed (1959–60)

Ranking Among 129 Nations	Country	Inhabitants per Hospital Bed
10	West Germany	100
15	United States	110
21	Italy	120
21	Japan	120
32	Argentina	160
53	Chile	260
57	Brazil	300
73	Peru	470
116	Mexico	1,900
117	Nigeria	2,100
119	India	2,200

Source: Ibid., pp. 207–210.

TABLE 1-19 Nutrition Consumption per Person

Country	Calories per Day	Grams of Protein per Day	Kilos of Meat per Annum
United States	3,110	91	97
Argentina	3,090	84	101
Brazil	2,860	68	27
Mexico	2,650	75	23
Peru	2,370	60	18

Source: Statistical Abstract of Latin America (1966), p. 42.

to a nation's technological achievements and cultural accomplishments and is often the result of the type and variety of its educational institutions. Literacy can be correlated with more modernization features than possibly any other single dimension.

TABLE 1-20

Country	Persons per Household	Persons per Room
United States	3.3	.7
Argentina	3.7	1.4
Peru	4.9	2.3
Brazil	5.1	1.3
Chile	5.4	1.7
Mexico	5.5	2.9

Source: *Statistical Abstract of Latin America* (1969), p. 131.

TABLE 1-21 Literacy in Population 15 Years and Over

Country	Per Cent
United States	98
Argentina	91
Chile	84
Mexico	62
Peru	61
Brazil	61

Source: *Statistical Abstract of Latin America* (1969), p. 108.

The generally very respectable literacy rates of Argentina and Chile are a result of a fairly good educational system, certainly one superior to that in the overwhelming majority of emerging nations. One important facet of high literacy is the system's ability to keep young people participating within the organized education for a minimum number of years.

The graduates of secondary schools are for the most part the bulwark of any society. They manage the middle-level positions of responsibilities from the civil service ranks to the vast majority of the white collar employees in private industry and commerce. Nevertheless a developing political system needs a minimum number of higher educated individuals from which society can draw its professional, scientific, administrative, and political leadership.

The remarkably high position of Argentina among nations points up its excellent human resource, putting it in a very special category equivalent to many nations far more economically developed. The inability of Argentina

TABLE 1-22 Primary and Secondary School Pupils as Per Cent of Population Aged 5–19 (1959–60)

Ranking Among 125 Nations	*Country*	*Percentage*
3	United States	81
10	Japan	73
10	West Germany	73
36	*Chile*	58
39	*Argentina*	57
55	Italy	50
64	*Mexico*	42
68	*Peru*	39
71	*Brazil*	38
89	India	29
94	Nigeria	25

Source: Russett et al., *World Handbook of Political and Social Indicators* (1964), pp. 217–220.

TABLE 1-23 Students Enrolled in Higher Education per 100,000 Population (1959–60)

Ranking Among 105 Nations	*Country*	*Number*
1	United States	1,983
7	*Argentina*	827
8	Japan	750
18	West Germany	528
32	Italy	362
44	*Mexico*	258
47	*Chile*	257
49	*Peru*	253
53	India	220
65	*Brazil*	132
102	Nigeria	4

Source: Russett et al., *World Handbook of Political and Social Indicators,* pp. 213–216.

to fully utilize and employ its educated class has resulted in a profound sense of frustration.[17] The university must accept its preparatory role and the

[17] This frustration is in many ways two-fold: firstly, the economic and social crises deteriorate the atmosphere for study at the universities in Argentina, and secondly, upon graduation, students either have not been prepared for assuming a technical or professional position or, if so prepared, cannot find adequate vocational absorption commensurate with their aspirations. One of the best studies made on this overall problem in Latin America is that of Robert C. Newton, "Students and the Political System of the University of Buenos Aires," *Journal of Inter-American Studies,* vol. 8, no. 4 (October 1966), pp. 633–656.

society must present opportunities for its newly educated citizenry if this acute problem is to be resolved.

In Argentina the July 1966 interventions by the Ongania military regime into the university system have accentuated the problem because it has undermined the independence of the universities and attempted to discredit leading scholars, teachers, and researchers. This heightened intellectual resentment to the new de facto government has resulted in a mass exodus and an inevitable "brain drain."[18]

Though Latin American educational standards are technically and physically inadequate and salaries and working conditions poor, the number of young people who continue to choose pedagogic careers at all levels continues to be impressive.

TABLE 1-24 Student-Teacher Ratios for Primary, Secondary, and Higher Education (1965–67)

Country	*Primary*	*Secondary*	*Higher*
United States	30	15	12
Argentina	20	7	16
Chile	—	—	3
Mexico	47	13	5
Brazil	28	16	5
Peru	38	14	30

Source: Statistical Abstract of Latin America (1969), p. 101 ff.

The very good ratio of teachers to students, particularly in the secondary and higher educational strata, can be misleading. The number of students who complete their secondary schooling is very small in all four countries, and indeed in all Latin America, with the exceptions of Argentina and Uruguay. Also, because salary scales are low, few university professors in Latin America can afford to teach or do research full time, and the majority of them hold down various other positions. Thus despite the promising student/teacher ratios, the reality is much more disturbing. University professors, because of the pressures of other responsibilities, have little time to thoroughly prepare themselves for classes or to do independent research.

[18] Frank N. Manitzas discusses the reactions of various distressed Argentine professors in *The New Republic* (November 19, 1966), pp. 12–15. The situation was particularly acute in the social sciences. For example, of the twenty-eight professors teaching and doing research in sociology at the University of Buenos Aires in June 1966, only four remained nine months later. Similar developments took place in other fields of social science. For a complete analysis of the contemporary state of the Argentine social sciences, see Juan F. Marsal et al., *El estado de las ciencias sociales en la Argentina* (Buenos Aires: Instituto Torcuato Di Tella, September 1969).

This weakens both the educators' commitments to higher education as a professional alternative and the eagerness of students to undertake and continue academic and professional studies.

Though the availability of higher educational institutions continues to expand in Latin America, the problems that confront the prospective university student remain.[19] Despite the fact that tuition at the national and state universities is nominal or non-existent other factors continue to discourage the potential student. An important consideration is the distance which the majority of students live from the university campuses and the student's inability to meet the added costs of transportation, food, and lodging.

The insulating qualities of rural life inhibit a fuller participation in a more modern environment. Physical encumbrances inhibit the rural student,

TABLE 1-25

Country	*Number of Universities*	*Millions of People per University* †*
United States	205	0.95
Chile	8	1.0
Peru	9	1.2
Argentina	15	1.4
Mexico	25	1.6
Brazil	27	3.0

Source: Author's compilation.
* Only those offering at least one doctorate program.
† Author's own approximation.

which affects educational opportunities, literacy, and a host of other civilizing paraphernalia of urbanization. Though the number of universities on the Latin American scene is rapidly increasing, there still is a need for locality diversification. Added to the urban-oriented university situation is the problem of the qualitative difference among universities. Again the major better equipped and better staffed universities are those state-run institutions of the capitals and other major cities. Regional and provincial universities have, until very recently, been sub par. Progressive strides are being made, however, to remedy deficiencies in several countries, particularly Mexico, Brazil, and Argentina.

There is a growing awareness of the connection between educational standards, that is the level of training in the arts and sciences, and the improvement of the society. This commitment to the improvement and expansion of education among the political leadership groups and educators is not always identified with the needs of an industrializing society.

[19] For a comprehensive report on the conditions of the universities of Latin America see the volume by Harold R. W. Benjamin, *Higher Education in the American Republics* (New York: McGraw-Hill, 1965).

Many very good private universities have been established with governmental sanction. Mexico's Ibero-American University and the University of the Americas have further added to the network of almost a score of state universities; the Pontifical Catholic Universities in Lima and Rio de Janeiro have been established; Brazil's national-state university system continues to grow at an astounding rate; and the Catholic communities of Chile and Argentina have also given higher education an imposing boost with the founding of good, and in some cases distinguished, private universities, such

TABLE 1-26 (Thousands) of Students Enrolled in Educational Institutions (1961)

Country	*Primary*	*Secondary*	*Technical*	*Teacher Training*	*Higher*
United States					
(total)	30,178*	(10,959)		—†	3,861
female	15,943	(5,446)		—	1,452
Argentina					
(total)	2,872	150	301	144	190
female	1,407	56	125	127	65
Japan					
(total)	11,811	8,741	1,302	—	757
female	5,783	4,321	507	—	156
W. Germany					
(total)	5,137	1,249	1,859	—	303
female	2,531	547	844	—	72
Italy					
(total)	4,494	1,767	504	118	206
female	2,172	730	131	104	59
Chile					
(total)	1,217	170	66	6	22
female	601	88	30	4	8
Mexico					
(total)	5,368	268	112	53	94
female	—	83	68	—	—
Peru					
(total)	1,392	141	37	—	27
female	—	—	—	—	5
India					
(total)	32,020	8,990	283	100	1,045
female	10,290	1,995	52	26	166
Brazil					
(total)	7,835	960	247	100	102
female	3,970	454	72	92	30
Nigeria					
(total)	2,806	167	6	28	3
female	1,063	40	.1	6	.2

Source: *Statistical Abstract of Latin America* (1966), p. 36ff.
* Includes pre-school children (nursery school, etc.)
† No statistics available for these categories

as the Federico Santa Maria University, Catholic University of Chile, and El Salvador University of Buenos Aires. In many of these instances, formerly rigid governmental attitudes toward religious sponsorship of higher education have been waived on behalf of multiplying professional training centers.

Despite these advances, educational training of the young continues to be strained at each level because of the lack of material resources and the absence of strong motivation toward earning an academic degree. The number of drop-outs at every level of the formal educational cycle is high.

The countries compared in Table 1-26 have been ranked in descending order according to an estimation of the numbers of students enrolled in higher education as a percentage of the total population in the *same* year. Later population figures might have unduly skewed the rankings in favor of nations with low to average birth rates. In all countries, with the exception of the United States, rarely more than 1 per cent of the total population was attending schools of higher education. Argentina again ranked exceptionally well in university attendance as compared to the more industrialized nations of Japan, West Germany, and Italy.

As noted earlier, the five Latin American nations have made sufficient progress in mobilizing the female in relation to urbanization and later it will be shown that the contribution of women to the economy is also rapidly increasing. At this juncture it is important to note their increasing participation in higher education. The reader is invited to make further calculations under such categories as teacher training and technical and secondary schooling, where female participation in many Latin American nations is truly impressive.

TABLE 1-27 Females as Percentages of Higher Education Enrollment (1967)

United States	40%
Chile	40
Argentina	40
Italy	38
Peru	34
Brazil	29
Japan	28
West Germany	27
Mexico	18
India	18
Nigeria	13

Source: Author's compilation based on figures reported in *United Nations Statistical Yearbook* (1970), pp. 716–740. Females often reach or surpass 50 per cent of student enrollment in such varied fields as languages, philosophy, architecture, medicine, and the social sciences.

In the communications media, the figures for the circulation of newspapers, the ownership of radio and television, and the general access to electronic and mechanical modes of mobility and information, indicate that the Latin American countries under study, with few exceptions, are not consistent with the generalities about the paucity of such technological advantages in the developing countries.[20]

TABLE 1–28 Daily Newspaper Circulation per 1,000 Population (1957–61)

Ranking Among 125 Nations	*Country*	*Number*
6	Japan	416
13	United States	326
14	West Germany	307
28	*Argentina*	155
32	*Chile*	134
40	Italy	101
47	*Mexico*	83
50	*Peru*	76
63	*Brazil*	54
91	India	11
97	Nigeria	8

Source: Russett et al., *World Handbook of Political and Social Indicators* (1964), pp. 107–110.

The figures in Table 1-28 indicate a substantial readership audience, profoundly different from that of India, Nigeria, or any of the lesser developed Afro-Asian nations. The type of audience in Latin America makes it much more accessible, manipulatable, and educable. There is a steady audiovisual link between the leaders and molders of public opinion and the community. More cautiously, it can also be added that the diversity of information received will make for more decisions that fall under the heading of universal-rational rather than particularist-traditional criteria.

The broad horizontal extensiveness of the Latin American family and the generally more familial environment further tends to increase the daily readership of newspapers beyond what the figures ostensibly establish. A

[20] John T. McNally, "Mass Communication and the Climate of Modernization in Latin America," *Journal of Inter-American Studies*, vol. 8, no. 3 (July 1966), describes the very high level of media use among professional, technical, and other urban groups in Latin America. Joseph A. Kahl writes of high mass-media involvement ("participation") as one pattern statistically related to other aspects of the modernity syndrome, such as activism, urbanism, and individualism. See his *The Measurement of Modernism: A Study of Values in Brazil and Mexico* (Austin: The University of Texas Press, 1968).

newspaper in Latin America will doubtlessly go through many hands before it ceases to be of informational use.[21] Even then its life is surely not ended. This is much more true than in the more autonomous and prescribed readership audience of, for example, the United States and West Germany. The position of Japan, of course, is noteworthy.

Radios are now quite common in Latin America and are more economically available to the working class sectors. Radios, more than newspapers, often provide the principal means of personal information-gathering, so it is quite common for the young adult to acquire a small transistor radio as one of his first major purchases after the more essential bicycle has been bought. Among rural familes, particularly, the radio plays a more important role than daily newspapers, and one may conjecture than an equal number of people are informed by radios as by newspapers.[22] In the hinterland, where newspapers are not normally delivered, radios have penetrated the physical barriers.

Tables 1-29 and 1-30 give an indication of the extent to which the post office and telephone services are employed.

Here again it appears that illiteracy and lack of formal education need not necessarily be impediments to communication. As with radios versus newspapers, telephones are of more immediate use than sending messages through the mail. Both means of communication are available at very reason-

TABLE 1-29 Radios per 1,000 Population (1959–1961)

Ranking Among 118 Nations	*Country*	*Number*
1	United States	948
6	West Germany	319
32	*Argentina*	175
33	Italy	170
37	*Chile*	130
40	Japan	107
43	*Mexico*	97
50	*Peru*	78
61	*Brazil*	64
103	India	5
107	Nigeria	4

Source: Russett et al., *World Handbook of Political and Social Indicators* (1964), pp. 118–122.

[21] It is also not unusual to see literally hundreds of people gathering before the business offices of a nation's leading newspaper reading the "free of charge" posted headline news and feature stories. Discussions and/or arguments frequently follow long into the evening.

[22] The Almond and Verba Study, *The Civic Culture* (Princeton: Princeton University Press, 1963), p. 94, cites Mexicans as informing themselves on public affairs mainly through newspapers, with radios a close second.

TABLE 1-30 Items of Domestic Mail per Capita (1960–1961)

Ranking Among 76 Nations	*Country*	*Number*
1	United States	350
10	West Germany	153
15	Italy	98
22	*Argentina*	65
23	*Brazil*	62
35	*Mexico*	19
42	*Chile*	13
47	India	8
61	Nigeria	3

Source: Ibid., pp. 111–113.

able costs to the consumer, as they are usually heavily subsidized and at least partly controlled by the government.

The movie and its visual impact is one of the most economical means by which great numbers of people may become familiar with different places and cultures. Since movie theaters in Latin America are, in many cases, partially subsidized by the governmental departments of either Tourism, Information, or Communications, ticket prices are usually maintained at a fairly reasonable level. Going to movies in urban areas is certainly a principal form of weekly entertainment.

TABLE 1–31 Persons per Telephone in 1962 (Author's Approximations)

Country	*Number*
United States	2
West Germany	8
Italy	11
Japan	13
Argentina	14
Chile	34
Mexico	57
Peru	75
Brazil	76
India	616
Nigeria	648

Source: Data calculated from figures presented in *United Nations Statistical Yearbook* (1965), pp. 488–491, and *United Nations Demographic Yearbook* (1966), pp. 120–131.

Producers of consumer goods, such as household furnishings, clothing, food and beverages, do a considerable amount of advertising on the theater screens between showings of the films. The disappearance of the short newsreel productions in United States movie theaters, related to growing TV coverage, has not occurred in Latin America. Government produced films are a very important means of political communication with the public. The emphasis is often on governmental projects, such as housing, health facilities, and public works, or on the daily routines and travels of the chief executive.

TABLE 1-32 Cinema Attendance per Capita (1960–62)

Ranking Among 104 Nations	*Country*	*Movies Attended per Year*
8	Italy	15
19	United States	12
21	*Mexico*	10
26	Japan	9
26	West Germany	9
35	*Argentina*	8
43	*Peru*	7
55	*Brazil*	5
60	*Chile*	4
61	India	4
102	Nigeria	.1

Source: Russett et al., *World Handbook of Political and Social Indicators,* pp. 128–131.

It is significant that those nations (e.g., Italy, United States, Mexico, and Japan) with high cinema attendance also have a plethora of domestic film makers, and all export their productions. Italian, United States, and Japanese films, of course, do very well before a world-wide audience. Mexican films are found mainly in Latin America, though they are also seen in parts of the United States.[23]

Television, by and large, still remains out of reach to most Latin Americans, though urban statistics should be taken separately to measure this media's recent influx into the major cities.

Another luxury item in Latin America is the automobile. It is approximately equivalent to an apartment in a cooperative dwelling or a modest home, and its purchase is usually limited to the middle and upper socio-economic groups. However, the North American method of time payment is becoming increasingly popular and is stimulating greater demand for

[23] Figures are available on the numbers of long films produced annually and theater locales among the sample of nations employed here. It indicates Mexico's prominence in the cinematic field vis-a-vis its leading Latin American competitors.

TABLE 1–33 Long Films Produced (1962)

Country	Number	Number of Theaters
Japan	652	6,742
India*	319	3,664
United States	254	21,106
Italy	242	10,571
West Germany	78	6,332
Mexico	56	2,005
Argentina	34	2,228
Brazil	28	3,232
Peru	—	399
Chile	—	336
Nigeria	—	67

Source: United Nations Statistical Yearbook (1965), pp. 727–728.

* It appears that India's film production is intended almost entirely for world consumption as a leading export commodity.

hitherto unattainable goods. The automobile, apart from its status connotations, is an important means of physical mobility, though general mass mobility in Latin America is still possible because of the relative abundance of cheap transportation. Though the average annual increase of passenger cars in Latin America far surpasses that of the United States or the world in general, the automobile still represents a rare commodity for the Latin American.[24]

The amount of communication that a society has with the outside

TABLE 1–34 Television Sets per 1,000 Population (1961)

Ranking Among 69 Nations	*Country*	*Number*
1	United States	306
7	West Germany	109
8	Japan	98
14	Italy	56
22	*Argentina*	34
27	*Mexico*	25
28	*Brazil*	22
38	*Peru*	8
63	*Chile*	.4
64	Nigeria	.2
69	India	.001

Source: Russett et al., *World Handbook of Political and Social Indicators* (1964), p. 118 ff.

[24] Example percentage increases in passenger cars between 1958–1964 are world (50 per cent), United States 26 per cent, Brazil 107 per cent, Argentina 86 per cent, Mexico 80 per cent, Peru 77 per cent, and Chile 65 per cent.

TABLE 1-35 Passenger Cars in Use per Capita* (1962)

Country	*Persons per Automobile*
United States	3
West Germany	9
Italy	16
Argentina	33
Mexico	66
Brazil	113
Peru	113
Japan	127
Chile	130
Nigeria	783
India	1,420

* Author's calculations based on absolute numbers of passenger cars.

world, in terms of visitors and foreign correspondence, gives some basis for assessing cultural modernity.

Naturally, contiguous countries supply most of the visitors to a given country. The only nations that appear to be able to provide visitors regardless of distance are the United States and England. This is a result not only of Anglo-American mobility and world-wide economic interests but also of the very favorable exchange rates available to spenders of dollars and pounds.

The principal external Latin American influence on Argentina and Chile is the United States, which has completely displaced the European powers. Spain dominated the scene in pre-independence days to be supplanted later by Franco-British cultural penetrations. Though the figures are not available in the *United Nations Statistical Yearbook*, it is quite apparent that the overwhelming percentage of tourists and visitors to Mexico are United States citizens (over 500,000 each year). Peru and Brazil also receive large quantities of United States visitors in addition to those from Latin America. The extent of United States cultural influence on these Latin American countries is not readily quantifiable, though there are such indicators as business practices, United States books translated, foreign economic assistance, size of United States embassy personnel permanently based in the larger cities, products available in department stores, and a general predisposition to mechanize in accordance with North American innovations.

The figures in Table 1-37 point to a cultural insularity in all parts of the world, particularly apparent in mainland Asia and Africa but including the Western Hemisphere. The relatively higher rates for West Germany and Italy are due partly to the growing success of the European Common Market and the continental commercial requirements of daily contact with six "foreign" nations which are near and accessible.

The confluence of civilizing paraphernalia tends to occur most often

TABLE 1-36 Visitors by Country of Origin to Sample Countries

Country	*Visitors*	*Leading Countries of Origin*	
Italy (1968)	28,800,000	5,576,000 from	West Germany
		4,457,000	France
		4,010,000	Switzerland
		2,600,000	Yugoslavia
		1,514,000	England
United States (1968)	10,711,000	8,500,000	Canada
		506,000	Mexico
		255,000	England
West Germany (1968)	6,557,000	1,082,000	United States
		953,000	Netherlands
		618,000	England
		608,000	France
Mexico (1968)	1,665,000	n.d.	
Japan (1968)	421,000	207,000	United States
		22,000	England
Argentina (1964)	231,000	40,000	Chile
(1968)	323,000	21,000	United States
		15,000	Brazil
		8,000	Spain
India (1968)	189,000	42,000	United States
		30,000	England
		10,000	West Germany
Brazil (1968)	134,000	34,000	United States
		28,000	Argentina
Chile (1964)	77,000	28,000	Argentina
(1968)		13,000	United States
Peru (1968)	114,000	46,000	United States
		9,000	Argentina
		9,000	Chile
Nigeria (1968)	23,000	6,000	England
		4,000	United States

Source: Figures gathered from *United States Statistical Yearbook* (1970) pp. 440–452.

in the larger urban centers of Latin America. It is in these developed cities and their satellites that the modernized one third of the population lives. Clustered in these administrative, industrial, and commercial hubs are institutional, social, and environmental facilities to prolong life, to succor the infirm, to educate the ignorant, and to inform the unaware.

Features of modernity in these countries are sufficiently evident that relatively moderate increases of productivity rates could sufficiently assure maintenance of these standards. A more basic obstacle to modernization is

TABLE 1-37 Items of Foreign Mail Sent per Capita* (1900–61)

Ranking Among 74 Nations	*Country*	*Number*
21	West Germany	8.1
27	Italy	6.3
32	*Mexico*	3.9
38	United States	2.9
41	*Argentina*	2.5
50	*Chile*	1.3
52	*Brazil*	1.3 (1957)
64	Nigeria	.5
68	India	.2

Source: Russett et al., *World Handbook of Political and Social Indicators* (1964), pp. 114–115.

* The incidence of foreign telegrams sent and received follows an almost duplicate pattern.

the more difficult political decision to distribute these civilizing paraphernalia more equitably throughout the society. Logically, a controlled, smooth transition to urbanization would tend to modernize Latin America incrementally. However, urbanization rates move along a haphazard and precipitous scale, stimulating their own momentum. The urban pressures to continue to keep pace almost rule out any solid commitment to comparable modernizing rates in the rural context.

These five nations, for example, all have an ultramodern sector of society. The question is how successfully their political leaders, be they civilians or military men, can transmit these goods and services to transitional areas of the country (smaller cities and towns) before the gap becomes sufficiently large to drain off sizeable numbers of professionals, technicians, businessmen, and students with their skills, know-how, capital, and initiative.

Political Development

Earlier we spoke of three criteria for contemporary political development in Latin America and suggested that, though political development is an integral part of modernity, it deserves special attention because of its crucial influence on the allocation of economic resources and societal values. We will examine the comparative state of political development in contemporary Latin America, and in the following chapters it will be treated within the context of an evolutionary historical process which has culminated in the type of governmental responses now being made.

One of the norms of a viable political process is the relative capacity of the national government to preserve its sovereignty against internal and external competitors, that is, to maintain political stability. Taking approximately four decades, or going back to 1930, which is a favorite demarcation year for distinguishing between recent Latin America and that of past periods, it is possible to make certain preliminary assessments of Latin American political stability.

Both Mexico and Chile have made notable strides in this direction. Mexico, with its predominant governing party, the PRI, has managed to sustain and fortify its governmental institutions. Since 1930, the predominant political leadership of Mexico has developed a farflung, coordinated party organization wedded to a reorganized governmental bureaucracy. Mexican stability was ensured through the monopoly of political power and bureaucratic control by a dominant party apparatus at a crucial period in the nation's development. The party was able to channel the aspirations and energies released by an extended revolutionary struggle.

Chile's success at political stability has quite another basis. Her political life has remained sufficiently open and competitive since 1931, giving her the opportunity to experience and digest several types of political orientations. Chile has been remarkably free of repression during this period of stability, which is based upon the fundamental values of political bargaining and open exchange.

Both nations have resolved in distinct ways the challenge of political transition and the need for civilian-oriented and authority-centered political executives. It is enough to say at this point that their profoundly distinct experiences demonstrate the variety of Latin American modes of struggling with the problems of political development.

Peru, Brazil, and Argentina, on the other hand, have had intermittent interruptions of their legal and governmental processes by incursions of institutional interest groups, such as the military or of personalist-inspired and often mass-supported populist movements.

Of the five Latin American nations one would find a high stability quotient in only two of five of the major Latin American powers, that is Mexico and Chile.[25]

[25] Ivo and Rosalind Feierabend have developed a statistical test to determine the cross-relationships between stability, permissiveness, and socioeconomic satisfaction on the one hand, and instability, coercion, and socioeconomic frustrations on the other hand. One could have reservations about the placement of various Latin American countries on certain stability-permissive-satisfaction indices (e.g., Mexico is classified as a moderately permissive political system—yet mid-level unstable; Chile is described as only slightly permissive—yet also as mid-level unstable; Argentina, along with Cuba, is called moderately coercive and unstable.) Despite this question of interpreting the same data differently, this is a major contribution to cross-polity investigation of the dynamics of political stability.

Stability profiles are yielded for 84 polities for the years 1948–1962. Very

TABLE 1-38

Country	*Unconstitutional Changes in Executive (1930–1970)*		*Duration of Unconstitutional Regimes*
Mexico	None	(0)	0 years
Chile	1931, 1932	(2)	1
Brazil	1930, 45, 54, 64	(4)	21*
Argentina	1930, 43, 55, 62, 66, 70	(6)	22*
Peru	1930, 31, 33, 48, 62, 68	(6)	20*

Source: Figures adapted from "U.S. Department of State Review of Illegal and Unscheduled Changes in Heads of State, 1930–1965," *Inter-American Economic Affairs,* vol. 19, no. 4 (Spring, 1966).

* Includes dictatorial regimes despite nominally free elections and imposed Constitutions.

The leadership in Mexico and Chile have managed, in most cases, to institutionalize the process of policymaking and to channel dissent and potential opposition to the government. Both societies have managed in the recent decades to undermine nonparty bases of power, known in Latin America as the extensive use of "personalismo." Mexico and Chile have both repeatedly awarded power to those political groups with relatively overlapping supports from various social strata and with commitments extending beyond the ambitions of a powerful few. The capacity to avoid the "cult of the personality" is not so much a result of the fact that individual charisma is absent in these two Latin American countries. To the contrary, the role of political personalities is quite striking in Latin American political change. However, certain factors, such as an apolitical military command, the political communication of a set of explicit value-orientations and the capacity to act pragmatically at crucial junctures, allowed Mexico and Chile to avoid demagogues and strongmen or "caudillos."[26]

---

relevant to the study of Latin America was the finding that low-levels of punishment do not serve as inhibitors of domestic instigation; only high levels of punishment are likely to result in anxiety and withdrawal. Punishment at mid-levels of intensity acts as a frustrating factor and stimulates further aggression, maintaining an aggression-punishment cycle.

Of further interest is the hypothesis that the highly permissive and highly coercive governments both tend to be stable if they provide high levels of socioeconomic satisfactions. On the other hand, the greatest tendency to political instability will result from a high level of socioeconomically caused frustration combined with mid-level amounts of governmental coercion. This, the authors state, pools two sources of systematic frustration: one socioeconomic, the other political. "The Relationship of Systemic Frustration, Political Coercion, International Tension and Political Instability" (Paper prepared by Ivo K. Feierabend and Rosalind L. Feierabend for delivery at the Annual Meeting of the American Psychological Association, New York City, September 2–6, 1966), pp. 1–22 and Tables 1–6.

[26] Defined by K. H. Silvert as a situation in which "party mechanisms, administrative procedures, and legislative functions are subject to the intimate and

TABLE 1-39 Public Educational Expenditures as Percent of Central Government Budget (1965)

Country	*Percentage*	*Dollars Expended per Student*
Peru	27	73
Mexico	24	39
Argentina	17	40
Chile	11	40
Brazil	7	15

Source: Socioeconomic Progress in Latin America, Social Progress Trust Fund Sixth Annual Report, 1966 (Washington, D.C.: Inter-American Development Bank, 1967), p. 39.

Related to governmental stability is the equally important political-development criteria of governmental responsibility. This concerns leadership legislation on behalf of a growing politicized community and the amelioration of social conditions. We have already covered the standard of living index of the five nations, including such quantifiable factors as health and nutrition, medical and living facilities, educational levels, and the availability and proliferation of communication media.

Particularly impressive in this are Argentina and Chile. Also in the last decade, Mexico and Peru have concerned themselves with the promulgation of health, social security, and educational measures. For example, they lead the other countries in annual public expenditures for education as a percentage of the Central Government Budget.

The five countries have made steady progress in the expansion of their available social services. In some, primarily in Argentina, there is a sufficient amount of coordination between private institutions, voluntary institutions, and various federal and provincial agencies. In addition, the community-development programs of Peru, "Cooperación Popular," and Chile, "Promoción Popular," were meant to acquaint people with the needs and requirements of social services. These projects according to the testimony of one expert, involved a reorganization and a restructuring of established government-to-people relationships, one based on increasing "grass roots" efforts.[27]

For this type of governmental policymaking, a more aware and active citizenry is required. One important measure of sensitivity to governmental concerns is the popular response to the electoral function. Through Argentina

immediate control of a charismatic leader and his cadre of mediating officials." "Leadership Formation and Modernization in Latin America," *Journal of International Affairs*, vol. 20, no. 2 (1966), p. 326.

[27] Virginia A. Paraiso, "Social Service in Latin America: Functions and Relationship to Development," *Economic Bulletin for Latin America,* vol. 11, no. 1 (April 1966), p. 92.

TABLE 1-40

Country	Voting Age	Literacy Requir.	Property Qual.	Female Vote	Military Suffrage	Suffrage Clerical	Year of Univ. Suf-frage**	Manda-tory Vote
Argentina	18*	No	No	Yes	No	Yes	1949	Yes
Brazil	18	Yes	No	Yes	Yes	Yes	1946	Yes
Chile	21	Yes	No	Yes	No	Yes	1949	Yes
Mexico	18* 21*	No	No	Yes	Yes	No	1958	Yes
Peru	18*	Yes	No	Yes	No	No	1955	Yes

* If the person is married, 21 if single.
** In essence, when females were granted suffrage rights.

and Chile both have relatively high indices of modernity as compared to the other three countries, for various reasons each shows a distinct response to the electoral process. Argentina has a low birth rate, which gives her a higher percentage in voting age brackets. In fact, with practically half her total population and over 80 per cent of her eligible population voting in the elections of 1963 and 1965, she claims among the highest voter turnouts in the world. However, in Argentina, voting is mandatory, as it also is in our other country samples. The voting mandate, however, is not uniformly enforced and severe penalties rare. A comparison of the five countries as shown in Table 1-40 indicates a general consistency in suffrage requirements.

Several observations must be made here. Argentina's waiver of the literacy requirement has no great effect on voters turnout because of the high literacy rate and compulsory voting. In Mexico, however, the absence of literacy restrictions enables several million essentially illiterates to vote. This allows for citizen building at an unusually parochial level. Governmental and political party officials reiterate policy objectives and bring leadership images to geographical areas that might otherwise be insulated from political exposure. Such political penetration into rural pockets of poverty and ignorance is no doubt an important factor in the shaping of the Mexican political culture.

Literacy requirements in Brazil and Peru have been consciously employed to disenfranchise large portions of the indigent Negro and Indian majorities and, of course, these requirements have been instrumental in shrinking the voting electorate. Because of the literacy requirement, most of the voters in Chile are from the Central Valley and those major urban sectors between Santiago, Valparaiso, and Concepción.[28]

[28] From figures presented by Charles J. Parrish, Arpad J. von Lazar, and Jorge Tapia Videla in *The Chilean Congressional Election of March 7, 1965* (Washington, D.C.: Institute for Comparative Study of Political Systems, 1967),

Complete suffrage for women has resulted in the growth in recent years of female politicians in Latin America, and her political behavior is the subject of much speculation and interest. The 1964 presidential and 1965 legislative elections in Chile made clear the power of women to affect the content of political campaigning and the outcome of competitive elections.[29] It has not yet been determined, however, whether women perform an essentially redundant political function, going along with their husbands, brothers, or fathers, or whether they present an autonomous political pattern.

It is interesting that in several instances throughout Latin America, women received their right to vote during the rule of dicators. This was the case in Argentina under Perón in 1949 and in Peru under Odría in 1955.

Mandatory voting is employed in all the sample countries. However, punishment for nonvoting of those registered and eligible is not equitably or universally imposed. Any punitive measures would largely affect those wishing to travel abroad and in need of documents, those who wish to enter a state-run university, and, in general, those most likely to vote anyway. In this context, Mexico with no literacy requirements but a compulsory vote system is attempting to increase political participation from even the most parochial elements. This indicates a high degree of self-confidence among the leadership in the stability of the Mexican political system and its capacity to absorb increasing numbers of nonparticipant peoples into areas of, at least, nominal involvement.

Presidential as well as legislative elections are compared which very much affect the percentages. For example, the figures for the United States, Peru, and Brazil are the result of presidential contests, whereas those of Chile, Mexico, and Argentina involve only the national legislatures.

Of course, where literacy rates are low and literacy remains a voting requirement, electoral participation, as in Brazil and Peru, will be on the low side. In the case of Argentina and Chile, voter participation has increased tremendously during the recent elections of 1963, 1964, and 1965—again an indication of the importance of literacy as a modernity factor related to levels of political development.

In 1970 over two-thirds of the voting-age population participated in the presidential election in Mexico. This, among other factors, seems to indicate a relatively high degree of popular mobilization at least at regular intervals. Peru and Brazil, on the other hand, are still relatively parochial and nonparticipant.

Voter participation, however, is not a direct indicator of active political

p. 34, it is possible to compute that the provinces of Santiago, Valparaiso, and Concepcion account for 57 per cent of the total vote.

[29] Ibid., pp. 36–37. For example, in the Chilean congressional elections of 1965, 45,000 more women than men voted for the Christian Democrats. On the other hand, the Communist Party received 60,000 less votes from the women than from the men and the Socialist Party 48,000 less votes.

TABLE 1-41 Votes in National Elections as Percent of Voting Age Population

Ranking Among 100 Nations	*Country*	*Percentage*	*Year*
10	Italy	93	1963
22	West Germany	87	1961
42	Japan	71	1960
48	United States	64	1960
50	*Argentina*	62	1960
59	India	53	1962
70	*Peru*	39	1963
71	*Chile*	37	1961
73	*Mexico*	35	1961
74	*Brazil*	34	1960

Source: Russett et al., *World Handbook of Political and Social Indicators* (1964), pp. 82–86.

TABLE 1-42 Presidential Election Votes as Percent of Total Population

Country	*Vote*	*Percent of Total Population*	*Year*
Argentina	9,300,000	43	1963
United States	72,100,000	36	1968
Chile	2,900,000	32	1970
Mexico	14,000,000	30	1970
Brazil	12,600,000	18	1960
Peru	2,000,000	18	1963

Source: Percentages calculated from figures presented in *Statistical Abstract of Latin America,* 1969, Federico Gil and James Parrish, *The Chilean Presidential Election of September 4, 1964,* p. 45, and James Rowe, *The Argentine Election of 1963,* p. 5 (Washington, D.C.: Institute for the Comparative Study of Political Systems) and *Latin American Digest* (vol. 5, no. 1, October, 1970).

involvement or even of continuing political interest. It is an index of the general level of nominal participation that a particular society has achieved. In any case, effective political socialization by means of voting can be best undertaken in a literate society, though literacy rates as such are no ultimate test of the speed at which groups are being mobilized into active public life.

The military establishment and labor unions also perform substantial functions of popular mobilization. The various branches of the armed forces give their personnel the opportunity to improve their literacy, technical skills, and level of political cognizance.

A further breakdown of these figures surveyed in the Russett volume of political and social indicators details the armed services as a percentage of the national population.

Labor unions, perhaps even more, bring the citizens into integrated

TABLE 1-43 Total Armed Forces Personnel

Country	*Number*
United States	2,375,000
Brazil	203,000
Argentina	128,000
Mexico	67,000
Chile	61,000
Peru	52,000

Source: Statistical Abstract of Latin America (1969), p. 138.

TABLE 1-44 Military Personnel as Percent of Population

Ranking Among 88 Nations	*Country*	*Percentage*	*Year*
17	United States	1.4	1959
23	*Mexico*	1.0	1955
31	Italy	.9	1961
41	*Chile*	.6	1959
43	West Germany	.6	1961
45	*Argentina*	.5	1959
57	*Brazil*	.4	1959
66	Japan	.3	1959
76	*Peru*	.1	1956
82	India	.1	1955

Source: Russett et al., *World Handbook of Political and Social Indicators* (1964), pp. 74–75.

social and syndical activities which teach the arts of organization, cooperation, and collective bargaining. There are also the obligations of membership, repeated pecuniary contributions for extra-personal goals, and constant commitment to social and political programs and issues.[30]

Peasant organizations also perform a politicizing function, particularly in Mexico where approximately 750,000 small farmers belong to the peasant sector of the governing PRI (Partido Revolucionario Institucional) party. In Brazil, perhaps no more than 100,000 peasants have been organized into peasant leagues of the type popularized by Francisco Julião. In Peru there are a few peasant organizations, but the overwhelming majority of the rural people have not managed to organize for any tangible group goals. The absence of permanent associations is true as well for the agricultural workers of Chile and Argentina, neither of which has shared in the general level of modernity of their countries and both of which have lacked political-party sponsorship on a continuing basis.

[30] Interest in broader societal issues which don't directly affect the individual concerned has been described as requiring feelings of "empathy," an important characteristic of modernization. Daniel Lerner, *The Passing of Traditional Society* (New York: Free Press, 1958).

TABLE 1-45 Organized Union Membership

Country	*Membership*	*Approximate % of Population*
Argentina	2,600,000	12%
United States	18,000,000	9
Mexico	2,250,000	6
Chile	500,000	6
Peru	550,000	3
Brazil	2,500,000	3

Source: Statistical Abstract of Latin America, (1966), p. 52.

Political parties, though usually limited in membership, perform a continuous role in the process of political integration. Mass parties of the Mexican type are still not very common in most of Latin America. Permanent membership lists are rare, and parties, though they are continuous mobilizers of the population, tend to be more active during crucial electoral periods. Aside from the PRI, the Peronista party in Argentina, with its permanent political and financial support from the largest labor unions, was also a mobilizing party, as are the Aprista and Acción Popular of Peru and the Christian Democratic and Frente de Acción Popular parties of Chile. All these parties are very active in winning wholesale endorsements of organized labor sectors. However, with the exception of the PRI, all must continue to activate (and are now doing so) other societal associations if they hope to continue to aggregate political sectors. Most of the other parties do not care to have, or do not yet have, large organizations of participating citizens. Some parties remain personal vehicles of a selected few who would rather see their party small and cohesive rather than large and loosely conceived, even if it should mean less chance to win power. However, these many small parties, with their marginal influence on a limited electorate, do serve a similar politicizing function as do other organizations interested in the political scene, like professional groups, business, landowners, and student groups.

All these groups, including political parties of whatever size, contribute to the "citizenship" training of members of society. They prepare the individual professionally, occupationally, technically, and socially for participating more fully in organized community life.

Political development, in addition to institutional stability and public and associated participation, requires a government that is capable of channeling discontent and opposition and also of broadening the opportunities for its people within a genuinely open and increasingly complex and interdependent environment. This is often a question of keeping the lines of communication open and allowing unfiltered information to be continually registered. It is helpful if development among the various regions is fairly equitable. The unevenness of development and the neglect of the Northeast have, for example, had substantial influence on Brazilian political development.[31]

An equitable promulgation of the law in rural as well as urban areas is also a means of stimulating a positive response from the populace. Political development is dependent often on the responsivenes and flexibility of the public administrators and upon their effectiveness in acceding to reasonable demands. This leads to, perhaps, a more basic problem of making sure there is a "proper mix" of public and private responsibility, activity, initiative, and a mutually satisfactory balance of overlapping national roles.

The relationship of a government to certain important institutions and groups give some indication of its relative openness. Political parties have been disbanded, for example, in Brazil, Peru and Argentina. In Brazil, governmentally conceived and sponsored party groupings have been allowed to organize. In Mexico, minor parties do exist. However, the Communist Party has not been granted the right to compete in elections on the grounds of insufficient membership, and a platform adherence to a foreign ideology and to a foreign country, the USSR, though the party's organizational existence is legal and recognized.

Only in Chile does the Communist Party flourish as a recognizable and forceful political entity. Along with certain Western European nations, Chile accepts the Communist Party as one of several parties within the political process. A recent comparative compilation notes the pattern shown in Table 1-46.

In terms of an independent legislative branch or an effective legislature, one would again have to single out the Chilean Congress, which performs a more important policymaking function than in the sister republics. The

TABLE 1-46 Votes for Communist Party as Percent of Total Vote

Ranking Among 44 Nations	*Country*	*Percentage*	*Year*
10	Italy	24	1963
15	*Chile*	12	1961
16	India	10	1962
26	*Brazil*	3	1958
26	Japan	3	1960
30	West Germany	2	1953
32	*Peru*	2	1962
40	United States	0	1952

Source: Russett et al., *World Handbook of Political and Social Indicators* (1964), pp. 89–90.

[31] For a highly stimulating analysis of this problem see Glaucio Ary Dillon Soares, "The Political Sociology of Uneven Development in Brazil," in I. L. Horowitz, *Revolution in Brazil* (New York: E. P. Dutton, 1964), pp. 164–195.

legislatures, as will be discussed in Part IV, do not usually initiate legislation. At best, they are partially effective in performing some of the subsidiary functions of lawmaking bodies. Striking examples of Chilean legislative independence occurred in January, 1967 when the Senate, controlled by opposition parties, voted 23 to 15 to prohibit President Frei's departure for an official visit to the United States. The refusal was based on a seldom used article 43 of the Chilean Constitution. Again in January, 1968, the Senate forced the withdrawal of a government-sponsored, 5 per cent anti-inflationary, forced-savings measure pegged directly to a 20 per cent wage increase.

Further, Banks and Textor have placed Chile in the company of two West European nations in regard to anomic behavior among interest groups.[32] Polities where interest articulation by anomic groups is frequent or occasional (64 nations) include India, *Brazil, Mexico, Peru,* Japan, and Nigeria.[33] Polities where interest articulation by anomic groups is infrequent or very infrequent (35 nations) are *Chile,* West Germany, and Italy. It may be cautiously observed that in Chile it is generally less necessary for interest groups, whether organized or not, to take direct means of forcing or preventing action by the government.

Banks and Textor further note the very significant articulation by institutional interest groups (e.g. military, church, bureaucrats) in Argentina and Brazil and their less active role in, among others, the United States, Chile, Peru, and Mexico. Peru's interest-group structure is, however, enfeebled by a generally weak articulation capability on the part of associational interests from the society-at-large. This might be the result, however, of a generally disinterested or politically uninitiated society rather than a symbolic capacity to satisfy private group demands.

The following countries are grouped according to independence of the press. Polities where freedom of the press is complete are West Germany, Japan, India, United States, *Chile,* Italy, and *Mexico.*[34] Polities where freedom of the press is intermittent, internally absent, or internally and externally absent are *Argentina, Brazil, Peru,* and Nigeria.

Certainly the events of recent years show this to be the case in Argentina and Brazil. Military controlled governments have thoroughly throttled the press both by insinuation and crackdown. In both countries several publications of importance have been banned. In Argentina, for example, newspapers and magazines are prevented from publishing accounts that may injure or

[32] Defined by Gabriel Almond and Bingham Powell as "The more or less spontaneous penetrations into the political system from the society, such as riots, demonstrations, assassinations, and the like." *Comparative Politics: A Developmental Approach* (Boston: Little, Brown, 1966), pp. 75–76.

[33] Arthur S. Banks and Robert B. Textor, A *Cross-Polity Survey* (Cambridge: MIT Press, 1963), Sec. 36, print-out p. 125.

[34] *Ibid.,* Sec. 13, print-out p. 50.

offend the heads of the government—admittedly a very broad basis for future prosecution. Restrictions of the press are even more comprehensive in Brazil. Under a new constitution, promulgated in March, 1967, there are stiff punishments for making any "damaging" statements that could undermine either the political stability or the economic and financial solvency of the nation. Furthermore, the military regimes of Generals Castelo Branco and Costa y Silva made extensive use of decree powers to suspend the political rights of numerous opposition-newspaper editors and reporters.

The press in Peru has been sufficiently developed to present a broad spectrum in regard to the news. Between 1956 and 1969 the major three newspapers, *La Prensa, El Comercio,* and *La Tribuna,* have constantly been at odds with each other but free from any continuous governmental restrictions. In fact, they tended to be highly partisan and eloquent on behalf of the groups which support them.[35] Under the military government of General Juan Velasco Alvarado the situation of the press has become much more precarious. Late in 1969 the government seized the offices and printing plants of two lesser known newspapers, *Expreso* and *Extra,* and turned the newspapers' management over to its unionized employees.

Mexico's press "appears" to be free, though Mexican newspapers have shown an abnormally high sense of respect for the country's institutions. Mexico's major newspapers, *El Excelsior, El Universal,* and *Las Novedades,* all avoid overt criticisms of the government. However, objections to the government are found in such weeklies as *Siempre.*

The right to basic human dignity and freedom of assembly and speech is most apparent in Chile, though this has also been, despite the temporary effects of military control, traditional in Argentina and Brazil. Mexico has had several decades of relative individual freedom, though the system has not been as severely tested as have the other four countries in the last thirty years. Among the five countries, Peru's status in regard to private rights has been the most tenuous of all in this century.

None of these major Latin American powers fits the patent definition of a totalitarian or a police state, though there is an appreciable increase of mass unrest and violence. However, civil unrest and violence have been much less frequent in Latin America than one would be led to suppose in reading the daily newspaper headlines. Organized group violence has occurred mainly in the Caribbean and Venezuela in the last several decades. In terms of group violence per capita Latin America certainly cannot be singled out from the rest of the developing world as being particularly prone toward nonpeaceful resolution of societal problems.

Tolerance of diversity appears to be a basic cultural ingredient in the Latin American political framework, and the continual formation of auton-

[35] See James Payne, *Labor and Politics in Peru* (New Haven: Yale University Press, 1965), p. 7.

omous economic and political groupings gives adequate testimony, despite the persistence of a stratified, closed structural arrangement, of essentially polyarchically disposed social systems. This will be referred to more extensively within the concept of political culture in Parts IV and VI.

Modernity and political development is difficult to assess with any degree of certainty. We have compared the five countries using simple single dimensions. We have not attempted to devise any multiple dimensions nor aggregate the unidimensional findings in order to arrive at some general measure of modernity and political development.[36] Rather, in summary, a rough attempt has been made to briefly discuss these five nations in terms of some of their modernity and political-development factors.

Based on our criteria for political development, Chile has come furthest. She has a visible and self-sustaining government which elicits a moderate degree of responsiveness and which oversees a relatively integrated society. Chile is a free society in most respects, its government is stable, and succession is orderly and predictable. Political bargaining is legitimate, and opposition parties and interests are recognized and sanctioned. Chile's governments have been responsive to public pressures and ostensibly dedicated to ending poverty, ill health, and lack of education. The society is fairly well racially mestizized.

Legal protection is given to publications, meetings, strikes, and general political activity, and the governments seem to be responsive to world culture, open to change, and willing to engage in self-criticism. Public debate is articulate and differentiated. In general, Chile seems to be approaching a pluralistic political community.

Mexico, although a less open society, ranks very close to Chile. Mexico has accomplished the yeoman's task of stabilizing her political institutions and maintaining the preeminence of her governing organs. Political leadership is effective, skilled, and motivated in areas of economic and political development. Mexico's governing elite is confidently and rapidly mobilizing and integrating the public. In the utilization of human and physical resources, Mexico has done more than Chile and has developed well despite the handicap of an uneducated, illiterate, peasant-based society.

However, we have placed Mexico behind Chile because Mexico is not as complex, pluralistic, or politically sophisticated as Chile. Mexico has had to rely on a sometimes repressive one-party government with no real alternative political philosophies. However, Mexico has tailormade her institutions to fit her needs profitably.

[36] One attempt has been made to compare nations on a continuum relating their political development potential (free elections, independent legislature, existence of political parties) vis-à-vis their communications level. Philips Cutright, "National Political Development," in Nelson Polsby et al., *Politics and Social Life* (Boston: Houghton Mifflin, 1963), pp. 569–581.

Using our political-development criteria, after Chile and Mexico would come Peru, Argentina, and Brazil. Peru as well as Argentina and Brazil maintains a military coalition in power. Her military is once again taking a predominant leadership role in society. Peru, however, is lacking in areas of social and political participation and in governmental penetration into and political communication with its vast hinterland.

Argentina, despite very high modernity indices, still flounders in political instability fostered by dissident social sectors, resulting in a dominant military establishment. Given better minority representation, viable political competition, and the willingness to compromise, Argentina at present has the socioeconomic wherewithal to quickly become the most politically developed nation in Latin America. Here is an example par excellence of "arrested development." Certain political aberrations exist, largely related to the residue of Perón-inspired revenge politics which continues to set one sector of Argentine society against another.

Brazil has no mass party that can mobilize sufficient sectors of society into a workable political mandate. Current military politics has disrupted institutional and constitutional patterns and will, regardless of the level of economic sophistication achieved by the governing juntas, most probably result in a stultification if not a regression of Brazilian attempts to attain political development.

In the last analysis, it is necessary to come to grips with the more complex and integral concept of modernity as it is manifested in the contemporary environment of these five nations. It is important to remind oneself that despite her political instability and lack of cohesion since 1930, Argentina remains the most modern nation among the major nations of Latin America.

Though Argentina has failed to resolve many of her political problems, her earlier political evolution has resulted in a sufficiently complex society. She is thus in line to becoming the preeminent country in Latin America. Argentine leadership in the century and a half since independence has created an advantaged society that, weighing all the factors, ranks very high among the nations of the world.

Chile ranks close with Argentina in many ways. Her political performance is superior, but her level of modernity does not match that of Argentina. Again the answer lies in the historical modernization process of these nations and the experiences that each underwent. In this longer view of national development one may be better able to find the answer.

Mexico is probably the most modern among the remaining three, followed by Brazil and then Peru. These modernity comparisons, of course, do not take into account the progress that each society has made in relation to its own natural and human resources but rather they are based upon those variants that make a modern state and distinguish nations like the United States and Sweden from the Soviet Union and Egypt. Thus, Argentina, politically arrested, is still sufficiently modern.

Historically, political leadership gives its people more or less a certain minimum civilizing paraphernalia which has been partly in the form of some sort of democratizing goals and/or procedures along with the more measurable socio-economic well-being. In this overall national task Argentina appears to have achieved the most by the year 1970 followed by Chile, Mexico, Brazil, and Peru.

What can be assessed is the combined political and socioeconomic achievements that a particular nation has reached over several generations. Modernity and political development historically attain a composite level. This is the modernization process. The blending of these two phenomena—modernity and political development—at a relatively high modernization level may be the result of two factors: (1) The absence of overburdensome and severe demands upon society, the value system and political competition for the sake of achieving higher or distant levels of development at some later date and (2) The unwillingness of the public to sacrifice and comply with the hardships and rigors of a socioeconomic policy, purposefully predicated on benefiting future generations.[37]

It is true, for example, that at times the continuing drive of a nation toward increasing modernity is purposefully inhibited because public policy-makers are called upon by either external, internal, or a combination of both factors to undertake political suppression and economic austerity measures. These measures may have salubrious short-run benefits, but over the long-run period in which development takes place, imposed demands and restrictions usually result in diminishing returns for sound political development. The contention here is that an increase of political and economic freedom with a large measure of interclass mobility will help to strengthen and integrate the political system.

Thus political development and modernity, though closely interrelated, are not synonymous. It is very important to distinguish between them in the Latin America context because they are really different aspects of the very complicated process of change. Political development involves the various approaches taken by political leaders, planners, technicians, and bureaucrats as they perceive and weigh alternative policies and the subsequent repercussions on society. Modernity is concerned with the pattern of acceptance, trust, and cognitions within a society which determines its needs, aspirations, and demands. It appears that neither political development nor modernity changes can occur long in a vacuum or without an eventual alteration in the other. Political development by nature, requires the optimization of authority, control, and legitimacy, whereas modernity pulls in a countervailing direction

[37] Touching on a similar vein, Martin Needler sees economic development as stimulating trends toward greater constitutional stability or higher political participation. The direction depends upon the degree of egalitarianism in the social structure. Martin C. Needler, *Political Development in Latin America: Instability, Violence, and Evolutionary Change* (New York: Random House, 1968), Ch. 4.

toward societal initiative, distribution of political and economic resources and the enhancement of individual prerogatives.

Inattention to either of these social forces for long periods of time will undoubtedly damage the overall construction of an organized political community and its continual pacific renewal. Political development is usually the result of past policies that have been successfully implemented. The skillful use of human and material resources over the years can lead to the advancement, educationally and technically, of the citizenry who, in turn, participate more, consume more, and learn more about the quality and dimensions of the good life.

PART II

Political Institutions in Preindependence Latin America

The preindependence era in the southern part of the Americas can be divided into two fairly logical political periods: the preconquest years have been termed the *indigenous period* and the settlement phase of the conquest the *colonial period*.

The indigenous period was characterized by Spanish political and cultural dominance over the native Indian societies. The Iberian conquerors could not, however, completely erase Indian influences on art, literature, agriculture, social stratification, and land ownership. That part of the Indian cultural heritage that did not disintegrate wove itself indelibly into the fabric of succeeding generations.

The colonial period very much influenced republican developments in the nineteenth and twentieth centuries. The deliberate and artificial nature of Spanish colonial policy thoroughly retarded Latin American economic development. Allowing all initiative to the crown's agents or, more often, to Madrid itself made innovation slow and progress labored. The amount of communication and correspondence before a decision was made was usually mountainous. Spanish-American bureaucracies even at this early date of social organization were already quite formidable. The formal and legal processes smothered the efficacy of decision making. The Spanish penchant for the immediate regularizing and systematizing of still experimental methods of trade and government often changed something tentative into something permanent. This resulted in a rigid framework which was less difficult to totter than to reform.[1]

[1] There is, however, much evidence suggesting that, despite a certain formalism, generous amounts of leeway existed in compliance with the law. See Frank J. Moreno, "The Spanish Colonial System: A Functional Approach," *The Western Political Quarterly*, vol. 20, no. 2, part 1 (June 1967), pp. 308–320.

CHAPTER 2 Indigenous Period

A variety of economic, political, and religious motives lay behind the Spanish movement to the West at the close of the fifteenth century and in the beginning of the sixteenth century. Fundamentally, the Iberian Peninsula did not offer the physical and material abundance to satisfy various elements of Spanish society. The soil was poor and the land had been devastated as a result of years of conquest and counterconquest. The conquest of the Americas offered an important outlet to portions of the military class and to those portions of the middle and gentry classes that did not have substantial investments in incipient industry and holdings of fertile land. Many of the leaders of the initial explorations and later conquests were entrepreneurial types and outright adventurers seeking to better themselves under the guise of settling new lands for the Pope and for Spain. It was widely rumored that the American continent offered this hope and challenge. This inquisitive spirit resembled the mood of the Renaissance, when Spain, France, and several Italian states were busily competing for trade routes and new lands to exploit.

In 1492, the last of the Moorish invaders were driven out of their stronghold; the Christian world had defeated the Moslems at Granada and had expelled them from the European continent. The military victory over the Moors left the Spanish with no outlet for their martial energy. For many Spanish soldiers it was necessary to find a new occupational outlet. The consolidation of Spain under Ferdinand and Isabella offered a new national impetus. Rampant nationalistic forces were let loose as Spain became more conscious of her strength and less concerned with domestic unrest.

Complementing the triumph over the "infidels" of the East, Catholic leaders initiated the Spanish Inquisition to purge Spain not only of Moslems but also of Jews and heretical Christian sects. With their zeal bestirred by triumph, the Spanish nobility turned toward newer horizons in the West. Thus the Spaniards turned to the new continent not only as an outlet for their materialistic and nationalistic ambitions but also as a means of perpetuating the faith that was threatened on the Continent by a new and dynamic reform movement that had the Papacy as its principal target.

What perhaps distinguished the Spaniards from other Europeans was the Spanish overriding quest for riches. Gold was not shunned by any country, but Holland and England, for example, moderated its quest by a search for other raw materials, by attention to the technical fields, and by a healthy respect for establishing shipping routes. It was Spain's obsession with gold which led to the eventual stagnation of the Spanish mercantile position.

The desire for wealth by the Spanish nobility went hand in hand with the Church's designs to gain new converts to the cross. The Spaniards forced upon the primitive cultures the Spanish conceptions of morality, society, and economic organization. The audacity with which they disseminated their cultural imperialism completely disintegrated and demoralized the Indians of the West Indies and, to a lesser extent, those of Mexico and Peru. The Spaniards lacked the social awareness of later French colonists and the skill for economic planning of their British counterparts.

Much of the Spanish failure to institute a calm and deliberate colonial policy was due to the character of the men engaged in the conquest of America. For the most part they were adventurers and the unemployed, many escaping one thing or another in Spain, and generally not representative of the finest flower of Spanish gentility. The great distance between Spain and the new colonies made it difficult to institute and maintain any semblance of discipline over these rapacious and raucous seekers of fortune.[1]

The exploration of America was an experience in the annals of conquest for which there was no precedent. Anarchy and a lack of discipline characterized the first years of the conquest. Room for personal judgment on the part of the early conquerors was immense. When the conquerors collided with one another or with the law, there was almost always violence or political rupture.

The first administrative and legal problem that the conquerors encountered was the position of the American Indians. A minority element among the clergy, led by Las Casas in the West Indies, opposed wholesale victimization and enslavement of the Indians, but the conquerors, being used to a fairly free reign over their expeditions, were distraught over what they considered a mere unimportant legality.[2] Subsequently in 1512, the Laws of Burgos were promulgated, giving Indians their freedom on the basis of their amenability to Christianity and self-government. The Indians, their cultural and social structure upended, failed to become politically sophisticated and morally "enlightened" overnight. Conveniently it was found that few Indians could achieve a civilization independently of the white man. Inquiries by the Crown were directed, of course, only to the white men who had something to lose by independent status for the Indians of the West Indies. Experiments were carried out in Cuba in order to determine the Indians' capacity for self-management. However, the balance was weighted so heavily against the Indians that there could be only one conclusion.

[1] See Charles Gibson, *Spain in America* (New York: Harper and Row, 1966), especially Ch. 3.

[2] Donald Worcester and Wendell Schaeffer, *The Growth and Culture of Latin America* (New York: Oxford University Press, 1956), pp. 31–34; Lewis Hanke, "Spanish Struggle for Justice in the Conquest of America," *Hispanic American Historical Review,* vol. 44, no. 3 (August 1964), pp. 293–340.

There is anthropological evidence that the civilization of these Indians of the West Indies was less developed than that of the mainland Indians to the west. All the native American societies had agriculturally based communities and, despite complete independence from one another due to miles of rough and uninhabited terrain, were comparable socially, politically, and theologically. Let us examine these cultures on the eve of the Spanish invasion of the Americas.

The Maya civilization of the Yucatan Peninsula had achieved a considerable proficiency in the abstract intellectual fields of astronomy, mathematics, and calendrics. The Aztecs were recording history through pictographs and the architectural displays which are evident in Tenochtitlan (Mexico City). The Inca Indians were the most advanced in the skills of building roads and bridges and were achieving amazing proficiency as military scientists.[3]

The Aztec lands were divided into three principal parts: one of which was set aside for the support of the government, one for the support of religion, and the remainder was reserved for the support of the people. As among the Aztecs, the Inca lands were cultivated wholly by the populace. Their duties were fully prescribed, and initial obligations required the cultivation of lands belonging to the Inca, the infirm, and the military before they could return to their own plots. In both these large Indian kingdoms the land was the chief source of wealth, social control, and political division. Among the Incas, food was the basic form of tribute, since its accumulation underlay the financing of all production and activities. The Mayas in similar fashion had obligations to pay tribute to the halac uinic (local administrator), to present the local lords with gifts, and to continually make offerings to the gods through the priests. The Mayan lands, too, were held as community property and were tilled in common.

However, the most salient and observable feature of all three of the Indian societies was the hierarchical despotism which pervaded their political realms. It was similar economically and managerially to the hydraulic despotisms of the East.[4] The hiatus between the masses and the ruling nobility was huge: For one there were only obligations; for the others only rights.

The most unmitigated and efficient despotism was that of the Incas of Peru. Inca society can be described as a perfect social pyramid. The Inca sat at the zenith of his official hierarchy. Below him were the four apocuna who

[3] See such illuminating studies as: V. W. Van Hagen, *The Ancient Sun Kingdoms of the Americas* (Cleveland: World, 1961); George C. Vaillant, *The Aztecs of Mexico* (Baltimore: Penguin Books, 1956); Manuel Moreno, *La organizacion politica y social de los Aztecos* (Mexico, 1931); John Eric Thompson, *The Rise and Fall of Maya Civilization* (Norman: University of Oklahoma Press, 1954); John Alden Mason, *The Ancient Civilizations of Peru* (Baltimore: Penguin Books, 1957).

[4] Karl H. Wittfogel, *Oriental Despotism* (New Haven: Yale University Press, 1957), pp. 246–250, 258–260.

managed the four quarters of the empire, and below them were the T'oqrikog who each ruled 40,000 families. As one descends the structural ladder, there are an increasing number of officials governing smaller and smaller segments of the Peruvian population. There were rulers of 10,000 families, of 1,000 families, of 100 families, and of 10 families. All owed allegiance to the person directly above them. Thus it was the perfect bureaucracy with authority filtering down and information, tribute, sacrifice, and subservience reaching upward. As Sally Falk Moore has said: the concern of the Inca society was not with the limitations of the power of government, but rather with the limitation of that of the individual. The fear was of insubordination rather than despotism.[5]

Though Inca society was despotic, the government mixed the employment of the carrot and the stick. It gave, in return for the passive obedience and tribute of the people, security, peace, plenty, and justice, as the Inca determined it. It was a paternalistic society that no monarchy in seventeenth century Europe could match in thoroughness and complete control. Though he was the be-all and end-all of Inca society, the ruler needed the strength and loyalty of the Inca nobility, who were usually his blood relations. They served as the upper aristocracy into which no one could move except by birth. They were distinguished from the rest of the Peruvians by dress, insignia, and language as well as origin. One always knew an Inca.

The Maya Indians seem to have been divided into four general hierarchical classes: the nobility, the priesthood, the common people, and the slaves. As among the Incas, power was hereditary and exclusively reserved for a limited class. The nobility served as local magistrates and executives who administered the affairs of the towns and villages. During periods of wars and other crises they all served under the one leader. In and around the Valley of Mexico the Aztecs, too, attained a well knit federation under the single leadership of Montezuma I. The power of the Aztec ruler was immense, though he depended greatly on his ruling council, more so than the Inca ruler. A weak Aztec ruler might be dominated by a strong inner council. The executive council, which was in on all policy decisions, apparently consisted of one representative from each of the twenty geographical clans (calpulli) which formed the Aztec nation. On the question of succession we see a variation from the Maya and Inca systems. The Aztec rulers did not necessarily succeed their fathers but had to be elected by an assembly of clan chiefs, old leaders, and leading priests whose vote had to be unanimous. However, the choice was limited to a single lineage. There was usually a logical successor such as a son or brother, but if he proved unsuitable, he was passed over. It was a despotic, oligarchic system with small leeway for political choice. On the other hand, the Aztec kingdom was based primarily on the calpulli.

[5] Sally Falk Moore, *Power and Property in Inca Peru* (New York, Columbia University Press, 1958), p. 117.

These, in more ancient times, were independent and at the time of Spanish Conquest were being finally absorbed under Montezuma II.

In geo-political terms, the Mayan confederation, as far as is known, was governed from the ruling circles in the political centers of Mayapan, Uxmal and Chichen Itzá. The Aztecs had extended their kingdom by conquering the Toltecs and absorbing much of their cultural heritage. The Aztecs, unlike the Incas, made many unresigned enemies in their conquests, which greatly lightened Cortez's task in overthrowing the Aztec empire.[6] Many parts of Montezuma's empire revolted or refused to fight the Spaniards whom they felt would save them from the Aztec domination and treachery. The Spanish alliance with the subject people, the Tlaxcalans, proved to be the key to the Aztec defeat.

William H. Prescott, who thoroughly studied both cultures, opts for the cleverness and intelligence of the Inca imperial policy vis-à-vis the Aztec. He speaks of the Inca substitution of negotiation and intrigue for violence and terror. The Incas dealt with antagonists with a view toward eventually pacifying them within the realm of their empire rather than by alienating them forever by unnecessary bloodshed and at best making them unwilling slaves. The Inca accepted defeated peoples with equal rights and obligations within the confines of the community. The Aztec system made the subjugated tribes forever aware of their slave status and demanded sacrifices which reached the limits of their endurance.

The most important cultural phenomenon found in these communities, as in most primitive societies, was religion. The societies were God-centered, the people concentrating on succeeding reincarnations rather than on the present. Religion played perhaps the most intricate role among the Maya Indians, where the priests were not only the interpreters of the word of the Gods but often outstanding scholars, astronomers, and mathematicians. Since their prestige was great and their words influential, the priests brought religion into the affairs of state. Their knowledge of and interest in public affairs was second only to that of the Halach Uinic. Religion for the Maya developed from simple nature worship and the personification of natural forces to a more organized and specialized structure. The change came about with increasing community life and greater time for leisure. Temples and ceremonial centers were built, and religion became the function of a special class which established an elaborate ritual. Apparently the violence of the Aztec religion was not practiced at the height of Maya civilization.

The Aztec priest was closely connected with the military. Religion and warfare were so closely interrelated that young men preparing for either re-

[6] A first-hand account by a lieutenant of Cortez has preserved for the reader a vivid experience of Spanish audacity in the subjugation of the Aztec empire. Bernal Díaz del Castillo, *The True History of the Conquest of Mexico* (New York: R. M. McBride, 1927).

ceived the same preliminary education. Aztec society was in every sense a theocracy with each calpulli having its own temple and priesthood. Thousands of persons served the various sacerdotal organizations. Apparently there were over 5,000 people employed in the service of the temple of Huitzilopochtli in Mexico City, including priests of various classes, vestal virgins, and altar boys.

In Peru, the priesthood was composed of men drawn exclusively from the body of Inca people, and it was a privileged order of the nobility.

Generally one could say that on the eve of the Spanish subjugation of the Americas, the Inca civilization had reached a formidable peak of achievement, the Maya civilization had long since gone into a steady deterioration, and the Aztec civilization was in the process of building an empire of great strength.

The Mayan organization and its military and imperial policies could not match those of the Incas. Nor did the Maya achieve the technical achievements and urbanized characteristics of the Aztecs. The Maya intellectual stimulus may have come from their lack of political conformity and control in the pre-Spanish period. Their achievements were less communal and more individual. The control of thought and activity was markedly less prevalent among the Maya than under the Inca and Aztec systems. There was perhaps less security but more creativity, less centralization, and more independence.

The Aztecs and Incas had built up vast empires from tiny holdings. Both had overwhelmed their neighbors and spread their civilization to these lesser-developed tribes. They had been thought invincible but had easily collapsed under a handful of white men from the East. It appears that both the Inca and Aztec myths spoke of the eventual conquest of their lands by God-like creatures from the East. This helped to subdue Indian leadership and gave rise to a negative and defeatist psychology which was dissipated too late.

Thus, the three Indian groups all managed to absorb their neighbors by force, intrigue, or cultural superiority. In a sense, all were imperialistic by modern standards. All were, however, upended and absorbed by the Spaniards within a period of fifty years. Each of these Indian groups was interrupted in its attempts to absorb, pacify, and conquer their immediate environment.

The actual conquest of Mexico and Peru was done with the greatest speed and deliberation.[7] It was rather the penetration and exploration which proved to be the greater problem for the Spaniards. In Mexico in 1521, Cuauhtemoc surrendered to Cortez after over 200,000 of his countrymen had perished. When the Spanish finally humbled the Aztecs, a wasted city and empire had to be reconstructed. Little of Aztec art, construction, or edifices were left standing as the Spaniards led the vengeful anti-Aztec tribes into the heart of a once magnificent empire. The completely disorganized and disintegrated Aztec nation was never again to be a special community of people but rather one faction of an integrated Spanish-American empire.

[7] Still the most detailed, literate account of the conquest are the two works by William Prescott. *History of the Conquest of Mexico* and *History of the Conquest of Peru* (New York: Modern Library, 1936).

The conquest instituted a system of repartimientos under which the Indians suffered deplorably.[8] However, under this new patriarchal-slave system a certain degree of normality returned to Mexico. Occupations and trades were resumed; canals were opened again and markets again displayed their wares. New forces and settlers from Spain arrived, as it was the Crown's policy to consolidate her conquests with a different group of men from those who had effected it. Those who conquered were adventurers and innovators. The new wave of men from Spain were of the upper class, skilled in administration, law, and trade, and they were there to make Mexico peaceful, lawful, and profitable. The conquest of Mexico was a marvelous, exciting enterprise that bolstered Spain enormously in her efforts to continue exploration of the New World.

No less daring was the audacity of Pizarro and his handful of men in the highlands of Peru. In addition to being outnumbered they undertook an uncertain enterprise with neither ships, artillery, knowledge of the land, nor possibility of retreat. Of course, the crucial and most unbelievable occurrence was the capture of Atahuallpa. With one bold act the Spaniards replaced the pinnacle of Inca hierarchy with Spanish power and controlled the empire. Had the Inca Empire been less closely knit and the subjects less obedient, Pizarro and his men might never have survived their initial adventure.

Pizarro set up a puppet Inca, Manco, and as the power behind the illusory throne, crowned the new Inca. The Aztecs like the Incas suffered indescribable hardships. The aristocracy became a tool in the hands of the Spanish soldiers; the commoners became little more than serfs; the dwellings were appropriated: it is said that their temples were turned into stables and the royal residence into barracks for the troops; the Inca religion was not tolerated, and its religious houses were wantonly violated.

The Indian cultures of the other major nations to be studied, Chile's Araucanians, Brazil's Tupi, and Argentina's Puelches, were more nomadic than sedentary. Little is known of their cultural contributions. Their importance in the eventual political developments of these three nations lies more in their being either opponents to governmental suppressive policies or being physically integrated populations (as in Chile) than as their being significant influences on later institutional developments.

[8] A royal grant of land including the Indian labor which was indigenous to it.

CHAPTER 3 Colonial Period

Unlike the colonizers of North America, who were individuals searching for religious freedom and economic independence, the colonizers of Latin America came to extend the land holdings, riches, and religion of the Spanish monarchy. The question of settlement and establishment of viable communities came much later and as a secondary concern. For many years the conquerors of these new lands saw them not as an alternative to Spain but as a mere interlude which could bring fame and fortune to those able to withstand the sacrifice and hardship. Thus the early colonial institutions bear the stamp of other-sea orientations and dependence entirely on the changing regulations and political options of the crown in Madrid and Sevilla. Any formation of independent institutions in colonial Latin America came by mere happenstance and by legal aberrations within the general framework of monarchical rule. Although the distance and relative isolation of the southern colonies provided a small margin of independent development, the self-reliance and immediate organization of a new political community observed among early settlers in New England were quite unknown in early Hispanic colonization.

The existence of large, organized, and usually wealthy groups of indigenous peoples, which to some extent counteracted Spanish lethargy, helped to create local communities. These Indian groups served as a built-in labor force with which the Spanish conquerors could revive an earlier Spanish feudalism. Immense wealth within easy reach made organization for survival quite unimportant and economic initiative unnecessary.

Mexico, known as New Spain, was the first territory to be totally subjugated and controlled by the first third of the sixteenth century. From the first the Indians were recognized as the foundation of a new society and as the base of an economic and social pyramid. Though the Mexican Indians were enslaved and exploited, the Spanish never doubted that they were a crucial cog in the community, and no other device was ever considered. Racial discrimination abounded throughout that first century and began diminishing thereafter. The economic contribution of the Indians and their relative docility at performing tasks far outweighed all other considerations for the colonial Spaniard. There was no effort made, as in the English colony of the United States, to implement extermination as a policy. The Indians were rather used and abused than driven off or killed. Their organization and level of culture, generally absent among the more nomadic Western Plains Indians of the United States, convinced the Spaniards, whose view of society was hierarchical, that the Indians could well serve as the laboring element in a society where the Spaniards were lords, landowners, and the leisure class.

The system of "encomienda," a type of responsible authority or delegated power established by the Spanish crown, defined the labor and legal relationship between the Spaniard and the Mexican Indian.[1] The majority of the more important and influential Spaniards received large land tracts with scores of Indians, the only proviso being that the owner feed, protect, and teach them the basic Catholic ritual. This proved to be the essential economic relationship in Colonial Mexico. From this system the authority system of Spanish control derived its strength. The Viceroy of Mexico was the chief executor of the Spanish will, and his role was the most prestigious in the Americas. Not only was he chief administrator but also president of the "audiencia," a type of judicial hearing-board which carried adjudicating and appeal functions, Vice-patron of the Catholic Church, Commander-in-Chief of the army, and supervisor of the royal treasury. In general he represented the physical embodiment of the monarch in Mexico.

The policymaking organ within the Spanish Empire was the Council of the Indies which formulated long-range decisions for Spain's overseas possessions. It was this body that decided the tenure of the Viceroy and passed on his more important plans. Emanating from the Council was the Casa de Contratación, located originally in Sevilla and then in Cadiz. This administrator for commerce and trade handled all trade to and from Latin America and kept a watchful eye out for contraband and indiscriminate and free trading among their overseas possessions. All trade followed the tortuous route from Vera Cruz, Lima or Panama, occasionally through Havana, to Sevilla. No alterations of that route were tolerated, and no other Latin American city was allowed to import or export Spanish goods. The Council of the Indies to which the Viceroy was ultimately responsible acted as the major legislative branch in the legal and political arena. Usually in collaboration with the Viceroy and certainly not with his opposition, the Council of the Indies appointed the regional and local officials of the new continent. A "Corregidor" was assigned to handle the administrative duties in the smaller villages and towns. He collected taxes, protected the Indians somewhat, and was responsible for fortifications and exploration. For newly explored, still virtually uninhabited territories, the Council of the Indies chose "adelantados" who administered the area until it was integrated within the realm of the Viceroy's charge. Very rarely, and with varying effectiveness, local committees of selected settlers would be allowed to institute committees of administrative

[1] As distinct from the "hacienda" system which gave legal status only to landownership and left "jurisdictional aspects to de facto patterns." See James Lockart, "Encomienda and Hacienda: The Evolution of the Great Estate in the Spanish Indies," *Hispanic American Historical Review*, vol. 49, no. 3 (August 1969), p. 427.

powers known as "Cabildos." These were responsible for local justice, education, health, and protection of the populace. With the development of Mexico and the other colonies, "Visitadors" and "Residencias" were introduced. The former, as direct agents of the monarchy in Spain, made periodic visits to the colonies to inspect and supervise the implementation of crown policies. Their ephemeral duties often conflicted with the same duties by the Viceroy, and the result was much conflict and aggravation for both the home and colony authorities. Occasionally these visits were established on a permanent basis, and the agents became "residencias." These peninsular (Spanish) personages would remain months and years at a time attending to local disputes, Indian complaints, boundary infractions, and malfeasance of funds or duties.[2]

In Peru an entirely similar hierarchical operation existed. Under the Peruvian Viceroys much of the Inca social system was reinstated, with the Spanish replacing the Inca nobility. Tributes were revived, and military and public works duty, known as "mita," was required on a revolving basis several months of each year. The strength of Inca ties made administration of Peru easier than that of Mexico once the Inca leaders had been subjugated. Both Peru and Mexico had abundant gold and silver that was made available to the crown. Little economic diversification was practiced throughout the colonial period. Inflation was rampant because of the lack of finished goods and even basic raw materials for everyday necessities were very expensive. Increasing consumption standards quickly pressured prices higher and higher. Small scale manufacturing was virtually a nonexistent practice, and tools and construction equipment used to edify Mexico City and Lima were generally imported from Spain or smuggled in by way of Holland and England.

Portugal's colony of Brazil offers a variation from the colonial models of Peru and Mexico. As in the United States, Brazil's original colonization was based upon a combination of feudal and capitalist concepts. Personal contracts were made with individual conquerors to explore and settle special geographical areas in which the explorer was welcome to the fruits of his labor. The only stipulation was that one/fifth of the earnings be sent to Lisbon and that the territory be settled for the King of Portugal. Colonial Brazil was originally divided into fifteen captaincies after which the modern Brazilian states were patterned. These were awarded to twelve "donatarios" or royal recipients who had to finance their own exploration, obtain their own soldiers and supplies, and provide for their own general welfare and protection. However, once they were established, they had much greater independence of action than their Spanish counterparts. The small patriarchies were controlled by one family and handed down through the generations, while the encomiendas, especially in Mexico, tended to revert back to the crown if there

[2] The rather involved Spanish colonial bureaucracy is helpfully diagrammed in Magali Sarfatti, *Spanish Bureaucratic-Patrimonialism in America* (Berkeley: Institute of International Studies, 1966), pullout page between pp. 22 and 23.

was any doubt about the lineage or some question as to the efficiency with which the land or the mines were worked.

The charters given by the Portuguese monarch to the captaincies compare to those given the Crown colonies of Massachusetts and Virginia. Only as the captaincies went bankrupt and failed to administer and protect its inhabitants were they absorbed by the Portuguese monarchical institutions. The Portuguese, as the Spaniards in the West Indies who had trouble with the Carib and Arawak Indians, were unable to exploit and absorb the Tupí or Ge Indians and therefore had no ready source of plentiful and cheap labor. Again as the Spaniards of the West Indies, the Portuguese instituted a profitable slave trade from the coast of West Africa and introduced millions of Negroes to the Americas. Indeed, the Portuguese became the leading slave traders for 300 years. The Negroes proved more adaptable and more amenable to European institutions and arduous labor than the indigenous peoples of the continent. Less ubiquitous than the Spaniards, the Portuguese tolerated much greater autonomy. Brazilian society developed within the framework of local authority. The plantation system, in which sugar was the central crop, was practically outside of the control of Lisbon. Also during the 60 years of "Babylonian Captivity" when Portugal was under the occupation of the Spanish monarchs (1580–1640), Brazilian colonists felt none of the normal allegiance to the mother country. The gigantic size of the country and its natural wealth further added to Brazil's national psyche.

The Spanish system of the Viceroyalty existed in Brazil, but the Brazilian Viceroy never had the authority of those of Peru and Mexico. Coupled with the decentralization in Brazil, the most important government posts were given to creoles (those born in Brazil) rather than, as in Peru and Mexico, to those from the Iberian peninsula.

The actual settlement of Chile, discovered during 1535–1540, occurred much later than that of the colonial focal point of Peru. In the absence of abundant precious metals, those settlers who remained in Chile had to develop methods of survival comparable to those of the pioneers of Western North America. They had to face the Araucanian Indians who stubbornly defended their territory and who failed to be pacified until midway in the nineteenth century. The Araucanians remain historically an unconquered people. The central valley of Chile, in which Santiago was founded, proved, as did the California valley of the United States, to be of inestimable agricultural value, and formed the basis of attempts to make Chile economically viable. In the absence of a subdued Indian population, much of the work had to be done by the Spaniards themselves. This made for greater democratic potentiality, though with a Creole superstructure the mestizo element later became the laboring class.

Because there was little mineral wealth, Chile was considered important only as a buffer state which could ward off possible British, French, or Dutch intrusions into South America. As historian John Fagg has said, Chile was more an armed garrison than a colonial settlement.[3]

The colonization of Argentina followed somewhat the same pattern as that of Chile. Having less mineral wealth than even Chile, Argentina at the southern end of the La Plata Viceroyalty was considered the most uninteresting settlement in South America. Until the initiation of free trade policies by the Spanish Bourbon kings of the eighteenth century, Buenos Aires remained a muddy, inconspicuous little village known only for the occasional smuggling that occurred there. The western cities of Argentina, notably Tucumán, Córdoba, and Mendoza, were of much more importance until the late eighteenth century because they lay on the overland route by way of the Andes from the point of disembarkation, Lima. Like the Indians of Brazil, the Indians of Argentina proved unwilling to urbanize and acquire domestic occupations. Distinct from other colonial Latin Americans and similar to those of North America, the Argentines early initiated an extinction policy by which the unamenable, indigenous peoples were either massacred or limited to certain (usually the most marginal) territorial reservations. Though intermarriage and miscegenation were common in colonial Latin America (with the Indian in Chile, Peru, and Mexico and with the Negro in Brazil), in Argentina there was much less.

The vast expanses of Argentina, as those of Chile, made tight colonial administration tenuous. The absence of governing focal points, such as Peru and Mexico, had resulted in a large degree of local freedom. It is no accident that the cabildos of Argentina developed large measures of local autonomy and independence long before the more tightly managed cities of Peru and Mexico. Buenos Aires "declared" for independence from Spain before Lima or Mexico City. From the start, Argentina's access to the fertile plains of her interior made life much less arduous than that on the arid lands of Peru, the unarable plateau land of Mexico, or the inaccessible and distant Amazon jungles of interior Brazil. In colonial Argentina there was no hunger for land or food and little of the class and race antagonisms that existed in her sister colonies.

With the replacement of the Hapsburg line by the Bourbons in the early eighteenth century the monarchy of Spain underwent several changes in its New World orientation. Principally, free trade was initiated within the whole of the Spanish Empire, which stimulated the development of countless secondary cities hitherto neglected because of Spain's former mercantile restrictions on trade. Buenos Aires, Valparaiso, Santiago de Chile, and others owe their early impetus to this relaxation of trade restrictions. Also taxes were reduced on all types of commerce.

Under the Bourbon dynasty the encomienda system slowly began to

[3] John E. Fagg, *Latin America* (New York: Macmillan, 1963), pp. 168–71.

wither as, because of abuses or technicalities, more and more of the descendants of the original conquistadores lost their land. Much of this land reverted to monarchical control. The Bourbons also replaced the Council of Indies with the new, more modernized Ministry of Marine and Indies which became the policymaking agent of the monarchy. Under the auspices of this Ministry, two new viceroyalties were founded: La Plata containing what is now Southern Bolivia, Paraguay, Uruguay, and Argentina, and New Granada within which can be found Venezuela, Colombia, and Ecuador. These efforts further decentralized and loosened the structure of the Hapsburg American venture and served to stimulate commerce and incipient industry. The Bourbons sought to regulate as much as to dominate, and they served warning to many officeholders that efficiency was the prime criterion in holding down a colonial office.

In 1767 during the Bourbon reign, the Jesuits were expelled from the Americas, and the monarchs pressured the Papacy to disband them. They were disbanded in 1772 and remained so for almost half a century. The Inquisition, so active a century earlier in the Americas, was practically nonexistent in the eighteenth century. However, though the Enlightenment influenced the French-oriented Bourbon dynasty of Spain, the reforms the Bourbons instituted were mainly confined to certain economic and religious matters and certainly did not involve political freedom or the development of a secular, equalitarian state. The Latin American independence movements were to make that especially clear.

In retrospect it becomes apparent that many features of the Iberian colonies influenced succeeding Latin American societies.[4] The Spanish obsession with direct trading practices between her and her colonies led to the isolation that existed among her overseas possessions. InterAmerican commercial contact, other than that of transporting Spanish goods into the interior or extracting precious metals and delivering them to Spain, remained miniscule among the American colonies. All contact was with Spain itself. Commercial routes followed a set pattern from the interior to the coast and vice versa. There was little initiative shown, nor did the Spanish encourage it, in developing trading routes from north to south or from one urban complex to another. Peru and Mexico had no contact, and Argentina had few contacts with Peru or Chile. The accent was rather on what the colonies could provide for European consumption and what in return could be sent to the colonies in the way of finished goods and manufactured implements.

Iberian America was further burdened by the large degree of nepotism and patronage in government. Positions were generally received because of

[4] Historians have long been concerned with the long-range effects of the Spanish colonial pattern. See, for example, Woodrow Borah, "Colonial Institutions and Contemporary Latin America: Political and Economic Life," *Hispanic American Historical Review*, vol. 43, no. 3 (August 1963), pp. 371–79.

favoritism or blood ties or through their outright purchase. Membership in the ruling caste was often closed to those on the American continent best qualified to govern, and colonial posts were regarded more as temporary gifts of prestige than as responsible and meaningful positions in a developing new society. Status and image were the usual awards in sixteenth to eighteenth century Hispanic America. The universal art of corruption and improbity was practiced everywhere. Privileges were misused and authority catered to personal predilections and ambitions. Perhaps the most fatal flaw in the colonial institutional framework was the personal connection between the local arbiter and a distant censor that controlled his activities and movements in the broad sense but failed to either lay down firm but flexible guidelines or give sufficient amounts of local control as colonial conditions shifted.

PART III

Political Evolution in Postindependence Latin America

In examining political development within an historical context, one can survey the patterns of political change over a period of many generations. As political development can be described as an achieved level of governmental maturity, it may also be useful to depict several historical phases in a nation's national development.

Every stage of national development, in many ways, appears closely related to another period, but some generalizations can be made.[1] One can refer to political development as a continuous and ongoing process of growth in complexity and effectiveness of the political structure as a nation advances from relatively simple forms of organized social life to more intricate and complicated patterns.

It appears that the Latin American nations, after emerging from indigenous and colonial stages of development, pass through three major postindependence periods of political development. In each of these three phases they achieve or absorb certain requisites for achieving political maturity.[2]

[1] A noted book by C. E. Black, though very broadly framed, nevertheless agrees with this basic premise of periodizing the processes of national political change.

Black attempts to isolate "political modernization" into four phases: (1) challenge of modernity; (2) consolidation of modernizing leadership; (3) economic and social transformation; (4) integration of society. He then places 170 politically organized societies into seven patterns of modernization which are conveniently categorized according to historical chronology, geography, independence struggles, revolutions, existence of colonial heritage, and fall of dictatorships. This allows Black the tool by which he manages to include the USSR, Ethiopia, Japan, and Afghanistan in one group, Israel and Yemen in another, Albania and Sweden in still another, and all the Latin American nations in a group by themselves. C. E. Black, *The Dynamics of Modernization* (New York: Harper & Row, 1966).

[2] Dankwart Rustow has been instrumental in influencing the author to see national developments in terms of historic sequences of leadership tasks. I am indebted to him by way of several conversations and a conference on political development at the Brookings Institution in 1963. See his *A World of Nations* (Washington, D.C.: Brookings Institution, 1967), pp. 120–132, where he considers the

First, consistent authority is wielded by a centralizing administration or group. Second, this group is able to elicit support from its people and achieve unity within its territory. Third, the central authority eventually reaches a point when it can begin to distribute social ameliorations after its primary governing and economic development functions have been sustained.

It does not seem that any of these steps can be bypassed by any developing nation. This is not to say that any of these phases must be arrived at exactly in the above sequence. They may be achieved concomitantly, or they may even on occasion be muddled or intermingled, but all must be dealt with.[3]

Can we chart these essentially political stages of growth using the example of five major Latin American nations? It is necessary then to first develop a scheme which allows for further comparisons; thus we shall be dividing Republican or postindependence Latin American development into three substantive periods:

(1) *The Authoritative Phase*—a phase in which a central focus of power and legitimacy are established and sustained. It is a phase which sees the slow evolvement of a constitutional infrastructure and the development of basic patterns of institutional relationships. This period is witness to the phenomenon wherein local interest groups recognize the expediency and necessity of subordinating themselves to a better equipped and more powerful centralizing group which has the wherewithal to speak for divergent interests. The challenges, during this initial period of postindependence or national development, involves achieving respect for institutions, laws, and geopolitical domains so that the hierarchical relationships between the rulers and the ruled may become increasingly defined. It is the period of organized political ascendancy and the promulgation of the rule of law. The emphasis rests largely on governmental control rather than economic development, societal integration, or political participation. Thus a major concern for the leadership is to keep the body politic together as a basic political unit by either coercion, persuasion or even bargaining. Governments were often suppressive in their policies, which often resulted in civil conflicts and regional antagonisms against the national government as the latter sought to establish its paramountcy and sovereignty.

The tasks of leadership during this phase are formidable. Frontiers had

---

quests for authority, identity, and equality as critical to the modernization process. A. F. K. Organski has also developed an historical model of four stages of political development concerned with unification, industrialization, welfare, and abundance. *The Stages of Political Development* (New York: Alfred Knopf, 1965).

[3] Samuel Huntington sees three phases of political modernization with (1) the rationalization of authority, (2) the differentiation of structure coming closely together, and (3) the broadening of participation coming later. "Political Modernization: America versus Europe," *World Politics*, vol. 18, no. 2 (April 1966), page 378.

to be guarded against foreign incursions, and national physical integrity had to be safeguarded by a mobilization of armed forces and the imposition of taxes to raise revenue for defensive deployment. Secondly, early postindependence leadership often sets the tone and style of political relationships that persist through several political generations. Almost invariably liberal leadership of the nineteenth century variety displaced conservative leadership. Both political philosophies accustomed the people to a pattern of authority and rule of a small elite. Lastly, leadership policies were implemented with a self-conscious motivation of creating goals oriented to sustaining central political power and persuasion.

(2) *The Aggregative Phase*—a phase in which a nation tends to discover its national identity and its leadership is free to attend to the tasks of promoting political communication between them and the societal economic interest. Force as the basic means of attaining social peace is no longer as necessary because the national interests intersect at various class and regional levels. Beneficial relationships develop among interdependent subnational communities, and a central authority is recognized as the creator of a new feeling of national community and social harmony.

In this phase leadership tasks usually focus on providing for the establishment of an economic infrastructure and a commercial basis for modernity. With social stability enhanced the goals of leadership are diverted toward developing the country's capacity for economic growth. Along with the economic change evident in the society comes the concomitant growth and development of new political parties and interest groups which represent the new urban industrial and commercial groups. This causes an evolving competition between those traditional economic groups and the incipient commercial groups seeking to share political dominance. These factors, though they increase friction among policymakers, have the effect of multiplying public cognizance and political responsibility toward increasing numbers of people. This increasing access to political communication on the part of more and diverse groups results in an increase in political participation and a general dispersion of political freedoms, such as voting, speech, assembly, press, and such rights as formally reproduced in legislation and sometimes in integral constitutions promulgated between the late nineteenth century and 1930.

(3) *The Distributive Phase*—a phase in which the government can concentrate on the political integration and socialization of the masses of the people. At this point in development the economic base has grown sufficiently large to divide along more equitable lines. Efforts are increased to mobilize the nation for mass participation. The people are expectant in terms of the government's ability to provide for the general welfare and to promote equitable justice among all its citizens. There is an equalization of opportunity and a better division of the fruits of society's collective labor.

This phase in national development sees a growth in leadership aspirations toward national self-determination and an increasing rejection of applying foreign solutions to domestic problems. Nationalism is increasingly applied as a development ideology predicated on its inherent "social value" of integrating all societal sectors into a more comprehensive, identifiable unit.[4]

A growing accommodation is perceived regarding such priorities as industrialization and the increasing requirements of state intervention into the economy. Mass political parties make their appearance in increasing numbers during this phase and the general level of political education rapidly reaches a large popular audience. All these factors serve to greatly politicize the national community and to increase its stake in economic and social alternatives.

[4] See Kalman Silvert's definition in this regard. *Expectant Peoples* (New York: Random House, 1963), pp. 21–24.

CHAPTER 4 The Authoritative Phase

As the North American revolution had middle class overtones, both in the mechanisms by which it was launched and carried out and in the aims and principles for which it was nurtured, so the Latin American revolts were aristocratic and leisure-class fulminations against a system which offered few opportunities for social advancement and recognition and fewer financial advantages. The Latin American variety contained a mixture of patriotic, French-instilled fervor with a predominance of fratricidal social revenge. As the Russian and French revolutions were primarily class conscious in content and the American independence movement significantly political and economic in motivation, so the independence movements in Latin America can be more than partially classified as primarily political in scope. Latin American aristocrats from Rio de Janeiro to Lima and from Buenos Aires to Mexico City had been repeatedly snubbed and depreciated in the courts of Spain and Portugal, whether a monarch was in attendance or whether an interim executive or parliamentary government ruled in his stead. The collective Latin American ego was mortified by this treatment. Seats of power in the Americas were often held by foreigners whose long-run goals included returning to the Iberian Peninsula to enjoy the fruits of superior education, culture, and social life. Latin American independence meant a reassertion of social class equality as much as it meant the basic freedoms. An underlying factor was the achievement of this unmeasured psychic equality. It was in the political arena that this equalization drive could have its outlet and rationalization.

It is interesting to note that the Spain against which the Latin American nations revolted beginning in 1810 was one of the most liberal and forward looking in Iberian history. America was revolting against Spain as much as against any particular Spanish institution or colonial policy. In the absence of exiled Fernando VII, the Spanish parliament had in fact abolished the Inquisition, ended many oppressive mercantile taxes with the colonies, and denied the Spanish church some of her most excessive privileges. In addition to this, the Spanish Constitution of 1812 was in the tradition of later, liberal European constitution making.

Despite the obvious shifts in the direction of social change in Spain and the possibility of the liberalization of her colonial policy, the various Latin American states launched their creole uprisings in the name of King Ferdinand VII, who was deposed with the help of Napoleon, against the interregnum (1808–1814) regime in Spain. It was a question of self-government regardless of the authority across the seas. The original attempts at autonomy failed in all the major centers of Latin America except Buenos Aires. Argentina was the least important for Spain both financially and commercially of all her colonies. Also Argentina had been able to slowly achieve a measure of independence because of administrative neglect. Elsewhere Spanish loyalist tradition prevailed for another several years, and it was usually native support of Spanish institutions rather than peninsular troops which aborted these revolts.

It was not until the exploits of Argentine General San Martín that Latin American independence movements began to succeed. The victory of his InterAmerican army at Chacabuco in Chile in the summer of 1817 led to a series of triumphs that culminated in the cessation of Spanish control in the Western Hemisphere. It was this type of personal heroism and individual achievement rather than any political ideology of national independence that furnished the Latin American independence movement with the necessary drive to oust a colonial empire. Private ambition and individual sacrifice provided the necessary stimulus to carry out this rather gigantic enterprise.

Mexico

In Mexico, independence was originally called for on behalf of King Fernando VII, good government, and the redress of Indian grievances, which certainly represented a mixture of political and social objectives. Led by a village priest Miguel Hidalgo, the first response to the initial stirrings of Mexican nationalism was abortive, though it influenced Mexicanism for generations to come. Today celebration of the deeds of Hidalgo form an essential part of Mexican ritual. Though another priest José María Morelos carried on the drive for independence, the movement bogged down because of insufficient organized support from the upper creole classes who were demonstrating everywhere in Latin America that they must lead the rupture with Spain if it were to succeed. Fathers Hidalgo and Morelos did not sufficiently demonstrate their loyalty to the new American aristocratic system as against the older and tottering European one. The proportions of Hidalgo's 50,000-man Indian army positively frightened and repelled the proponents of an administrative revolution against the intrenched bureaucratic structure of Spain in America. Mexican independence had to await the more controlled maneuvers of Augustín de Iturbide, an upper class military figure who was intelligent enough to include Vicente Guerrero, a representative of the disgruntled Mexican mestizo. Together Iturbide and Guerrero issued the first of many historical Mexican "plans"—the Plan of Iguala which called for independence, the primacy of the Catholic Church, and the equalization of opportunity for all classes.[1]

[1] Lesley Byrd Simpson, *Many Mexicos* (Berkeley: University of California Press, 1960), pp. 198–199.

This ephemeral tactical alliance was to bloodlessly and almost effortlessly achieve independence for Mexico and gain the title of Emperor Agustín I for Iturbide who, after quickly discarding Guerrero and his program, settled down to a short and unspectacular reign in which no changes in the social system were carried out. The Mexican experiment with a monarchy was short-lived, and in 1823, after one year, it was replaced by a conservative-liberal alliance led by General Santa Anna, whose leadership at that time, and subsequently, had no ideological justification.

The Mexican Constitution of 1824 was federal in orientation and provided for a bicameral congress and indirect presidential elections. Catholicism was declared the state religion. By 1828 a Conservative-Liberal political competition had evolved, but frequently military interventions, assassinations, and coups marred the chances for both peaceful governmental transitions and basic social reform. Neither side seemed sufficiently ready to provide Mexico with sound constitutional government. Neither group concerned itself with the mass of Mexicans, and their power disputes had little to do with the needs of the countryside. Social and political unity as well as federal authority were constantly being put to the test by provincial and local competitors.

During its authoritative phase, from independence to the mid-nineteenth century, Mexico suffered a series of harsh, corrupt, and ineffective administrations that provided a minimum of central authority but didn't advance economic progress or social justice. Fiscal corruption was rampant as governments and federal troops were bartered and sold. Government programs and party platforms were mere shibboleths meant to attract momentary support. The fraudulent behavior of General and President López de Santa Anna was typical of much of the deception and dishonesty within the whole government. His continual sallies into political power inhibited normal administration whether by the liberals or the conservatives.

There were, however, some attempts at national legislation between palace coups, military revolts, and foreign wars with the United States and France. The conservative Lucás Alamán managed to establish a national credit bank for agriculture and industry to stimulate investments and development of Mexico's incipient textile mills and traditional mining enterprises. From within the ranks of the liberal faction, Gómez Farías sought to colonize Mexico's vast northern lands which were, however, lost to the United States in the Mexican-American War of 1846–47. Gómez Farías also reduced the number of commissioned generals and put an end to the payment of church tithes. However, the majority of his reforms were blocked and consequently never enacted into law.

Between 1830 and 1855 Mexico was so absorbed by her trying and frustrating relations with the United States that her national politicians were either discredited or worshipped according to their ability to cope with the North Americans. What occurred was a complete distortion of normal development and its replacement by abject demagoguery and extreme forms of personalism. A strong defensive posture against the United States would strengthen the worst leader, while support for the most perceptive legislator would dwindle if he showed any weakness toward the north. The loss of Mexican territory to the United States drained Mexican capital, men, and most important, the pride and self-confidence of her people in their government and national destiny.

The ouster of the Santa Anna dictatorship was accomplished by 1854 under the Plan of Ayutla, which called for the convening of a congress to revise the constitution of 1824.[2] At the same time the liberals issued the Juárez Law, a series of decree laws named after the impassioned, single-minded leader of the Liberals, Benito Juárez. The Law ended jurisdiction over civil cases by ecclesiastical and military courts. Fast on the heels of this measure came the Lerdo Law of 1856 which required the Church to divest itself of all landownings, one half of usable Mexican land, not used strictly for religious purposes. This land had remained for years in the hands of the clergy and had never been exploited for the benefit of the nation but was rather a source of inestimable value in real estate for the Church. These lands were now to be sold into private hands with a heavy sales tax, the proceeds of which would go to the liberal government. It was an antifeudal measure based on the principle that individual ownership of private property is natural and most efficient. The law, though directed principally at the Church's widespread control and inefficient management of the land, also covered all corporate landownership. Paradoxically this latter aspect affected the indigenous "ejidos" whose common ownership of the land dated back to precolonial times.[3]

The results of the Lerdo Law were quite unforeseen. While the Church was deprived of much of her land (though she did manage to hide titles to the land through "created" individual ownership rights), it was the communal Indian who fared the worst. The Church became the leading capitalist class in Mexico through the accumulation of payments for her lands, while the Indians were usually defrauded of their traditional lands without adequate compensation. The law, quite unconsciously, fostered the concentration of land in the hands of fewer and fewer individuals, while it created thousands of landless Indians in nineteenth century Mexico. This was responsible for the landhunger that was to stir others in the twentieth century to the Mexican Revolution.

The constitution of 1857, the most liberal of nineteenth century Latin America, reaffirmed the Juárez and Lerdo Laws. Aside from its anticlerical measures, the military arm of government was subordinated to the civil author-

[2] Henry Bamford Parkes, *A History of Mexico* (Boston: Houghton Mifflin, 1960), pp. 227–229.

[3] See E. N. Simpson's *The Ejido, Mexico's Way Out* (Chapel Hill: The University of North Carolina Press, 1937).

ity, a problem that was to occupy liberals of nineteenth and twentieth century Latin America. Hereditary land titles were abolished to further break up the monopoly of landownership, though it did little to nullify some of the unforeseen ill effects of the Lerdo Law.

Thus though the constitution of 1857 represented the most institutionalized attack on aristocratic privileges during any authoritative phase in Latin America, it did not contain any solution to problems of the landless Indian and the challenge of integrating him into nineteenth century Mexican economic and social life. The natural preoccupation had been with political rather than social reform. However, the 1857 constitution marked the coming of age of Mexican liberalism which in the 1820s had been so obsessed with a formal need for a federalistic structure and in the 1830s with anticlericalism of one or another variety, but now gave evidence of a growing awareness of the need to establish a middle-class basis for landownership as a more viable support for a politically liberal regime.

Under Juárez's leadership, then duly elected president, the reform mongering persisted in the Reform Laws of 1859. These more radical measures called for expropriation without payment of all church property not used for worship purposes, for the nationalization of cemeteries, and for the legality of civil marriages. The liberals were temporarily eclipsed by an alliance between the conservative forces and the French Empire occupation forces of Louis Napoleon as France sought, through the Austrian Archduke Maximilian, to launch a far-reaching French empire in America having as its initial base the Republic of Mexico. Combined United States diplomatic and military support of Juárez and his liberal followers ended five years of French occupation. Surprisingly Maximilian shared the liberal ideas of Juárez and the liberals and did nothing to rescind the reform measures instituted shortly before his arrival.

The triumphant return of Juárez was a milestone in Mexican national developments. Liberalism had triumphed again over a potential long-range monarchist revival, the people had unified to defeat a foreign occupying power, and abolition of certain of the worst church abuses had been written into law and carried out by the leading individuals of this period. The concentration of land in the hands of a few and the abominable living standards in the rural areas, however, remained the unresolved social issue.

The implementation of authority in Mexico was a long and arduous process made difficult by the lack of legitimate federal leadership. However, though continuous liberal-conservative confrontations gave the appearance of the imminent collapse of authority, power gradually became concentrated in the central government in Mexico City. Indeed, despite the obstacles of foreign incursions and domestic turbulence, Mexican governmental institutions continued to gain strength. Occasionally, help came from strong leaders such as Juárez. In several ways, Juárez was a prototype of the aggregative phase leader but foreign interventions and military engagements so dominated decision-making in the latter part of his administration that the consolidation (and often, perversion) of his public policies paradoxically took shape under the advent of the Díaz dictatorship of 1867 to 1910.

Peru

In Peru, Spain's rule was most deeply entrenched, and the independence was achieved not by her own efforts but by the incursions of republican troops from Argentina and Chile and from Colombia and Ecuador. The converging forces freed Peru from Spanish control by 1824 in the famous last battle with Spanish forces in South America—the Battle of Ayacucho. Foreign influences were essential in the ousting of Spanish dominance in the Americas and provided the necessary psychological conditions to close one epoch and initiate another. Under the successive mandates of San Martín and Simón Bolívar several reforms were initiated in Peru, though the majority remained on paper and were never implemented. Under the aegis of San Martín slaves born after 1812 were to be freemen, and in general the Indian's protection under the law was fostered. Bolívar closed many convents and turned them into schools in which primary education was provided. Indians were often allowed to take possession of the lands on which they labored. Under Bolívar a constitution with a president chosen for life was written. The executive was given overwhelming administrative, judicial, and legislative powers.

With the end of Bolívar's influence, the new constitution of 1828 was drawn up, and most of Bolívar's personal appointments were ousted from the government. Bolívar had not been able to demonstrate the same ability in administration as he had in the organization of armed encounters.

Bolívar's withdrawal left a power vacuum in Peru that was not filled for two decades during which time his former lieutenants in the independence campaigns jockeyed for control of Lima. Peru, more than elsewhere, returned to a social and political structure very similar to that of preindependence days, while economically, she had fared better under the Spanish Viceroyalty. The gap between the whites and the mestizo remained as broad. Privilege and wealth were still shared by a tiny minority of Lima's upper society; the rest of the nation remained poverty ridden. Military rule predominated for almost half of Peru's authoritative period and the country was continually unstabilized by the intermartial warfare.[4] As Mexico suffered by its constant preoccupation with United States aims, so Peru remained unsettled because of Bolivian intervention schemes and Chilean counterthrusts against any Bolivian influence so close to Chile. Like Mexico, Peru depended for the

[4] James C. Carey, *Peru and the United States, 1900–1962* (Notre Dame: University of Notre Dame Press, 1964), pp. 3–4.

solution of her many problems on the established elite, consisting of the clergy, the army, and the large landowners, all of whom agreed on what must be preserved but who found no agreement on what had to be accomplished. With the removal of the Spanish in Mexico and Peru, both countries were left to their own devices, but both had been poorly prepared for government by the former colonial power.

Social dissolution and short-lived military governments continued to dominate the national scene in Peru where there were fewer signs of liberal stirrings so apparent under Juárez in Mexico. Though richly endowed, Peru made no significant advancements by the latter half of the nineteenth century. The Peruvian governments did, however, manage to enact some social legislation, such as the abolition of slavery and the Spanish encomienda tradition of exacting forced tribute from the Indians. The Peruvian government also closed church courts and discontinued the necessity of paying church tithes, though no antichurch measures were as dramatic as those in Mexico. A strong presidential system was established whose electorate, as elsewhere in Latin America, was severely limited, and Catholicism became the official religion.

As in Mexico, it was essentially Anglo-American interests that exploited Peruvian natural resources and initiated the capitalization of the nation. Though she suffered a severe setback during the War of the Pacific in which she lost over a quarter of her territory and inestimable wealth in nitrate resources to Chile, Peru by the turn of the twentieth century began to show some signs of economic achievement. In this she was aided by exorbitant British loans which were to make it necessary for Peru to concede economic privileges to the British in order to cancel her huge debts.

It was the influence of foreign capital which was responsible for change in Peru. Vast parts of her nation were lost to Chile in the War of the Pacific which had been embarked upon apparently at the insistence of those Chileans invited by the Peruvian government to develop Peru's nitrate mines. Also it was foreign capital which allowed Peru to initiate a program of economic development. However, lethargy overcame Peruvian society after the fall of Lima as the commercial and cultural center of South America. The little wealth derived from her tremendous natural riches placated the landed gentry but did not touch the poor.

Of the five nations under study, Peru has been the last to enter a period of steady economic growth and the last to seriously attempt to resolve the problem of the huge gap between her rich few and her many poor. Also Peru has not undergone the social changes that are so intimately linked to the development of Mexico, Brazil, Chile, and Argentina. Dominated by a satisfied minority and their country dominated by its military establishment, the people of Peru were again governed by the civilian dictatorship of Augusto Leguía from 1919 (the year of many military coups in Latin America) to 1930. Though suffrage was extended by the Constitution of 1920, elections were rarely honest, and in fact, Peruvian elections remained dubious through the presidential elections of 1962.

During the Leguía dictatorship a new party was formed which, for the first time, did not merely represent some faction of the same upper class. The founder of the APRA party (Alianza Popular Revolucionaria Americana) was a young Marxist Victor Raúl Haya de la Torre. The party and its leader represented a blend of old world socialism, warmed-over Marxism (without the Lenin concept of a trained elite), a genuine concern for the conditions of the American Indian, and an amorphous anti-imperialist orientation.[5] Though the members of the APRA party, the Apristas, had InterAmerican if not international pretensions, the party never took root anywhere but in Peru. In Peru, however, the Apristas found a yawning gap in political representation which they managed to fill for over a generation, and they probably still remain Peru's most important mass party. The evolution of the APRA party parallels that of Peru and is a guide to the understanding of misfortunes that have befallen her since the inception of the party. In a real sense the APRA has been Peru's social conscience for more than three decades.

The economic catastrophe of 1930 reverberated in Peru and resulted in a military coup against Leguía. The military government was led by Luis Sánchez Cerro who ran the country with an iron hand until his assassination in 1933. While dictator he intervened to annul the elections of 1931 in which Haya de la Torre was victorious. Sánchez Cerro was succeeded by another military dictator Oscar Benavides who ruled until 1939. During Benavides' administration the Aprista leadership was either exiled or jailed, while the party itself was labeled "international" and driven underground. The party flourished in illegality and strengthened not only its pyramidic organization but also its popular following which had no alternative choices within the political arena.

The Peruvian case is an example of the difficulty of achieving and sustaining autonomous political institutions within a social system very dependent upon a single geographical, cultural and political elite. Not until the middle sectors, strengthened by foreign investment, and the military forces began to grasp for a share of power could the extended authoritative phase of development meaningfully blend into the aggregative phase.

Brazil

As the exile of Fernando VII had simplified Latin American resistance to the Spanish interim governments, so the Napoleonic occupation of Portugal gave the final impetus to Brazilian dissatisfaction with a tiny monarchy which

[5] Harry Kantor, *The Ideology and Program of the Peruvian Aprista Party* (Berkeley: University of California Press, 1953).

ruled Brazil from a distance of thousands of miles. In 1808 the Portuguese court in exile moved to Brazil which flourished under its newly achieved prestige. Not even the most conservative Portuguese monarchists could expect a return to the status quo ante-bellum. After the Napoleonic influence and occupation were toppled, João VI, King of Portugal, did not wish to leave Brazil and decided to conduct his affairs from there. From all accounts it was love for Brazil and its people that lured João to remain when it was no longer necessary.[6]

By 1820 the Portuguese version of the Spanish "cortes" (parliament) had virtually adopted the liberal Spanish constitution of 1812 of Cadiz, and though the parliament took a liberal domestic position, its foreign policy was geared toward preserving Brazil as an integral part of the Portuguese empire. Finally, fearful for his crown, João VI returned to Portugal leaving his son Pedro as regent. The Portuguese Cortes maintained its dominant position and after the departure of João VI managed to antagonize Brazilians within the colonial empire as well as the Brazilian deputies to the Lisbon Cortes. Under these worsening relations, Pedro was ordered by the Cortes to return to Portugal for his education; but he refused, declaring in 1822 that he would remain in Brazil. This instituted proceedings which, in 1822, resulted in Brazilian independence and the crowning of Pedro I.

As Brazil's own monarchy replaced that of Portugal, there were no large-scale political changes other than the institutionalization of what already existed. The new American empire did not balkanize as did its Spanish American counterpart mainly because Brazil's various subdivisions never had political ambitions but rather sought economic self-determination. This economic freedom they were able to maintain under the new Brazilian monarchy. As in the United States, where Confederation developed into Federation, there was in Brazil a spirit of entrepreneurial rugged individualism mixed with abundant national sentiment which took some time to be viably absorbed into a greater economic union. The task of the central governments in Brazil was made easier by the lack of politicalization among the various captaincies and their plantation owners. Due to the traditional economic leeway given to "fazenda" (hacienda) groups, they did not measurably concern themselves with the nature of monarchical government in Rio.

The Fazendeiros of Northeastern Brazil combined with the cattle ranchers of the Southeast, the merchants and artisans of the Eastern Coastal region, and the mine owners of Minas Gerais to form the economic and political backbone of the Brazilian Empire in America. Pedro I promulgated the Constitution of 1824, much as Wilhelm I of Prussia would in 1871, as a "gift" to the people. The essence of the 1824 Brazilian Constitution that was to last the 65 years until the fall of the Empire was the overwhelming

[6] See for example C. H. Haring, *Empire in Brazil* (Cambridge: Harvard University Press, 1958), pp. 9–14.

powers given the Emperor. The monarch could overcome any ministerial or parliamentary impasse, and he had use of the suspensive veto for any piece of legislation. He could dissolve parliament at will, and senators were chosen by him from lists submitted by the various Brazilian states. The Chamber of Deputies was popularly elected, but the electorate was limited by property ownership. The church, as distinct from Mexico where it was predominant, was under the Emperor's control and patronage.

Subsequently Pedro II assumed power in 1842 from a regency ruling in his name when he reached the age of 16. His reign lasted without interruption until the fall of the Empire in 1889, the longest uninterrupted rule in the history of Ibero-America. During the early years of his reign the liberals gave him complete support in return for influence within his council of ministers, and the conservatives backed his monarchy as the strongest element for preserving authority and avoiding disintegration and civil war.

A master administrator and leader, Pedro II filled his government with effective leaders and parliamentarians. He improved Brazilian commerce, banking, and industrial capitalization. Through patronage he kept the loyalty and interests of the northeastern sugar-planting elite as well as of the newer coffee and cotton groups of central Brazil. He supported protectionism for incipient industrialists and sponsored free trade policies for exporters. In contrast to the situation in Mexico and Peru, property and life in Brazil were safe from marauders and local caudillos. The basic freedoms were assured, and more than in any Latin American nation racial integration was a fact of social and political life. Moreover the government managed to maintain civilian control over the military groups during this period.[7]

Under Pedro II the Brazilian Empire made significant strides in her economic development. As a constitutional monarch, Pedro II showed a marked predisposition toward economic liberalism and political leniency. He never committed the excesses of the Latin American national dictator or local caudillo, and throughout his reign he stimulated and encouraged innovative ideas in all areas of social life. He supported railroad construction, shipbuilding, and other necessary industries which helped to develop the urban middle classes of Rio de Janeiro and São Paulo. He relied on these groups to counterbalance the fazenda owners of the Northeast whom he felt he needed too much for public support.

Some of the most startling economic advances undertaken during the reign of Pedro II were those administered by the self-styled Baron Mauá, a financier, banker, and a minister of Pedro II's government. In the tradition of the Morgans, Carnegies, and Rockefellers, Baron Mauá (to be so dignified at the height of his contributions) built roads, ports, and canals; introduced gaslighting to Rio and telegraph lines to the Brazilian interior; and had a

[7] Edwin Lieuwen, *Arms and Politics in Latin America* (New York: Praeger, 1960), p. 17.

transatlantic cable completed. He was responsible for establishing Brazil's first stock companies and real estate firms which grew to great size and power. It may be said that he originally taught the Brazilian people their tremendous speculation consciousness.

The United States experience convinced Mauá that Brazil should link her farm industry with her other industries, and that exchange between them should flourish. He wanted Brazil to consume more of her own production and was one of the original and eloquent Latin American voices raised against the colonial economy in which the colony produced raw materials that they sold at relatively low prices abroad and bought expensive finished goods. Also, under the influence of Pedro II, Baron Mauá and others hoped to encourage immigration from Europe. Beginning in the 1850s, inducements were given to Europeans to settle in Brazil, and at the fall of the Empire of Pedro II the number of immigrants was to reach over one-half million, far exceeding immigration to Mexico, Peru, and Chile.[8] In Latin America this was only surpassed by Argentina whose immigration reached truly fantastic proportions by the turn of the century. As was the case in Mexico in the latter half of the nineteenth century, foreign investments poured into Brazil since under Pedro II she presented the picture of economic and political stability.

Again, however, we have a repetition of the Mexican picture in that the general prosperity among the urban middle classes did not trickle down to the mass of Brazilians who lived in the backlands. For these people educational standards were very low, literacy no more than 15 per cent (as in the Mexico of 1900), and the general condition of life completely impoverished.

In areas of foreign policy, Pedro II showed moderation and skill. Once having defined the borders of Brazil, he showed no imperialist aspirations as did two of his southern neighbors, Solano López of Paraguay and Manuel Rosas of Argentina. He respected Uruguayan independence, though his support of an Uruguayan faction caused a Paraguayan attack on Brazil which resulted in the Paraguayan War of 1864–1870 that virtually devastated Paraguay.

However, slavery, which had been outlawed in the other countries discussed, continued and was very profitable in Brazil until British pressures on the Atlantic finally forced its abrogation. It is apparent that Pedro II did not share the northern owners' views that slavery was a necessity but kept his peace in order to satisfy this important sector of the Brazilian national community.[9] A supporter of Lincoln's Emancipation Proclamation,

[8] Celso Furtado, *The Economic Growth of Brazil* (Berkeley: University of California Press, 1963), p. 140.

[9] A well-documented account cites the process of urbanization and the growing commercialization of coffee as the principal causes for the movement toward

he had long ago (as George Washington and Thomas Jefferson) freed his own slaves. However, Brazil was to wait until 1871 for the first full-scale legislative act regarding slavery. It stated that all who were born slaves would be free upon birth, though they might be required to serve an apprenticeship with their master until twenty-one years of age. In 1885 all slaves over sixty-five were freed. By passing piecemeal legislation it was hoped that an all out confrontation could be avoided, and it was not until 1888 that all slaves were given their immediate freedom without compensation to their owners.

The slavery question was the major reason for the subsequent fall of the Brazilian Empire and its replacement by the Brazilian Republic. With their plantation economy in jeopardy, the northern planters fought abolition until the end, and when they had lost the fight they saw no further need to support the monarchy. They perhaps envisioned that under a republic a conservative policy might emerge victorious.

The Catholic Church did nothing to defend the Empire, as a gradual cooling of relations between it and Pedro II had developed since the church-state crisis of 1872.[10] As freemasonry, which was open and popular in Brazil, had been denounced by the papacy in 1864, a local bishop had used punitive measures against a Brazilian priest who celebrated a mass in a freemason lodge. Under the patronage system, Pedro II had never published the papal decree in Brazil, thus making the bishop's action illegal. Two other local bishops joined the fray ordering all Catholics to sever any connection with freemasonry, but since this was illegal and would affect thousands of Brazilians who had seen no conflict between Catholicism and freemasonry, Pedro II intervened and had the offending bishops arrested and jailed. They were later pardoned; but Pedro II was never pardoned by diehard Catholics, and another essential support of his Empire was weakened. Catholics reasoned that under a Republic, Brazil might be able to end the patronage relationship between church, state, and monarchy.

It is not strange that the forced resignation of Pedro II in 1889 was precipitated by the military, an event that was to associate Brazil more closely with other Latin American republics who were generally dominated by the armed forces. Influenced in part by liberal European positivism and to a greater extent, after decades of accepting a civil-dominated society, by a taste for power, the military revolted. Looking on approvingly were the disgruntled landowners, the frustrated clergy, and, possibly, a group of genuine republicans who now, with the twentieth century approaching, looked upon a

slave abolition. The cities required abundant and cheap labor. Richard Graham, "Causes for the Abolition of Negro Slavery in Brazil," *Hispanic American Historical Review*, vol. 46, no. 2 (May 1966), pp. 123–137.

[10] For an excellent analysis of this crisis see J. P. Calogeras, *A History of Brazil*, trans. P. A. Martin (Chapel Hill: University of North Carolina Press, 1939), pp. 234–245.

monarchy as an anachronism. Possibly an additional factor was Pedro II's failing health and the imminent succession to the throne of his daughter Isabela and her French-born husband, Count d'Eu. The idea of being ruled by a woman who was perhaps dominated by a foreigner may have not been received very well within the army barracks.

In retrospect, after the initial pacification of the various state rebellions and following the long drawn out efforts of Rio Grande do Sul to secede, Brazil's Empire was never again troubled with the kind of civil strife that beset Mexico, Chile, Peru, and Argentina. Contrary to the Mexican and Peruvian experiences, Brazil's successful ventures in diplomacy and her victories in border disputes and wars hastened to strengthen her sense of governmental authority and competence which was essential for a country of such sprawling territory.

As in Mexico, there were two separate political philosophies in Brazil: liberalism and conservatism. What assisted Brazilian unity under the monarchy was that the conservatives stood for the defense of the monarchy as a stabilizing and moderating force, while the liberals were looking for a constitution that could organize and preserve a modern federal system. Both groups supported the enlightened policies of Pedro II who was probably the most thoroughly admired leader of nineteenth century Latin America. Under this constitutionally endowed empire, Brazil was able to avoid the terror, bitterness, rivalry, and disintegration that prevailed in Mexico, Peru, Chile, and Argentina. Under the rather enlightened monarchical leadership of Pedro I, a short-term regency, and Pedro II, Brazil was able throughout the nineteenth century to find the formulas for peaceful change and continuity.

The Brazilian monarchy of Pedro II was a successful example of authoritative government not only because it worked out acceptable relationships between the center and its subdivisions, but also because the subdivisions remained politically unmobilized, primarily economic units, and were therefore able to accommodate the center. The preservation of this durable Brazilian unity thus seemed to depend quite heavily on low political mobilization and participation rates.

Chile

Chile declared her formal independence from Spain in 1818. The Cabildo of Santiago offered the leadership of the state to San Martín, Chile's liberator. He declined, however, in favor of Bernardo O'Higgins who assumed the title as Supreme Director. As in the other newly independent Latin American nations, power lay basically in the hands of a powerful executive. As Bolívar had done, O'Higgins attempted some basic reforms during the initial period of his control. Also like Bolívar, O'Higgins recognized the importance of primary and secondary education. He required all monasteries to establish private schools, and town councils were also expected to establish teaching facilities. European periodicals and books were allowed to enter Chile duty free in the effort to disseminate education. Mildly anticlerical, O'Higgins restricted the number of religious processions and permitted the burial of noncatholics in cemeteries. Many landed nobility titles to estates were nullified, and in many cases these lands which had previously been handed down to members of the same family were distributed to others.

However, continued unrest and finally an uprising caused O'Higgins to resign in 1823, after which followed 10 years of civil turmoil. By 1830 the Conservative faction of Chile's landed oligarchy under Joaquín Prieto and Diego Portales took power which they were not to relinquish for three decades.

Chile's political developments, after almost a decade of confusion following the withdrawal of O'Higgins, were the most stable and substantial of any in the Latin American Republics. Under the powerful leadership of Diego Portales, Conservative governments between 1830 and 1860 were able to ward off divisional revolts, civil war, and political anarchy. A railroad between Valparaiso and Santiago was completed and the modernization of the harbor of Valparaiso undertaken. Banking institutions were created, and trade was fostered with Europe and Peru. Minister Portales and Presidents Prieto, Bulnes, and Montt were all from the Conservative Party, which basically represented the large landowners, upper clergy, and military hierarchy. These men sought to instill as much of the monarchical traditions as feasible into Chilean republican institutions. Their principal opposition, though it was negligible for a generation, came from the Liberal Party. Though devoted Catholics, the Liberals were anticlerical in regard to the Church's role in government, and many were imbued with vague notions of British parliamentarism and French revolutionary concepts which led them to pursue a less centralized presidential system.

Under Portales overly individualistic army officers were exiled, landowners were again assured primogeniture, and the Church received all its past privileges. Portales sought to devise a formula for social peace so that Chile might make economic progress. Though the large masses of people made no social gains, the urban and commercial upper classes benefited and prospered under these changes. In 1833 a constitution heavily influenced by Portales was prescribed. It lasted with amendments until 1925, lasting longer than any Latin American constitution with the exception of the Argentine constitution of 1855, which lasted until 1949. By indirect vote and a literate, propertied public, the president and the two houses of congress were elected. Provincial and municipal authorities were directly responsible to the national president. The president had an absolute veto power and full appointive powers at all levels of government. The Conservatives maintained their monopoly of power until the mid-nineteenth century with the Liberals serving as a loyal opposition. Religion and the role of the Church was the basic issue that separated these two aristocratic parties.

In Chile the beginnings of a liberal philosophy of government and society came as the result of a religious dispute which took place in the latter part of the administration of Manuel Montt. President Montt, though conservative, began to accede to some of the moderate liberal demands of the 1850's. New capitalist groups had developed by then, partially because of the increasing commerce by way of Valparaiso and, to a lesser degree, as a result of the incipient mining interests in the northern Chilean nitrate fields. These groups combined to demand mild administrative and tax reforms as well as some electoral changes.

The ecclesiastical dispute involved the ouster of a sacristan from the cathedral of Santiago. When the Archbishop refused, President Montt threatened to expel him from Chile. Nothing came of it, but the rancor remained, splitting the conservative party into those supporting Montt and opposed to the Church's political interference and those favoring a proclerical orientation.[11] The former group soon combined with a more moderate (though anticlerical) liberal faction to establish Chile's third party—the National Party. The religious affair was actually symptomatic of the shifting alliances in a society changing from feudalism to capitalism and for which the Conservative Party could not provide all the answers.

As a result of the societal shifts, the Liberal Party and some of the newer coalitions of parties which were created to meet the needs of the economic and social classes began to gain strength. Many religious reforms were made, including the use of cemeteries for non-Catholics in the late 1850s, the right of non-Catholics to worship freely in 1865, the abolition of church courts in 1875, the nationalization of cemeteries in 1880, and the legalization of civil marriage in 1883.

The liberals also began winning victories by various amendments to the Constitution of 1833. In 1868 a president was forbidden to run for reelection. In 1871 proportional representation was instituted, aiding the cause of several newly-formed parties and weakening presidential authority. In 1885 and 1891 other measures increased home rule of the municipalities and gave Congress the power of overriding a presidential veto on legislation. Also in 1885 suffrage requirements gave the vote to all males over twenty-five and excluded the property qualification.

By 1890 President Balmaceda conceded to Congress that the cabinet had to be directly responsible to parliament; but that same year Balmaceda, faced with a divided cabinet, ousted the cabinet while Congress was adjourned and appointed one more congenial to his view of a strong executive. In fact, he

[11] Luis Galdames, *A History of Chile*, trans. I. J. Cox (Chapel Hill: University of North Carolina Press, 1941), pp. 294–295.

did not call Congress into session to approve his budget for 1891 but simply announced that the 1890 budget would remain in force. As a result of these actions, in January 1891 a large group of deputies declared Balmaceda deposed as president. A civil war ensued with military forces fighting on both sides of the issue. Lacking support from the most influential social and economic groups, Balmaceda was forced into exile in the Argentine legation. When permitted to leave, he committed suicide leaving behind a statement which said that his nationally oriented economic development plans were correct despite the profound opposition they evoked from the traditional power groups.

Balmaceda, during his time in office, had embarked upon a program of railroad and highway building, water works, health and sanitation, and universal schooling. His programs were rejected at the hands of the traditional elite who resented the increased taxes they would mean.

Though he failed to establish a modern executive system, Balmaceda was representative of the almost phenomenal economic changes in Chilean society after its victory in the War of the Pacific (1779–1783). With the great acquisition of new lands and resources, especially nitrate, Chile, at the expense of Peru and Bolivia, launched itself on an economic drive without par in its whole history, quadrupling, for example, its national income in a decade. The psychological boost the war gave the national mentality was a very important factor.

The Chilean commercial revolution of the latter half of the nineteenth century resulted in a proliferation of political parties.[12] Besides the creation of the National Party in 1856, which mainly represented the urban upper classes, the higher bureaucrats, and the banking interests, there was the founding of the Radicals in 1861 and the Democrats in 1887. The former represented the professional sectors and some of the landowners and the latter the developing middle classes of the largest urban centers of Chile. After the reform of 1885 which extended suffrage the Radicals and Democrats began to consider the worker as voting potential.

In a sense, the Balmaceda-congressional war represented the replacement of religious factors by political ones. The clerical-anticlerical issue was beginning to recede on the eve of the presidential-parliamentary struggle of 1891. The coup ousting Balmaceda came as a result of the conflict between the entrenched nineteenth century landed groups and a modernizing president who sought national above class interests. Because the mass of the people still remained politically and economically powerless, Balmaceda was sacrificed to the more traditional sectors of Chilean society.

Authoritative Chilean governments were substantially bolstered by the quality of their political leaders from O'Higgins to Portales. During the

[12] For an account of this period see Fredrick B. Pike, *Chile and the United States* (Notre Dame: University of Notre Dame, 1963), pp. 16–46.

authoritative phase and subsequent liberal-conservative competition for governmental control these early political leaders accustomed the country to peaceful political transition and policy resolution. At the same time the populace accepted the legitimacy of this limited ruling group, thus allowing constitutional regularity and longevity to keep pace.

Argentina

The most powerful and localized thrust for independence, however, was centered in Buenos Aires. Argentine society was quite different from Brazilian, Peruvian, and Mexican societies in that there were very few large-scale haciendas based upon abundant servile labor. The Argentine economy was based rather upon merchants in the cities and individual cattlemen in the rural pampa areas. Neither of these occupational groups ever accepted the restrictive and limited Spanish mercantile policies. Both needed export and import markets with which direct trade could be established.

There was also the psychological boost given the Argentine independence movement by the victory over the British occupation attempts in Buenos Aires in 1806–7. The defense of Buenos Aires was led mainly by Creoles rather than Spanish troops, and the successful repulsion of the British immeasurably strengthened the hand of the porteños for controlling their own political destiny.

However, the announcement of independence by the Buenos Aires junta in May of 1810 caused little echo in the other major Argentine cities of Mendoza, Córdoba, and Tucumán. Nor was there any reverberation in the other important centers of the La Plata Viceroyalty, namely, Montevideo and Asunción. Buenos Aires leadership in independence from Spain was rejected. Later her leadership within the Argentine nation was to be rejected for many years. The special nature of Buenos Aires society, her European orientation, and advanced commercial policies were a continual threat to eventual Argentine national unification.[13] In the interim years between the independence proclamation of Buenos Aires and the official Argentine pronouncement in Córdoba in 1816, Argentina lost a fair share of what would have been a nation comparable in size to Mexico. Uruguay was lost in a war to Brazil and later was assured independence by the British who rushed to create a buffer state between the giants of Brazil and Argentina. Paraguay initiated her own national drive by 1811. Upper Peru, which had been detached from the area under Lima's control and integrated into the La Plata colony, was later absorbed under Bolívar into a new state called Bolivia.

Aside from these considerable losses, Buenos Aires was faced with strong

[13] See Raul Puigbo, *Historia social y economica Argentina* (Buenos Aires: Ediciones Esnaola, 1964), pp. 91–94.

opposition from within Argentina itself. Rural cities opposed the Buenos Aires port duties on exports. Buenos Aires was distrusted because it preferred materials from Europe, which were both cheaper and of superior quality. During the early period British investments were concentrated in Buenos Aires with the virtual exclusion of interior Argentina.

Bernardo Rivadavia, chosen by Buenos Aires to be leader of a loosely aligned group of provinces, instituted policies much like those of O'Higgins, Bolívar, and San Martín. Taxation rights of the church were terminated as were her ecclesiastical courts, civil authorities were given the power to regulate the church, and church cemeteries were secularized. Under Rivadavia's leadership public-works projects were initiated as well as a national university system. As could be expected, however, Rivadavia's attempts to initiate a constitution which would form a unitary national state with Buenos Aires as the capital were rejected by every one of the recognized provinces of Argentina. The failure of Bernardo Rivadavia to gain acceptance of his plan for a unitary government in Buenos Aires determined successive political events and fostered one of the more severe Latin American dictatorships in the nineteenth century as well as the most overt abuse of power anywhere during the authoritative period.

As a leader of the federalists who opposed unitarian policies, which originated in the city of Buenos Aires, Juan Manuel Rosas led Buenos Aires province and other federal-oriented provinces to reject Rivadavia's leadership. The legislature in Buenos Aires called on this popular caudillo of the province to lead the federalist forces as governor. Under Rosas' leadership from the province of Buenos Aires, a loose confederation was created among all the provinces to combat any unitarian proposal by the city of Buenos Aires. The local federalist leaders of the various provinces were mainly interested in ensuring their local autonomy and defending free trade without tax and customs interference from the port of Buenos Aires. Under Rosas they established their own armies and coined their own currency. However, Rosas maintained control of foreign policy and commercial trading with Buenos Aires.

Though a federalist in name, Rosas developed into a strong unitarian in fact, though he replaced the city of Buenos Aires with the province and thus maintained a rather artificial alliance with other provincial governors. Rosas' leadership was a reaction to the internationalism of liberal Buenos Aires and, it was in the style of the most anti-liberal of the European monarchs in the post Napoleonic restoration. A book burner despite the ideological currents of revolutionary Europe, Rosas' use for Europe was based on selling beef and hides and buying manufactured goods—nothing more. As a very wealthy and powerful rancher and the creator of the first Argentine salting plant for preserving beef, Rosas was principally responsible for setting Argentina along the seemingly irreversible path as a monocultural exporter of beef to Europe's industrial centers.

Rosas for all intents and purposes was a dictator until 1852. He sought a federal complex in the sense that all provinces were to be equal, but one (Buenos Aires) was to be more equal than the others. Through his own army, spies, large public wealth, and his own personal fortune, Rosas was able to keep the other provincial governors quiet for 18 years. Reelected governor of Buenos Aires Province by popular demand in 1835, he took this as a mandate to further centralize the government and enforce his tyranny over the Argentine nation. During the balance of his rule, the Buenos Aires cabildo and the provincial legislature were disbanded. However, Rosas continued to avoid a strictly unitary regime and avoided any title higher than governor of Buenos Aires province. Yet as Governor, he was to wield more power than any Argentine, until the advent of Juan Perón in 1946.

Throughout the late 1830's and 1840's Rosas pursued a policy of aggressive Argentine nationalism and discouraged foreign technology, immigration, and ideas.[14] Lands recovered from the Indian wars were dispersed by Rosas on a strictly arbitrary basis. Tremendous tracts of land were controlled by a very few individuals, a phenomenon still very evident in Argentina. With the consolidation of Rosas' power, he was able to finance his administration almost totally from the revenues received by the ships entering and leaving the Paraná and Uruguay Rivers at the mouth of the La Plata estuary at Buenos Aires. This allowed him to ease the already "feathery" tax burden on his fellow estancieros with their all-important cattle herds for export. Rosas' foreign policy was as forceful as his domestic policies. Though he won no clearcut diplomatic or military victories, he entrenched himself with the Argentine masses by his occasional foreign forays.

The eventual downfall of Rosas came largely because of the many foreign enemies he had made during his 20 years in office. Brazilian and Uruguayan support of a caudillo José de Urquiza of Entre Rios Province combined to send Rosas into exile. The many liberal Argentines in exile in Montevideo and Santiago aided the fight against Rosas as did numerous provincial governors who resented the increasing unitarian developments under Rosas' leadership.

In retrospect, Rosas gave impetus to Argentine nationality by his aggressive domestic and foreign policies.[15] Despite his federal claims he accustomed the provinces to look toward Buenos Aires province, if not toward the city

[14] See James R. Scobie, *Argentina: A City and a Nation* (New York: Oxford University Press, 1964), pp. 80–87.

[15] Marcos Merchensky, *Las corrientes ideologicas en la historia Argentina* (Buenos Aires: Editorial Concordia, 1961), pp. 81–95. Beezley, for example, states that the mark of a successful "caudillo" is one that enforces stability, aids the growth of nationalism, demonstrates the availability of national wealth and power, and often contributes to material progress, while the unsuccessful caudillo divides the society and intensifies its breakdown. Here again it would be difficult to evaluate Rosas with certitude. See William H. Beezley, "Caudillismo: An Interpretive Note," *Journal of Inter-American Studies*, vol. 2, no. 3 (July 1969), p. 352.

itself, for national leadership. In this respect he merely reaffirmed an existing geopolitical tendency. He initiated Argentina on its traditional role as meat supplier for European dinner tables, he reinforced the inequality of landownership, and he inhibited indigenous industry and commercial advancement. When measured against the potential the Rosas regime had for economic development and political advance, the record shows a substantial deficit.

In Argentina much of the second half of the nineteenth century was taken up with the federal-unitary struggle that had absorbed her early independence years. The victory of Urquiza over the Rosas forces in 1852 was a victory of legitimate federalism. A constituent congress was assembled, and Urquiza was named provisional director of the confederation. In an effort to unify the nation, Urquiza ended trade restrictions between provinces, freed trade up and down the Paraná, and nationalized all customs duties which Buenos Aires had formerly monopolized. Under the leadership of the governor of Buenos Aires, Bartolomé Mitre, Buenos Aires denounced this plan for a more unified national entity. With Urquiza's plans repudiated by Buenos Aires, the Confederation of the United Provinces moved its capital up to Paraná in Entre Rios from where Urquiza governed for 8 years without the participation of the province of Buenos Aires. Thus a decapitated Argentina developed in an unnatural manner with a confederation of the poorer provinces that sorely missed Buenos Aires with its monopoly of educated people, lucrative exports, and rich farm lands. However, Urquiza made statesmanlike efforts to formally organize the nation into an organic whole into which someday Buenos Aires might wish or be forced to join. The fourteen provinces proceeded to meet in Santa Fe in 1852 and drew up the Argentine constitution of 1853.

Very similar to the North American Constitution, the Argentine constitution was to last until it was abrogated by Perón. It was reinstated in 1957. If anyone qualifies for the title of father of his country's constitution, it is Juan Bautista Alberdi whose book *Bases and Points of Departure for the Political Organization of the Argentine Republic* laid down close guide lines for the constitutional convention in Santa Fe. A great number of Alberdi's suggestions were incorporated into the Argentine Constitution. The president's term of office was limited to 6 years, and he could not serve two consecutive terms. The federal government was given a great deal of power in administration and provincial affairs, and many implied powers were given to the president. There were articles on stimulation of immigration and the elimination of trade barriers among the provinces. The responsibility for education was given to the national government as well as the obligation to develop industry and trade, import foreign capital, and explore and colonize public lands—all very specific duties not often catalogued in constitutions.

The difficulties of running a government with a weak economic base became all too clear to Urquiza who valiantly attempted to go it alone for a time, even though many of his economic schemes were failing. Finally in order to bring about a compromise with Buenos Aires, he resigned the presidency. With Urquiza in the background, Mitre as governor of Buenos Aires province assumed the provisional presidency and moved the capital back to Buenos Aires. In 1862 Mitre was formally elected and installed as the first constitutional president of a newly united Argentina.

Under Mitre's presidency (1862–1868) congress again attempted to integrate the city of Buenos Aires by federalizing it, but porteño opposition made it necessary to locate *both* the national and the provincial capitals at Buenos Aires. This arrangement continued until the Presidency of Julio Roca in 1880 when Buenos Aires was finally separated from the province of the same name and federalized, and the provincial government of Buenos Aires Province was moved to La Plata. Under the forceful leadership of Mitre and Domingo Faustino Sarmiento (1868–1874) Argentina made important strides in stimulating European immigration and capital.[16] Railroads flourished, telegraph lines multiplied, and the port of Buenos Aires was refurbished. President Sarmiento, in particular, took great interest in making Argentina's educational and specifically her university system the most advanced in Latin America. An extremely cultivated and talented individual himself, Sarmiento was the major impetus behind the construction of museums, libraries, and educational institutes which still dot the Argentina cultural landscape.

Though Argentina was prospering by the turn of the century, her politics were left to a small ruling oligarchy which maintained itself, despite intraparty bickering, as an inbred power group that limited popular participation and neglected both the needs of the middle and lower classes.

In Argentina in the 1880's and 1890's a new movement, the Unión Cívica of Leandro Alem, had been formed. This party represented the aspirations of a new wave of immigrants and merchant classes which were becoming prominent in the large urban hubs of eastern Argentina. Alem sought the services of Bartolomé Mitre who, at seventy, returned from Europe to run for the presidency of Argentina in the 1892 elections. The Unión Cívica learned an important lesson when Mitre eventually sidestepped this middle class party to throw his prestige and fortune behind one of the existing traditional parties which had ruled Argentina since the fall of Rosas in 1852. At loggerheads with each other, Mitre and General Julio Roca eventually decided on a third choice, a compromise candidate, Luis Sáenz Peña. The conservatives won a dubiously run election, but the Unión Cívica Radical, as it was now called, touched off a civilian revolt which, though quickly suppressed, represented the first mass uprising against the monopoly of power held by the landed

[16] José Luis Romero, *A History of Argentine Political Thought*, trans. Thomas McGann (Stanford: Stanford University Press, 1963), pp. 169–170.

interests.[17] The suicide of Alem in 1896 paved the way for the ascension to power within the party of Hipólito Irigoyen and the radicalization of the movement to one of abstention and noncompliance under the existing conditions. This was brought out in the 1898 elections when Roca won a second term in office while the Unión Cívica Radical, or Radicals, abstained under the leadership of Irigoyen. As the Roca administration was succeeded by others within the ruling elite, the Radicals in 1905 attempted another surge for total power and were again crushed.

Two important splinter groups whose break influenced much of twentieth century party politics arose within the ranks of the Radicals. Opposed to the charismatic leadership of Irigoyen and to what they felt was a paucity of program and a mere demagogic adherence, while electoral fraud existed, to "no electoral participation," two influential Radical party members broke with the parent organization. Juan B. Justo, greatly influenced by the Socialist tide in Europe, founded the Argentine Socialist Party in 1905. Lisandro de la Torre, disgruntled with the personalist party dictatorship of Irigoyen, also left the party to establish the Progressive Democrats, an influential but minor party in twentieth century affairs. By the estrangement of these two groups, the Unión Cívica Radical lost much of its ideological fervor.

Thus the Argentine struggle for authority and legitimacy lasted longer than those of Peru, Brazil, and Chile, while it responded to more genuine local and regional differences than was true in the Mexican case. Development of interior interests (on trade routes from Lima, Peru) in Argentina preceded the formation of or predisposition to any national governmental organization in Buenos Aires, and thus laid the foundations for a veritable struggle for dominance. The compromise of federalizing the city of Buenos Aires marked the end of the authoritative struggle that had seen a leader of a confederational league stimulate the development of a strongly centralized federal regime. It represents an excellent case study of the kind of mixture of command, persuasion, and bargaining necessary to establish political control over disperse national interests.

Summary

Early in the authoritative period, Peru, Chile, and Argentina had leadership which, however well-intentioned, failed to really gain control, and these nations often succumbed to factional and fratricidal warfare. These leadership elements instituted mild reforms and anticlerical policies in hopes of breaking

[17] For an excellent interpretation of this new mass movement see Oscar Cornblit et al., "La generacion del 80 y su proyecto," in Torcuato S. Di Tella et al., *Argentina, sociedad de masas* (Buenos Aires: Editorial de la Universidad de Buenos Aires, 1965), pp. 37–38.

down some of the more virulent aspects of feudal society. All these early leaders were eventually ousted and their policies superseded by more traditional ones. Mexico had poor leadership and the most widespread insurrectionism and local turbulence, while Brazil demonstrated the viability of a constitutional monarchy as an initial focal point for both authority and legitimacy.

Change has usually been induced by either external influences that have resulted in the adaptation of new institutions or by ideological shifts on the parts of modernizing elites. In Mexico incessant foreign pressures during her formative years when her sense of nationality was as yet not fully realized affected her policy and leadership. Successive penetrations of Mexican soil by North American and French occupations had a powerful effect on Mexican national consciousness. Through American expansion Mexico lost over two-thirds of her territory—from southern Oregon to the Rio Grande River. She reacted to this by a reaffirmation of her nationality and a need to consolidate her nation as an independent entity. The defeat at the hands of the Texans taught the Mexican leadership that they must not only settle Mexico's vast remaining frontier but also provide a more disciplined, socially concerned political administration that could genuinely represent the national interest rather than class and personal interests. Mexico's national entity was in much less danger by the mid-nineteenth century, and though she was again occupied, this time by the French soldiers of Maximilian, she overcame this temporary infringement to emerge with a more confident view of her statecraft.

In Brazil the conscientious leadership of Pedro II combined with the capitalist visions of Baron Mauá provided the peace and economic drive which allowed Brazil to overcome the immense national reverberations following the abolition of slavery. The end of slavery, combined with the republicanism of the military, initiated a series of changes that culminated in the demise of the monarchy. Here, too, positivism provided the ideological bind that brought forth the new Republic from a monarchy that had provided the basic groundwork for republicanism.

Chile's foreign successes, notably the War of the Pacific, brought her by the turn of the twentieth century economic development and basic political stability. The nitrate boom was one of those fortuitous occurrences that shapes and alters the life of a nation. It provided the spark which brought Chile to the threshold of economic modernization. Throughout the nineteenth century occasional personalistic leaders carried her on separate waves toward national maturity. From the paternalistic leadership of Diego Portales, through the anticlerical policies of President Montt, to the "anti-oligarchic" conceptions of President Balmaceda, Chile developed in spite of the natural disposition of the landowners and church to defend the status quo.

Argentina went through perhaps the most "typical" phase of national development. The spirit of nationalism provided by the xenophobic character of Rosas allowed for a later transition to a constitutional refinement of Rosas' primitive attempts. Under presidents Mitre and Sarmiento, Argentina achieved the national unity which was necessary for her material expansion which took place first under the agrarian beef exporters and later by the urban merchant classes that clamored for tariff protection and governmental paternalism.

CHAPTER 5 The Aggregative Phase

The aggregative phase is characterized by the growing impact of new interests. These interests are a result of policies fostered by authoritative governments but which slowly take on an independent direction. They often counteract and even confront existing governmental leadership. Central governments recognize these incipient interests that perform functional development services yet do not represent direct threats to the established leadership groups controlling the public administration.

Foreign capital (and/or immigration in some cases) has also been an important innovative input into resource exploitation and infrastructure investment. The ownership of land was conceived of as another potential resource of productive rather than residual wealth.

Characteristic of these new interests was the development of reformed middle-class parties. They represented no immediate challenge to the power structure but rather diverted national interests toward economic problems that faced conservative governments. They were instrumental in channeling into the political process the new urban middle-class groups which might otherwise have found their aspirations completely incompatible with those of the more traditional ruling groups. In addition, the military's role became more ambivalent during the aggregative period by developing a more professional commitment that represented a countervailing form of pressure on the still dominant traditional civilian groups.

The impact of European liberalism as represented by the events of 1848–1875 subjected the traditional authoritative governments to strains that were to be manifested more and more often between 1860 and 1916. As the authoritative phase had demonstrated the capacity of governing elites to deal successfully with the problems of concentrating political power in a social group centered in the national administration, so the aggregative phase witnessed the advent of groups within society who were directing their attention to the priorities and decisions made by the central governments. This funnelled hitherto dispersed, or sometimes latent, interests into the national policy-making process. This had two major effects: It resulted in a growing national arena for political activity. At the same time it increased instability as central decision-making became more crucial to economic interests who were competing for scarce natural and material resources. Political confrontation became more widespread as increasingly large payoffs were derived from political involvement. This development was reinforced by the proliferation of new parties. The Conservative and Liberal parties were joined by Radical, Democratic, and Socialist parties who contributed much to the expanded political dialogue.

Mexico

In the struggle for power after the death of Juárez, General Porfirio Díaz was to rule Mexico for 35 years, bringing to Latin America a modern dictatorship as opposed to the conservative rule of a Rosas of Argentina, a Francis of Paraguay, a Melgarejo of Bolivia, and others of the preceding generation.

The Díaz regime represented a sophisticatedly organized, unwritten confluence of interests among the landowners, church, military, and foreign economic interest.[1] The key to Díaz's overwhelming power lay in his skillful use of the Lerdo Law which deprived thousands of Indians of their traditional lands and gave them to individual landowners already controlling haciendas that extended sometimes for hundreds of thousands of acres. Church property was also gradually returned by the same mechanisms, the Church by now having the wherewithall to make the nominal payment. In return for these favors Díaz received the unequivocal support of the largest and most influential landowners. In addition he seemed able to keep the countryside free of marauders and caudillos. Surveying companies were hired to find cause for confiscation of Indian communal properties by some technicality and were given one-third of all the land they so freed for individual sales and private accumulation.[2] The expropriation of Indian lands forced thousands of Indians to hire themselves out as peons and day laborers under the worst conditions. Because the 25 centavos daily wage forced the Indian to take out small loans with excessive interest rates, the hacienda owner-Indian relationship often forced the Indian into serf-like conditions which continued unabated during his lifetime and was often assured his sons. As a result of these Porfirian

[1] Moisés Gonzalez Navarro et al., *Historia documental de Mexico* (Mexico: Universidad Nacional Autónama de México, 1964), p. 341 ff. The Diaz period marked foreign domination in all the important sectors of the economy, such as the banks, petroleum, mining, railways, and public services. Anglo-American and French interests were the prime movers in the Mexican economy. See for example, David H. Shelton in Raymond Vernon, *Public Policy and Private Enterprise in Mexico* (Cambridge: Harvard University Press, 1964), pp. 130–131, and Alfred Tischendorf, *Great Britain and Mexico in the Era of Porfirio Diaz* (Durham, N.C.: Duke University Press, 1961). The fourth largest foreign investor, though much out-distanced by the other three, was Germany. See Warren Schiff, "The Germans in Mexican Trade and Industry During the Diaz Period," *The Americans,* vol. 23, no. 3 (January 1967), pp. 279–296.

[2] Jesús Silva Herzog, *Breve historia de la revolución Mexicana* (Mexico City: Fonda de Cultura Económica, 1960), p. 16; Gonzalez Navarro et al., *Historia documental de Mexico,* p. 343.

policies, statistics demonstrate that at the turn of the twentieth century an average of 85 percent of the Mexicans were engaged in agriculture, while less than 1 percent owned the land.

The church remained a staunch ally of Díaz, because though he refused to abrogate the Reform Laws instituted under Juárez, he never applied the Laws against the church. The church flourished in extent of its landholdings, number of new clergymen, and in the creation of new bishoprics. Since anti-clerical liberals favored a continuance of the Reform Laws within the legal framework and the conservatives favored a tolerant view of the church within Mexican society, neither found enough fault with Porfirio Díaz's policy on religion.

Díaz's third area of support came from the military arm of the government. His generals were a highly privileged group of men who received excellent salaries, generous fringe benefits, such as expense accounts, and other accouterments in line with their imposing positions. The members of this fraternity were assured the best kind of life known to Mexican prerevolutionary society. Not one to depend on positive persuasion alone, Díaz also relied on a scheme he instituted of continually rotating his officers throughout the country. Thus, no general could elicit extraordinary loyalties from his command, which, if he did, was tantamount to admitting disloyalty against the central government in nineteenth and twentieth century Mexico.[3] The proof that Porfirio Díaz's scheme was successful is demonstrated by the fact that there was only one large-scale rebellion against his dictatorship, and that one succeeded in overthrowing him when he had reached the age of 80.

In terms of Mexican economic development and the modernization of the country, the Díaz regime developed special relationships with foreign economic interests in Mexico. To stimulate cattle ranching, oil development, and the mining of precious metals, British and American interests were given special dispensations within the first years of the Díaz government. One was the controversial right to the ownership of the subsoil; however, oil production, for example, jumped from 10,000 barrels in 1901 to 13,000,000 barrels in 1911. Aside from the American and British involvement in the extractive industries, French capital assisted in the development of the textile industry which had originally been started by Padre Hidalgo at the turn of the nineteenth century. Many of Mexico City's largest department stores were also begun by French businessmen. The Germans were influential in many of the hardware and drug businesses, while Spaniards were noted for their involvement in various retail trades and tobacco farming in the rural areas. Public utilities were usually controlled by American or British companies; thus the great preponderance of business and manufacturing in Mexico was in foreign hands.[4]

[3] Lieuwen, *Arms and Politics in Latin America*, p. 104.

[4] For an authoritative compilation of foreign investments during the Díaz

The large-scale web of foreign commercial interests which was tied to Mexican political power was basically the work of the "cientificos," a group of young intellectuals and economists who sought to achieve a British-type laissez-faire commercial revolution for Mexico. They apparently held high positions in Porfirio Díaz's administration and were very influential in establishing sound financial, investment and developmental practices that helped to strengthen the urban middle sectors of Mexican society who were, they felt, the only capable group in a progressive Mexico. Immersed in the spirit of French positivism, the cientificos sought "order and progress" for the middle classes at the expense of Mexico's vast majority of people who, though they indirectly benefited from some of the commercial measures and innovations, were never the object of any economic changes during the aggregative phase of Mexican development.

The opulence into which Mexico City grew under the administration of Porfirio Díaz did not find a counterpart in the surrounding countryside where millions still remained poorly housed and educated with no alternative but to eke out a threadbare existence in a country where rural wages were frozen and costs were rising of products manufactured by a combination of foreign capital and middle class Mexican skills.

The Díaz government was most markedly aggregative in its guidance and stimulation of new foreign and domestic economic interests. Because of the tightly controlled nature of the Mexican government, these interests did not challenge the Díaz government directly or develop independent directions of their own. However, the "cientificos" did represent, more than Díaz himself, the formation of modernizing attitudes and they laid the groundwork by which the newly developing economic interests shared increasing power with the political administration. Thus, in lieu of acting as a political organization, these cientificos behaved as a parapolitical factor of power that guided Mexico by the turn of the twentieth century. Their economic preoccupations, more than Díaz's political and administrative concerns, were to outlast the fulminations of the imminent Mexican Revolution.

---

regime, consult Volume 7 in the series under the general editorship of Daniel Cosio Villegas, *Historia moderna de Mexico. El Porfiriato: La vida económica* (Mexico: Editorial Hermes, 1965). See Chapter 10 written by Luis Nicolau D'Olwer, pp. 1003–1152. United States, British, and French investments, for example, in commercial banks approximated 92 per cent around the turn of the century. The comparable investments of these three countries in other crucial economic sectors were as follows: railroads 87 per cent, of which half was North American; mining 98 per cent, of which 62 per cent of total investment was North American; industry 79 per cent, of which France's share was 55 per cent; petroleum close to 100 per cent with the inclusion of some Canadian interests; commerce and retailing, in which the French contributed 66 per cent of total investments; and public services in which Britain's share was 89 per cent. In all, American and British interests alone contributed about 85 per cent of total investments in Mexico.

Peru

In Peru, civilian governments returned between 1939 and 1948 though the armed forces still retained their veto power. The deciding factor in the elections of 1939 and 1945 were the Aprista votes which elected president Prado, in return for ending the exile of Haya de la Torre, and Bustamente, in return for the legalization of the APRA party and APRA's receiving several cabinet posts in Bustamente's government. The APRA in positions of responsibility in government did not demonstrate as much acumen as it had in its role of forceful opposition. Another military coup, led by Manuel Odría, ended the unsuccessful Aprista participation in government. It must be added that the Aprista people were not masters in their own house and thus the final word regarding their administrative skills must be withheld.

The military government of General Odría was a necessary respite for Peru.[5] Though his administration did not legislate on behalf of the social and political integration of the masses of Indians, Odría did preside over a period of accelerated economic growth, and he used the funds of increased exports of copper, cotton, and sugar to build roads, power plants, and initiate heavy industry.

Odría—as Aramburu in Argentina and Ibañez in Chile—allowed his regime to come to an end within the prescribed time allowed by the constitution. He was followed by Manuel Prado, who returned for a second time and whose administration appeared merely to mark time and made few changes in Peruvian society. Prado did, however, allow the Apristas to act in public after years of suppression under Odría. When the Apristas returned a plurality for the presidential elections of 1962, the military again intervened, as they had in 1931 and 1948, to forestall increasing Aprista influence both within and outside the government. Continual Aprista compromises with Bustamente in 1945 and Prado in 1956 failed to legitimize them in the eyes of the military. When elections were again held in 1963, the Acción Pópular of Fernando Belaúnde Terry won the presidency against the Aprista party allied with its erstwhile enemy, the Odría forces. The Belaúnde Terry administration, though faced with overwhelming opposition from congressional majorities, appeared, at the time of the 1968 military coup, to be overcoming the Aprista–anti-Aprista dialogue of three decades, and with a minimum of ideological warfare, to be consolidating economic gains.[6]

[5] Charles Anderson states that Odría was supported by most major power contenders except APRA. See his sophisticated interpretation of Peruvian policies in the 1950s in *Politics and Economic Change in Latin America* (Princeton, N.J., Van Nostrand, 1967), pp. 248–255.

[6] John Gunther observed the effective manner in which Belaunde Terry carried out legislation despite his coalition's minority position in congress. See his *Inside South America* (New York: Harper and Row, 1966), pp. 330–332.

Peru has only comparatively recently made the transition from authoritative to aggregative stage which, more than in her sister republics, gave rise to almost coincidental distributive pressures best represented by the rise, crises, and fall of the Aprista party fortunes. This can be partially explained by the effects of many years of authoritative rule that had accustomed the populace to the rule of a relatively small elite. Thus the aggregative and distributive phenomena emerged in very rapid succession—within one generation or so—between World War II and the early 1960's. The Odría dictatorship of the 1950's, however, was typically aggregative in style in that it released economic interests, both commercial and industrial, which, under the aegis of Belaúnde Terry's party, the Acción Popular, and certain sectors of the military, were to manifest themselves in competition with the upper classes by the end of the 1950's.

Brazil

The Brazilian military revolt which ended the Brazilian Empire in 1889 initiated a series of perceptible changes not only in the political sector, but in the economic decision-making sector as well by bringing about a shift toward middle-class control.

What had been an essentially sugar export economy until the mid nineteenth century now was challenged by the coffee export sector of the Southern states of São Paulo and Rio de Janeiro. Complementing the growth of coffee as king were important cattle and cotton growing developments in Minas Gerais and Rio Grande do Sul. This resulted in a waning dominance of the northeastern sugar growers of Pernambuco and Bahia who had been the most opulent and powerful of the traditional nineteenth century oligarchy. Whereas the northeastern planters had been quite satisfied to be the economic ruling class, allowing Pedro II's political rule, the rising financial elites of the aggregative phase, represented not only by the cattle, cotton, and coffee interests but by the newly powerful urban commercial classes, sought political control and status as well. With the demise of the empire's moderating and unifying factor in the person of the monarch, early twentieth century Brazilian development gave rise to a new and vigorous interplay and struggle for political power and economic status.

The new republican constitution of Brazil in 1891 resembled in many ways the constitution of the United States in its articles on federalism, division of powers, and the principle of states' rights. This was also the case with so many of her sister republics. Despite the formal constitutional framework, military control persisted during the early years of the aggregative phase, and ostensibly the only visible shift in policy from the last period of the authoritative phase was the growing preponderance of the military within the centers of public power. After the nominal reassertion of civilian control in 1895, a pattern of military ascendancy in Brazilian politics developed which was to last until after the Vargas coup of 1930. The coffee interests of São Paulo combined with the mining and cotton interests of Minas Gerais to rotate among themselves the highest offices of the land. The control by these two states spread to the national level.[7] The military along with these powerful interest groups first asserted influence in São Paulo and Minas Gerais. It was an easy transition from there to the central seat of government in Rio de Janeiro, and there was no competition, except possibly from the state of Rio Grande do Sul. However, three decades passed before the cattle-dominated Rio Grande do Sul could make a successful and long-range bid for power.

Characteristic of 20th century Latin American political and economic development, world wars have not only given impetus to the process of capital accumulation and consumer power but have shifted control from one group to another by stimulating the export sector in foodstuffs and other raw materials. This not only has enriched the private entrepreneurs but the central government as well and has either meant an increase in the standard of living of much of the population through full employment and possibly higher wages or, something not immediately observable from the consumers' point of view, an effort by the central government to capitalize and modernize the country's infrastructure by dispersal of social overhead capital. Thus World War I enriched Brazil. It marked the beginning of a growth period which went unhampered until the depression of 1930.

Brazil's boom during the aggregative phase was uneven in the sense that it was confined largely to the urban areas, which represented probably not more than a quarter of Brazil's population, and to the leading coffee and cotton plantations scattered throughout Eastern Brazil. The so-called "demonstration effect" determined much of the revolutionary fervor that paralleled this economic development in the 1920's. During this decade the rising expectations of the masses allowed the fomenting of numerous military and filo-Communist uprisings. The most famous of these was the attempted officers' revolt led by Luis Carlos Prestes who led a group of military rebels through the Brazilian countryside for two years in order to foment a mass uprising against the government. Never entirely defeated, and never successful at stirring up the people, the column eventually disappeared. Many of these rebellious junior officers remained politically active and combined in support of the 1930 revolt.[8]

[7] See the memoirs of Brazilian President Manoel de Campos Salles (1898–1902), reprinted by Alfred C. Stepan in Fredrick Pike (ed.), *Latin American History: Select Problems* (New York: Harcourt, Brace and World, 1969), pp. 276–278.

[8] See an interpretation of this movement by John D. Wirth, "Tenentismo in the Brazilian Revolution of 1930," *Hispanic American Historical Review*, vol. 44,

The unwritten code of alternate succession to the presidency between São Paulo and Minas Gerais was carelessly neglected by president Washington Luis of the state of São Paulo. In 1930 he sought to be succeeded by a fellow Paulista, Julio Prestes. This miscalculation gave other sectors of the country the hope that their day to control was not far off, and thus a new pattern of power was initiated. Incensed at this break in a gentlemen's agreement, the state of Minas Gerais banded together with Rio Grande do Sul which bargained to get the presidency for itself.

The leader of the new elite was a cattle baron from Rio Grande do Sul, Getulio Vargas, who governed Brazil from 1930 to 1955 with a lapse of five years (1945–1950) when Marshall Dutra took control for the military. The reforms which Vargas made in political and economic system affect Brazil today. The more important changes occurred in the federal framework, in the greater unification of the states, and in the emancipation of the working classes to the point of their self-recognition as an important and consequential part of the economy and political structure of Brazil.[9] All this, however, was achieved within a dictatorial system which, in varying degrees, imposed control over Brazilian citizens during the initial stages of the distributive period.

The aggregative phase in Brazil marked the rise of the formerly less important states as they began to compete successfully for political influence. The monopoly of São Paulo and Minas Gerais was further assaulted during the distributive phase under the dictatorship of Getulio Vargas. This growing pluralization of Brazil's political structure was based on the proliferation of diversified class, economic, and regional interests. Moreover, military concern for economic and social change was evident toward the end of the aggregative period. Under the leadership of the junior army officials, these lieutenants, along with elements of the urban middle classes, acted as a countervailing influence on the traditional rural upper classes.

Chile

In Chile, the 1891–1925 period is popularly known as the period of parliamentary government, though the whole experiment took place under the presidential system established by the Constitution of 1833. What occurred was the passage of a series of parliamentary measures and amendments to the old constitution that weakened the president's control over congress and gave congress important auditing powers over the executive's tax and appropriation

---

no. 2 (May, 1964), pp. 161–179. Wirth's thesis centers about the accommodation made between the nationalist aspirations of the lieutenants and the political pragmatism of Getulio Vargas.

[9] For a summary of the import of Vargas' policies on the working classes, see E. Bradford Burns, *Nationalism in Brazil: A Historical Survey* (New York: Praeger, 1968), pp. 85–89.

program as well as his choice of cabinet officers. Distinct from a traditional parliamentary system, there was no prime minister nor a built-in system of parliamentary dissolution or censure of the executive. This period, better described as one of weak presidents or parliamentary ascendancy, resulted in a political and administrative anachronism. Chile moved toward greater decentralism and away from effective executive leadership at the same time that many of the other nations were strengthening, though often with tyranny, the executive office.[10] It has been said that this period gave Chile, more than her republican sisters, a real taste for democratic procedures. However, an examination of political participation, electoral rolls, and the unrepresentative nature of the parliamentary parties suggests that it was rather a power struggle between a declining landed elite and nationally oriented and middle class-supported presidents. "Parliamentary democracy" meant the absence of necessary executive programs in economic and social areas, blocked as they continually were by the aristocratic forces who had the power within the Chilean national legislature.

World War I gave Chile the opportunity for greater economic development. The wealth from the discovery of nitrate, which followed Chile's great imperialist effort in the War of the Pacific (1879–1883), broadened her economic potential and export capacities and found fruition at the beginning of the twentieth century. New groups, such as mine owners, mineral exporters, and financiers, all very rapidly attempted to penetrate the national economic elite which had been made up of predominantly large landowners. A second major group which helped distribute national wealth and political power were the newly arrived immigrants from Central and Eastern Europe and Spain, who rather quickly developed the land of Southern Chile into small efficient farms. These groups began to compete with the large landowners in the political arenas, although the economic strength of the landowners remained predominant for several more generations. For the landed elite the pre-1925 period was a time in which the balance of power, for the first time in Chilean history, seemed to be veering dangerously away from them. Though the landowners preserved their basic political strength until the latter 1920's and the 1930's, economic changes continued to occur which eventually altered the political landscape.

The Radical party represented a political response to the middle sectors and an incipient awareness of the growth of the popular sectors. The Radicals became the prime competitors of the two-party Liberal-Conservative dominance. The Liberals and Conservatives, as the clerical question was gradually losing force, found comfort in each other and became inveterate political and economic companions. In 1912 the Socialist Workers party appeared and by

[10] For an analysis of this thirty-year period of parliamentary "government" see Federico G. Gil, *The Political System of Chile* (Boston: Houghton Mifflin, 1966), pp. 47–56.

1921 reconstituted itself as the Communist party. The advent of the Radical party as well as various smaller traditional parties which developed under the stimulation of parliamentary dominance resulted in a situation where party interests became more differentiated and identifiable.

This aggregative phase provided the Chilean people with a tradition in which parliament was not to be a rubber-stamp institution for presidential initiative. The parliamentary experience proved a valuable testing ground for democratic schooling, free debate, and juridical normality, which in the long run probably strengthened Chilean democratic institutions more than those of Brazil, Mexico, Peru, and Argentina.

However, the slow, unwieldy congress proved unequal to the task of dealing with the social and economic problems that cried out for quick and effective solutions. Thus the more articulate middle class and the growing urban proletariat (which amounted to about 1 million by World War I) shifted the center of political debate. These groups rapidly began to organize, each defending its own interests but both inimical to the landed aristocracy. As labor became more organized, strikes became more common. For example, between 1910 and 1920 there were close to 300 strikes called.[11] After the Mexican and Russian experiences of 1917, the poorest sectors of society began to clamor for a greater share of the national wealth.

It was against this background of social pressure that, following the depression after the close of World War I, a strong presidential system was restored. The elections of 1920 were won for the first time by a candidate who ran a campaign geared specifically to gain middle class and lower class votes. The discovery of synthetic nitrate had resulted in a tremendous economic letdown since nitrate had an 80 per cent share of all foreign exchange. Arturo Alessandri, elected under a combined Radical-Democratic Party with a faction of Liberals support, addressed himself to this economic dislocation. The continued resistance of parliament brought on the crisis of 1925 which led to military intervention and the writing of Chile's present constitution. For the first time in one hundred years the Chilean military interfered in political affairs for a number of reasons—concern for the country, distrust for the self-seeking parliamentarians, and self-interest.[12] Chilean affairs were deeply affected by this uprising.

In the new constitution a strong executive was created, control by congress over financial legislation was greatly weakened, suffrage for males was made universal, direct elections were instituted, the state and church were separated, and the presidential term was increased to six years. From 1925 to 1931 General Carlos Ibañez, who was overwhelmingly elected in 1927, con-

[11] Ibid., pp. 53–54.

[12] See the account by Frederick Nunn, "Military Rule in Chile: The Revolution of September 5, 1924 and January 23, 1925," *Hispanic American Historical Review*, vol. 47, no. 1 (February 1967), pp. 14–21.

trolled the government. His stated goal was "to purify Chilean politics." His methods allowed for no party interference in administration, and he suppressed extremist groups and cowered unfriendly critics, clubs, and newspapers. However, his administration has been called the most efficient since that of Balmaceda in the 1880s. Under Ibañez vast public works programs were undertaken in areas like harbor facilities, railroads, and canals, immigration was encouraged, the University of Chile was made autonomous, and educational facilities were greatly enhanced. In a sense Ibañez hoped to compensate for what was being lost in terms of political freedom, and thus his administration significantly compares with the Vargas period of Brazil and the Odría period in Peru.

The economic depression, according to a League of Nations report, was most deeply felt in Chile of all the nations of the world.[13] It cost the Ibañez government its life. A series of passive strikes led by students and later joined by doctors, lawyers, teachers, engineers, and finally civil servants toppled the government in what was an excellent example of Chilean civic consciousness. Ibañez's Minister of Interior took over for fifteen months and was, in turn, ousted in 1932 by another group of military colonels who established a Socialist Republic lasting only one hundred days. During this period Congress was dissolved, and the military junta passed a good deal of decree legislation, much of which was advanced for its time. They strengthened the organizational rights of the trade unions and proposed to nationalize with compensation the coal, copper, and nitrate industries, though they made no outright attack on private enterprise as such. A series of tax measures was proposed, most important of which was a tax on large landholdings.

Another coup prepared the nation for the election of 1932 in which Arturo Alessandri, supported by the Radicals, center groups, and some faction of the Liberals, was again victorious. The runner-up was Marmaduke Grove, a Socialist and member of the Socialist Republic junta of early 1932.

The initial development toward a Popular Front in Chile began in 1936 at the same time as similar developments in France and Spain were taking place.[14] Chile was the only Latin American nation to establish a workable, majoritarian Popular Front. The principal power behind the Front was the Radical party, which had disaffiliated itself with the Alessandri government, leaving Alessandri with the support of only the Conservative and Liberal parties. The Socialists and Communists made up the other two important political groups. For the Communists it meant the end of their political isolation imposed upon them since their formal creation in 1922.

[13] P. T. Ellsworth, *Chile: An Economy in Transition* (New York: Macmillan, 1945), p. 9.

[14] For a survey of the development and program of the Popular Front see John R. Stevenson, *The Chilean Popular Front* (Philadelphia: University of Pennsylvania Press, 1942).

Without the Radical party, the Front could never have had any electoral pretensions because of its basic protelariat and working-class orientation. The Radicals provided that important element of political legitimacy. An intraparty struggle within the Radical party developed over Front participation and finally was resolved with a "progressive" victory and the acceptance of Radical participation in the Front. Two important events of 1937 ensured Radical integration with the Front's more socialist elements. First the Front achieved an important victory in the municipal elections of the 1937 election which demonstrated its national appeal. Secondly, and probably more important, the Economics Minister under Alessandri, the Conservative Gustavo Ross, used his influence to oust the remaining Radical ministers within the government. The Radicals had tried to maintain this administrative foot in the door to respectability, since they had originally not been sure of the Front's durability.

After the establishment of the Front, the question arose in late 1937 as to who would provide its presidential leadership. Neither the Socialists nor the Radicals, the two most powerful parties within the Front, could muster an immediate majority for their candidates. There was at that time a good deal of feeling that the Front would collapse for failing to agree on a candidate. Eventually, however, Marmaduke Grove, the Socialist candidate, renounced his candidacy for the sake of the Front's unity and thus paved the way for the Radical candidate, Pedro Aguirre Cerda. Running against Aguirre Cerda in 1938 were Gustavo Ross, the Conservative Party candidate, and Carlos Ibañez, the former military strongman who had formed his own party vehicle of the right, the Alianza Popular Liberador.[15]

A suppressed Nazi takeover in September 1938 in which Ibañez, being sure his party could not win, played (as in 1925) a conspiratorial part, provided the Popular Front with the necessary margin of victory. It put several thousand right-wing votes into the Popular Front's margin from those who were protesting against the government's suppression of the Nazis. Chile was never unduly threatened by Nazism, but its democratically committed population was more incensed at the suppression of a political group than the existence of such a group.

The Popular Front experiment lasted but two years, from 1939–1941. The Communists withdrew in 1939 as a response to the Molotov-von Ribbentrop nonaggression pact between the Soviet Union and Germany. The final breakup followed the decision by the Radical party to leave the Front and establish, in early 1941, its own independent party. Thus the Radical party had used the Popular Front as a vehicle to the party preeminence it was to maintain until 1964. Though it did not always occupy the executive mansion throughout these years, it was the most powerful single political party.

[15] See the interesting biographical sketch of Grove by J. R. Thomas, "The Evolution of a Chilean Socialist," *Hispanic American Historical Review*, vol. 47, no. 1 (February 1967), pp. 22–37.

Chile's aggregative phase was characterized by considerably more institutional distribution of power than elsewhere among the five nations under study. There was much evident sharing of political responsibility and democratic bargaining among two branches of government at a time when few countries in the world, not to speak of Latin America, lived by these formal mechanisms. Within this incipient pluralist political structure, newly emerging urban and rural groups with concomitant political party representation increased their rates of political mobilization and participation. There was noticeable growth of political cognizance as the middle and lower classes began to assume new civic roles politically and new consumer roles as economic entities.

Argentina

In Argentina, despite the loss of some of his most able men, Irigoyen's abstention strategy succeeded, and his party was finally allowed to compete without restrictions. The president of the conservative groups from 1910 was Roque Sáenz Peña. In 1912 he passed the so-called Sáenz Peña Law that declared secret and universal male suffrage and initiated a system of two-thirds-one-third representation from each electoral district and was an indication that Irigoyen's policy of electoral abstention within a system of electoral restrictions and fraud had been successful.[16]

In 1916 at the next presidential election Irigoyen won the presidency. He was a powerful executive and his administration introduced Argentina to many innovations within the economic and political realm. Politically Irigoyen had developed a very large, disciplined party, and upon election he provided employment for a great majority of his followers. This resulted in a large influx of inexperienced and patronage-hungry politicians, but it also provided an opening among the middle classes for political-leadership recruitment that had been all but closed before. The Irigoyen administration instituted an internal political revolution by intervening in a record number of provinces in order to oust Conservative governments and to replace them with his own party followers.

The Radical administration from 1916 to 1922 was highly nationalistic economically and remained independent of the central powers and the allies during World War I. Under the aegis of Irigoyen the Argentine Petroleum Corporation, YPF (Yacimientos Petroleros Fiscales), was established. YPF provided for exclusive Argentine control over further exploration, drilling, and marketing but did not disturb any concessions made since 1905. Labor gains under Irigoyen despite high exports during World War I were small. He did little for organized labor and less to develop an industrialized economy,

[16] Alfredo Galletti, *La realidad Argentina en el siglo XX: La política y los partidos* (Buenos Aires: Fondo de Cultura Economica, 1961), pp. 29–47.

being content to continue Argentina's dependence on grain and meat exports to Europe.

Rather, the Irigoyen administration symbolized the growing mobilization of the urban groups toward political participation. For example, the 1916 election returns provide a correlation between the Radical vote, the urbanization index, and the number of foreigners in the electoral district. Thus the Radical party represented the middle sectors as they made their initial legitimate entry into political influence. However, many educated, literate people, a large number being university trained, remained for the most part within the ranks of the Conservative party.[17]

However, the Radical Party, despite its call for reform during twenty-five years of electoral abstention, did not initiate any major social reforms and did little to improve the institutional framework of the country. One of its achievements was the granting of autonomy to the universities of Argentina, by which university administration, faculty, and students took a major share in determining university curriculum and policy. This major innovation in 1918 became widely adopted soon thereafter in the rest of Latin America.

Irigoyen proved to be much more autocratic and strong-man style of president than most of his conservative predecessors. He intervened in and often suppressed labor strikes and in his foreign policy, which was to remain neutral during World War I, he laid the framework for a tough, ultranationalist position in world affairs for Argentina. Thus the Unión Cívica Radical, which had organized electoral resentment against political fraud, once in power was more instrumental in shifting the political culture and psychology of the nation toward a clear self-awareness of her basic middle class nature rather than in achieving any specific program.[18] It certainly represented the participation of the urban, immigrant, and nonindustrial, commercial sectors into the realms of political and economic influence.[19]

The Radicals were the mass, popular party in Argentina from the 1916 election until the 1946 election of Juan Perón. Despite this the 1922 election showed a definite conservative shift within the government as the presidency was assumed by Marcelo T. de Alvear who retained the office until 1928.

[17] An exhaustive sociological analysis of electoral statistics is provided by Ezequiel Gallo, Jr. and Silvia Sigal, "La formacion de los partidos contemporaneos: La U.C.R. (1890–1916)," in Torcuato S. Di Tella et al., *Argentina: sociedad de masas* (Buenos Aires: Editorial Universitaria de Buenos Aires, 1965), pp. 124–176.

[18] For a negative interpretation of the accomplishments of the Irigoyen administration see Sergio Bagu's contribution in a colloquium published as *Tres revoluciones* (Buenos Aires: Emilio Perrot, 1959), p. 21.

[19] Oscar Cornblit points out that no party, not even the Radicals, between 1880 and 1930, represented the Industrialists. "European Immigrants in Argentine Industry and Politics," in Claudio Veliz (ed.), *The Politics of Conformity in Latin America* (New York: Oxford University Press, 1967), pp. 221–248.

Although he had the endorsement of Irigoyen, Alvear took a more traditional stance on the major social problems as he supported the goals of the largest landowners. In fact, once in power he was author of an antipersonalist movement within the Radical party which was directed against the hegemony of Irigoyen.[20] This ideological shift from the paternal leadership had important implications for future crucial splits and divisions within the Radical party. Irigoyen won the internal battle over the "antipersonalistas," was renominated, and won the presidency in 1928.

The short, unhappy government of Irigoyen existed only two years when he was overthrown by a military coup. For the following thirteen years the Conservative Party retained control under presidents Agustín Justo, Roberto Ortiz and Ramón Castillo. Under Conservative rule, the 1930s saw widescale changes in both the economic and social pattern of society. The actual military blow against the Irigoyen government was led by General José Uriburu, a Conservative, who, in the Ibañez style, intervened in order to moralize and depoliticize society and, if need be, to rule above parties entirely. However, it was obvious to the military leadership that the Radical party, no longer abstaining from elections, was the most prominent political force, so when elections were again allowed, the method used during the thirties to ensure Conservative victory was election fraud.

During these years of frustrated opposition, the Radical party developed within its conglomerate movement a group known as FORJA, Fuerza de Orientación Radical de la Joven Argentina. This faction opposed the milder reform-minded Alvear leadership and initiated a return to the strongly nationalist and popular conceptions that marked the Irigoyen administration. This perpetuated a "personalista–anti-personalista" debate among the Radicals until the very eve of Perón's advent to power. FORJA led several abortive revolutions during the thirties and called for a return to political abstention and resistance to electoral fraud. The deep split within the ranks of the Radicals allowed the Conservatives to slowly woo important members of the Alvear wing of the Radicals into positions of importance in the Conservative movement. The most important of these converts was Roberto Ortiz, an anti-Irigoyen Radical who became the Conservative nominee for president in 1938.

Thus the FORJA, though small, became the most eloquent faction within the Radical party, which was becoming a large, inchoate mass of followers with little coherent ideological cement. The program of FORJA in the mid thirties bears remarkable resemblance to the political platform later espoused by Perón in his campaign in 1945–46. FORJA called for a

[20] José S. Campobassi, "Historia de los partidos políticos Argentinos (1810–1943)," in José S. Campobassi et al., *Los partidos políticos: estructura y vigencia en la Argentina* (Buenos Aires: Cooperadora de Derecho y Ciencias Sociales, 1963), p. 27.

return to the vague nationalism of Irigoyen during World War I, a rejection of Anglo-American interests and ideology, and a reassertion of a true Argentine national culture.[21] They believed that a true Argentine social revolution must include and be supported by the masses from the cities and countryside and must be accompanied by a strong assertion of economic independence from Great Britain. With the advent of Perón during the post–1943 period, most of the members of FORJA moved into his camp and provided much of the ideological content of Peronism which was later refined and developed. In an act of self-conscious political suicide they dissolved their movement and supported Perón's candidacy in late 1945.

Perón participated in the Uriburu revolt of 1930 as a captain. Later he became assistant to Uriburu's Minister of War and continued in that position under President Justo's Minister of War. Between 1936–1938 he was military attaché in Chile. It is interesting to speculate what Perón's views might have been of Chile's Popular Front which was developing in those years.[22] It is probable that he favored the Front as a second choice after the Ibañez nationalist party had been suppressed and outlawed by Alessandri's government. Between 1939 and 1941 Perón served as military attaché in Rome under Mussolini's dictatorship, and it is certain that this two-year experience influenced him profoundly in the succeeding years. The military, which had been unleashed in 1930 after a century of aquiescence to civilian rule, became the principal power element in Argentina as either the government or the power group behind the government.

The concentration of labor and capital within the periphery of Greater Buenos Aires specifically and the Eastern Litoral generally was tremendously accentuated in the thirties. The Litoral, which makes up about 20 per cent of Argentine territory, contained close to 70 per cent of the population, 90 per cent of total grains grown, 63 per cent of all the cattle grazed, 46 per cent of the sheep, 77 per cent of the hogs, 54 per cent of the railroad lines, 71 per cent of all telephones in operation, 79 per cent of all automobiles running, and about 80 per cent of all capital invested in extractive industry and manufacturing.[23]

Until the year 1930 there existed three labor federations: La Federación Obrera Regional Argentina (FORA), which was Communist inspired, La Unión Sindical Argentina (USA), run by nationalists, and La Confederación

[21] For a favorable exposition of the significance of FORJA see J. J. Hernandez Arregui, *La formación de la conciencia nacional (1930–1960)* (Buenos Aires: Ediciones Hachea, 1960), Ch. 4.

[22] It is perhaps significant that a leader of the Popular Front was Marmaduke Grove who led the military uprising in Chile in 1932 and who has been described as a precursor of Justicialism. See Ernst Halperin, *Nationalism and Communism in Chile* (Cambridge: MIT Press, 1965), p. 123.

[23] Alberto Ciria, *Partidos y poder en la Argentina moderna: 1930–1946* (BA: J. Alvarez, 1964), pp. 266–67.

Obrera Argentina (COA), Socialist in orientation. With Communist FORA refusing to join, USA and COA combined to create La Confederación General del Trabajo (CGT), which remains Argentina's powerful central labor federation today.[24]

During the thirties the Communists infiltrated the CGT and dominated the construction, meat, woodworking, metallurgical, and printers unions, while the Socialists held power among the Commercial Workers Union, municipal workers, and government employees union. The Syndicalists controlled the railway brotherhoods, the public transport unions, and brewery workers. The mass of workers in the late thirties could be divided into two large subdivisions. The first consisted of the older organized groups whose origin was European and whose base of operation and residence had always been the city or suburbs of Buenos Aires. They were generally anarchists and international socialists. They supported the classical, international socialists line of action and were led by a rigid, long-entrenched leadership. The bulk of these workers were found in public service unions, such as gas and transport, and were state employees, commercial workers, and printers. Many were partisans of the Argentine Socialist Party founded by Juan B. Justo in 1905, and most tried to perpetuate the traditional class-conscious Marxist interpretation of Argentine society. The other faction of workers was usually younger and less skilled and usually were natives of Argentina who had migrated very recently from rural areas to accept the poorer paid, less attractive jobs in Buenos Aires. They lived in conditions generally much poorer than the first group, their mentality was in a sense "virgin," and their experience with international socialism was completely nil. It is this second group that made up the bulk of Peronist support in the post-1943 period.

Urbanization rates of the middle class and working class had reached truly monumental proportions by the end of Argentina's aggregative phase, far outstripping that universal phenomenon in any Latin American nation. During the 1930's the laboring class in Argentina had also achieved significant politicalization rates far more significant than even in Chile. The proliferation of a vast gamut of ideological perspectives was evident in Argentina's capital Buenos Aires, and its immediate surroundings. Organized interest groups developed mobilization capacity. The legislative and political party institutions were as viable as those in Chile and political participation was superior. The role of the military became ambivalent as it leaned increasingly toward a broader, more nationalistic interventionist role. This, in addition to Latin America's highest modernity indices, made for an extremely volatile and dynamic aggregative phase of national development. By the eve of the peronist era, Argentina had already achieved the level of an incipient mass society with civil or military governments increasingly susceptible to societal pressures.

[24] Ibid., p. 303.

Summary

Certain dimensions of political evolution thus emerge during the aggregative phase. This post-authoritative period of change lasted in most cases from one to two generations, ranging approximately from a quarter of a century to half a century.

In Mexico a convergence of sophisticated political elites with harnessed economic groups provided a rather long and, in many ways, successful preparation for subsequent decades of distributive politics. The stability wrought by this powerful marriage of money and might resolved many of the hitherto outstanding ideological and institutional questions of the Juárez and Santa Anna eras. The decades of peace from political strife and turmoil provided the backdrop to the rapid capitalization of urban Mexico. The framework by which the military would subsequently be integrated into a party-government was laid during the Díaz dictatorship. The armed forces were coordinated as a controlled political arm rather than a random pressure group. Lastly, rather than working at loggerheads with each other causing multiple sociopolitical disturbances, foreign and domestic capital collaborated under the guidance of the elite establishment.

In Peru, legitimacy was never as clearly achieved as it was in the other four countries. Political leadership was neither strong enough to sustain power or allow for a peaceful rotation in power of politically diverse groups. The Odría administration represented perhaps the most successful of Peru's aggregative-phase governments. It succeeded at combining the development of the economic infrastructure while it presided over a relative degree of political harmony.

Brazil's aggregative phase was marked by a growing predisposition of political leadership to act with a national orientation. It roots increasingly represented the new urban classes. However, popular participation was still strictly, as in Mexico, an unknown quantity. Parties assumed more ideological stances and, in general, the competition for influence became a more open and serious matter. Whereas public policy in Mexico and Peru was handled by a more definitive, ascertainable leadership group (one effectively and one ineffectively) in Brazil competition existed among several economic and political groups centered in distinct geographical regions.

In Chile and Argentina one can observe a more rapid widening of political freedoms essential for group identification. In Chile, particularly, there was little recourse to any imposition of unity as occurred under Díaz in Mexico and no dependence on electoral fraud as passed under the Conservative rule in Argentina during the 1930's. A noteworthy amount of capitalization and investment occurred in Argentina and Chile. In the former country this was complemented by large infusions of European immigration not seen to any great extent elsewhere in Latin America.

Common to the experience of all five nations during the aggregative phase of political evolution is the increase of political recruitment from the middle classes, forcing the upper classes to share the power and influencing a decided shift in policy-orientation. This altered base of political gravity was largely spurred on by the conglomeration of urbanization trends, educational opportunities, and increasing social mobility.

CHAPTER 6 The Distributive Phase

During this period of national development increasing attention is paid to providing and fostering meaningful economic linkages between rural and urban communities. This is meant to augment the productive capacity of the agricultural sector and to speed up the distribution and dissemination of capital and consumer goods, labor, and technical assistance.

With the growth of urban-rural societal interaction, the migration pattern to the cities became very pronounced. This influx of rural migrants had the effect of slowly shifting the focus of economic development to commerce and industry rather than agriculture. The growth in the workers' share of national income under such paternal administrations as those of Cárdenas, Belaúnde Terry, Vargas, The Chilean Popular Front, and Perón give evidence of the basic economic restructuring that occurred. These massive infusions of laborers and the parallel growth of the industrial middle class in the cities resulted in population pressures that had, for the first time, a recognizable impact on governmental decision making.

Mobilizational political parties continued to flourish under these changing sociopolitical conditions. The increasingly politicized urban groups provided one of the principal bases of support for such political parties as the PRI, APRA, PTB (Brazilian Labor Party), the FRAP (Communist-Socialist Coalition), and the Peronistas. This widening political representation of industrial economic groups considerably altered the concerns of the political elites by convincing them of the necessity of considering different approaches toward economic development.

A growing accommodation is noticeable among such politically influential groups as the church, the military, and the bureaucracy as they engage each other on the problems of economic development in ways that mitigate class and ideological commitments. The military in particular became massively involved in the operations of public administration and the techniques of economic development.

Mexico

Mexico underwent the most profound distributive changes among the major nations of Latin America. Beginning with what was essentially a movement for electoral reform, suffrage rights, and the abrogation of dictatorial rule, the Mexican revolution brought about real and momentous changes in the social and political structure.

The leader of the revolt against the Porfirio Díaz regime was a respectable landowner Francisco Madero. He, however, was unable to assess the content of the revolution he had unleashed and the staggering pressures that were building up from the surrounding conservative and radical forces. His presidency was short-lived and wrenched from his control. He failed to assuage the basic social discontent around which the revolutionary leaders of the countryside—Emiliano Zapata, Pancho Villa, and Álvaro Obregón—were beginning to rally.[1] In a most unMachiavellian style he awarded governmental positions to ideological enemies, such as Generals Felix Díaz, Bernardo Reyes, and Victoriano Huerta, while he displayed only cool tolerance toward sectors that could have strongly supported his program and policies.

Though a revolutionary by intent, Madero neither consolidated his administrative control or too quickly embarked on a program of land and governmental reform and a policy of full employment. This inability to initiate either a peaceful administrative overhaul or, as Díaz had done, establish a stable economic environment brought several powerful groups against him. Foreign investors from Europe and the United States, the landed aristocracy, the upper military class, and the wealthiest entrepreneurs aligned themselves against Madero and did nothing to protect him against the military coup that ended both his government and his life.

A tradition was shattered by the Madero revolt, but there was no replacement for at least a decade of the ousted by a new elite.[2] During the interim period Mexico suffered a considerable loss of life and property, and economic development was arrested. Interfactional fighting was common, and no new group was able to lead from strength or resolve the leading social issues. Yet the miracle of Mexican development is that out of this morass of conflicting interests emerged a group that has been able to lead Mexico ever since.

Much criticism has been directed against what many call the senseless violence of the Mexican scene between 1910 and 1920. Her contortions, however, can be compared to those of the French and Russian Revolutions and were equally important in their influence on Mexico's institutions. The excesses of the Mexican Revolution can no more be condemned than can

[1] Moisés Gonzalez Navarro, "Mexico: The Lop-sided Revolution," in Claudio Veliz (ed.) *Obstacles to Change in Latin America* (New York: Oxford University Press, 1965), pp. 209–211.

[2] However, within the context of Chalmers Johnson's interesting typology in *Revolutionary Change* (Boston: Little, Brown, 1966), Ch. 7, one would certainly have to speak of Madero's leadership as marking the "simple" phase of the Mexican revolution where both the authority and the constitutional system of the old order were replaced. It was not until the violence subsided that the ideological or "total" phase of the revolution was reached.

any eruption which arises because of human suffering and aspirations. The stability of Mexican institutions since that initial assault on privilege and injustice may be somewhat symbolic of the long-range impact of such thoroughgoing changes. The tremendous shift in social-power relations and the economic landscape made subsequent societal convulsions much more remote.

Under the military leadership of Venustiano Carranza, Álvaro Obregón, and Plutarco Elias Calles, Mexico was able to more and more channel the original revolutionary fervor. First the more progressive sectors of society were won over to the Revolution, and finally the traditional sectors accepted the inevitable. From the period of Obregón's consolidation of the Revolution to its centralization under Calles, attempted coups emanated from only the traditional sectors. The Constitution of 1917, with its defense of the subsoil, lay education, agrarian reform, and labor rights, immediately won the continuing support of large parts of the middle sectors and eventually won over the conservative groups when it became apparent that, barring injury to the national patrimony, rights of private property and enterprise would be guaranteed. The great flexibility of the Mexican Constitution made it adaptable to changing social needs and provided her future leaders a great amount of leeway.

The elimination of Zapata and Villa signified the establishment of a mixed socioeconomic system for Mexico rather than one that was purely socialist or peasant oriented. The Obregón (1920–1924) and Calles (1924–1934) administrations solidified a pragmatic, power-conscious conception of governmental responsibility, one which tolerated little localism or division of power. Parties did not represent definable ideological consistency but were composed of individuals who in the rural areas supported Obregón or, in the more urban centers, favored Calles.[3] There was, however, never an open schism between these two orientations.

Though the Obregón-Calles years established political continuity and finally gave Mexico a reputation for stability after a decade and a half of turmoil, there was a lack of clean, honest government. Perhaps the most telling criticisms of this decade of control are contained in the ample writings of Obregón's one-time Minister of Education, José Vasconcelos, who depicts the Mexican leadership as a group of corrupt, dissolute men who lived by the revolution, making their livelihood from it rather than for it to better Mexican conditions. Vasconcelos describes a decade of personalism and corruption when governmental morality was almost nonexistent.[4]

[3] Frank Brandenburg, *The Making of Modern Mexico* (Englewood Cliffs, N.J.: Prentice-Hall, 1964), p. 60.

[4] Consider, for example, his disillusionment at losing what he considered the fraudulent 1929 presidential election. "El Excelsior" (Mexico City: November 18, 1929), and José Vasconcelos, *Indología: una interpretación de la cultura Ibero-*

Officialism was given legal status by the formation of an official national party—the Partido Nacional Revolucionario. This newly organized party was created to broaden the scope of the leadership control. By this new, ubiquitous machine, Calles was able to create a clear line of authority from the party to its various sectors and to society in general. The organization grew and survived many individual presidents and policies.

Under Calles the church was significantly weakened as laws were imposed limiting the number of priests per state, preventing their participation in elections and their presence in habit on the streets. The resulting bitterness lasted many years and was more intense than the days of the Reform Laws under Juárez. In the latter years of the Calles administration relations with the church became slightly more amicable as the government chose not to enforce all the measures it legally could have.

All organized labor groups were centralized under the Confederación Regional de Obreros Mexicanos (CROM), which claimed over two million members by 1930. However, as time went on, the administration of Calles became less progressive. Almost no land was distributed, generous foreign oil concessions were easy to get, and labor made few if any gains. It was in its anticlerical attitude that the Calles government upheld the intent of the 1917 Constitution. Also with the promulgation of the Labor Code of 1931, Calles laid the framework for those labor gains made under President Lázaro Cárdenas.

The Calles administration had its most significant impact in the submission and professionalization of the military. Commands were frequently changed, and loyal commanders were amply rewarded. The Secretary of War became the principal military figure rather than commanders in the field. Also, Calles used his broad political power to intervene in any economic sector of society, be it petroleum, electricity, foreign investment, or agricultural credit. Cárdenas later made full use of this governmental power. Calles initiated Latin America's second (Uruguay was first) governmental development corporation, known as Nacional Financiera in 1934, which also played a major role in Mexico's development from the Cárdenas administration through that of Díaz Ordaz.

With the reform in the president's term of office made during the Calles period, Cárdenas, following three relatively weak puppet presidents who served two years each (1925–1934), was easily elected to a six-year term in 1934. As Calles had dominated Mexican politics for a decade, so Cárdenas had even greater political control, lasting until 1946 and the inauguration of President Miguel Alemán, a power in his own right.

---

americana (Barcelona: Agencia Mundial de Librería, 1934), p. iii. His critique of the arbitrary quality of Mexican revolutionary leadership is found in many of his speeches. See his *Discursos: 1920–1950* (Mexico: Ediciones Botas, 1950), especially pp. 136–141.

Under Cárdenas a new, more powerful Workers' Confederation, Confederación de Trabajadores de México (CTM), was established. The first secretary-general, Vicente Lombardo Toledano, was a Marxist-Socialist. Originally the organization included peasants, civil servants, and teachers. However, these groups were gradually replaced by industrial and commercial workers. In addition to his organization of the laborers, Cárdenas made it a point of his administration to aid the rural peasantry. Land was divided at the fastest rate in Mexican history into both small, private farms and semicollective "ejidos." Ejidatários, or owners of parcels of land, often worked the land in common and were required to participate in the national peasant organization, Confederación Nacional Campesina (CNC). The CNC and CTM became the backbone and support of the Cárdenas government and two of the three basic sectors of the official Mexican party. The third prong of the party is the Popular sector which unified otherwise autonomous groups, such as civil servants, intellectuals, artists, teachers, and women.

Significantly, Cárdenas altered the name of the Partido Nacional Revolucionario to the Partido de la Revolución Mexicana. The shift corresponded to a change in emphasis from that of "nationalizing" the party, already accomplished, to giving the party a Mexican content. The party under Cárdenas made great strides in integrating large sectors of the rural masses into governmental programs and securing at least a type of parochial interest. The military lost its status as an integral part of the official party, but in compensation it received the right to nominate the president of the official party.[5] The ministries of national defense and the navy became other vehicles for policy making.[6]

Under Cárdenas, the distributive phase in Mexico reached its apex. The nation began its economic development programs at this time, and social equalization was pursued with vigor. The building of an infrastructure begun under Calles was carried on by Cárdenas. An ejido credit bank was established in 1935 to give loans to the peasants under programs sponsored by the government. Labor flourished as its leader Vicente Lombardo Toledano, found a sympathetic ear in the Mexican president until their temporary fall out in 1939 when Lombardo Toledano supported the Nazi-Soviet Pact of 1939–1941.[7] The Cárdenas government took control of the Mexican railroads and nationalized the oil properties with compensation in 1938. It was also under Cárdenas that the Mexicanization legislation was first developed. This

[5] Frank Brandenburg, *The Making of Modern Mexico*, p. 101.

[6] Miguel Aleman, "Informe del presidente de la republica" (Mexico City: Oficina del Presidente, 1952), p. 51.

[7] Lombardo Toledano's views toward Nazi Germany corresponded intimately with the going Soviet foreign policy. Robert Paul Millon, *Mexican Marxist: Vicente Lombardo Toledano* (Chapel Hill: University of North Carolina Press, 1966), pp. 108–116.

flourished during the Lopez Mateos government and is today the Mexican instrument for dealing with foreign capital. Under this legislation, foreign capital is allowed into the country and directed toward the more essential economic areas, and 51 per cent of the stock and control in management is consigned to Mexican capital and Mexican capitalists.

The Cárdenas government generally proved the most popular one in Mexican history. The government and its "jefe maximo" were always visible to the public, as they attended local events, opened highways, inaugurated new public works and awarded titles of lands to the ever-increasing army of ejidatarios. Cárdenas maintained power through the presidency of Ávila Camacho during the war years until the beginning of the Miguel Alemán government.

Miguel Alemán presided over Mexico's capitalistic explosion. The first civilian president since Madero, Alemán's ascendance marked the institutionalization of the Mexican Revolution, as the change of her party name from the Partido de la Revolución Mexicana to Partido Revolucionario Institucional symbolized. During the Alemán years there was a leveling off again of revolutionary criteria and a drive toward industrialization despite the costs to the masses of the people. The agricultural sector was squeezed, and wage rates did not keep pace with productivity.

The Alemán six-year administration, ending with the election of Ruiz Cortines in 1952, provided Mexico with its period of greatest economic growth. It gave Mexico the impetus to make important industrial advances throughout the fifties and sixties. The spectacular growth affected urban renewal, university buildings, dams, roads, airfields, harbor facilities, petroleum industry, steel production, and the development of hundreds of small enterprises from soft drinks and textiles to paper products. Radios, televisions, and automobiles became a common sight in the cities of Mexico. The Ruiz Cortines era emphasized more social goals as it undertook school and hospital construction, slum clearance, the development of sewage and water systems, and the beautification of the urban hubs. The Lopez Mateos government (1958–1964) stimulated Mexican industry and, while not doing anything rash enough to affect a serious flight of capital, enacted legislation designed to control foreign capital. Land was distributed at the fastest pace since distribution under the Cárdenas government, and government agencies were established to sell basic commodities at wholesale prices in the poorer neighborhoods of the large cities. Now, two added factors complement the political stability Mexico has enjoyed for over three decades: Its increasing exports being faster than its imports and rapidly growing United States tourism.

The Diaz Ordáz administration (1964–70) continued to consolidate the economic gains achieved under the previous regime. It continued the priorities of industrial development first conceived by the Alemán government while following up the Lopez Mateos lead in the area of rural irrigation projects, soil-conservation programs, transportation facilities, and electrification to assist the small peasant farmer.

Thus it can be said that a cyclical pattern was being established within the hierarchy of the PRI party government. An innovative administration which emphasized either welfare politics or capital accumulation was usually followed by a transitional and consolidating administration less intent on dramatic policy changes. One administration makes advances in vital areas of society while its successor performs the role of securing and refining these advances. The innovative regimes of Obregón, Cárdenas, and Alemán were followed by the consolidating regimes of Calles, Avila Camacho, and Ruiz Cortines. Finally, the innovative measures undertaken by Lopez Mateos were consolidated under the Díaz Ordaz administration (1964–1970). The innovative governments differ as to their emphasis, which has been either on distributive-social goals, as under the Obregón, Cárdenas, Lopez Mateos, and Echeverría governments, or an industrial and development goals, as, so far, only under the Alemán administration. The consolidating governments usually act as the transitional authorities linking the more innovative regimes. The consolidators, with their linkage function, form a majority, and this allows for a methodical and careful approach to contemporary Mexican politics, one which avoids any precipitous action.

The generally excellent economic growth rate in Mexico has undoubtedly helped to stabilize and legitimize her political institutions. Industrialization has thus become a value in itself, one that not only stimulates economic growth but assists in solidifying the position of the Mexican political leadership. However, it has not solely been Mexican productivity that can explain the policy successes during its distributive period of political development. Even as far back as the aftermath of the Madero challenge to the "cientificos" of Díaz's administration one can perceive the impingement of rural considerations upon an urban-dominated national administration. This is exemplified on the many structural and policy changes undertaken by the Carranza, Obregón, Calles, and Cárdenas administrations as they evolved means of mitigating rural pressure for land, agricultural assistance, and political representation. In the purely political realm the PRI party passed through several organizational stages under Calles, Cárdenas, and Alemán, each of which represented a growing awareness of linking the rural states with the urban centers. Particularly the Mexicanization of the party under Cárdenas was specifically aimed to broaden constituent support and it did initiate the instruction of rural Indian and mestizo social classes in political organization. Lastly, the distributive phase was prominently marked by the economic policies pursued by an interventionist-minded Calles government and by noteworthy labor gains achieved under Lombardo Toledano in the thirties and forties.

Peru

With the accession to the presidency of Peru by Belaúnde Terry, his political party vehicle, The Acción Popular, appeared likely in its coalition with the Christian Democrats to co-opt the middle of the political spectrum. The party maintained relations and received support from hitherto antagonistic forces within society, and Belaúnde Terry managed to generally pacify the political atmosphere.

The military, until late in 1968, supported the Belaúnde government and lent consequential assistance in the government's overall development goals. Under governmental supervision the armed forces conducted geographical surveys, extended communications facilities to the hinterland, colonized unexploited regions, and provided needed medical assistance in the backward areas.[8]

Students as well developed their dissertations around some problem of national interest, in such fields as architecture, city planning, and engineering. A National Institute for Advanced Studies had been created to provide the facilities for the completition of such scholarly research, which would be published and placed in a library dedicated to the treatment of national problems of development.[9]

Political participation of the populace had also received new interest as demonstrated by the 1966 municipal elections in which 2.1 million voted as compared to 1.8 million in the hotly contested presidential elections of 1963. No doubt the increased interest is related to the general health of the economy, the very good record that Peru had achieved in the mid sixties of currency stabilization, and the growth of employment opportunities. The economy has made particularly impressive strides in its mineral exports, fish meal industry, various agricultural produce, such as cotton, and the increasing production of petroleum.[10]

The Belaúnde government had managed, though watered-down by the legislature, to pass several measures dealing with land and tax reform as well as laying the basis for a multinational north-south wilderness road that would link fifteen hundred miles of Peru's eastern territory to her altiplano and coastal regions.[11] Feeder roads would allow the passage of men and materials from east to west and be instrumental in integrating Peru's domestic economy. The augmentation of such means of communication would serve to mobilize her population and mitigate the obvious hardships of such stark

[8] Fernando Belaúnde Terry, *Peru's Own Conquest* (Lima: American Studies Press, 1965), pp. 198–208.

[9] Ibid., pp. 208–212.

[10] Belaúnde Terry chose to negotiate for better terms rather than expropriate the U.S. petroleum interests.

[11] In cooperation with Colombia, Ecuador, and Bolivia.

alternatives as the urban shanty-towns of Lima and the rural backwaters of the altiplano.[12] The growth of development in the interior with the subsequent creation of jobs for the altiplano population was of crucial priority among Acción Popular leadership.

The military intervention in October, 1968, not many months before the culmination of the Belaúnde administration in 1969, was caused by a series of both economic and political factors. The junta led by General Juan Velasco Alvarado made apparent in the early weeks of the military government its dissatisfaction with the inability of the previous government to get its social and economic programs through the opposition-controlled legislature and to reach a satisfactory resolution between the Peruvian government and the American-controlled International Petroleum Company.

Because of Aprista-Odriista opposition in the legislature, the previous Acción Popular government had to soften its land reform measures, exempting the large coastal sugar and cotton estates and extending the periods of land resettlement beyond the administration's original intentions. In its negotiations with the International Petroleum Company (IPC), the Belaúnde government conceded the question of back taxes owed to the country in exchange for a new leasing arrangement of the oil fields.

The military apparently responded to deep-seated Peruvian nationalism and to dissatisfaction with the slow and cautious approach of the constitutionally-delimited government of Belaúnde Terry. After consolidating its power, the military junta proceeded to identify the petroleum and land reform issues as the central concern of the first year of its government. In late 1968 they seized the IPC petroleum fields, replaced much of the American management staff, and assessed over half a billion dollars in back taxes owed the government, an amount which far surpassed the American assessment of the worth of the United States companies. The seizure and tax assessment was based on the implementation of the 1933 constitution which reserves all subsurface mineral and petroleum rights to the state but post dates the 1924 agreement reached with the petroleum concerns. This "past debt" theory is thus predicated on oil extracted in Peruvian fields for over forty years. On the question of land reform, the military government promulgated in June 1969 what amounted to a very inclusive series of measures geared to distribute land held by large estates. In promulgating the new law, the military government emphasized the universality and extensiveness of its application, includ-

[12] Richard Patch has dramatically shown the overwhelming obstacles that face rural migrants who feel the economic need to pursue their livelihood in Lima yet are unprepared emotionally, socially, and technically for the skills needed to survive in this huge metropolitan center. See the remarkable vignettes of "marginality" in Lima's slums in his "La Parada, Lima's Market," *American Universities Field Staff Reports* West Coast South American Series, vol. 14, nos. 1, 2, 3 (February 1967).

ing export-oriented crop farms and foreign-held properties such as the W.R. Grace Co., producer of 18 per cent of Peru's sugar crop. The means of reimbursement was to be in government bonds unless the former owners agreed to invest 50 per cent of an immediate cash payment into the industrial sector. The beneficiaries of this act were to be peasant cooperatives and communities as well as individually qualified peasants, with the minimum size of the plot to be distributed amounting to seven acres.

In the second year of the military government's tenure it visibly radicalized its distributive policies by adopting novel approaches to industrialization and private enterprise. Under a new industrial law of July 1970, the Peruvian junta decreed a series of industrial priorities. First priority included heavy essential industries such as steel, chemicals, and cement as well as industries manufacturing equipment, e.g., machine tools, crucial to further research and development. Second priority is consigned to industries fulfilling such basic social-service needs as housing, food, clothing, transportation, education, and recreation. Third and fourth priorities encompass enterprises producing nonessential goods and outright luxury goods. High priority industrial sectors will come under the state's jurisdiction or in some kind of public-private partnership, but always at the government's discretion. In addition, all industries must distribute 10 per cent of their net income before taxes to their employees and 15 per cent to an "Industrial Community," whose board oversees investment policies. As the industrial community for each enterprise attains more shares in the industry its investment voice will grow proportionately.

Quite similarly to the Brazilian and Argentine military governments, the Peruvian junta has not hesitated to enact far-reaching economic measures which it deems beneficial to the society without recourse to organized political and social organizations. Again as in the other two nations, the military government does not tend to see itself in interim terms merely preparing the way for the accession of a newly elected civilian government but rather as an instrumental leadership group which plans to perform a crucial policy-making role.

The politicization of the Peruvian military has found its preeminence in the distributive phase and historically appears to serve somewhat as a predictable extension of the growth of Peruvian nationalism, expressed in more incipient form under the Belaúnde Terry administration from 1963 to 1968. The military government, as its predecessor, has taken a concerned approach toward agrarian reform and the incorporation of the countless altiplano indigenous communities into the national domestic economy. Concomitantly there has been increased emphasis on enhancing the efficiency of the commercial export-oriented estates of the coastal regions. Using the ideology of nationalism as a purposive mechanism of the distributive period, the military has launched Peru on a national policy racing to gain control of the nation's economic resources.

Brazil

Vargas represented a new elite in Brazilian politics which had heretofore suffered virtual political exclusion. Apart from the apparent patronage requirements of the new group, the Vargas revolution opened positions of power and influence to the new middle sector and lower economic groups. Political recruitment was widened, but the traditional ruling elite's monopoly of political power though greatly restricted was not removed.

Through the termination of interstate custom duties and the imposition of stiffer national taxes, Vargas was responsible for the investment in a growing Brazilian market where internal consumption increased as the market grew. Though he hesitated at first to use full powers and governed under the constitution of 1934, which allowed him a four-year term as president, Vargas soon assumed full authority and eventually in November of 1937 promulgated his own document.[13] Extreme nationalists, one group finding their inspiration in Moscow, the other in Berlin, attempted abortive coups between 1935 and 1937, giving Vargas the pretext to assume dictatorial control. Establishing a state of siege for three months in late 1937, Vargas refused the offer of Plinio Salgado, leader of a Fascist group called the Integralistas, to dispatch one hundred thousand "brown shirts" to quell any possible communist uprising.[14] Apparently Vargas had learned well the lessons of the Kerensky government of 1917 and the Weimar government of 1930–33 about calling in extremist groups to quell local disturbances. Vargas assumed full control himself.

Vargas's document known as "Estado Novo" was in many cases just that. This highly personalist constitution gave Vargas full decree powers until a national plebiscite would sanction the constitution and until a new congress was elected. These issues, however, were quietly buried.

The exploitation of Brazil's unlimited resources combined with the wealth brought in by the conflict in Europe brought to Brazil a period of economic growth and, what was equally important, a series of social security and wage measures that increased the workers' share in the national income.[15]

Party politics emerged as a result of the military uprising which ended the Vargas dictatorship. Vargas had promised to hold free elections in December, 1945, but as election time neared, he let it be known that he would continue to rule despite his earlier promise that a new president would emerge

[13] A good description of this event can be found in José María Bello, *A History of Modern Brazil: 1889–1964* (Stanford: Stanford University Press, 1966), pp. 297–299.

[14] Ibid., p. 294. Bello's well-rounded definition of the "integralistas" is the best available in the secondary literature.

[15] This period of economic change is detailed in Helio Jaguaribe, *Economic and Political Development: Theoretical Approach and a Brazilian Case Study.* (Cambridge: Harvard University Press, 1968), Ch. 10.

from the election. The coup allowed for a full-fledged election campaign to take place, and this 1945 electoral campaign marked some decline of state politics and the control of executive authority based on regional ties rather than on political association. The post-1945 period has not been any more ideologically-oriented than the Vargas government, but three important parties—the União Democrática Nacional (UDN), the Partido Social Democrático (PSD), and the Partido Trabalhista Brasileiro (PTB)—now became the principal means to power.

With Vargas's backing, General Eurico Dutra, candidate of PSD, won the election from the UDN's candidate, Air Brigadier Eduardo Gomes. In 1946, under Dutra, the Estado Novo was abrogated and replaced with Brazil's 1946 constitution. After the dictatorship of Vargas and the agitation both for and against Vargas during the War years, the Dutra administration was accepted with some relief. Restrictions on the basic freedoms were ended, and Brazil enjoyed a relatively uneventful five-year moratorium from strongman policies. Economically Brazil experienced very rapid growth which paralleled that under Miguel Alemán in Mexico. This and subsequent periods of economic progress gave rise to the saying in Rio de Janeiro that "Brazil grows at night," the implication being that Brazil's economic momentum is so great that all the imaginable pilfering, corruption, and poor administrative procedures could not brake it.

In the 1950 elections Vargas reentered the political arena with his own party, the PTB. He defeated Gomes who again received the support of the UDN. Vargas, apart from his many social and economic innovations on behalf of the working sectors, has been responsible for the extension and further diversification of political power which, since his own demise, has increased Brazil's potentiality for democratic development. Not only did he interrupt the bi-state monopoly of São Paulo and Minas Gerais, but he developed Brazil's tolerance and capacity to support labor parties, primarily his own original vehicle the PTB.

While serving as democratically elected president, Vargas gave his support to the establishment of Pétrobras, the Brazilian Petroleum Corporation, though Brazil has not been as successful as Argentine and Mexican petroleum corporations have in discovering oil reserves.

As Vargas's term drew to a close, charges of nepotism and corruption became ever more widespread. It was in this atmosphere that Vargas was identified with an attempted attack on the life of Carlos Lacerda, the very influential editor of one of Rio's most important newspapers. This charge precipitated military demands for Vargas's retirement and was probably the cause of his suicide, because he apparently did not wish to submit to a military ouster twice in one generation.[16]

[16] For a detailed summary of the events leading to Vargas's suicide, see J. V. D. Saunders, "A Revolution of Agreement Among Friends: The End of the

Juscelino Kubitschek of PSD and João Goulart of PTB became the presidential and vice-presidential candidates respectively in 1955 after an interim period of military rule. Opposed to this combination ticket were candidates of the UDN and a newer party, the Partido Social Progresista. The very strong Kubitschek-Goulart team won the election because of their dual appeal to the middle and working classes. João Goulart, a favorite of Vargas and his Minister of Labor, received much popular support, and Kubitschek received strong support from the middle sectors, both electorally and financially. The military, with a certain amount of mixed feelings and apprehension, allowed this pair to take power, and Kubitschek and Goulart, along with strong opposition from editor turned politician, Carlos Lacerda, dominated politics and public debate for the next decade.[17]

Under the guidance of Kubitschek, Brazil continued to develop economically at one of the fastest rates in Latin America. Its only rival in terms of steady growth was Mexico. Venezuela has also enjoyed an extended rise in her GNP, because of the very special factor of her oil exports, though her internal development has been uneven. Kubitschek managed to conduct a popular administration marked by policies that inspired Brazilian nationalism and audacious economic changes. As a monument to Brazil, and perhaps to himself, Kubitschek undertook the building of a new capital five hundred miles inland in Goias. It was inaugurated in 1960 and represents a far-reaching effort to expand Brazil's hinterland and populate the vast expanses between the new capital, Brasilia, and the east-coast metropoli of Rio and São Paulo.[18] It is one of the few examples in the contemporary Western world, outside of the Australian capital of Canberra, of an entire city created on an architect's and engineer's drawing board and planned in terms of design and location. It was not a decision which followed any marked population, economic, or political shift but was rather a rational move to establish a new focus and pattern for the subsequent civilizing paraphernalia that would emerge in the new setting.

The elections of 1960 saw the strange phenomena of the first victory of the UDN with Jañio Quadros elected as president while opposition party leader João Goulart gained the vice-presidency. This may be the reason for Quadros's almost unexplicable resignation in the winter of 1961 after only a half a year in office. Elements of the military who feared the growing influence of labor-oriented João Goulart put unusual pressures on Quadros who,

---

Vargas Era," *Hispanic American Historical Review*, vol. 49, no. 2 (May 1964), pp. 197–213.

[17] For a full treatment of this ten-year period see Thomas E. Skidmore, *Politics in Brazil, 1930–1964* (New York: Oxford University Press, 1967), pp. 163–302.

[18] President Kubitschek's decision to create Brasilia is examined in Nathaniel H. Leff, *Economic Policy-Making and Development in Brazil, 1947–1964* (New York: John Wiley, 1968), p. 49 ff.

hoping his popularity would allow him, like Perón in 1945, to return with strong executive authority.[19] He assumed that fear of Goulart would be sufficient to stimulate the military to bring about some changes in the constitutional framework, which would give Quadros an easier means for dealing with an obstreperous congress that opposed most of his fiscal and administrative reform and his unaligned foreign policy. Other Latin American nations have also had this problem of the president and vice-president coming from opposing parties and increasing the danger of internal dissension and intrigue.

Quadros's plan failed, and he left by boat for England in August of 1961. Thus the military strategy appeared to be to get rid of Quadros and weaken Goulart, which they proceeded to do by constitutionally instituting a parliamentary system in which a new office of prime minister was created directly responsible to Congress and under which Goulart was kicked upstairs. Similar to Chile's failure with parliamentary innovations of 1891–1920, the Brazilian parliamentary experiment resulted in legislative stagnation and a complete disintegration of responsibility. It allowed Goulart to take his case to the people, by way of a plebiscite, which changed Brazil once more to a presidential system. The military, uneasy over the five to one vote favoring Goulart, finally intervened a year later and has since gradually imposed a tight military dictatorship.

The military uprising against the Goulart government represented frustration with governmental ineffectiveness as much as it did a general malaise attributed to Goulart's increasing tendency to cultivate a labor, peasant, and military-recruit bases of support. The actual event which, ostensibly, triggered off the coup was Goulart's refusal to discipline a group of enlisted sailors who had revolted against the naval command demanding certain ameliorative measures during their term of service in the armed forces.[20]

The coup was fashioned with consummate deliberation, speed, and resulted in no apparent popular unrest. Few institutional changes in Brazilian history have ever aroused any such reactions. Under the leadership of General Castelo Branco, who was imposed as the first military president since the election of Marshal Dutra in 1945, the new government gave immediate indication that its reasons for seizing power were deep rooted and consequential. There was little doubt that the military leadership planned wholesale personnel and policy changes.

Using the economic powers of military decree, the government undertook measures to arrest inflation, rationalize the governmental bureaucracy, restrict consumption, and multiply the economic investment level. These measures necessitated taking very unpopular attitudes, designed to hurt the economic position of the mass society. Wage freezes were imposed, removal

[19] Skidmore advances several other hypotheses on Quadros's resignation in his *Politics in Brazil, 1930–1964*, Ch. 6, pp. 202–204.

[20] Ibid., pp. 294–302.

of subsidies to consumer-products industries released prices upward, and excessive government personnel were cashiered. In the area of inflation the military government has been quite successful, reducing the rate from 86 percent in 1964, its first year at the helm, to 45 percent in 1965, 41 percent in 1966, and 24 percent in 1967.[21]

In its economic policies plans have been made to develop both the Amazon interior and the impoverished Northeast. Both public and private agencies have been created under governmental surveillance to foster private investments into these undercapitalized regions. It is also apparent that achievements have been made in inducing an increasing measure of governmental efficiency in the various ministries. These steps are geared to centralizing decision making within the various ministerial jurisdictions much like an army chain of command. The focus for decision making was consciously centralized in two interrelated administrative groups: the president and his closest military advisors and the economic and technical specialists that were under the guidance of the Ministry of Planning, presided over by economist Roberto Campos.[22]

Though the gains in the economic sector of Brazil since 1964 are undeniable, with its commensurate increase in foreign financial assistance, they have in many cases been made at the expense of a democratic society. With the culmination of military control, a series of four Institutional Acts were decreed that severely altered the constitutional framework established by the liberal 1946 document. In essence the acts, decreed in April, 1964, October, 1965, and February, and October, 1966, provided for the right of the government to strip individual politicians of their constitutional rights (of running for office or holding elective office), required the chamber of deputies to act within thirty days on all proposed legislation, provided for the indirect election by national and state legislators of the president and governors, and gave military courts jurisdiction over civilians where questions of national security are involved. These stern and extreme measures further included the abolition of existing political parties and the right to deprive any Brazilian of his civil rights for a period of ten years. By mid-1970 over 1,100 private citizens had been so deprived.

Opposition to some of these measures has only witnessed continuing governmental moves to further impose and consolidate its powers. Repetitive suspension of deputies caused organized congressional protest. Subsequent governmental reprisals included the "recessing" of parliament in October,

[21] *New York Times*, 6 January 1968.

[22] Roberto Campos' measured and undogmatic economic views are perhaps best assessed in his short contribution to the "structuralist" versus "monetarist" debate among Latin American-interested economists in Albert O. Hirschman (ed.) *Latin American Issues: Essays and Comments* (New York: Twentieth Century Fund, 1961), pp. 69–79.

1966 until such a time that the administration was prepared to present its new constitution for nominal legislative amendments in late 1966 and early 1967.

The results of these stringent measures were very imposing. By the end of 1966 one could speak of the dismissal from office and deprivation of political rights from over fifty federal deputies. A total of over four hundred other high political officials were shorn of their political prerogatives for ten years. Further, one observer notes the firing of nine or ten thousand other civilian and military officeholders.[23]

By the process of indirect elections to executive offices, a successor to President Castelo Branco was elected in October, 1966, and inaugurated in March, 1967. Marshal da Costa e Silva took office as the second successive military ruler[24] by receiving a majority of two hundred and ninety-five votes out of the four hundred and seventy-five members of the national Chamber of Deputies and Senate. Despite the fact that many of the outstanding opposition leaders had already been politically purged, the election was boycotted by considerable numbers of the "government-sanctioned" opposition legislators belonging to the Brazilian Democratic Movement (MDB).

In November, 1966, the first direct national elections since the presidential elections of 1960 were held. At stake were the full Chamber of Deputies and a third of the Senate. Again as in earlier state bi-elections many potentially popular candidates were deprived the right of standing for elective office, among which were such obvious luminaries as former presidents Kubitschek, Quadros, and Goulart. Based on such restrictive measures, the victory scored by the government sponsored and supported Alliance for National Renovation (ARENA) proved rather indecisive. In any case, the legislature that would work with the da Costa e Silva administration seats 277 ARENA deputies out of a total of 409 and 48 such affiliates out of 66 senatorial seats, clearly a dominant majority for a government that had already seriously weakened the legislative branch.[25]

It is of interest to note that the 1970 Congressional elections fortified again the recurring phenomena of Brazilian politics—an urban-rural electoral dichotomy. The MDB as the principal opposition group did very well in the more

[23] James W. Rowe, "The Revolution and the System: Notes on Brazilian Politics," *American Universities Field Staff Reports,* East Coast South America Series, vol. 12, no. 5 (August 1966), p. 16.

[24] It is interesting that there is a marked influence in both these administrations of the majority faction of the "tenentes" groups who have been instrumental as the leaders of the anti-Vargas and PSD/PTB party alliances from 1937–1964. See this interpretation by Christopher George, "Brazil: The Revolution and Political Party Structure," *The World Today* (June 1967), p. 264.

[25] James W. Rowe, "Brazil Stops the Clock," *American Universities Field Staff Reports,* East Coast South America Series, vol. 13, no. 1 (March 1967), pp. 11–12.

politically conscious urban centers, such as Rio de Janeiro, São Paulo, Santos, Belo Horizonte, Salvador, Recife, and Pôrto Alegre. This tendency described the political attitudes of Brazilians in past elections. In areas with high rates of industrialization and modernity, voters have been known to give greater weight to translating attitudinal frustrations into protest votes. It is important to reiterate that civilizing paraphernalia relate to commitment and voter interest. On the other hand, the obverse situation in Brazil's rural areas mitigated any great voter propensity to challenge the status quo as represented by the military government.

Discontent with the military government, though it was not yet pronounced since approximately 30 percent of the voters in 1966 and 40 percent in 1970 abstained in cities like Rio de Janeiro and São Paulo, continued to be manifested in areas where the Goulart and Quadros followers banded together to object to the rural traditional policies advocated by the PSD.[26]

Tensions between the military government and the populace, however, were substantially increased by the radicalization of the military policy, which was made evident in the proclamation of stringent new decrees in December, 1968 and early 1969. A series of Institutional Acts were promulgated which expanded the original four acts passed in the first two years of the military government. The events that culminated in the new government measures followed the refusal by the Chamber of Deputies, by a vote of 216 to 141, to deprive Congressman Márcio Moreira Alves of his legislative immunity, which would have made him liable to military punishment. The case reached national proportions after the deputy had made disparaging remarks about the character of the military leadership. In the final vote in the Chamber of Deputies approximately eighty ARENA legislators voted against the military request. The day after the vote, the military regime issued its fifth Institutional Act since 1964, suspending indefinitely the national congress as well as all state legislatures and giving the executive extraordinary powers, among them the right to suspend provisions of the 1967 Constitution.

The sixth Institutional Act, decreed in January, 1969, reformed the make-up of the Federal Supreme Court, suspending three Supreme Court justices and leading to the resignation of the Chief Justice and one other justice. In the seventh Institutional Act, promulgated in February, legislative salaries were regulated for maximum ceilings, and all interim elections to municipal and federal offices were abolished to be replaced by interim executive appointments instead. The eighth Institutional Act decreed the means for rapid expropriation of large landed estates. In other actions, the military furthered its hold on labor union affairs, implemented increased censorship

[26] Such an urban/rural discrepancy has been notably examined by Glaucio Ary Dillon Soares, "The Political Sociology of Uneven Development in Brazil," in I. L. Horowitz (ed.), *Revolution in Brazil* (New York: E. P. Dutton, 1964), pp. 164–195.

of the press and films, and lay the groundwork for dismissing supernumeraries in the federal civil service.

Thus from the beginning of the Vargas era to the present Garrastazú Médici administration sees the growth of military influence, then dominance, over Brazilian decision making at the highest levels of government. The whole of Brazil's distributive period has witnessed the accretion of political responsibility devolve upon the military services. It was they who twice ousted Vargas, played a significant power factor under Kubitschek, and again dominated the Quadros regime before their final intervention against Goulart's government. Under the aegis of the military establishment, the Brazilian governments since 1964 have sought to undertake revolutionary policy changes from above while maintaining a tight, sometimes terroristic, largely undemocratic control over the extent and speed of such reforms.

The strategy of Brazilian military administrators is very distinct from past military-controlled administrations. It may mark the eclipse of Brazilian public policy symbolized by a type of "politics by concession" and practiced by ruling traditional groups attempting to co-opt more competitive urban groups. In any case, there is no reason to believe that distributive politics under Garrastazú Médici by means of increased expenditures for housing, education, and land reform, will not reassert itself in subsequent "stages" of Brazilian reformism. However, there is a greater likelihood than before that the military will maintain their predominate political position; their leadership certainly does not give the impression of merely "caretaking" between civilian governments.

The Vargas upheaval and its political residues are probably too powerful to allow the military to maintain for long its very monolithic, apolitical approach to public responsibility. However, it is just as apparent that the military has succeeded in doing with its domestic policies what former President Jãnio Quadros wanted but failed to do.

Chile

The accomplishments of Chile's Popular Front marked the real inception of its distributive stage of political evolution. Considering the Front lasted less than two years, its contributions were of considerable importance for subsequent decades of development, both politically and economically.

Probably its most important contribution was the creation in 1939 of Corporación de Fomento (CORFO), a governmental development agency which directed its efforts toward developing modern industrial and agricultural enterprises. Furthermore, as its counterpart the Nacional Financiera of Mexico created in 1934 had done, it sought to widen the industrial base, to coordinate industry with agriculture, to exploit raw materials in a more rational manner, and to fulfill a whole gamut of intermediary goals in the development area. The Corporación de Fomento creates new industries with key loans and expands and develops other essential industries. In most of the newer industries, CORFO will own 50 percent of the stock, but once the enterprise becomes a "going" concern, CORFO will sell out to predominantly private capital.

Another important but more limited program of the Front was the free school breakfast and lunch policy which affected thousands of grade school children. The Front also extended Alessandri's program of social security which was paid into by employees, employers, and the state. Several huge low-cost housing projects were also initiated.

Another remarkable achievement of the short-lived Front was the stimulation (similar to Britain's Labor Party in post-War England) which it gave to organized workers. In the two years 50,000 workers were organized into 100 new unions, rural workers were also organized into incipient unions, and strikes increased four times.

In the area of civil liberties there was absolutely no limit. Civil liberties had always been ample in Chile but never to this degree. No party headquarters were shut down, no papers were closed, and no individual exiled for his political beliefs. Even the worst enemies of the Front enjoyed these amenities. In retrospect the Popular Front created a climate of political opinion that made all parties realize that they themselves would have to meet the pressing national and social questions if they hoped to bid for and remain in power. It instilled into the politics of Chile an open atmosphere that is still prevalent today and demonstrated to Chileans the value of allowing the Communists to work in the open rather than as an irresponsible underground movement.

With the death of Aguirre Cerda in 1942, another Radical, Juan Antonio Rios, was elected. He, too, died in office in 1946, and a third Radical candidate Gabriel Gonzalez Videla was elected with cross-party support extending from the Communists to one faction of the Liberals. Though the Communists were given cabinet posts for the first time, Gonzalez Videla found it necessary within the context of the Cold War to oust them from his administration and to outlaw the party in 1948.

The economic situation worsened as the demand for copper and nitrates declined after the end of the War. The Korean War again served as an important stimulus to Chilean copper which was rapidly outstripping nitrate as the overwhelming single Chilean export. However, inflation set in on the eve of the 1952 presidential election, and the venerable General Carlos Ibañez emerged victorious as he ran with his own socialist agrarian party. His winning formula was based on discrediting existing parties, promising to legalize the Communist Party, and pledging to control Chile's rampant inflation. In many respects running as a man above party as Perón had done in Argentina in both the 1946 and 1951 elections, Ibañez drew support from all sectors of society. He received votes from both extremes of the Communists and most conservative parties.[27]

Several important political changes were made during the Ibañez term in office (1952–1958). Reminiscent of the Popular Front days, a new electoral alliance was formed between the Communists and the Socialists which is still known today as the Frente de Acción Popular (FRAP). The FRAP also included a minor Socialist Party, the Workers' Party, and the Peoples' Democratic Party. Also, of historical importance was the renovation of the old Falangista Party (offshoot from the Conservative Party), which took on the goals of Christian Democracy and the new name of Christian Democrats. This development had long been in the making, but the formal change in name and program took place in 1957. Thus in the 1958 elections there were three main contending groups. The Conservatives and Liberals, anxious to make a comeback since their presidential eclipse of 1938, named Jorge Alessandri, son of Arturo Alessandri, as their presidential aspirant. The Christian Democrats chose Eduardo Frei. The FRAP put forward Senator Salvador Allende, a Socialist. By 1965–66, the competition was between the Christian Democrats who were gaining steadily and the FRAP as principal opposition. The Radicals were in apparent eclipse, and the future of the Conservatives and Liberals was none too secure.

The 1964 presidential election and the 1965 congressional election reaffirmed the growing preponderance of the Christian Democratic movement as a viable alternative to traditional conservatism and organized protest groups, such as the existing factions of communism and socialism. The very impressive victory of the Christian Democrats in early 1965 punctuated the continuing "middle way" taken by Chilean participatory society.[28] Given the policy alternatives, as presented by the principal political advocates the Christian Democrats and the FRAP, it seems apparent that the voters made the choice in favor of a reasonable and conciliatory position as opposed to a rabid and impetuous one.[29]

The 1970 presidential electoral victory of Salvador Allende again typified

[27] There is substantial evidence that Ibañez and his followers were committed to Perón's political and economic outlook and that Justicialismo as a doctrine had considerable appeal with the Chilean masses. Donald Bray, "Peronism in Chile," *Hispanic American Historical Review*, vol. 47, no. 1 (February 1967), pp. 38–49.

[28] For a very comprehensive run-down and analysis of Chilean elections of 1964 and 1965 see Federico G. Gil, *The Political System of Chile* (Boston: Houghton Mifflin, 1966), Ch. 7.

[29] Ibid., pp. 299–304. Here the economic and social programs espoused by the Christian Democrats and FRAP are compared. For an appraisal of the ideological roots, contemporary intraparty dialogue, and confrontation as they pertain to the Communists, Socialists, and Christian Democrats see the study by Ernst Halperin, *Nationalism and Communism in Chile* (Cambridge: MIT Press, 1965).

Chilean distributive politics; the political atmosphere was open, democratic, very hotly contested, and offered the populace a genuine choice among several leadership groups. The three major ideological positions were again in competition for political preeminence: the Christian Democrats in the center of the political spectrum with Radomiro Tomic as candidate, flanked by Jorge Alessandri of the Liberal-Conservative National Party, and Senator Salvador Allende of the Communist-Socialist FRAP coalition.

Allende's September 4, 1970, victory, with 36.3 percent of the vote to Alessandri's 34.9 percent and Tomic's 28.8 percent constituted the first Communist-Socialist triumph under democratic-parliamentary processes anywhere in the world. This particular aspect of the election heightened the implications of this triumph in both of the world's major ideological camps. It was Allende's fourth attempt for the presidency, going back to his initial entry against the Ibañez candidacy in 1952. Under the Chilean Constitution he needed the majority support of Congress in its balloting on October 24, 1970, since he received a plurality and not a majority of the popular vote total. Both Tomic and Alessandri released their partisans in Congress in a demonstration of Chilean consensus regarding the legitimate and established rules of democratic procedure. Typical was Alessandri's message of support on October 19, just five days before the Congressional balloting for the presidency, which was printed in the *New York Times* the following day: "My best wishes for success go to the next President of Chile, whose long and proven democratic conviction, reflected in attitudes of constant respect for the Constitution and the laws are well known."

The Allende cabinet posts were distributed among the six parties (Unidad Popular) that supported his candidacy. His own Socialist Party received four posts, among them the important ministries of interior (José Toha) and foreign relations (Clodomiro Almeyda). The Communists and Radicals each received three posts in the cabinet. Two cabinet ministries went to the Social Democrats and one each to the Independent Popular Action Party and the Unified Popular Action Movement (MAPU), a splinter group of the Christian Democrats. The MAPU group's leader, Jacques Chonchol, former director of the Frei agrarian reform agency, received the sensitive agricultural ministry.

The Socialist-Communist coalition government under Allende has emphasized that the nationalization of the copper mines and other essential industries would be high on the administration's agenda. Agrarian reform appears as the second item of concern. However, as Frei before him, Allende lacks a working majority in Congress, controlling but 90 out of the 200 seats. As a candidate Allende reiterated that despite the acknowledged frustrations his government is bound to experience with the legislative branch, he is committed to its independent role in the Chilean political process. Allende, after his inauguration, made similar assurances of autonomy in the direction of the military, mass media, and educational establishments.

More than any other country in South America, Chile continues to demonstrate political stability combined with increasing leadership concern for economic and political modernization.[30] The nation appears as a very progressively inclined entity forced, particularly by the Christian Democrats between 1964 and 1970, to consider major distributive decisions in the next several years that will mightily affect Chilean developments in succeeding decades. The Christian Democrats seem to be appropriately grounded in fundamental skills to undertake major societal changes within the limitations of scientific management. Its leadership is thoroughly grounded in the urban middle class. Though in most cases they are of a traditional Catholic background, their subsequent training in such fields as business administration, law, and journalism has tended to moderate any previous disposition to follow a dogmatic policy approach. Similarly, politically, many in the Frei administration were former adherents of the Liberal and Conservative parties. Changing social conditions and requirements, however, aroused their social consciousness and marked them for new commitments to the Christian Democratic alternative. An argument can be advanced that the more enlightened, less tradition-bound, more flexible, and pragmatic elements of the Conservative and Liberal parties have formed the nucleus of the governing party.

The Christian Democratic formulas for political and economic change have seemed particularly suited to fostering social consciousness (based on the recent papal encyclicals), achieving popular support and identity (by means of a built-in Catholic constituency), and moving forward incrementally and marginally, thereby mitigating major social dislocations and/or disruptions (assisted by the movement's avoidance of being labelled as either strictly socialist or capitalist).

Chilean distributive politics has witnessed the growth of a sophisticated labor movement, the beginnings of a land redistribution, the capacity to deal effectively with foreign capital without inhibiting its influx, and the ability to channel the needs and demands of the armed forces. It is significant that these and other advances in policy have been achieved without aborting constitutional procedures. Despite the drawbacks of an inflationary economy and a well-organized FRAP opposition, the 1964 to 1970 Frei years of leadership have been one of the most positive examples of distributive politics undertaken within the confines of civilian, political party leadership in Latin America. Many of the advances achieved in recent years occurred with an opposition-dominated Senate that forced the type of ceaseless bargaining known in only a handful of countries in the world. The tactics of coalition politics that put a premium on resolving institutional conflicts between the

[30] K. H. Silvert cites the observable pluralism of Chilean society and lists several signs of an achievement of political maturity. He mentions legislative independence, an apolitical military, free elections, an essentially professional bureaucracy, and modern and effective political leadership. *Chile: Yesterday and Today* (New York: Holt, Rinehart and Winston, 1965), pp. 191–193.

presidential administration and the congress, and compromising policy and personality differences by patient persuasion were evident throughout the Frei administration.

Argentina

On the eve of the Peronist takeover in Argentina, several things were apparent: A vast inequality appeared between the urban and rural regions of Argentina in both material and human resources;[31] massive migrations from the interior were at their peak flow; Argentina's trade pattern was still heavily dependent upon British imports of beef and grains; within the infrastructure, British capital was foremost in practically every area; and the thousands of suddenly rootless rural peons transformed into industrial workers were experiencing economic advancement without finding any institutional outlets or political recognition.

The years immediately preceding the advent of Perón were thus fertile ground for the growth of socioeconomic disintegration: There was class warfare on the economic front, there was an ideological battle over the Allied-Axis struggle which divided Argentine society, and from 1932 to 1943 every successive government was unrepresentative. The upper classes ruled, the middle classes were momentarily defrauded and disenfranchised, and the mass of people were almost entirely unrepresented.

The Perón regime represented this very mass of new urban migrants, which outnumbered the other two sectors by early 1940s. The government of Perón widened public interest in politics and irrevocably initiated Argentina into the era of mass politics.[32] Mass European immigration, industrialization, and the emergence of a stronger middle class further laid the ground-

[31] Mario S. Brodersohn explains the historical reasons for this difference. He compares Argentina's urbanized Central-East region to other sections of the country. He traces the wealth of the Central-East to the pampa area (mostly situated in Buenos Aires province), which contributed about 95 per cent of the country's total agricultural production. In "A Regional Analysis of the Economic Development of Argentina," his paper prepared for the International Conference on Comparative Social Research in Developing Countries, Buenos Aires, September 7–16, 1964, Brodersohn states that this early advantage ". . . permitted the region to absorb a large part of the social overhead capital and human resources." Statistics are provided to show the Central-East region's monopoly in such factors as literate population, European immigrants, capital, and railroads.

[32] This is the view of many Argentine intellectuals. However, the most lucid and scientific explanation of this phenomenon belongs to the dean of Argentine sociologists, Gino Germani, *Política y Sociedad en una Epoca de Transición: de la Sociedad Tradicional a la Sociedad de Masas* (Buenos Aires: Editorial Paidos, 1963).

work for the representation of hitherto unrepresented or underrepresented classes.

It is important to acknowledge the difference between Perón as one of the leaders of a military coup perpetrated against a conservative government and Perón as the demagogic leader of a newly evolved power complex. The palace coup of 1943 was launched by an ostensibly Fascist-tainted military who feared the ambivalence of a government which maintained neutrality toward the Allied-Axis world split. Perón and his associates were anxious over the growing governmental solicitude toward Great Britain, and when Patrón Costas, a conservative with British leanings, was put forward as the most likely successor to President Ramón Castillo, the retinue of Axis sympathizers within the military intervened. The Socialist and Radical parties were impotent and the ruling Conservative party discredited. Any counterforce was conspicuously absent. The revolt paved the way for Perón's eventual election as president in 1946 and his ten-year dominance of Argentine society.

It is fair to say that though Perón contributed to a Fascist-type military seizure, his leadership was of a unique nationalist nature which, with the defeat of Germany and the evolution of domestic developments, sought a series of social goals which were massively supported. Perón's regime was within the tradition of authoritarianism, and he ruled as a man above party. This began with his overwhelming victory in 1946 over the Democratic Union Coalition, representing the Communists, Socialists, Progressive Democrats, Radicals, and Conservatives. Perón claimed that he was the only candidate that did not represent a party or a vested interest but all the Argentine people. He sought to become the leader, in word and deed, of the European immigrant and the rural migrant as they swelled the ranks of the urban centers in search of economic self-sufficiency and social recognition.

Perón led Argentina through a nationalist and then socialist phase of political development. With or without Perón, Argentina would probably have gone through this period of growing national integration and consciousness, but Perón telescoped several decades of peaceful political evolution into a dozen years of rather demagogic governmental activity.

Though his political philosophy was neither revolutionary nor original, it did gradually develop a workable series of beliefs and practices. In its initial formulations, Perón's idea of government was highly simplistic, based on the need for order, discipline, and morality. It was this triumvirate of values that laid the foundation for the military coup of 1943.[33]

It was only as Perón broadened his sphere of interest between 1945 and 1949 that he and his associates gradually felt the need to develop a social statement that would encompass past and future actions. Within this frame-

[33] George I. Blanksten, *Perón's Argentina* (Chicago: University of Chicago Press, 1953), p. 48.

work, "justicialism," as it came to be called, was created. Justicialism can best be described as a "third position" nationally placed between the polar attractions of Marxism and Capitalism, as de Gaulle's "third position" described a similarly self-conscious road between Eastern and Western international alternatives. Justicialism espouses the doctrine that idealism, individualism (of the capitalist system), materialism, and collectivism (of the Communist system) cannot stand alone and that each separated from the others results in a form of tyranny over man in society.[34] Justicialism, as a political ideology, has not made a sufficient philosophical contribution to warrant a detailed analysis. However, its historical importance rests in its flexibility and pragmatism which allow it to adjust the means to the end. It paved the way for a facile integration of huge sectors of Argentine society into the Peronist camp and allowed an "all things to all men" interpretation which is still observable in contemporary Peronismo.

Perón left his mark on almost every political, economic, educational, and social apparatus of Argentina. He intervened into the affairs of the labor confederation, he displaced Congressmen at will, he controlled provincial and local elections, he abolished social clubs and societies, he harnessed the universities and their professors, he suspended newspapers, and he issued decrees in the areas of individual liberties that affected all Argentine citizens.

At the same time, though he augmented class tensions, he contributed considerably to the lessening of class divisions based on money and status. Perón's policies tended to equalize income and spread the incidence of purchasing power which created new social and economic groups with new social commitments and an increased stake in the society. Perón has been especially credited with his extensive public works program and his strengthening of the organization of the labor movement.[35] In addition his administration, as was its wont, managed to cut through the sloth and red tape of the traditional bureaucracy.

Complementing his paternal treatment of organized labor was Perón's expectation of extraordinary loyalty from the armed forces and complete subordination from his political party, the Peronista Party, and public administration sectors. His control over the judiciary branch of government made his decade in power a highly personalistic one in which the normal activities of the political institutions were greatly reduced. With the establishment of the Peronista Party in the aftermath of the victory at the polls in 1946, Perón liberally made wholesale prizes of the judiciary, all but eliminating its autonomy as an effective countervailing branch of government.

[34] Ibid., p. 286.

[35] The reorganization of the unions was achieved by refusing recognition to unfriendly unions, sponsoring rival unions, and centralizing them into a reconstituted labor confederation dominated by loyal Perón people. George Pendle, *Argentina*, 3rd ed. (New York: Oxford University Press, 1963), pp. 98–99.

Legislative leaders were impeached and imprisoned for making "seditious" antiPeronista speeches in Congress, less and less criticism was tolerated, and all parties were considered disloyal and subject to continual harassment. The Peronistas, without subjection to judicial restraint, legislated into all areas of human activity.

However, Perón's regime eventually antagonized several important political power centers. It was a community of antiPerón sentiment that resulted in the fall of his regime. The Catholic Church was severely offended by Perón's policies of legalizing divorce, granting equal civil rights to illegitimate children, and by his occasional insinuations of separating church and state. The military was antagonized by Perón's continual threats to arm the organized workers if the need arose to defend the "revolution." The political parties were only too eager to divide the spoils of an entrenched regime. The affluent classes could not pardon Perón for giving the workers their great opportunity for organized action in both the political and industrial spheres.[36] The nationalists resented Perón's policy after 1954 of inviting foreign oil companies into Argentina for the exploration and sale of oil to the National Petroleum Corporation.

The combination of these dissatisfactions was sufficient to topple the Perón hierarchy.

Perón: A Case Study of Distributive Politics

An important change produced by Perón was a shift in political ideology. Though the Perón government was less than radical in its conception of who would lead and who would follow, it surpassed itself in its desire to appear progressive in the eyes of the popular masses.[37] It is necessary to recall that Perón, though a nationalist, was not a revolutionary. His reforms came from a position of power and from above, and his ideological commitments developed out of the international and national circumstances of that period. The development of a mass industrial base with a large politically unrepresented working force provided the political substructure upon which a regime could build its public support. On the international scene, Argentina was

[36] Luis Reissig, "Punto clave en la evolucion politica Argentina," *Cuardernos Americanos* (July–October 1958), p. 129.

[37] As a leader of one Socialist party wing states the case: ". . . Perónismo was a horizontal movement—in its popular base and in its hopeful expressions—it tended toward the left. As for its vertical aspect, in its tendencies and actions, it served to maintain the middle class and augment its privileges." Abel Alexis Latendorf, in Silvio Frondizi et al. (eds.), *Las izquierdas en el proceso politico* (Buenos Aires: Palestra, 1959), pp. 114–115.

embarking on a highly nationalistic period in its history, and Perón in many ways filled this need.[38]

Perón's policies were, in one manner of speaking, double edged. His public philosophy exuded the workers' creed while he privately assured the middle sectors.[39] He railed against the large landowners, capitalist investments, and the elite social clubs while he moved against them only as acts of reprisal. Much of Perón's more radical policies against private enterprise, the church, and the military were made more in the heat of revenge than within the confines of philosophical deliberations. One is aware of his innate distrust of the worker. Perón, apparently, did not intend to build a national labor party of stated ideals.

In its most philosophical sense, Peronismo represented the revolt of romantic nationalism of an integrative sort against a liberal and hierarchical tradition of individualism. It played upon the anxieties and frustrations of atomized individuals and sought to bind them tightly to the overwhelming attractiveness of the collectivity. Peronismo uprooted the urban masses from lethargy and aroused them to a pitch of unsurpassed loyalty by manipulating latent antagonisms and funnelling them into service for the state. Above all, Peronismo made the masses feel represented and a part of the councils of government.

Economic changes are secondary in comparison with the profound changes in social mentality. Though he increased the consumptive standard and the social security of the laboring masses, Perón failed to alter Argentina's monocultural livestock export sector. The basis for heavy industry was not initiated nor was essential development in heavy industry, petroleum, transportation, energy, electricity, and communications carried out. Rather the huge government reserves which were built up during World War II by the heavy exportation of beef and grain to the Allies at the very time that Argentina was unable to import industrial goods from these same belligerents were spent in the nationalization of a sorely outmoded British railway system, in such gestures as increasing worker bonuses and holidays and in the rapid growth of a new governing bureaucracy. Perón's economic policies were more symbolic than deep rooted. Though he destroyed the leisurely landowners' symbol of opulence, "the Jockey Club," he left their land undisturbed. If he expropriated traditional enterprises in the name of the state, he usually handed them over to large-scale "sympathetic" capital enterprises.

[38] See Enrique Díaz Araujo, "Las relaciones de la Argentina con Estados Unidos de Norteamerica," *Boletín de Estudios Politicos y Sociales,* no. 16 (1967), especially pp. 53–66.

[39] One Argentine observer makes the analogy that Perón was attempting to invent the classic imperial formula of subjugating without humiliating and humiliating without subjugating. Bruno C. Jacovella, "Los ingredientes de la historia Argentina," *Dinámica Social,* no. 117 (June 1960), p. 13.

The more formal and significant economic approaches under Perón consisted of the first Argentine attempt at economic planning and the nationalization of much of the financial structure (banks, foreign commerce). If not successful in Perón's time, it paved the way for subsequent governmental concern for a rapid rate of economic development and a knowledgeable distribution of scarce resources.

Also in the field of labor, Perón's influence was far reaching both in his time and for the contemporary period.[40] In what was, perhaps, the most positive contribution of his ten years in office, Perón was instrumental in adopting a whole range of social legislation ensuring a modicum of social services, employee benefits, pension funds, and varying aids to the needy.

Markworthy as well, as Perón's organization of the workers of Argentina. Approximately 300,000 workers were unionized before World War II. With the inception of the Perón-dominated regimes several million had been organized, and there is little doubt that Perón had the support of the majority of workers.[41] The laborers gave sustenance to Perón's policies because of a variety of welcomed gains and avoided discriminations. Those who abjured his lead were soon ousted from positions of control within the Confederación General de Trabajo. He converted this confederation of scores of unions into the strongest labor movement in Latin America. For all intents and purposes it was under his control and served as an arm of the Labor Secretariat of the administration. The price of better conditions and improved organization was a free and independent labor movement.

Regardless of their lack of autonomy, the coordination of the majority of labor into a central body gave the working man, whether politically captured or not, a serious and unified voice with which to make its opinion heard in public affairs.[42] This produced a concomitant evolution of labor's social consciousness. Once the move toward organization had been achieved, it devel-

[40] Bertram Silverman has documented the differential advantages enjoyed by the industrial sector, both labor and capital, throughout the Perón decade. Significantly real wages surpassed output per worker for the entire period, thus productivity considerations did not deter Perón's distributive policies. *Labor Ideology and Economic Development in the Peronist Epoch* (St. Louis: Washington University Studies in Comparative International Development), vol. 4, no. 11 (1968–1969), pp. 243–258.

[41] Torcuato S. Di Tella, *El sistema político Argentino y la clase obrera* (Buenos Aires: Editorial Universitaria de Buenos Aires, 1964), pp. 39–40. According to Arthur P. Whitaker, 10 per cent of all workers were organized into the labor movement at the beginning of Perón's dictatorship and 70 per cent by its conclusion. See his *Argentine Upheaval* (New York: Praeger, 1956), p. 71.

[42] Although the majority of Argentine workers may still be captured in the sense that they are loyal to Perón, this does not necessarily mean that they are "prenational" in their level of political consciousness as David Butler seems to imply. See his "Charisma, Migration, and Elite Coalescence: An Interpretation of Perónism," *Comparative Politics*, vol. 1, no. 3 (April 1969), pp. 438–439.

oped a life of its own apart from the nature of the regime that gave it birth. This has had a profound sociological impact on contemporary Argentina.

Post-Perón Politics

The coup against Perón was led by a military junta which installed General Eduardo Lonardi as president in September, 1955. The ouster of Lonardi two months later by a military faction led by General Pedro Aramburu, signaled the beginning of the post-Perón antiPeronista revolution. The Aramburu provisional government of 1955–58 sought to annihilate the Peronista movement in fact as well as in ideology. It paid little attention to the psychological and social residues of Peronismo, and many of Aramburu's repressive measures seem to have been motivated by the need to mete out justice rather than to reinstill in the populace the virtues of democratic institutions. Under the uncompromising nature of the antiPeronista government of Aramburu, the proportional strength of grass-roots elements of Peronismo increased.[43] The masses of workers rallied around the last banner which had afforded them social standing and psychological identification. However, the Aramburu government did prepare the way for a return to the 1853 constitution and did hand over power to a civil government elected in February 1958.

The two major candidates in the 1958 presidential elections were Arturo Frondizi, who represented the Unión Cívica Radical Intransigente (UCRI), and Ricardo Balbin of the Unión Cívica Radical del Pueblo (UCRP). The UCRI and UCRP represented the split which took place within the Radical party prior to the 1958 election. The Frondizi faction took a tolerant view of Peronismo and sought to woo it into the ranks of the UCRI. The UCRP of Balbin, on the other hand, was adamantly antiPeronista and refused to direct any appeal to the Peronista voter. As was expected, Frondizi won a landslide victory, having the solid support of the Peronista leadership, of Perón who was in exile, and the mass of Peronista voters.

Two factors determined the direction taken during the Frondizi years. The first was the growing desire within the military to take over the leadership from the civilian constitutional authority. The second was the erosion, sector by sector, of what once was Frondizi's very broad political support until

[43] Peronism in the post-Perón years has more than ever maintained its position as the foremost mass party in Argentina. Though it is essentially class-based, it is by no means confined to the lower classes. According to a recent public opinion survey the Peronists, along with the labor unions, are perceived as a second ranking power in society after the military, church and "oligarchy." All are considered more influential than the middle class entrepreneurs. See Jeane Jordan Kirkpatrick, "Peronist Politics in Argentina: Composition, Expectations and Demands of the Mass Base." (Columbia University Ph.D. Dissertation, 1968), p. 189.

his basis of power was too fragmentary to hold his weight. The outstanding dilemma that presented itself throughout these years remained that of Peronismo. The dialogue centered on the methods of dealing with this phenomenon which was now several years old and, in a real sense, a post-dictorial movement of great strength. How does one confront a powerful yet clearly unrepresented sector of the Argentine public? Should they be integrated into the political system? Should they be outlawed? Should they be allowed to enter coalitions with democratic parties? These were the deep-seated political questions which faced the Frondizi administration between 1958 and 1962.

Frondizi finally decided that since his movement had once absorbed Peronista votes, it could do so again even though it was planning to oppose Peronista candidates. The Congressional elections of March, 1962 were a test case for that theory. The calculations proved incorrect, and the Peronistas within various political groupings received over 30 percent of the vote and won over ten important governorships, including that of Buenos Aires province. The massive vote total in favor of Peronista candidates forced the military's hand, and it intervened to oust Frondizi and establish a military government which oversaw the elections of July, 1963. In these elections the Peronistas were prohibited from running as one massive bloc and prevented from running as part of an electoral alliance. Though Perón in exile eventually called for abstention on the part of his followers, a group of new parties began to develop in several of the rural provinces. These neoPeronistas, despite Perón's plea, entered candidates in legislative and gubernatorial elections and did very well. They achieved sixteen deputy seats, nine senatorial seats, and two governorships in an election won by the UCRP presidential candidate Arturo Illia.

The period between 1963 and 1965 saw the deterioration of the hard won economic advances made under the Frondizi administration and a growing incapability of the Illia government to take firm decisions in either the administrative or political arena. By the March, 1965, elections a bipolarization of the electorate resulted in Peronista and Radical parties absorbing around 60 percent of the total vote and many of the smaller parties finding it increasingly difficult to compete with either of the two main parties. The weakness of the minor parties, combined with the paucity of UCRP economic and social programs, augured well for a continued preeminent political position for the Peronistas.

The military coup of June, 1966, was precipitated as much by the inadequacies of the Radical government of President Illia as by the continued electoral predominance anticipated for the Peronistas in crucial elections to be held for governors in 1967 and for the presidency in 1969. The governing party, by 1966, was the target of almost universal reprimand, and discontent with its leadership capabilities. Inflation remained as an uncontrollable ingredient. The two largest government monopolies—the railways and petroleum (nationalized under Illia)—were running cumbersome deficits. Foreign investments had increasingly evaporated under the Radical administration. The government, furthermore, demonstrated little aptitude for rational economic planning.

On the other hand, the initial dePeronization period commenced the contemporary confusion as it failed to distinguish seriously between the Peronista machine bureaucrat, the Peronista supporter and the large-scale Peronista following. The revenge-oriented policies initiated since 1955 had given recent governments pause at allowing Peronistas to take positions of executive control for fear of Peronista retributions for past antiPeronista deeds.

This then was the background to the military's decision in 1966 to formalize their discontent with Argentine civil leadership. They hoped to avoid the continual confrontation with the Peronistas and at the same time lead in the transformation and modernization of the economy. The military government has virtually replaced politicians (from the preexisting parties) with military careerists, technicians, businessmen and intellectuals.

The military government at first was generally well accepted by most sectors of society and it even received a good deal of support from most political parties and even factions of the Peronistas (at whom the coup was chiefly aimed). Much of this acceptance was, no doubt, because of the public's weariness with unconstructive governments marked by unmitigated political hassels and continual efforts to legitimize their policies.

The military, without the need of constantly attracting widescale public support, made no clear efforts at popularizing its regime until the coup of June 1970. Such attempts at eliciting support had been largely confined to relating to and channeling the various societal leadership elements under a corporate structure. The masses, on the other hand, have been virtually untouched and unapproached, distinct from the policy-making styles of Perón and Frondizi.[44] Further, the regime of General Juan Carlos Onganía did not appear to have any distinct ideological commitments, any fixed notion of which political sectors it was beholden to nor any iron-clad promise to work through certain institutions, though it made clear its distaste for traditional methods of representation (i.e. parties and congress).

The military government, under the leadership of Onganiá, had been largely constituted by individuals that have not served in previous governments. This gave the administration the additional aspect of appearing uncommitted to any special interests. However, in the orientation of its personnel and in the direction of its policies the government is quite openly attempting to strengthen foreign and private investment aid to stabilize the value of the Argentine peso. They have followed these principal economic goals within an atmosphere of political tranquility, often imposed by undisguised authori-

[44] For a theoretically-focused analysis of the military government see Mariano Grondona, "El dialogo," *Comentarios*, vol. 3, No. 111 (August 30, 1966), p. 4.

tarian measures. The more harshly applied dicta have been directed at the political parties, the labor movement, students and, in some cases, the daily press.

In the tradition of the Brazilian military, the Argentine government dissolved all political parties, closed their headquarters, and seized all financial and property assets belonging to them. Distinct from the Brazilian example, Argentina has thus far not allowed a resurgence of "controlled" party activity. Neither has the Argentine military government taken away civil and political rights from large numbers of citizens. Argentina, again in variance from the Brazilian situation, has, for the near future, dissolved congress and suspended electoral activity, though none of these changes have yet been or are likely to be documented as constitutional reforms and amendments. They have been promulgated, rather, as de facto decrees.

Because of the government's pursuit of monetary stability and fiscal restraint the CGT workers confederation has taken an increasingly hostile position vis-à-vis the military's policies. Imposed wage freezes in 1967–68 led to increasing work stoppages, strikes, and public demonstrations. In reprisal the Onganía government has severed relations with several of the more volatile unions, divested them of their legal status while freezing their central bank assets. They have, thus far, with one exception, distinct from the policies under Aramburu, not intervened in the internal affairs of the labor unions. However, by their superiority of power they have rendered the labor unions weaker and more subordinate than at any time since 1940.

The universities of Argentina have also come under strict surveillance, as already alluded to in Part I.[45] The government has promulgated a new law thoroughly revising the organization of the national universities. Students and graduates have been stripped of their voting rights under the "co-gobierno," tripartite system, in which students voted along with faculty and university administrators. Absolute university autonomy has been abolished. The government may intervene for determined time periods. All forms of student political activity, agitation, militancy, propaganda, and proselytizing have been prohibited. Furthermore, the university rector and deans are to be nominated by the national government.[46]

Thus the Onganía military government, though its policies remained only partially defined, had demonstrated its desire to revitalize the Argentine economy by a variety of measures (reminiscent of Frondizi's administration) geared to free the economy from unwieldy exchange controls, an over-

[45] For the views of American academicians resulting from their trip to Argentina shortly after the military intervention into the universities see *A Report to The American Academic Community on the Present Argentine University Situation*, L.A.S.A. Special Publication no. 1, Austin, Texas, 1967. Also see an interesting coverage in the *New York Times*, September 23, 1966.

[46] A complete listing of all 126 articles contained in the university law is found in *La Nación* (*Edicion Aerea International*, April 24, 1967), pp. 1, 5.

burdensome bureaucracy, a weak export sector in manufactured goods, and inefficiently run government-owned corporations, in such fields as transportation, communication, and energy.[47]

The implementation of these measures, of course, called for generally unpopular steps as far as the laborer class and fixed income, white-collar workers were concerned. The military government had the power to enforce such policies better than any of its predecessor governments but not without paying the price of increasing alienation among workers, students, and portions of the middle sectors.[48] Thus the crucial weakness of the military regime was its growing isolation from important sectors of the political community and its estrangement from still other large portions of the general populace. This lack of regularized channels of communication and dissent (particularly in the absence of political parties, a congress, and an unfettered press) stultified and hampered the regime in domestic policy.

These mounting societal pressures, in addition to the kidnapping and assassination of former president General Pedro Aramburu, provoked a palace coup within the military establishment in June 1970.[49] By mandate of the armed forces' three commanders, the heads of the joint chiefs of staff, it brought General Roberto Marcelo Levingston to the presidency. The coup, which was the fifth such military operation in fifteen years, was provoked not only by the increasing isolation and alienation of the Onganía administration from important societal interest groups, but also by the increasing "personalist" strain of the ex-president's administration. As in the period from 1962

[47] One general observation defines the Argentine and Brazilian military solutions as political absolutism mixed with economic liberalism. Antonio Garcia, "Las clases medias y la frustracion del estrado representativo en America Latina," *Cuadernos Americanos*, vol. 150, no. 1 (January/February 1967), p. 17.

[48] Eldon Kenworthy presents the thesis that any contemporary Argentine government is going to have trouble industrializing the economy. The groups who invariably must pay the cost of rapid industrialization (e.g., landowners, high-consumption-oriented middle class, and the labor unions) are already too well defined, sophisticated, and organized to sustain very heavy sacrifices. "Argentina: The Politics of Late Industrialization," *Foreign Affairs*, vol. 45, no. 3 (April 1967), pp. 463–476.

[49] Among many hypotheses for Aramburu's assassination, these are three: 1) a revenge-inspired tactic by militant Peronists who wished to avenge Aramburu's anti-Peronist sponsored violence of 1956; 2) a militant revolutionary group, related to urban guerrilla groups throughout Latin America, who wished to demonstrate the weakness of a supposedly strongman military government; 3) a right-wing, nationalist group seeeking to eliminate Aramburu as a possible leader of a movement favoring a return to civilian rule or at least to competitive elections. Before his kidnapping, Aramburu had increasingly associated himself with the position of resuscitating full scale political life. By resort to this act they hoped to cause a severe governmental reaction weakening the expansion of any dialogue with traditional political sectors. (Forty-eight hours before his ouster, Onganía had instituted the death penalty for political crimes.)

to 1963, the power rested with the military chiefs who sought a relatively unknown general to take up the governmental reins. This undoubtedly assured them an ample amount of flexibility to devise new policies and strategies.

From mid-1969 the erosion of societal support for Onganía was increasingly evident and indicated the inability of any Argentine government, whether civilian or military, to long postpone distributive policies, whether in the arena of increasing political participation, upholding a more nationalist outlook on the economy and foreign capital investment, or socioeconomic bread and butter demands. Political violence increased measurably in Argentina from 1969 to 1970. For example, a total of fourteen people were killed in the labor and student strikes of Córdoba in May 1969, the highest incident of civil violence in contemporary Argentine history. Labor demands for salary adjustments and student demands for an independent university system were eventually complemented by political party demands for a return to political normalcy and a reconstitution of the parties. Concurrently the middle sectors were ambivalent because of the failure of the Onganía administration to demonstrate its ability to modernize the economy as it had promised in 1966.

Within the confines of the military sector, it was apparently the armed forces' commanders who sought the beginnings of an accommodation with Argentine political parties and leading interest groups. They considered that Onganía had no specific political plan for reestablishing constitutionality, but rather was merely hinting vaguely at a corporate restructuring of societal organizations–from labor to business to industrial to regional and community interests. The military appeared to opt unequivocally for a fairly rapid return to the legitimization of traditional modes of representation—namely by way of political parties and congress. It seems proper to conclude that the military has not found it possible to avoid fundamental distributive pressures and that arrangements had to be made to suit these demands without major societal disruptions.

Summary

The five nations we have examined are all aspiring nations of the twentieth century. They share many common goals among which industrialization may be placed first. They all desire to increase their productive capacities which would allow them to make a substantial saving on their foreign exchange expenditures which so burden each of their national accounts. In order to better achieve rapid industrialization, they all have shown a leaning toward the active and progressive role of government as principal capital accumulator in the country's economic structure. They are all quite aware of the uncertain markets for their few money-making raw materials, minerals, and foodstuffs and thus are intent in diversifying their exports. This would allow them the financial wherewithal to capitalize not only their industrial sector but their agricultural sector, which is now suffering from a lack of technology and is making it increasingly difficult for these rather huge nations to feed their own growing populations. Their valuable national income is spent on food imports which does little to develop their own economies.

Their politically dominant leadership groups all share the belief that a strong centralized government is the best hope toward economic and social development. It is widely believed among their leaders that power must be centralized to better engineer necessary and vital innovations in all sectors of society. There is a common reaction that dissipated and highly decentralized power only leads to social stagnation and economic ruin. Though they do not all agree on the organization of the central administration, they usually support the idea that presidential authority must not be delimited if it is to master the technical detail of the modern age and overcome the backwardness characteristic of many remote areas in each of these societies.

The leadership in these five nations not so long ago learned that the area from which decision makers are recruited can be expanded and that this increase in social mobility is important if the population as a whole is expected to be an active participant in societal change. The base from which the future elites emerge can be expected to progressively broaden and be less and less related to ideology. This will be the result of governmental policies that stress merit rather than ascription, class mobility rather than rigid class stratification, and educational rather than strictly familial background.

It is evident that the five Latin American nations have had very long periods of authority and aggregation, as shown in the drawing on page 145. Several of the Asian nations, on the other hand, developed more quickly to the distributive period despite the presence in many cases of colonial regimes. Thus Republicanism, achieved quite early in Latin America, is not a key factor of political development, nor is there an unmistakable relationship between economic development, total democratic processes, and the absence of authoritarianism. Popular Bonapartist regimes often play a major role in modernization, whereas functionally representative republics may inhibit certain modernizing innovations which are prerequisite for political change. This may be so because in several cases the populist leader heralds the inception of the distributive phase and the end of the aggregative phase of development. Under his leadership there frequently occurs a transference of the concept of nationality from the preoccupation of a relatively small economic elite to the growing concern of the popular masses. What appears as important as the type of political system is the degree to which the traditional elites are eventually surpassed and replaced by modernizing elites. For example, in Brazil and Chile, and to a degree in Argentina, the traditional elite groups when capable and willing have usually been absorbed into the modern governing structure. In Peru and again partially in Argentina, the

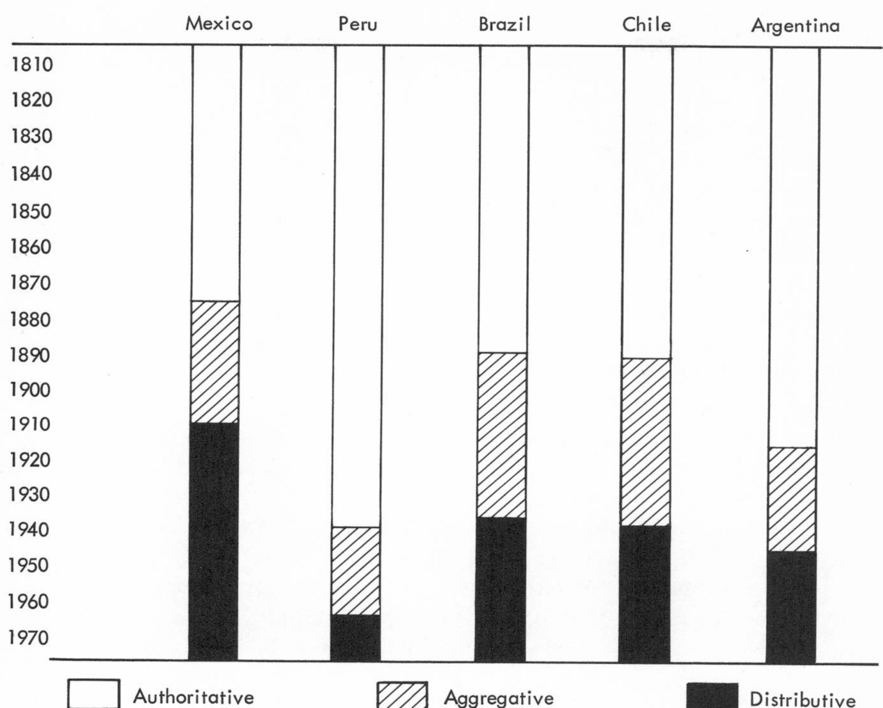

traditional groups have been ignored, skirted or detoured and replaced by newer governing groups with a more refined view of twentieth century requirements. In Mexico, the old elites were isolated, quarantined, and even destroyed. The relative power roles shared by traditional and modern elite groups have a major bearing not only upon modernity and political development but upon the political culture itself, as will be discussed in subsequent chapters.

Mexico, Peru, Brazil, Chile, and Argentina, for example, all have reached the distributive stage in national development, though they differ as to the permissiveness or rigidity of their governors. Mexico and Peru tend toward more permissive approaches within their distributive policies. Chile has achieved permissiveness for more than a generation, while Brazil and Argentina have lately reverted to rigidity after a permissive period of twenty to thirty years. However, none of these countries can contemplate a return to an earlier stage of national development.[50] Table 6-1 is a concise table, then,

[50] Bruce Russett places all but Peru (which he views as a "transitional society") into the category of "Industrial Revolution societies." See his *World Handbook of Political and Social Indicators* (New Haven: Yale University Press, 1964), pp. 294–298.

TABLE 6-1 National Development

Country	*The Authoritative Phase*	*The Aggregative Phase*	*The Distributive Phase*
Mexico	Independence (1821) to the administrations of Juárez (1855–1876)	Porfirio Díaz regime (1876–1910)	Since 1910–1917 (Madero)
Peru	Independence (1822) to the Prado government (1939)	1939–1963	Since 1963 (Belaúnde)
Brazil	Independence (1822) to the fall of empire (1889)	1889 to the Vargas regime (i.e., 1930–1937)	Since 1930–1937 (Vargas)
Chile	Independence (1817) to the Balmaceda administration (1886–1890)	1890–1938 and the inception of the Popular Front	Since 1938–1941 (Popular Front)
Argentina	Independence (1816) to the Irigoyen administration (1912–1916)	1916 to the initiation of the Perón era, 1946	Since 1946 (Perón)

of the three stages of development as applied to these five Latin American countries.

It is appropriate to reiterate that the arbitrary separation of the three phases of political evolution has been employed as a pedagogical device to better conceptualize what might otherwise be a morass of often unrelated historical data. Naturally the phases tend to overlap, and certain features of the earlier periods still exist in later stages of political evolution.

However, the major deep-seated change that distinguished the aggregative phase from the authoritative phase was the growth of the entrepreneurial private sector of society. This occurred at the same time that the public authorities were becoming increasingly concerned with modernizing the state administrative apparatus. The government had at its disposal increasing financial and personnel resources and could actively stimulate private economic initiative. The national government, during the aggregative phase, became the crucial fulcrum in the general impetus toward economic development. Also, during the aggregative phase external cultural influences and economic stimuli made an impact on national economic development. As a result of the "demonstration effect," foreign techniques and methods became ever more widely used. During the distributive phase, there was a return to the earlier paternalistic concept of government but with more emphasis on defending the "national interest." There occurred a synthesis of the earlier two periods: Government assumed a more energetic role in developing society, yet it avoided making the social and political systems synonymous. The distinction became clearer in the twentieth century as competing elite groups in the political, economic, social, educational, and military fields proliferated.

Governmental self-restraint and respect for societal pluralism began to develop in the period from 1860 to 1930. This nonauthoritarian role of government has been increasingly strained since 1930 under the impact of Latin America's industrial revolutions. However, evidence since World War II indicates that the temptation of Latin American governments to functionally overpower society has continued to be resisted.

PART IV
Political Culture

Introduction

The term *political culture* has been defined in numerous ways but almost all the definitions seem to include certain common principles. Though many definitions contain similar propositions, a typical but highly serviceable discussion is found in the writings of Lucian Pye, though he acknowledges in various places his indebtedness to the groundbreaking contributions of Gabriel Almond. According to Pye, political culture represents a set of attitudes, beliefs, and sentiments that help to give order and meaning to the political process. He further discusses the importance of political culture implanting upon society certain norms and ideals. It thus constitutes the psychological and subjective dimensions of politics. Political culture is then the product of both the collective history of the political system and the aggregate life histories of the members of that society. It is to the political system, says Pye, what general culture is to the social system.[1]

There appears to be general agreement as to its usefulness in understanding political institutions and processes. Further, agreement seems to be emerging as to how political culture is particularly suitable to the study of developing nations. As a device in the assessment of political systems, the study of political culture involves sociological, psychological, and anthropological investigations. These areas of interest often cast new light and offer new perspectives as to how a political system operates and under what constraints and by what alternatives it must function. Of particular interest is the realization political culture turns our attention to individual characteristics among constituent members of society and to their impact on general social attitudes of citizens in the aggregate.

The special suitability of the analysis of political culture in the study

[1] Lucian W. Pye, *Aspects of Political Development* (Boston: Little, Brown, 1966), pp. 104–5. For a more detailed definition of political culture see Pye's expanded remarks in Lucian W. Pye and Sidney Verba, *Political Culture and Political Development* (Princeton: Princeton University Press, 1965), pp. 3–26.

of emerging nations, such as these five Latin American nations, is even more meaningful. Political culture studies stress the importance of beliefs (a combined system of attitudes, opinions, and not to be neglected, sentiments) that people in particular geopolitical regions share about the historical and contemporary phases of their national development. As discussed in an earlier part of this book, the historical stages of authority, aggregation, and distribution in Latin American countries are not only subject to the concerns, aspirations, and cognitions of the national citizenry at a given time but, in turn, alter and change the lives of the respective peoples.

Certain historical crises, for example, during the authoritative phase may alter not only the success of an independence struggle but also affect the type of leadership available at the particular time. These historical crises affect not only that evolutionary phase but subsequent periods right down to the contemporary distributive period. The very concept of the nation-state is deeply involved in these kinds of historical relationships between a country's leaders and its people. At each historical period this delicate interrelationship has important bearing upon subsequent successes and failures at nation-building and modernization—defined earlier as the combined level of political development and modernity. Political culture is the result of circumstances, particularly acts of leadership, stretched over interlocking stages of national development. Political history, or what one might call major events of crucial national significance, has much to do with the mental associations that people have of their society. The psychological attitudes of the people, which are the result of past events, serve as essential reference points in contemporary social conduct.

Perhaps the major problems of the authoritative phase of national development involve the nurturing and sustenance of governmental legitimacy and the initial creation of national goals and aspirations. In the aggregative phase the leadership requires institutions that enhance and stimulate, primarily, identification with the national polity and, secondarily, participation of the people in sociopolitical life. The governing powers must also furnish the resources to assure reasonable independence from potentially domineering outside forces. During the contemporary distributive stage (for some of the countries well established, for others just beginning), the crises center about the pressures to allocate the economic benefits of the period and also to enhance the opportunities for full integration of the masses of people.

The political culture by various patterns of socialization, in Latin America, has thus been gradually established throughout the three stages of development. Perhaps the authoritative phase is most instrumental in affecting the general pattern and make-up of the political culture, while in the aggregative and distributive phases these patterns are usually slowly transformed under "normal" nonbelligerency, nonrevolutionary conditions. However, using these five countries as an example, it is clear that events, circumstances, and situations occur that have had long-lasting, consequential effects of altering patterns of political culture and even creating new patterns.

Political culture also offers another means by which to study contemporary politics in developing countries. It focuses upon the interstitial, cementing patterns of dynamic behavior between political leadership and the general public, serving, as was discussed in Part I, as the usual countervailing forces in the achievement of modernity and political development. These societal patterns (knowledge of government, feelings toward political leadership, emotional attachments toward the nation, etc.) are related to the dynamic tension between the forces of political development that emphasize legitimacy, predictable policy making, and the channeling of acceptable dissent and the forces of modernity that emphasize the expansion of societal comforts (civilizing paraphernalia) and the broadening of spheres of political license and economic security. It seems rather clear that political culture relates closely to the modernity features of a country and these levels of modernity often determine the constraints and checks within which the political leadership operate to promote further political development.

Given these general implications how can we further define the many ramifications that make the concept of political culture so valuable? An understanding of political culture assists the observer in comprehending the bearing of popular perceptions upon the society. It may help explain why and how a society arrives at institutional and political decisions as well as define the outer limits of permissible political behavior. By reviewing a society's traditional themes and contemporary predispositions, one can better isolate social characteristics which augment the study of the institutions of a nation.

CHAPTER 7 Latin American Political Culture

Each of the five countries studied, though it has certain important unique features, also represents shared traditional and contemporary cultural themes that effect nation building in Latin America. They offer many contrasts and still more numerous similarities. Significantly it is Latin America's heritage which makes up a large measure of her contemporary political culture. This is not due solely to the fact that Latin American nations are necessarily tradition-oriented but rather because they value and propagate the understanding of how they got where they are. Latin Americans are very much aware of their heritage, family tree, and individual blood ties. History for them lives and is meaningful. They look upon the past in order to revere it and to better put the present in perspective.

The Spanish and Portuguese conquest was their beginning. Racial intermingling, Euro-American fusion, marks their developments through periods of separation, autocracy, rebellion and reform. Spanish-Portuguese cultural ties have outlived the Spanish and Portuguese empires, and these European languages merely typify the old world melting into the new world. Though the Ibero Peninsula's political dominance was rejected, its institutions and ideologies persisted.[1] The Catholic religion, the patriarchal family, the drive toward ownership of the land, the mystic strain, the love of embellishment, the creative conversation, the importance of personalism, the persuasiveness of opulence, and the distinction of class have all waged their persistent war against the onrush of modernity and the egalitarianism of industrialization.[2] The drive toward economic and political development does not square with this tradition. Thus contemporary political culture in Latin

[1] One historian has noted " . . . certain attitudes or principles . . . appear more viable, less changeable, than the institutions that express them because they occur at higher or more durable levels of abstraction. The truth is that it is impossible to think of anything social or cultural that has not been modified in some degree in Latin America since the colonial period. But it is also possible to see some of these changes as superficial adjustments that do not affect underlying uniformities, or as variations on constant themes." Charles Gibson, "Colonial Institutions and Contemporary Latin America: Social and Cultural Life," *Hispanic American Historical Review*, vol. 43, no. 3 (August 1963), p. 382.

[2] These national traits are, of course, in some measure stereotyped assessments of some pervasive characteristics. Their importance, however, lies in the fact that they are generally acknowledged by the Latin Americans themselves. A sociologist sees such national characteristics as bases for behavior within countries. See Don Martindale, "The Sociology of National Character," *The Annals*, vol. 370 (March 1967), p. 35.

America is ambivalent—it is a competition, a strain, and an intellectual battleground between the old order with its aristocratic weave and the new with its popular thrust and national banners.

Today's Latin America, however, belongs as much to the innovative and novel cultural stream as to the past. The shoeless Indian, the landless peasant, the meat packer, the chain store manager, the Secretary of Interior, and international economists all have left their mark on Latin American society. However, the new interpreters of modernization are increasingly influential, and their support is proportionally more visible.[3] To speak then of political culture in Latin America today is to recognize the values of the old as they are confronted by the challenges and offensive of contemporary requirements.

The emotional perceptions of the Latin American people are also a factor of Latin America's political culture. Whether it is antiYanquism in Cuba, the fierce factional skirmishes in Santo Domingo, or electoral campaigns in Santiago political conflict is highly emotional. It is almost essential for one who would tackle the political problems of his country to inspire the emotions of the people. Emotionally charged politics is expected and approved, and issues become meaningful as they become more personal. The Latin American brand of nationalism, independence, and economic development all must dip into the reservoir of human emotionality in order to help justify any new policy decisions on a national or local level.

Juxtaposed with the importance of Latin America's heritage, its apparent commitment to change, and its propensity to emote is the cultivation of the intellect and the subservience to dogmatism. Both these tendencies act as deterrents to the pragmatic, problem solving and often pedestrian approach that accompanies commitments to improvement. Cultivation of the intellect is a goal rather than a tool for change,[4] which results sometimes in short

[3] Sidney Verba, in Pye and Verba, *Political Culture and Political Development*, pp. 521–525, discusses the problem of distinguishing between cultural beliefs adhered to by the mass of people vis-à-vis the implicit ideological direction fostered by the political elites.

[4] John P. Gillen, as an anthropologist, sees this as one of the prominent human aspects of contemporary Latin American culture. He notes the high value assigned to goals and lower values to instrumental patterns for carrying them out. "Possible Cultural Maladjustments in Modern Latin America," *Journal of Inter-American Studies*, vol. 5, no. 2 (April 1963), pp. 156–157. Frank Tannenbaum writes of the Latin literary and theoretical traditions wherein ideas are not the bases for formulating definite policies. *Ten Keys to Latin America* (New York: Alfred Knopf, 1966), p. 135. Also Glaucio Ary Dillon Soares analyzes data on Latin American students which suggests that those students who see themselves as "intellectuals" rather than "professionals" or "scientists" are those most likely to champion diffuse, extreme solutions to society's problems. "Intellectual Identity and Political Ideology among University Students," in S. M. Lipset and A. Solari (eds.), *Elites in Latin America* (New York: Oxford University Press, 1967), pp. 431–453.

circuits in the process of daily policy management. Intellectuality courted as a virtue and displayed as an attribute serves to dampen its effectiveness in the requirements of modernization and economic organization. The "Renaissance Man" is often an overt and sharp-eyed critic but a poor organizer and a worse technician.

Dogma also plays its pervasive role in Latin America's political culture. The certainty of the "true" solution and the quick description of the malady leads to a certain myopia which is visible in party politics, labor-business disputes, public versus private sector conflicts, and adds to a general malaise in intercountry disputes. The dogmatic approach cared for by the easy and traditional class relationships is opposed to the variegated shades of what appears to be the truth. The shades of gray are not yet admired, for, among many, relativity in the pursuit of the truth is comparable to a faint-hearted pursuer of feminine beauty.[5]

These stereotypic traits then serve as one important indicator in the study of Latin American political culture. Another approach observes the importance of sociopsychological outlooks on political behavior. Though this problem has not been fully investigated, it is acknowledged as consequential in its impact on political development. Robert Scott recognizes the importance of cultural traits when noting the dichotomy among Mexicans between the parochial members of society who hardly relate to the political process and the subject and participant people who do relate to the political process, the former in a more rudimentary fashion of acknowledging governmental functions and programs and the latter by actively seeking to influence the content and direction of such functions and programs.[6]

There is in all likelihood this ambivalence regarding the degree of political enculturation among all the Latin American countries. These differences are in large measure due to the shaping effect of private and

[5] Discussion of the Latin American temperament and psychology has been extensively covered in numerous books. The reader is advised, for example, to consult such authors as Robert Scott, *Mexican Government in Transition* (Urbana: University of Illinois Press, 1959), pp. 56–95 on such concepts as *personalismo* and *hombres de confianza;* Samuel Ramos, *Profile of Man and Culture in Mexico* (Austin: University of Texas Press, 1962) on Mexican *machismo* (ostentatious maleness); Gilberto Freyre, *The Masters and the Slaves* (New York: Alfred Knopf, 1956), and *New World in the Tropics* (New York: Alfred Knopf, 1959), on Brazilian psychological propensities; Charles Wagley, *Amazon Town* (New York: Macmillan Co., 1958), on the rural pace of life in Brazil; and William R. Crawford, *A Century of Latin American Thought* (Cambridge: Harvard University Press, 1961), on the content of Latin American philosophical and literary thought.

[6] See Robert Scott's section in Pye and Verba, *Political Culture and Political Development,* pp. 330–395. Gabriel Almond and Sidney Verba's *The Civic Culture: Political Attitudes and Democracy in Five Nations* (Boston: Little, Brown, 1965), presents massive survey data on the Mexican's civic attitudes, competence and participation.

public societal institutions from the family upward to more and more impersonal relationships. The average human being is continually influenced in his attitudes toward society by any one of a number of sources. Some of these beliefs are instilled subconsciously (by his mother's relationship to his father for example), others consciously (by his elementary school social studies teacher). Some influences are long lived and constant (like that of an older brother), others massive but of a short time span (police brutality, death in the family, a university lecture). Some sentiments are inculcated chiefly at home and in childhood, others away from home in the adult years.

The formation of such attitudes in a person has been labelled as the process of political socialization.[7] An apt definition states that political socialization describes the way in which values are learned and "internalized," social norms regarding politics are implanted, political roles institutionalized, and political consensus created, either effectively or ineffectively.[8] Quite early in a person's life he acquires certain attitudes toward authority which certainly affect the legitimacy of any political system. It furthermore tends to have a bearing on his volition both to participate politically and to take up responsible positions in occupational and social groups. These propensities to act in a certain manner politically and socially are often engrained in childhood. Children learn such basic attitudes as "give and take," flexibility, institutional respect, extrafamilial involvements from their earliest days through imitating adult behavior, specific instruction, and the method of trial and error which has very significant and crucial punishments and rewards.[9]

In general, it is quite clear that Latin America's participant citizenry is still a somewhat abbreviated percentage of the total population. But passive understanding and a semi-interested viewpoint are certainly quite extended among the populace. National pride and identification with historical and contemporary symbols are high in Latin America because it requires little attention and no active support or participation in national, regional, or local organization. Latin America so far is not a "participation culture." Its population is still largely in the client state, hoping to receive benefits from the government but unable, short of uprisings and violence, to modify local conditions.

Despite the fact that most Latin American nations are short on economic benefits, they are long on the distribution of government information. Though education, especially in rural areas, is generally poor, the

[7] For an excellent annotated review of the literature see Gerald J. Bender, "Political Socialization and Political Change," *The Western Political Quarterly*, vol. 20, no. 2, part 1 (June 1967), pp. 390–407.

[8] Harry Eckstein and David E. Apter, *Comparative Politics: A Reader* (New York: Free Press, 1963), p. 26.

[9] See the thesis presented by Robert Levine, "Political Socialization and Cultural Change," in Clifford Geertz (ed.), *Old Societies and New States* (New York: Free Press, 1963), pp. 280–303.

governments attempt to inculate patriotic fervor and respect for national history and contemporary institutions.[10] Above all, there is loyalty for and identification with the person who occupies the presidency. In the rural sections of Latin America, education for politics amounts to a crude form of teaching the basics of voting, to meeting important dignitaries, and to listening to the government radio programs on Sunday.

Of course, urban Latin America is a much more participatory and active social element. However, the evermore crowded conditions of the urban centers had made social stability and a climate of tranquillity increasingly problematic. The urban masses, more intellectually emancipated and less indulgent, are a greater challenge to central governments who wish to simultaneously stimulate production and distribution. With improving dissemination of a nation's political culture through better means of transportation and communication, this function of the governmental communication is now easier. With government's greater share in the economy, the government receives a greater share, for example, of praise and support for its efforts in the building of a new bridge, highway, tunnel, airstrip, or public square.

Latin American public administrators are today, as in the rest of the developed world, the largest focus for business, education, culture, and information. They are the foremost articulators of the public's will as it is recorded by the government communications networks, be they tuned correctly or not (as in Haiti, for example). But this concomitantly brings with it a greater concentration of power. There are few major interest groups in Latin America outside the public sector, for example, that would not be affected by some major institutional change. Again few of the major interests have coped fully with the challenges of "reformmongering," as described by Albert O. Hirschman.[11] The more these groups appear and are tolerated, the more reforms and transitions may occur in society without the accompanying social dissolution and violent change. Up to the present the Mexican government appears to have best understood this need as an alternative to abrupt change and social distortions.

Political parties, in the absence of an articulate public, have a special monopoly on the representation of the public will. In Latin America these too, until recently (and with the exception of Chile and Uruguay), have had

[10] The Mexican government, for example, seems to have succeeded in implanting respect for Mexican institutions, the Mexican revolutionary tradition, and is eliciting interest from its citizens. Almond and Verba, *The Civic Culture: Political Attitudes and Democracy in Five Nations*, pp. 66–67.

[11] Albert O. Hirschman, *Journeys Toward Progress* (New York: Twentieth Century Fund, 1963). According to Hirschman "reformmongering" applies to those individuals or agencies that learn how to solve problems, enact changes, and make crucial advances without employing revolutionary tactics or stimulating massive resistance or opposition.

a dichotomous view of political participation. Parties have either not been able to aggregate a majority, or they have tried for some unreal and mythical unanimity. A multifaceted factionalism or a monolith has usually been the rule. Parties often do not cut across sectional, class, or occupational interests and too often have been content with appeals to the powerful or the organized. They have been too specialized in their appeal, and no large effort has been made to integrate larger social groups. Espoused ideology, in word at least, has kept otherwise compatible parties from amalgamating. However, party politics shows many encouraging signs. Party programs and grass roots organizations are becoming more common, and parties strive more to educate and inform as well as to widen loyalty to their banners. In fact, party development in most Latin American countries demonstrates the potential for mass national organizations which are rapidly filling a necessary gap in articulating the public's will.

Thus, though we have discussed certain significant national traits and characteristics and distinguished among some of the more important institutional purveyors of national attitudes, we have yet to examine the comparative dynamics of Latin American political culture. As this stage of social science research in Latin America only certain very tentative assessments can be even attempted regarding both the historical developments and contemporary factors that affect political culture. Elite culture and mass culture are often two quite distinct concepts; however, much of the discussion is based on some composite picture of the two sets of attitudes and beliefs. Furthermore, only those attitudes and beliefs are examined that have been instrumental in shaping the politics of Latin American nations. Though these necessarily overlap, we have divided the effects upon a nation's political culture into three, historical, institutional, and behavioral groups.

Historically, as depicted in Part II, strong, intact, indigenous cultures formed an imposing backdrop to the investiture of Spanish political control in Mexico and Peru. The existence of these highly structured and organized indian societies mitigated the possibility of duplicating the Spanish political culture of the Iberian peninsula. The stratified indigenous cultures served as the substructure upon which economic and political policy making was later built. The relative ease with which the native populations were first subdued and then subjugated testifies to the facility of integrating a feudal culture to the essentially viceroy-oriented Iberian patrimonialism.

The very structured social environment of Mexico and Peru was unlike the much more haphazard foundations of Argentina, Chile, and Brazil. In these areas dispersed, nomadic indian groups were either socially quarantined or slowly eradicated over the years so that the impact of their cultures upon the basic colonial patterns of settlement was minimal. The viability of the socioeconomic institutions of indigenous Mexico and Peru made it quite unnecessary for Spanish settlers to innovate and experiment with novel socioeconomic arrangements. Rather they grafted their political control upon a generally subservient culture which provided the material and human resources that buttressed the colonial regime. The settlement pattern in Brazil, Chile, and Argentina was very different. The absence of established cultures forced the early colonial settlers to take upon themselves the commercial and agricultural roles otherwise filled by the native peoples.

The compact and sedentary nature of the indigenous groups in Mexico and Peru had the effect of greatly centralizing authority in the respective country's administrative centers. The experience in Brazil, Chile, and Argentina was one of much greater political diversification as control and authority developed centrifugally among competing and sometimes warring settlers. The absence of both abundant cheap labor plus sought-after mineral resources, such as silver and gold, required the early search for exportable raw materials and foodstuffs rather than precious metals. It was no accident then that early viceroyalties were established in Lima and Mexico City and not in Santiago and Buenos Aires or Córdoba.

The paternal, hierarchical nature of the Aztec and Inca communities was easily adaptable to the patrimonial Spanish pattern of settlement. Agricultural crops continued to be raised collectively, land ownership for the individual indian was still nonexistent, and the royalty and military elites maintained their social status as had the Inca and Aztec nobility. In Argentina, Chile, and Brazil, Spanish culture met no ostensible countervailing force, and thus its need to supersede and absorb was missing. This left these areas with less social cohesion, less stability in intergroup relationships, and less continuous and predictable class hierarchies.

The pattern of a large, almost completely inarticulate, passive majority was thus evolved over the early centuries of Spanish colonial rule, particularly in Mexico and Peru. First native fatalistic religions and then Catholicism had the general effect of creating submissive cultures with attitudes based on predestination. A slightly less authoritarian and more democratic culture developed in Brazil, Chile, and Argentina because of the absence of large masses of subordinated indians and the lack of tightly controlled political and religious life. In Brazil, however, the introduction of African slaves to replace the unavailable indian labor, mitigated the development of small handicrafts, petty industry, and general autonomy from the hacienda-based economy that gradually occurred in parts of Chile and Argentina. In many ways Brazil contained aspects of both types of political culture with the employment of slave labor in the northeastern states and the adoption of free labor and entreprenurial skills in the southeastern states.

During the colonial preindependence phase, the five colonies shared experiences which were more similar than distinct. Firstly, the political leadership was largely made up of men born in Spain and Portugal who had loyalties, interests, and in some cases families in Europe, which tended to heighten alienation among the native born, participant sector of the population. This distrust and suspicion of bureaucrats and administrators became over the years a deeply ingrained part of the Latin American political culture. It also, except for portions of Brazil, Chile, and Argentina, tended to weaken the development of local government, its economic initiative, and its general self-confidence in its ability to act independently.

The colonial administration relegated the mestizo and indian segments of society into merely receptive, subject roles from which they did not emerge for many generations. The Viceroy and his staff, for example, exercised not only rule-making functions but had a principal role in applying and adjudicating the rules for the colonies. Again the Chileans and Argentines, because of their relative isolation from seats of the Viceroyalties, were able to develop habits of self-government much earlier than their Mexican and Peruvian counterparts.

In most of the colonies the indigenous populations were "protected," Christianized, and "supervised"—that is, they were the *passive* recipients of mediation and arbitration external to their own control. Again, in Brazil, because of the colonial settlement pattern (discussed in Part II) and the vast distances between captaincies, a greater degree of administrative leeway was established and fostered. More quickly than in Mexico and Peru, local "notables" were given administrative responsibilities in Brazil.

Thus with the Bourbon reforms in religion, economics, trade, and finance, it was not surprising that the Argentine and Chilean colonies should have flourished most, since the institutions in these colonies had developed the rudiments of self-government, economic initiative, as well as the apparent psychological basis for modifying their institutions to fit the times.

It was in Argentina and Chile, too, that national independence movements could best find sustenance and support. Though, with the exception of Hidalgo's abortive leadership of the people of Mexico, the uprisings against Spain were essentially elite movements without full mass involvement. Nevertheless, the victory at Buenos Aires, Ayacucho, and elsewhere stirred the first feelings of national pride and solidarity among the general population. The major postindependence, internal conflicts, however, were not sufficiently "penetrative" to have any major effect upon the nonelite portions of society.

The more important disputes revolved about questions of governmental organization, regional representation in the councils of government, and other legal and procedural problems. The landslide of paper proclamations, for example, in Mexico, beginning with the Plan de Iguala in 1821, did not really serve to inspire the society as a whole. Moreover, the organizational questions were the prime issues in each of the countries under examination. In Mexico, the Federalists were confronted by the Centralists. The same pattern appeared in Argentina with the Unitarians and the Federalists and in Chile with the "Pelucones" and the "Pipiolos."

In many cases in the latter part of the authoritative period these organizational conflicts led to regional conflicts, as the unitarian-centralists usually were represented by the governors and administrators of the capital and its environs while the federalists came from the interior provinces. This was particularly the case in the struggle of several generations between Buenos Aires and the Argentine provinces for control of the Republic as well as in Mexican developments during its authoritative phase.

The early organizational and regional conflicts had little impact in terms of mass mobilization. Public concern and involvement of the more participant sectors was initiated rather by the evolving religious and economic disputes in the latter part of the authoritative phase. The clerical-anticlerical arguments and the competition between protectionism and free trade served to build up a noticeable degree of public concern. The religious struggles were most visible in Mexico where the anticlerical forces attempted to meet the needs of hitherto impoverished peoples by combining the struggle against church dominance with that of social and agrarian reforms. Under Pedro II in Brazil and Manuel Montt in Chile secular and religious forces also found themselves at odds. The secular force gained the ascendancy, but the religious force effected a noticeable regroupment of political interests along a Conservative-Liberal line—a regroupment which became most evident in the subsequent aggregative stage of development.

The free trade-protectionist competition was apparent to a greater or lesser degree in all the countries and served, along with the religious question, to involve a growing urban constituency. The incipient urban manufacturing interests with their working-class allies stimulated governmental paternalism and protection for their investments from foreign competition, while the agrarian-landed interests clamored for unrestricted trading, both in the sale of their commodities and in the purchase of what they considered superior finished imports. The struggle between the "porteños" and the provincial-based federalists of Argentina was the most marked of these economic bifurcations.

Political participation increased considerably during the aggregative phase of national development. International linkage factors had an impact on the growth of national identity and consciousness. Universal male suffrage was granted, for example, in Argentina by 1912, in Mexico by 1917, and Chile by 1925. These political changes were partly in response to the growth of a more involved and interested middle class and an incipient industrial proletariat. For instance, in Mexico the Madero-led insurgency, supported by local popular caudillos as Zapata, Obregón, and Villa, found reverberations among many popular forces. Chile and Argentina, in particular, showed early signs of public involvement. In 1890, a civil revolt inspired by the Radical Party against the Conservative government of Argentina was forcefully repressed, but it had demonstrated widescale popular support. Massive labor strikes occurred against the Irigoyen government, involving by 1919 over 300,000 workers.[12] In Chile nonviolent protests by citizens (including doctors, lawyers, students, and teachers) helped to topple the Ibañez government in 1930. Again the suppression of a planned Nazi conspiracy evoked public outcry and protest so that it assured the defeat of the Conservative party identified with the Alessandri government then in power.

Argentina and Chile, with their relatively higher levels of modernity, had greater rates of mass mobilization during the aggregative period. Much of Argentine mass political participation was initially inspired by the election campaigns and propagandizing of the Radical party and the Socialist party between 1910–1930. The so-called "parliamentary period" in Chile also was responsible for increased interest among the populace in political alternatives while, at the same time, it stimulated the development of new political parties which survived because of their increased influence in the legislature. The charismatic leadership of both Irigoyen and Alessandri further helped to emancipate the populace from civic indifference.

Certain international linkage factors, such as the two world wars, other foreign wars, the Bolshevik Revolution, the depression, and the anti-Fascist European Popular Front, all had an impact on the changing Latin American political culture. In Mexico the military incursions of the French in the 1860's and the United States disembarkation in 1914 served to heighten national consciousness. In Peru bad experiences on the battlefield with her neighbors Chile and Bolivia brought on increased awareness of an identity with the nation state. The Paraguayan War in the 1860's had a similar effect on Brazil and Argentina. We have already discussed the major impact of the War of the Pacific on Chilean development.

World Wars I and II energized Latin American export industries and stimulated the growth of a larger and more involved urban proletariat, while the depression made clear to the Latin American countries their close relationship to the world economy and their need to reach amicable political and economic agreements with the major industrial powers. After 1930, as demonstrated time and again during the distributive period, the political affairs of Western Europe, the Pacific, and the United States became an indelible part of the Latin American political calculus. The Bolshevik Revolution as well as the European Popular Front greatly affected the ideological currents of the five countries, particularly Chile with its relatively more cosmopolitan world outlook. These events inspired countless numbers of workers, students, professionals, and intellectuals in Latin America who then disseminated these ideas, identifying them with the economic and social goals of the masses. The East-West competition after 1945 again continued the process of socializing the populace toward greater awareness of the purposes and effectiveness of Latin American governments.

[12] Samuel L. Baily, *Labor, Nationalism and Politics in Argentina* (New Brunswick: Rutgers University Press, 1967), p. 30.

During the distributive period of political evolution one can better see the confluence of the historical impact on political culture and the effects of both institutional and behavioral characteristics in these Latin American nations.

Since the mid 1930's, and particularly under the stimulus of World War II, these countries have been heavily engaged in the process of industrialization. This has often resulted in a dichotomy between an industrial and an agrarian culture, which appears to be more marked in Latin America than elsewhere in the emerging nations. This dichotomy, already noted in Part I, is due in great part to the extended colonial and postindependence pattern of centralizing commerce and trade in already established administrative centers. The industrial and agrarian social structure and economy (as will be discussed in detail in Part VI) are very different from each other, and this has important effects on the rural and urban political culture.

Politics in the agrarian sector is often patronal, undifferentiated, and ideologically quite unsophisticated. Peer group relationships and social interaction is not complex, and many of the dimensions of the urban polity are represented here only in incipient forms. Voting turnout is lower, extra-familial ties are fewer, and class mobility is slight. This urban-rural hiatus is often reinforced by regional differences in human and natural resources; thus the cultural bifurcation is complicated by geographical considerations and this has continuing consequences for politics. The national political culture is then an aggregate of underprivileged and more privileged areas of the country. In Mexico states such as the Federal District, Nuevo León and Sonora are much more prosperous and advanced than, for example, Chiapas, Guerrero, and Oaxaca. In Brazil it is well known that immense differences exist between such states as Pernambuco and Bahia and those of the more modern Southeast, such as Guanabara, Rio de Janeiro, and São Paulo. In Peru, Chile, and Argentina similar differences exist between the capital city and certain contiguous areas and many of the outlying provinces.[13]

Ethnically the Spanish-Indian mestizo represents the prototype of the Latin American, with the predominant cultural group being Indian in Peru and the mestizo in Mexico and Chile. Brazil is largely white and mulatto with a significant black minority. Argentina is mostly white with a rather small minority of mestizos. Immigration has been largely European with Spanish and Portuguese settlers forming the overwhelming majority. A substantial Italian population exists in Eastern Argentina, a smaller number of Germans live in Chile, and some Japanese and East Europeans are in Brazil. Chinese and Japanese families have settled in Peru and Mexico as well. Though small in number, several other nationalities from Europe, the Orient, and the Middle East live in these five countries of Latin America.

It appears that countries like Chile and Argentina have achieved high

[13] On these questions the reader is referred to the writings of Wilkie, Scobie, Dillon Soares, Patch, Gil cited in Parts V and VI.

indices of modernity because of the high percentages of the total population of Europeans. Many of the immigrant waves to these two countries and to parts of Southeastern Brazil have provided the needed expertise, the innovative outlooks, and the entrepreneurial psychology necessary for sustaining modernization. Mexico, without this demographic advantage, has made substantial advancements because of the effectiveness of its leadership policies since the 1917 Revolution. Peru, with no large-scale European immigration and no long run impetus of a social revolution, has modernized at a much slower rate.

The urban centers in which the immigrants tended to conglomerate are also the most participant sectors. These urban immigrants wield considerably more political pressure than their native-born rural counterparts who live under a highly stratified Spanish patrimonial system. The urban environment nurtures greater critical and ideological capacity. It is in these areas, for example, that minority parties, such as the Socialists or Communists, receive the most votes. The urban centers also support a more cosmopolitan world outlook. Its inhabitants are more familiar with events abroad and exhibit a greater willingness to experiment with foreign innovations both in politics and society.

The political culture of most of the large cities of Brazil, Chile, and Argentina is largely secular rather than religious. The religious factor plays a much more crucial role in the rural areas. In Mexico and Peru where the Catholic Church has had great historical impact, the cities still contain neighborhoods (mainly lower class) which are predominantly socialized by the church and its various agencies. However, the religious impact on political culture has declined considerably in the last several decades. The rise of politically competitive christian democratic parties has served to channel certain Christian beliefs and attitudes into various forms of political policy rather than the parties in any way promoting any aspect of religion itself.

The secularity of the urban environment tends to have come about not only by the impact of industrialization and the scientific revolution but by the church's own circumscription of its former totalistic view of its role in society. The Catholic Church, which is the only major religious denomination in Latin America, has given up its preeminent political role. It has successfully adopted social service techniques that rival those of trade unions, peasant cooperatives, and educational institutions in their ability to advance partisan interests in areas that apparently do not challenge the political monopoly of the state.

Despite the increasing social mobility in Latin America, its societies still remain highly stratified. The gulf between the middle and lower classes is even greater in social interrelationships than it is in the objective socioeconomic status sense which is measured by per capita income, housing, and consumption. Contacts are usually limited between employer-employee, landlord-tenant, and homeowner-servant. Exploitation of the poorer classes is a familiar pattern. Except possibly in Mexico, darker-skinned peoples can usually be found in the more unskilled types of occupations, and despite student-labor compatibility in goals for society, there has been very little real interaction and association between these groups. As Jordan Young aptly writes:

> The *paulista* students favor land reform in the northeast. The northeastern students agitate for reforms in the slum areas of Rio de Janeiro. But relatively few students become activists in the sense of doing something concretely to ameliorate conditions of the lower-income groups.[14]

In Mexico, Brazil, and Peru class distinction is still very common and can be easily seen in modes of travel, use of leisure, types of memberships, and in many other things that physically separate one class from another. In Chile and Argentina it is much harder to distinguish between the skilled machine operator, the mechanic, the accountant or the lawyer. There is a "bougeoissification" occurring in these two countries that at first glance is very striking. But here, too, as in the other three countries the social pyramid is a very real thing. Rather than de facto social interaction, feelings of equality exist more on an intellectual, moral, and even ideological-political level. Slum settlements, social club segregation, sporting activity (the poor play and attend soccer matches, for the better off there is tennis and rugby), and different sources of information all tend to strengthen interclass stratification.

Nevertheless, in the face of these restrictive institutionalized cultural patterns, Latin America has consistently been avoiding the return to autocracy, modern or traditional, and is continuing to preserve the overall polyarchical social system. Despite some of the actual rigidities of the class system, there appears to be little predisposition to establish closed political systems with monolithic institutions. "Democracy," "liberty," and "equality" are continually promoted political concepts by men who seek to preserve a more traditional society as well as by those who reject contemporary society as unjust.

The goals of most political leaders in Latin America do not seem very distinct from those espoused by leaders in most Western democracies. Temporary legislature suspensions, aborted political agencies, and interference in the freedom of the news media have continually appeared in monotonous succession; but legitimacy of parties, associational pressure groups, elections, legislatures, and constitutions seem to be well established and under no permanent threat of extinction.

[14] "Brazil" in B. G. Burnett and K. F. Johnson (Eds.), *Political Forces in Latin America* (Belmont, Calif.: Wadsworth, 1968), p. 472.

In Mexico, particularly, the goals of leadership groups have been successfully wedded with the values and attitudes of the people. There is a good deal of pride in the political and economic institutions in Mexico, despite Mexico's still "developing nation" status. Though the average Mexican's cognitions of the political world and his ability to affect political decisions are low, he nevertheless has an unusual faith in his country.[15] The revolutionary turmoil of 1910–1930 has been well integrated into the national memorabilia and, perhaps, is second only to the Bolshevik Revolution in representing a striking example of the impact of an historical occurrence. The secular political faith embodied in the revolutionary tenets of the Juárez and Lerdo Laws were actually sanctified in the Constitution of 1917, which became an almost irrevocable permanent document and guide to the future. The revolution and its aftermath, especially the Cárdenas years, brought about the identification of several decades of political paternalism with the PRI party and, in the minds of much of the Mexican people, legitimized the two in a seemingly indissolvable union. The patterns by which the people of Mexico are being politically socialized will be further examined in the case study below.

Overall, Argentina and Chile represent a relatively modern, mixed participant-subject political culture, particularly in their urban areas, when compared to Brazil and Peru. Mexico, too, has successfully achieved a more modern political culture with increasing political participation and mobilization of hitherto parochial groups. In terms of how open the political system is and the amount of dissent and competition tolerated, Chile and Argentina again, with their better-than-average political experience with a multiplicity of parties, the freedom of interest groups to organize, and the safeguarding of individual liberties, are the more polyarchically oriented societies with large-scale public understanding of the political process. Mexico, though exhibiting very high mobilizational rates, has over the years lacked any real open, free-wheeling, competitive political system. It has continued to deny to opposition groups the full advantages of dissent, the means to socialize the public, and the freedom to present alternative societal goals. Brazil and Peru show a somewhat similar cultural pattern. Both countries, despite the impacts of Vargas and the Apristas, have been very slow to mobilize the vast majority of peoples, particularly in the interior regions. The recent governments of Brazil and Peru have administered over a national constituency that has yet to understand, relate to, and affect the political process. Yet in both countries, despite military governments, it can be said that competing and even dissenting groups have maintained themselves, interests have proliferated, and there has been no dearth of ideological struggle and political conflict.

[15] Gabriel A. Almond and Sidney Verba, *The Civic Culture* (Boston: Little, Brown, 1965).

Transferring Political Culture: A Case Study of Political Communication in Mexico

Certainly a complex historical background has peculiarly affected Mexico. The various strains and innuendoes of that history still influence the societal characteristics of the Mexican—his life, his work, and his endeavors. The mestizo, for example, knows he is not a pure indian but realizes he is not a European as well. This halfway station of life is of vital importance in understanding the Mexican as distinct from the Argentine, and the Peruvian Indian of the Andes Region.

The proximity of the United States also plays a profound role in the investigation of any topic in Mexico. As Cosio Villegas has said, the North American is always present in all that Mexicans think and do. The omnipresent nature of the United States' existence is marked in all areas of Mexican society.[16]

The poverty of the land, the political fragmentation of its social institutions, and the isolation of its cultures all have perceptively touched the problem of political communication in Mexican society.

It may be of interest to list the results of a survey taken in Mexico two decades ago and quoted in a book by Jose E. Iturriaga. The polls' findings demonstrate some of the differences between the Mexican and the North American approach to life. A large sample of Mexicans were interviewed and asked to express an opinion on what one idea or motivation was the central wellspring of their lives.

The greatest majority (34.4 per cent, based on a total of 100 per cent) felt that their sexual drives and the eroticism which they actively cultivated were the most important aspects of their lives; the second greatest area was religion and mysticism (17.7 per cent); the role of "imaginative adventures" (11.4 per cent); the love of good food and a healthy and sane life (8.63 per cent); the raising of one's economic standard of life—usually rated near the top on similar United States polls—(6.92 per cent); family life (5.6 per cent); the importance of the self or the gratification of the individual's ego wherever possible (4.88 per cent); the drive toward artistic endeavors (4.27 per cent); the search for power (3.80 per cent); and political and social interests (2.82 per cent). Apparently there was no expression of any consequence about the concept of "security," important in a comparable North-American poll.[17]

[16] See Daniel Cosio Villegas, *Change in Latin America: The Mexican and Cuban Revolutions* (Lincoln: The University of Nebraska Press, 1961).

[17] The Almond-Verba survey responses have come up with similar Mexican emphases on "hobbies" and other noncivic interests. See the table in *The Civic Culture*, p. 210.

The possible difference in basic motivations is thereby discerned from the above results. Of course, the above concepts may be slowly vitiated by increasing modernization through fuller industrialization. However, it is fairly certain that there are national differences among people and nations; motivations in Mexico are not necessarily the same as those in North America.

Psychologically, the Mexican works within a varied framework of political values. With the preeminence of the individual and his self-assertion Iturriaga has stated that certainly the Mexican has not developed his "social I" as has the North American, whose social sense and more vigorous citizenship is contrasted remarkably to the Mexican's lack of it.[18] The life of the Mexican is more personalistic than ours. The information he gets comes from his friends and personal contacts rather than from printed matter. He places extreme confidence in the opinions of his friends and tends to distrust the distant voice of authority.[19] Scott has shown that the average Mexican tends to limit his social and even political relations to a few persons he knows and trusts, "hombres de confianza."[20] The Mexican's friendships appear to be of more value to him than the subservience to any idea in the realm of public life. As his life is often limited to personal circles and private associations, the Mexican often is helpless before a crucial political, civil question. As Iturriaga states, the Mexican often has an incapacity to express his disagreements and his aspirations through active civil means and thereby is open to adventures against authority whenever its weight upon him becomes overburdensome.[21]

The Mexican is a staunch individualist in the social sense, though friends and community are essentials to him. However, his aloofness to organization and compatible membership of civic groups makes him in a sense culturally isolated from his fellow Mexican.[22] Scott has demonstrated that in the village, and to a great extent in the city, the average Mexican has little direct contact outside his immediate social circle.[23] His family and close friends remain his major source of political and social contact. This is still the working force even with the advent of newspapers, radio, movies, and television. The Mexican does not belong to a multitude of associations and clubs which would bring him into contact with persons of different beliefs and attitudes that might implant conflicting interests in his mind. The danger inherent in

[18] Jose E. Iturriaga, *La estructura social y cultural de Mexico* (Mexico: Fondo de Cultura Económica, 1951), p. 234.

[19] See the survey responses in Almond and Verba, *The Civic Culture*, pp. 45–46, 62, 68–78.

[20] Robert E. Scott, *Mexican Government in Transition* (Urbana: University of Illinois Press, 1959), p. 93.

[21] Jose E. Iturriaga, *La estructura social y cultural de Mexico*, p. 235.

[22] See Almond and Verba, *The Civic Culture*, on Mexican organizational membership and civic competence, esp. Ch 10.

[23] Scott, *Mexican Government in Transition*, p. 92.

this situation is that once a person has his confidence, he becomes an easy mark for manipulation by small town political bosses and *caciques*. In another sense the Mexican's cultural isolation often adds to his individualism, because his mind has not yet become homogenized into a facet of the social mass mind of more mechanized societies.

Two factors are however responsible for the recent acculturation of the Mexican. The growth of the middle class has been from about 10 per cent of the population in 1940 to Howard Cline's figure of close to 50 per cent in 1960.[24] Particularly interesting has been the rapid rise of the middle class in the rural areas. Secondly, there is the evolving economic independence of women. Their ability to earn a living both before and after marriage, a rarity before World War II, places them well in the arena of political communication apart from their matrimonial and fraternal connections.

Given the basic importance of Mexico's physical, psychological, and historical difference from the Anglo-Saxon tradition, it is possible to further examine the role of communication in the political process.

The function of political communication in its broadest sense encompasses all the functions performed in the political system. As Almond and Coleman state: ". . . political socialization and recruitment, interest articulation, interest aggregation, rule making, rule application, and rule adjudication are performed by means of communication."[25] Political communication is not necessarily a sophisticated transferal of ideas. In fact it begins at a very tender age—perhaps subliminally—and continues, in one form or another by means of one medium or another, all one's life. According to Almond and Coleman the role of parents is cited as the first source of political communication, and one has reason to believe that this may be a tremendously strong source of influence on the younger generation in Mexico. Since Mexico is a socially traditional, historically conscious nation, its family structure is highly integrated and strongly paternal. The father, when he is the nuclear head, and the mother are the centrum of the family.

The Mexican family arrangement allows for little real independent thinking. A colleague of Eric Fromm's, Michael Maccoby argues that in many families the mother is the active core person. His psychoanalytic studies allow him, then, to persuasively theorize about the relationship of this mother-centered societal feature to not only machismo but to certain other male-oriented civic attitudes. Maccoby's thesis is so convincing that it merits repetition. He states in part: "Ramos (this and other names cited are noted Mexican social-psychologists) . . . and others who build their constructs of the Mexican around the idea of inferiority or insufficiency traced its origin

[24] Howard F. Cline, *Mexico, Revolution to Evolution: 1940–1960* (New York: Oxford University Press, 1963), Ch. XI.

[25] Gabriel A. Almond and James S. Coleman, *Politics of Developing Areas* (Princeton: Princeton University Press, 1960), p. 45.

to the Conquest, to the crushing of indigenous culture, to humiliation by foreigners, and to malinchismo, the tendency to betrayal, to imitate conquering overlords. . . . Gonzalez, who bases his evidence on vignettes, stresses the role of the Revolution of 1910 in breaking up the family and increasing the mother's power and influence over the children, while separating the father from his family. Ramirez emphasizes the Conquest, when the Spanish conquerors took Indian women for wives or concubines and left the Indian male displaced and impotent. The mestizo offspring of the union would ambivalently idealize and resent the Spanish father, next to him he felt inferior and would both depend on and denigrate his Indian mother. The origin of the Mexican male's glorification of the mother but predatory domination of women, according to Ramirez, is the mestizo's compulsive attempt to imitate the powerful Spaniards while at the same time preserving his only real affective link, with his mother. . . . Only 11% of the men have the extreme traits of machismo, and another 30% express these traits to a lesser degree. In turn, machismo is correlated with two more deeply rooted character factors: intense dependence on the mother and the authoritarian-exploitative syndrome. . . . Dependence on the mother is also favored by the lack of trust within a society's social and political institutions. When individuals feel that authority is irrational, that they cannot expect fair treatment from the police, the courts, and from administrators, the image of the mother is strengthened as the one person who loves unconditionally, who will never betray, and who will always provide protection. The mother stands for the safe haven of the home and, regressively, of the womb. The father stands for the society, for contract and structured authority. The father's ability to adapt successfully to the society is a powerful lesson for his children. If he fails, they reject not only him, but also their faith in rational authority, in law and contract."[26]

The sons and daughters often develop into "little liberals" or "little conservatives" owing to the political coloration of their parents. Children remain in the family until they are married, so the influence has many years to make itself felt. A daughter or son living away at a boarding school or university is a rarity for anyone from the middle classes down to the lowest classes. Primarily it is a question of financial inability, and secondly, dormitories rarely exist at the "colegio" and university levels in Mexico. Therefore the students are not able to develop an independent political personality as readily as they might, for example, in the United States.[27] This all means that while attending school, children living at home are continually offered a countervailing influence (if it should be different from the school). The

[26] Michael Maccoby, "On Mexican National Character," *The Annals*, vol. 370 (March 1967), pp. 68–72.

[27] Although the extent of children's independence, even in the U. S., has been shown to be similarly attenuated, given the findings by such investigators as Easton, Hess, Greenstein, Campbell, Lane, and others.

children don't have the chance to maintain themselves in a state of physical distance in order to assert a separate political entity. Though children express independence and a private personality on any given nonpolitical topic, they usually conform to their parents on the larger social issues. They just haven't the opportunity to be bombarded from the multitude of pressure and opinion groups that children in the United States experience.

Also, the youth of Mexico cannot usually afford to live independently. Again they are confined to the political and social environments of their homes. Even well-earning private secretaries in their mid twenties and unmarried continue to live with their families. Independence for Mexican children under this system can come for them only if they definitely embark on a "revolutionary" career or when they marry. Basically the reason that the youth in Mexico tend to marry very young is to free themselves of their traditional, paternal environments. It is the only "accepted" means to chart an independent existence, and even then, housing offers a major problem so that they must often continue to live with their families.

Next to the family, and often in opposition to parental teachings, are the school masters, teachers, and professors. Political communication is a very subtle feature of the educational system, because traditional patriotism is usually a strongly indoctrinating force within the primary, secondary, and preparatory schools in Mexico. The picture radically changes at the university level. The giant Universidad Nacional Autónoma de México, one of the largest universities in the world (including the universities of California, Buenos Aires, Bombay, Tokyo, Moscow and others) with a student population estimated at over 80,000, is a major source of political communication and an essential institution in understanding the function of political communication in Mexico today. It has morning, afternoon, and evening sessions, special student programs, and a school of philosophy which presents courses on literature and language to foreign students the year round. Each school or "facultad" has its own student officers and newspapers, and each has a varying degree of political sophistication and influence. Each school presents its own films (an easy way of determining political leanings of the school), holds periodic political rallies, and otherwise manifests its vivacity. The varying schools all are by consensus easily labelled according to their political viewpoints. The faculties of medicine, architecture, engineering, dentistry, biology, and chemistry usually tend to be more pro-American, anticommunist, and generally fairly conservative on other issues. The faculties of political science, commerce, philosophy, law, and economics are more outspoken, better organized, tend to be more radical, and are anti-United States. This was most easily observed in those who demonstrated on and around April 17th of 1961 against the United States intervention in Cuba. The focal point of anti-United States political communication is the school of economics. It was in their auditorium that the larger university meetings were held.

University professors may also use their podiums to put across political beliefs and are partially protected by the autonomous nature of the university. In general the university is one of the focal points of political communication in the Mexican nation. After the domestic influence, it has the strongest influence on that 1 per cent of Mexicans who really go as far as receiving university training. But in terms of numbers one can see that the home is yet more influential. The point in favor of the university is that it is one of the major stepping stones to a political career, thus giving it preponderance in the shaping of the minds of the future political elite.

The church is another major formative purveyor of political communication in Mexico. Many students in Mexico have gone to confessional and parochial schools, such as the private "Universidad Iberoamericana." The products of those schools are, with few exceptions, politically conservative. The students readily admit that the priests and nuns take political stands of one kind or another in class. The Jesuit academic hierarchy is apparently an intellectually aggressive and vital force in Mexican academic circles, even though constitutionally parochial schools are illegal as well as the dissemination of religious material in the public schools. The government has winked at a new effort of mutual coexistence and tolerance since the 1940's. The church on its part has cut down on much of its political interference. However, the church mass in the urban areas and the parish priests in the rural sections still are important sources of political communication. The direct influence of the rural priest is a familiar one; however, urban-centered religious mass also takes on significance. Particularly noteworthy was the mass on Sunday, July 2, 1961—the day of nation-wide elections for the national legislature. It is known unofficially that the church does not look with favor on the preponderance of the PRI party and finds its spiritual and political home more in accord with the Partido de Acción Nacional (PAN). Though fellow political scientists have witnessed sermons against the PRI, others have not. The author mentions a particular sermon not because it was against the PRI per se, but because it was an unmitigated defense of the status quo and a warning against revolution and the unbalancing of the social system. The sermon's central point was that the workers (congregation made up of humble, working class elements of the Coyoacán section of Mexico City) should be thankful for their jobs and their bosses, who are righteous men put there by God to preserve them from evil and maintain them in security.

The priest praised capitalism as the fruits of man's labor and asked that each man give his full loyalty to his employer or his company so as to merit its continued trust in him. He warned the audience against disrespect toward their superiors as going against God's law on this earth. He concluded that the owners of enterprises had risen to their positions through God's will and that they, the workers, could serve God best by serving their bosses well.

Almond and Coleman describe the role of secondarily influential groups, such as business groups, political leaders, and bureaucrats. From this vital sector of the upper middle classes come the most successful political manipulators in Mexico. There is in the Federal District, which is the focus for political communication, a powerful elite made up of the business community, party leaders, and bureaucrats. Scott has shown that the government bureaucrats are the most powerful single union in the country. The business sector since Alemán has continually prospered as compared to other professional groups. Political candidates are usually recruited from the business and legal communities in Mexico. Politicians and bureaucrats receive huge pensions, traveling allowances, business write-offs, and the right to vacation at low-cost pension hotels at Acapulco and Vera Cruz.

Lastly, there is the need to mention face-to-face groupings and the role of neighborhoods. Oscar Lewis in his book *The Children of Sánchez* has shown the close intermingling of the poorer people in the urban "vecindads." Whether this has a great effect as far as political communication is concerned is hard to determine. Lewis seems to feel that the political sophistication of the urban populace on matters concerning them is acute. As stated earlier face-to-face groups have importance in political communication because they are an essential forum for opinion making. Other face-to-face groupings that were noticed in Mexico to have cultivated similar political positions were the American, German, and Spanish communities.

The role of the Mexican Press as a source of political communication also deserves mention. The leading newspapers of Mexico are conservative in tone and contain wide international coverage.[28] *El Excelsior,* with a circulation of over 135,000, is pro-United States oriented and highly in favor of the PRI regime. The paper rarely has a really harsh editorial against the United States, nor is there ever a strong scent of criticism against the Mexican president himself. Though its coverage is extensive, it is often very impersonal, getting a good deal of news from the AP and UPI wire services. Its merit is its extent of Latin American news, the total absence of demagoguery, and its general respectability. William S. White, Walter Lippmann, Drew Pearson, and others in the past have been regularly syndicated, and it is through such foreign columnists that one can read some criticism of United States foreign and domestic policies.

The *Excelsior* stands for an independent, socially progressive, and cultured Mexico—goals with which no one could disagree. *El Universal,* with a circulation of over 145,000, is another large paper in Mexico. It is similar to the *Excelsior,* but less complete and not written as well. *Novedades,* with a circulation of more than 60,000, published by the Ramón Beteta family, a leading component of the Mexican intelligentsia, has the most interesting

[28] A run-down of Mexican newspaper sources exists in the appendix of Robert E. Ward, *Studying Politics Abroad* (Boston: Little, Brown, 1964), p. 213 ff.

and independent editorial page but less total news coverage. It is also not as uncritically pro-Western in its orientation as the other two leading newspapers. The other two important newspapers, *La Prensa* and *El Nacional,* are not as independent. *La Prensa,* with a circulation of 185,000 is not much more than a tabloid, and *El Nacional* is little more than a government organ.

Unofficially it is well known in Mexico that the government has a monopoly on domestically grown lumber and lumber imported from Canada. It proceeds to sell it at a nominal fee to the newspaper publishers. It is said that should the government be in any way displeased with statements in the newspapers, it could easily ask a normal, conventional price for the paper thus bankrupting all of them because they work on a small marginal-profit basis.

In Mexico, with no visible opposition press, periodicals have had to take up some of the slack. It is possible to single out certain monthly, bimonthly, and weekly journals of opinion that carry a very diversified amount of political material and have done much in keeping the political climate more genuine and controversial. First in mind was *Política,* an extremely critical, Marxist, antigovernmental magazine that, though at times irresponsible, provided a needed radical editorial position vis-à-vis government white washing of some of the more delicate issues. In international questions they frequently took the Soviet position and were consistently anti-"Yanqui."[29]

Two socialist journals more moderate in tone and perspective also contribute much to political communications in Mexico. They are *Siempre* and *Mañana.* These magazines are close to being independent, criticizing wherever they see the need. Outside of these exceptions, however, one cannot say that there is an autonomous press reporting neutral information. In fact, on many occasions certain United States journals offered a more relevant and perceptive understanding of sensitive Latin American issues than many publications existing in Mexico.

Mexico from one point of view might be included under the category of a homogeneous cultural system, if one excludes certain geographical and indigenous inconsistencies. Mexico is basically Hispanic-American and much more racially and linguistically homogeneous than the United States with its mixture of Anglo-Saxon, Germanic, Nordic, Mediterranean, Semitic, and Negroid people. However, despite having a homogeneous racial stock, Mexico does not have, as has been said, a homogeneous political culture nor a differentiated and objective media of communication. The PRI party controls almost all official political communication, and there is little heard of the minor parties of Mexico. Certainly the press does not perform an independent political communication function. The medias of communication are kept under the watchful eye of the government which maintains that it is

[29] *Política* ceased publication in early 1968 because of internal rivalries and declining circulation. *Latin American Digest,* vol. 2, no. 4 (March 1968), p. 1.

merely trying to protect the "Revolution." Under this concept, students and intellectuals, as artist David Siquieres, have been thrown into prison in the last decade. They are imprisoned under the provisions of the "Dissolution Act" which makes any abnormal criticism, rally, or disturbance subject to penal reprimand and punishment. What occurs is a monopoly of information given to the people—not necessarily ill advised, but not heterogeneous or diversified either. Publicity serves not to expose private interests but to reinforce them. Of course these private interests have for over a decade become the "revolutionary" public interest of all Mexicans, and they are not challenged by any vocal major group. Following this logically one would arrive at the concept of Mexico as a kind of semitotalitarian state. Within the Almond-Coleman framework, Mexico would qualify for such an onerous label.[30] But of course Mexico does have several saving features. There is no racial persecution, no aggressive foreign policy, minor parties are tolerated, there is no overt police state, no large army is incorporated (8 per cent of budget), and no governmental terror exists.

Taking all this into account, one finds the Mexican middle class well informed as to international events and often personally critical as to events at home. The problem remains that this personal position usually does not reach the point of organized and legal action. It has often been said that Mexico is a "vocal democracy" but not a "practicing democracy."

Much of what has been said above, as forewarned, applies to the mestizo Mexican and not to the most parochial elements of the society. Mexicans receive much "particularistic" political communication not readily comprehended by all in a like manner. In the filtering of communication, Mexico's whole population does not receive all the news as in a more developed society. In developing societies much political communication is transferred by "kinship, lineage, caste and language groupings performing the political communication function intermittently, diffusely, and particularistically."[31] It must be kept in mind that almost a million Mexicans still don't speak Spanish, and three million still speak it as a second language; railroads have still not cut through parts of the jungles of Chiapas, Yucatan, and Quintana Roo; illiteracy in Mexico is 35 per cent; some towns have no schools; and several states only one major hospital. Many people still sleep on floors and go barefoot, never having eaten bread, tasted beer, or ridden in a motor vehicle. Thus as Frank Tannenbaum has said the problem in Mexico is not the urban-rural hiatus as much as it is the modern and archaic cultures meeting in the same twentieth century. The cultural gap in many sections of Mexico is very apparent.

[30] The Almond-Coleman view states "One might even argue that the crucial control in the totalitarian political system is not coercion but the monopoly of media of communication." *Politics of Developing Areas*, p. 47.

[31] Ibid., p. 50.

Naturally then the inflow and outflow of political communication is slow and unwieldy, and some news "never fully penetrates diffuse and undifferentiated networks of the traditional and rural areas. . . . Much information remains covert and latent and it is consequently difficult to make political estimates accurately and quickly."[32]

The Mexican government, as the prime source of political communication, has greatly inundated the countryside by means of the "output" function but has not nearly received a comparable amount of "input" into the political system.[33] It is in this latter area that the acid test of a growing democracy is met.

[32] Ibid., p. 51.

[33] See the conclusions reached by the Almond-Verba survey, *The Civic Culture,* pp. 310–312.

CHAPTER 8 Federalism, Legitimacy, and Political Culture

In Chapter 6 we spoke of political culture as a composite of social and individual behavioral characteristics that affect the political process. We must also determine the effect on social attitudes and beliefs of structural and authoritative political relationships.

The historical as well as the contemporary experimentation with a federalist structure of government seems to indicate that in Latin America there has been a pattern of negotiation and compromise in political settlements rather than arbitrary linear lines of hierarchical subordination to authority. Though in many countries it is the local notables, the state "caudillos," the nonparty interest groups, that have been in positions to bargain with national administrators rather than legislators and party officialdom. The Latin American decision-making pattern has leaned, in general, toward a dispersal of legitimacy among one or more power centers. Though the dominance of the national executive branch has been relatively uncontested over the long haul, there has been a general agreement that distinctive local and regional aggregations should be reflected in the overall political calculus.

In Latin America, particularly in Mexico, Brazil, and Argentina where federalism still remains the political mechanism for administering very large physical domains, adoption of the federal political structure has been more to accommodate a personalist political culture than to impose any inhibitions on a unitary power. Under federalism more patronage is available, authority may be harmlessly divided, and subsidiary governmental units act as buffers between local and federal power centers.

Thus federalism in some areas has served to give the appearance of cultural pluralism by allowing the proliferation of more functionaries than there were, in fact, functions. This nominal dispersion of political responsibility had a negligible impact on the maintenance of the economic resource balance among the various interior regions. Nor did any political subdivisions act as a court of last resort in disputes of any consequence. Thus the central powers have held the monopoly over most decision making. Local cultural differences and diversities were recognized, but there has been no genuine *political* pluralism.

As such, federalism is quite a common phenomenon in the world today, and its creation and development is not confined to area or type of ideology.[1]

[1] For an extensive study of federalism see K. C. Wheare, *Federal Government* (New York: Oxford University Press, 1953).

Nigeria, the USSR, the United States, West Germany, and India for example are federal systems. There are many different degrees of centralization that a federal system may employ. Some are so centralized in favor of the national government as to verge on unitary systems, and others are so weak that they approximate confederational or simple dissolution.

In its basic structure federalism can be defined as a series of concentric power circles encompassing several levels of governing authority. With varying degrees of control and responsibility, national, state, and local governments jointly manage overlapping geographical areas and the same people. In Latin America overwhelming power and control over the duties and responsibilities of the state and local governments are relegated to the national government. As distinct, however, from the centralization of unitary governments, where most authority and responsibility rests with the national government, there are specific formal functions usually set aside to be administered by the constituent governments of the localities. These provincial nuclei of control receive some sense of autonomy in the formal aspects of local legislatures and local elections which have local issues as the focus of political campaigns. They have limited bases and usually jurisdictional control over police, health, sanitation, entertainment, adornment, and other administrative functions. In no case do they fix national revenues, administer defense or foreign policy, or negotiate treaties. In all federal systems, provincial powers survive by the sufference of national governments.

Among the three federal countries, Brazil has kept up the greatest semblance of a true federal structure, but its federal system, like that of Argentina's and Mexico's do not approach the state-national relationship which exists in West Germany and the United States. Chile and Peru, on the other hand, have very strongly centralized national governments of the unitary type.

An external stimulant to the creation of the Latin American variety of federalism came directly from the North American experience in establishing a successful federal system before the turn of the nineteenth century. The national surge of the original British colonies was admired in Latin America and later emulated by its independence leaders, though the most famous of the liberators, San Martin and Bolivar, favored either a monarchical system or at least a highly unified unitarian state structure. The early nineteenth century Latin American creations were quickly besieged with conflict between the proponents of federalism and those favoring a unitary state. Chile experimented with a federal structure but found it lacking and changed to a unitary system under the determined leadership of Portales. Peru, the most centralized and controlled of the Spanish colonies in the Americas, found a unitary structure more compatible with her strong colonial tradition. In Mexico, Brazil, and Argentina, the struggle between the unitarians and the federalists was in each case, though not immediately, won by the latter. By 1860 all three had constitutions and governmental structures which can be described as federal.

The creation of many federal governments usually entailed a compromise by the national government by which it was able to amass greater territory in return for constitutional promises for provincial control over particular administrative functions.[2] The smaller provincial governments received security from foreign attacks and a feeling of vague belonging in return for which they relinquished autonomous powers in vital state matters. This bargaining relationship was important in the unification of Argentina, Brazil, and Mexico. It gave the government the wherewithal to collect greater tax revenues from newly acquired territorial units, to raise nationally conscripted armies instead of relying on caudillo-backed mercenaries, and, with more territory and an army, to better assure and protect its national boundaries against foreign intrusion.

In the subsequent years there has been a decline in the power of the states and provinces. However, all three countries have, if only nominally, maintained their federal structures which have been weakened by strong presidential systems under such men as Sarmiento, Irigoyen and by dictatorships like that of Perón. The frequent interventions into provincial life by Pedro II and the basically antifederal, pro-unitarian policies of Getulio Vargas weakened federalism in Brazil, while the omnipotence of the PRI party has had the same effect in Mexico.

Looked at formally, the legal framework of the constitutional system of Mexico, Brazil, and Argentina still carries the signs and symbols of a federal structure. Each has had the full range of national, provincial, and local governments, provincial legislatures, and a senate which represents regional as opposed to popular constituencies; each allows either specific (Brazil and Mexico) or implied powers to its constituent states; and each refers in greater or less detail to the role and functions of individual executive, legislative, and judicial responsibilities on the provincial level. All three have federalized capital cities which geographically belong to the nation and are not a part of any state. Argentina, in conformance with the original United States constitution, still elects her senators indirectly by provincial legislators. The former Brazilian Constitution of 1946 and the Mexican Constitution of 1917 provided for the direct election of senators by the population of their districts. The same is provided for in the United States constitutional amendment 17 of 1913.

[2] I am indebted for this interpretation to William H. Riker's stimulating essay, *Federalism: Origin, Operation, Significance* (Boston: Little, Brown, 1964). Of particular value in understanding Latin American federalism is his Ch. 2. Also see his excellent bibliography on pp. 157–162. Riker's strongest statement on federalism is included in his review article, "Six Books in Search of a Subject or Does Federalism Exist and Does It Matter?" *Comparative Politics*, vol. 2, no. 1 (October 1969), pp. 135–146. He states unequivocally that federalism is significant only at the beginning of a central government as a way to bring in regional governments with a promise of autonomy. After this development it is the political culture that has a greater bearing on the viability of true federalism.

Several institutions, which in some federal systems, such as the United States and West Germany, allow for a certain amount of decentralization, are not as viable in Argentina, Brazil, and Mexico. The tradition of strong presidents, subservient legislative and judicial branches, and the presence of tightly disciplined national parties all obviate any real counterbalancing strength from provincial and local sources. For example, few legislatures, with the exception of the opposition to Presidents Quadros and Goulart in Brazil (1961–1964), some sporadic Socialist and Radical opposition to the Justo government (1932–1938) and parties' opposition to the Illia government in Argentina (1963–1966), have presented much of a countervailing force to the tremendous leverage of the national government and the presidential party. A free and independent judiciary branch, representing objective constitutional interests and potentially antithetical to the government, has also been absent in Latin America's federal systems. Rather the federal court has acted as a mere rationalization for presidential governments. In fact, judiciary branches have usually assisted in the further centralization of powers so evident in Latin America since 1930.

As the political culture of Latin America becomes increasingly dominated by middle class values, already the case in its urban centers, there is likely to be more and more support for centralizing powers within the federal system. The growing massification of society will increase not only the burdens of central governments but also the pressure upon them to assume greater and greater degrees of power.[3] As this occurs the powers of the provinces and the municipalities may further decrease. As political communication becomes more direct between the central government and the electorate, regional ties and loyalties will be superseded and possible national confrontations more likely.

Mexico

Of the four Latin American federal nations (Venezuela is the fourth), Mexico's federalism is probably the weakest. This may be because her institutions were actually created first and then federalism was appended, almost as an afterthought. Mexico had no viable provincial centers of authority during the preindependence period outside of Mexico City and Vera Cruz, and even Vera Cruz was more Mexico City's distant port than an autonomous power center. Federalism came to Mexico as a cultural import from the United States and was grafted upon Mexican traditions. Years of mercantile relations with Spain had also served to sharply dampen regional autonomy which has so often been a concomitant to genuine federalism. The Mexican Wars in the

[3] The first expression of this view can be found in the writings of John J. Johnson. See his *Political Change in Latin America, The Emergence of The Middle Sectors* (Stanford: Stanford University Press, 1958).

nineteenth century against the United States and France also strengthened the central government at the expense of regional caudillos. Mexico's failure to explore and settle its frontier territories to the north further weakened any regionalism north of the Rio Grande River. In fact, the first signs of Texan regionalism led to its breaking off from Mexican control and to its absorption by the United States where a more decentralized and genuine federal structure made assimilation of Texas easy. With the development of the Mexican Revolution and the creation of the one-party government, regional caudillos and local power sources were even further weakened. The ubiquity of the PRI party in Mexico virtually displaces any local aspects of Mexican federalism. As the Communist Party in the Soviet Union cuts down and across the political and administrative apparatus of the Soviet federal system, so the PRI performs a similar function making regional representation generally superfluous or, at best, subordinate.

However, the sheer size of Mexico allows federalism to play a limited role. It is significant, for example, that the greatest local demonstrations of resistance to Mexican centralism has come from two states very distant from the capital—Baja California, and Chihuahua. It is also in these two states that the Partido de Acción Nacional, Mexico's far outdistanced "second party," seems to do the best in national elections.[4] A phenomenon in Mexico which does nothing to further regionalism or centralization is the attachment of the people to parochial ties, to their birthplace known as "mi tierra" or "my land and home." This type of very personal identification to locality competes with both regionalism and centralism for the loyalty of the Mexicans. The competition will most likely be won by national agencies, represented by the PRI, who are making more of a determined effort to integrate Mexico's parochial masses than are the regional associations who lack the financial or ideological independence to undertake the effort. Lastly, Mexico has never absorbed European immigration to the degree that was absorbed by Brazil and Argentina. Thus there was no overt impetus to ameliorate the gap between the few rich and many poor. The absence of middle class European immigration allowed Mexico to pursue more traditional politics up to the Mexican revolution. Parties were not mass parties, and there was little communication between the elite structure and the popular base. One could even say that the new Mexican ruling class fathered by the Revolution tried several decades before the PRI (1934–1940) became a really popular, cross-sectional party. However, it should also be mentioned, that small immigration may have vitiated against the earlier development of a centralized government which new immigrant groups can stimulate in leadership, something that occurred in the United States and Argentina. The absence of new groups from Europe and their influence on mass parties, labor unions, and commercial organizations, helped to extend Mexico's federal

[4] Pablo Gonzáles Casanova, *La democracia en México* (Mexico: Ediciones ERA, 1965), pp. 257–259.

impetus and its reliance on regional caudillos as the backbone of national politics.

Argentina

Argentina's federalism is slightly more functional although it was also imposed. Argentina spent several decades as an uncertain and warring confederation of local caudillos who were occasionally unified but always bickering, usually for personal reasons. By 1860 and the firm establishment of the Argentine Republic, most of the regional loyalties had been broken down. The nationalistic and nationally oriented policies of Irigoyen, who represented the newly arrived European middle-class immigrant, and Perón, who represented the newly urbanized rural peons, did much to erase regional loyalties and replace them with a party ideology and national identity. Today there are few regional loyalties which would make for a genuine diversification of national interests. Except for the special wine-producing regions of Mendoza and the sugar cane farmers of Tucumán, much of Argentina is collectively interested in cattle, wheat, petroleum, and industry and there is generally an underlying agreement in these areas. It is in Mendoza and Tucumán that some of the more prevalent feelings of regionalism still exist in Argentina. However, the common languages (Spanish and Italian), customs, religions, and nationality of the Argentines make them a very culturally homogenous society. The modern aspects of Argentina make mobility very common, the middle class, whose ranks were swelled by mass European immigration, predominates, and the nation is over 60 per cent urban. All these factors have appeared to assist in breaking down the supports of true federalism. The growing governmental control over the exports of grain and beef through governmental "juntas," which were first initiated under Perón, has assisted in the growing centralism of Argentine federalism. The courts have been traditionally weak when the presidents have been strong so that they have done little to prevent the assumption of more and more powers within the hands of the executive. Parties have in the past also been centralized in the capital with most of the major ones (e.g., Peronistas, Radicals, Conservatives, Frondizi's MID) having had strong bases in at least three-fourths or more of the providences at election time. Again, national parties, who responded to the commands of the party's central headquarters in Buenos Aires, have controlled provincial governors and legislatures.

At first glance, one can see few signs of vital federalism. However, there are a few provincial parties that managed year in and year out to elect one or two deputies to the national legislature. For example, the provinces of Corrientes, Missiones, Chaco, and Mendoza have at one time or another developed a provincial offshoot from a national party or an indigenous party which have maintained some independence. However, their power has been too marginal to weaken that of the central government. There is also in Argentina a vague but definite antagonism to the preponderance of Buenos Aires on the national political map. However, since the nineteenth century, this sentiment has never been developed into a definite, observable movement but relegated to feelings of hostility, jealousy, and suspicion of the "unArgentine" behavior of the people of the capital. This is an amorphous but surprisingly widespread feeling in contemporary Argentina, but it does not in the least threaten the preponderance of the Argentine national government.

Brazil

Brazil has the closest approximation of federalism in Latin America, though it is a far cry from North American, Canadian, or Australian federalism. Brazil's colonial captaincies existed centuries before the establishment of Brazil's Republic in 1889, and this long traditional regionalism certainly struck a responsive chord in the federal development of the modern Brazilian state. The ties to territorial jurisdiction were strengthened in the twentieth century because of the regional relationship to the various economic and agricultural interests of Brazil. For example, sugar is associated with Pernambuco, coffee with São Paulo, minerals with Minas Gerais, and cattle with Rio Grande do Sul. The alliance of political tradition with economic interests gives some genuine meaning to regionalism. Brazil's central government has recognized this and has created a special North East Development Agency to try to uplift the economy of the Northeastern states in order to bring them more equitably into Brazilian union. The fact that Brazil has moved its capital 500 miles into the interior is a possible concession to potential centrifugal forces emerging from the interior.

However, as in Argentina of the twentieth century, Brazilian governments, especially the dictatorship of Getulio Vargas, have done much to overcome regional ties and supplant them with national loyalties and/or loyalties to parties with national roots. Here, too, as in Argentina, immigration, mass labor movements, and nationalism in general have vied with federalist tendencies for predominance in Brazil. It can be said that since 1930 the old regional structure has taken a subordinate position and Brazil's federalism, as that of Argentina and Mexico, has become so centralized as to put its viability in danger.

Looking at federalism in general, it seems to work well, or at least develop in nations with great extensions of territory having some cultural diversity or a marked regional tradition in its prenational period. However, over half the world has relied on a unitary form of government, usually for ease of administration and uniformity of laws, regulations, and governmental programs. Unitary governments have presented a more solid defense against regionalism and local disorders, and they have rarely needed the constitutional provisions which federal states have, allowing for national intervention into state affairs should their federalism or republicanism be threatened.

Unitary proponents have argued that the defenders of federalism, those who conclude that only federal systems can provide grass roots development, state experimentation, and a genuine representation of local interests and differences, are often defending rather vested interests.[5] In fact, nineteenth century federalism in Mexico, Brazil, and Argentina did very often defend the particular and minority interests of the large hacienda owner, the plantation owner, or the large cattle rancher. It was the centralizing revolutions of the twentieth century in Latin America which have had as one of their chief credos the breakdown of dominant rural minorities. An argument can also be made that local experimentation and the representation of local interests have been achieved under unitary governments in Great Britain and Chile as well as under the federalism of West Germany and Argentina.

It appears that federalism played an expansionist role during the authoritative period of a nation's development as the government bargained with local caudillos and gave up certain rights in return for the assurance that national boundaries would be made secure and that rule of law would exist throughout the length and breadth of the newly formed nation. Federalism continued to play a lesser role during the aggregative period as immigration, capitalization, and urbanization combined to nationalize politics and try the resources of the federal government. Today, with the distributive period well underway in the Republics of Mexico, Brazil, and Argentina, the requirements of social justice, production distribution and political uniformity make it paramount that a federal system be centralized. Thus federalism, as envisioned by the Latin American constitutionalists is fast growing obsolete. The establishment of these structural political arrangements can be observed in the composition and orientation of the Latin American constitutions written during the authoritative, aggregative phases, and even during the distributive period.

Certain conditions underlay the foundations of the Latin American constitutions at the beginning of the last century. As has been discussed, the independence movements were usually led by disgruntled but privileged classes who differed from their colonial masters mainly in their American origins. However, in the midst of consolidating their victories, they turned to what was essentially a rational, middle class revolutionary ideology.

After victory was in hand, principles were sought that would guide the young nations through the harrowing experiences of early adolescence and manhood. The leaders of the independence movements were basically anti-European rather than against an aristocratic pattern and view of life. It was

[5] William H. Riker, *Federalism: Origin, Operation, Significance,* see Ch. 6.

coincidental, however, that their drive for independence was launched against European aristocrats. The American leaders thus found spiritual solace and revolutionary fervor in the antiaristocratic philosophers and idealogues who were so influential in Europe on the eve of the American and French Revolutions.

Borrowed in toto were some of the leading political statements of the time, the majority of which found currency in the American and French Constitutional Conventions in the late eighteenth century. Montesquieu's conception of that delicate balance of power which would ensure an equitably run government was a main source of inspiration, yet this conception was an anathema to those earliest Latin American independence leaders who sought to indelibly centralize authority. In no other source however could these leaders find such well defined and formulated political conceptulizations. Thus for want of a good, developed aristocratic philosophy of government, Latin American schizophrenia was nurtured. The Lockean view of a government which would serve the commercial and propertied classes but infringe as little as possible also found its way into Latin American constitutionalism. However, Locke's benign view of human nature and of a society freed for the most part from government surveillance was not in tune with those of the framers of Latin America's constitutions who saw a middle class revolution as an implied threat. Perhaps more kindred in spirit was the Hobbesian concept of an all powerful government, absolute monarchy, which would lead the unaware, unwashed and potentially dangerous masses toward prescribed social norms and thus avoid major social disruptions. Along with Madison and Hamilton, the leaders of early Latin America distrusted an essentially equalitarian society which might unleash classes unable to govern and unfit to pursue the arts and sciences.

Despite the cautious view of social progress best expounded by Edmund Burke, Latin American revolutionaries received surprising inspiration from Voltaire, Condorcet, and Rousseau. The philosophies of these Frenchmen, the forerunners of modern political philosophy and social change on the European scene during the nineteenth century, were instrumental in later spawning the ideas of social justice developed by Proudhon, Marx, and even Sorel.

The originators of a philosophy of government which encompassed reason, rationality, indelible social progress, the perfectibility of man, the rights of man, and popular sovereignty became the ideological forerunners of Latin American political culture despite the lack of any strong relationship between Latin American sympathy for such eloquent social sermons and a natural predisposition of its early leaders to govern in opposition to these European concepts.

As the fathers of the Latin American constitutions met (and there were many fathers, stepfathers, and sons of fathers who were again fathers of new constitutions), they agreed on three principles in framing these documents.

Primarily they believed it essential to be *explicit* and *substantive* rather than implicit and procedural. Duties, responsibilities, rights, and activities were to be spelled out verbatim within the constitutions. Secondly, they agreed to incorporate *guidelines* for the future into the constitutional pattern which would serve as a source of revelation and inspiration for years to come. Lastly, the Latin American constitutional fathers felt that the constitutions themselves might hold the *solutions* to societal problems. All three of these guiding concepts tell us much of the political culture of Latin America. As has been discussed previously, the concern for political absolutes, the intellectual euphoria surrounding a well-turned phrase, the desire to promulgate a total, emphatic statement of the present as well as a guide to the future, all left their impact upon Latin American constitutionalism.

Mexico's third major constitutional statement of 1917 is its present guiding document and all later Latin American constitutionalists were to look to this document as a basis for their own revisions. The guarantees of the Mexican Constitution are completely explicit and are set forth in great detail. They pertain to legislative proposals and legal precepts, and there is a generous amount of discussion on the present and future rights of Mexicans, including such items as the forbidding of slavery, freedom of religion, secular-mass education, nondiscrimination on basis of race, creed, class, or sex, forbidding of religious training in state educational systems, right to work, sanctity of contracts, freedom of press, right to petition, bearing arms, free and unrestricted travel. Aside from these major statements are sections outlawing titles, establishing due process of law, trial by jury, and the right to face one's accuser, confront the witness, and not to testify against oneself. The inviolability of the home, the right to bear arms, and the privileges of life, liberty, and property are further guaranteed in this large section.

Perhaps the most noted and well known article under the section devoted to guarantees is Article 27 which goes into exhaustive detail in defining the government's inviolable ownership of the lands, waters, and subsoil of Mexico. All property ownership is thus defined as a type of long-term bargain, concession, or privilege in accordance with Mexican laws under their surveillance. This article also deals with land distribution to the dispossessed and landless and the illegality of any type of monopoly over the nation's economic resources.

This section, which is in many ways the heart of the Mexican Constitution of 1917, goes further than any constitution in the world in setting forth a definitive catalogue of human rights, extending in many cases far beyond purely legal and procedural statements. It is so full of detailed prescriptions and proscriptions that it places in jeopardy practically any successive legal interpretation within Mexico's changing social framework. Though influenced by the United States Bill of Rights and the French Rights of Man, it goes beyond by giving a special social and Mexican character to the Constitution which antedates the social character of later Soviet constitutions, specifically the Stalin Constitution of 1936. It is in every sense a constitutional section to deal with twentieth century political concerns. Needless to say, it is contradicted every day, perhaps not intentionally, but because of its very specificity. It was, in a sense, created as much for future unborn Mexicans as it is a legal framework which is generally and universally applicable.

Subsequent sections of the Constitution define in detail the concept of Mexicans and the duties and rights of citizens. Later articles are assigned to national sovereignty, a delineation of Mexico's federal structure, and the organization of its separation of powers, election, and methods of representation. A very large section is devoted to the general powers of Congress, the Chamber of Deputies, and the specific powers of the Senate. Following this section are the prerogatives of the executive and the judicial branches of government.

Following the traditional Western pattern of the division of national power, the Constitution follows with a detailed section describing the duties and responsibilities of public officials. The subsequent part dealing with the role of the states in Mexican federalism includes Article 122 which gives the executive the right to intervene in the states in order to "protect the States against all foreign invasion or violence." It goes on to state "In any case of internal uprising or disturbance, they shall give equal protection, provided it is requested by the legislature of the state or by its Executive if the former is not assembled." This provision has been much more liberally interpreted than the same provision written into the United States Constitution, Article IV, Section 4.

Following are the important and innovative labor and social security articles which, like the articles on individual guarantees, are hallmarks of the Mexican Constitution. Article 123 fixes maximum hours at eight, protects against child labor, enforces workers' sabbaticals once a week, provides for maternity care and time off from work, a minimum wage, equal pay for equal work regardless of sex or nationality, and doubletime for overtime employment. The Article goes on to require that all agricultural, industrial, and mining enterprises of over one hundred workers establish schools, hospitals, and other services to care for its workers. Those with more than two hundred, probably including families, who live in particular work centers have to provide municipal services and recreation centers. Concomitantly employers are responsible for labor and occupational hazards, accidents, and diseases. Legal requisites are also established for hygiene and safety.

The powers of the official sector include the recognition of the right to organize and strike (excluding government workers), the responsibility to arbitrate in labor-management disputes, the intervention on behalf of a fired worker (without due cause) to ensure him an indemnity of three months' wages, and the obligation to enact a complete social security law.

This section has been widely praised as not only revolutionary but far-sighted and has in actuality since the Calles regime in the early 1930's provided a necessary constitutional framework for much labor and social security legislation provisions. The paternal nature of the Mexican government has at the same time prevented the development of a solid, independent, free trade union movement. However, within this important limitation, the organized labor movement of Mexico has achieved meaningful advances, particularly in the areas of housing, medical assistance, and social insurance. It is this section that has become most recognized outside of Mexico for giving the Mexican Constitution its twentieth century flavor and social content. There is no doubt that it was the most progressive constitution of its day.

Title VII of the Constitution which comes at the end, covers an assortment of subjects that the 1916 Constitutional Convention was not able to integrate into other headings and is appropriately entitled General Considerations. Included here are the very important references to the military and to the church. The military is admonished that in time of peace it may only perform functions directly connected with military affairs. The record since 1930 has shown that this constitutional aspiration has been fulfilled, and a problem so serious in other Latin American societies has been avoided. Perhaps the most proscriptive and fervid part of the Constitution is reserved for Article 130 referring to the church and clergy. Within its rather long declarations appear a number of sharp, unmitigated rebukes directed against the church. Specifically, the federal government is given complete supervision over all matters relating to religious worship. Mexico does not provide for the establishment of any religion (Catholicism) or the denial of any (Protestant sects or Judaism). Marriage is a civil contract, and religiously affiliated people must, apart from their religious vows, register with civil officials. Complementing this is the legality of civil divorce. Churches are juridically unrecognized, while the number of priests allowed to practice in the various states is fixed by state legislatures according to local requirements. All priests or ministers must be Mexican by birth, and clergymen are forbidden in any public or private meeting to propagate religious propaganda or criticize the fundamental laws of the country. They are also denied the right to vote. The building of new places of worship must first be approved by the Secretary of *Gobernación* (Interior). Periodical publications of a religious character may not comment on national political matters or publish information related to the functioning of public institutions. Lastly, the formation of any kind of political group related to any religious denomination is strictly forbidden as are political meetings to be held in places of worship. These strictures for the most part have been somewhat relaxed in their implementation because of the confident position of the governing party vis-à-vis any political rivalry and the cautious attitude of the Catholic Church since the promulgation of the 1917 Constitution. It is mainly in the field of private education that the church has again been allowed to play a greater role despite constitutional limitations in Article 3.

In Peru the last full-fledged adoption of a new constitution dates to 1933 and was promulgated, interestingly enough, under the dictatorship of Marshal Benavides. As in the Mexican Constitution, guarantees are specifically delineated and definitions are given as to who is Peruvian and what this implies for citizenship. In the Peruvian Constitution the guarantees are divided into national and social guarantees and individual guarantees.

National and social guarantees merely indicate the degree to which the government may enter societal functions to assert its position and to keep any one sector, be it labor, capital, or foreign enterprise, from becoming too powerful. The Constitution assures the government in its managerial role in society. A part of the Constitution is devoted to the right of the state in money matters, collection of taxes, the supervision of the banks, and the prohibition of commercial or industrial monopolies, national or foreign. The state is given the power to guarantee the right of free association, property, commerce and industry, and the right to work. At the same time it requires property to be used in harmony with the "social interest" and can acquire and transfer property when it is in the "national interest," as has been done by the present military administration. As in the Mexican Constitution, the Peruvian Constitution in Article 37 states that mines, lands, woods, waters, and all the country's natural resources belong to the state and that the state decides their utility, for example, in private concessions. The section continues with a grab bag of motley articles which are difficult to categorize, the most interesting of which outlaws internationally organized political parties. This is a direct reference to the Aprista Party which was driven underground and its leaders exiled during Benavides' term in the 1930's.

Though the Peruvian governmental structure is not federal, there is a provision under the powers of the legislature that makes it incompatible to hold executive and legislative posts concurrently. This is in conformity with the usual federal-presidential systems rather than with the continental parliamentary types of unitary governments of, for example, western Europe. However, under the section devoted to the powers of the president, the unique Peruvian feature of the creation of a Prime Minister is established. He is chosen by the President to represent him in Congress and to function much like the Premier in the French Fifth Republic.

In contrast to the Mexican Constitution, little is said regarding the obligations of the government vis-à-vis its indigenous people, even though there is a special section on the subject. It is mentioned that the state legally recognizes the Indian communities and has the right to either apportion land or with indemnization seize it from them according to needs of "public utility." The Constitution thus has left the door open to the rather sorry treatment of Indian communities in Peru during the last three decades. It has caused a large exodus of Indians from the altiplano areas of eastern Peru to the coastal urban areas where they may better participate in the country's modernization and development programs which, in many cases, are generations away from the Indian's traditional culture.

The armed forces also receive special attention. Constitutionally they are given the duty to assure the rights of the Republic, defend the laws of the constitution, and maintain public order. Military activity in Peru has been quite open and continuous based partially on a loose interpretation of their constitutional role.

The chapter devoted to religion confirms the Roman Catholic Church as the established church, while the other religions are given the freedom to worship. Distinct from the Mexican Constitution that severely restricts the activities of the church, the Peruvian Constitution has no restraining articles.

Meanwhile, on March 15, 1967, Brazil promulgated its fifth constitution since the inception of the Republic in 1891. The military-imposed document consists of 189 articles as compared to the 218 articles in the 1946 post-Vargas constitution and its subsequent 75 or so amendments preceding the military coup of April 1964. Perhaps the most paternalistic of the Latin American constitutions, it purports to seriously regulate the political sector while increasing the prerogatives of the national government over the state and municipal constituent authorities.

The Constitution alters the name of the country from the United States of Brazil (the constitutional name, for example, of Mexico and Venezuela as well) to simply Brazil or the Republic of Brazil. The President and Vice-President, who now must run together on the same ticket, will be chosen by indirect elections by means of an electoral college composed of members of Congress and delegates appointed by the state legislatures, instead of by direct, popular vote as prescribed by the 1946 Constitution.

The executive receives exclusive initiating powers in the legislation of budgetary, fiscal, and security matters. The national government receives exclusive rights to collect all taxes except those on real estate. Thus the national government claims responsibility for collecting 80 per cent of all taxation due, which then is distributed to the states and municipalities on a supposedly equitable basis. This was to ensure a more overall and common fiscal policy than that under the more centrifugal taxation system of the 1946 Constitution, which allowed the states and municipalities a greater proportion of direct incoming revenue. An interesting feature of the budgetary procedure grants the government the right to request multiyear appropriations for allocation to Brazil's underdeveloped regions.

Within the legislative sphere, the Chamber of Deputies and the Senate each have but forty-five total days upon which to act on an executive measure. However, if the President so wishes, he may ask action to be taken on an "urgent" piece of legislation in forty days in a joint session of congress. The legislators may not hold any other elective post, whether federal or state. A legislator loses his mandate if he fails to attend more than half of his chamber's ordinary sessions during each legislative period. The Chamber of Deputies are still elected by direct elections, serve four years, and each state must receive a minimum of seven deputies regardless of its population. The Senate, also directly elected, serves eight years with three senators apportioned to each state.

The president, in cases of declared public interest, may issue decrees (even while Congress is in session) in the areas of national security and public finances. As expected, the President has sole effective responsibility for the activities and functions of the armed forces. One of the President's more controversial powers allows him to permit foreign armed forces to pass over or remain temporarily on Brazilian territory. He may also decree a state of siege and order federal interventions. A new National Security Council has been formed to assist the President in the formulation and conduct of national security. The Constitution also provides that military men may remain on active service for up to two years while serving in any nonelective public civil employment. This is a particularly favorable article for an administration intent on utilizing military officials for the top bureaucratic posts. Should such an official serve longer than two years, he would merely be transferred to a reserve or retired list.

Furthermore, military court jurisdiction may extend to civilians accused of crimes against national security or military institutions, though an appeal to the Federal Supreme Court is allowed. This particular article, under conditions of institutional normalcy, has no constitutional precedent in Latin America and is perhaps the most single controversial clause in the entire document.

The Constitution of 1967 also contains a special chapter on political rights which withdraws the vote and the right to seek public office from those who have been deprived, temporarily or permanently, of their political rights,[6] something usually decreed at the discretion of the President. A political party in order to qualify for political competition must have received the support of 10 per cent of the electorate who voted in the last general election for the Chamber of Deputies. These votes must be distributed over two-thirds of the states, with a minimum of 7 per cent in each of them, as well as 10 per cent of the elected deputies in one-third of the states and 10 per cent of the senators. Added to these rather severe restrictions is the prohibition of alliances between parties. These provisions are geared to establishing an

[6] Assumed to mean an attempt against "democratic order" or to "effect corruption."

ideologically recognizable, two-party system. But they are hardly rooted in an organically conceived construct aimed at the furthering of mature and responsive party development.

Martial law and its inherent extra powers[7] may, during a period of normalcy, be extended for up to 120 days.[7] During such a period if two-thirds of the members of each house so vote, immunities for congressmen could be suspended.

Under the section labelled "The Economic and Social Order" the revolutionary government makes clear its economic philosophy. It seeks to suppress any abuse which might tend to eliminate competition. Expropriations can only be decreed by the federal government, thus making impossible the confrontation between a state governor (expropriating some utility) and a foreign government (asking indemnification). Intervention in the economic sector is permitted only when indispensable, for reasons of national security or extreme inefficiency. Profit sharing in industry is provided for as well as occasional management participation on the part of the workers. These provisions have been introduced in Brazil (as in countries as disparate as Mexico, France, and United States) to blunt possible class antagonisms and confrontations.

On the other hand, Chile has had only two major constitutions in its one hundred and fifty year Republican history. The first was promulgated in 1833 and lasted until 1925 when a successor document was written which still is the constitution. It is one of the more concise and simple documents in Latin America running less than half the length of the Brazilian Constitution. As in the previously discussed constitutions, first come the definitions of sovereignty, nationality, and citizenship. This is followed by a section called Constitutional Guarantees which also follows the pattern discussed. Within its articles, privileged classes are abolished as is slavery, and freedoms of religion, expression without censorship, assembly, association and right to petition governmental authorities are all provided for. Education is construed as a governmental responsibility, and primary education is obligatory. Personal property, the home, and personal correspondence are inviolable.

Article 21 established a unique Chilean institution called the Comptroller General. Appointed by the President, it is an autonomous institution which performs legal-administrative functions, controls the revenues and expenditures of the national treasury, and acts as a general censor and keeper of the nation's accounts. The Comptroller's decisions are binding on the President of the country, though it is rare that there is any conflict between the two. Should there be, the differences are worked out in private. All money bills and decrees pertaining to the nation's finances may be ruled upon by the Comptroller General as to their constitutional legality. The

[7] See article 152, paragraph 2.

constitution also provides that public forces are essentially obedient and that no armed force can deliberate. Obviously as a response to the 1925 military intervention into the Chilean parliamentary session, the constitution of that same year states that any resolution taken by governing or legislative powers by the demand of or in the presence of the armed forces, with or without arms, is null and cannot take effect.

So that there would be no repetition of the delaying powers of parliament which were so flagrantly employed after 1891, the Constitution of 1925 provides that if Congress does not act upon the budget within that prescribed amount of time the budget automatically passes into law. Again to avoid any excess by parliament, deputies and senators may not vote salary increases for themselves during the current legislative period but only for the following one.

In the section devoted to law enactment, the Chilean Constitution further weakens the prerogatives of Congress by allowing it the right to only accept, diminish, or reject executive policies that advocate new expenditures for government programs or salaries. Congress, in other words, may not amend the character of an executive initiative nor augment the quantity involved. As in the other Latin American constitutions, the president of Chile is given the right to intervene in the provinces and in case of foreign attack or internal disturbance, he may declare a state of siege. Because the provinces and departments of a unitary state are more administrative than political jurisdictions, such intervention has a much more legal justification since the provincial intendants, comparable to nonelected governors, are presidential appointees.

The Chilean Constitution is amended much more easily than constitutions of federal systems. Amendments are approved by a simple majority of both houses of Congress the same as any other law, the only distinction being that if Congress and the President disagree, if he has vetoed the original amendment and Congress has again approved the amendment by two-thirds, the President has the prerogative to put the issue before the people by way of a popular plebiscite, something President Allende has promised to do.

Similarly, the Argentine Constitution is one of the shortest Latin American constitutions, the most readable, and that most patterned after the brief United States Constitution. The constitution was written in 1853 with short amendments made in 1860, 1898, and 1957. It is the oldest Latin American constitution in operation today, briefly supplanted by the Perón Constitution of 1949 and reestablished in 1957. It is a well organized document with a preamble and two major parts, the first dedicated to rights and guarantees and the second to the governmental authorities of the country.

The preamble is an almost exact replica of the preamble of the United States Constitution with some added references to peculiarly Argentine preoccupations. For example, it refers to the existence of preexisting pacts among member provinces as if to emphasize that any new found unity would not be at the expense of provinces committed to a new nation-state. As the North American founding fathers, the Argentine constitution makers were deeply concerned with the need to strike an effective compromise that would last. The preamble also differs from the North American one in that it ". . . secures the blessings of liberty" not only ". . . to ourselves, to our posterity" but ". . . to all men in the world who wish to dwell on Argentine soil." Here is a direct reference to the Argentine hope of stimulating immigration from Europe, which it felt would be necessary to a developing nation. This was the fervent hope of Alberdi, the principal architect of the Argentine Constitution.

In the first part of the Constitution, the Roman Catholic Church, as in Peru, is given support by the Argentine state. Each province is guaranteed the right to adopt its own constitution. The federal government reserves for itself the right to intervene in the provinces in order to either guarantee a republican form of government or to repel foreign invasions. Article 6 has been frequently invoked throughout Argentine history by democratic and dictatorial administrations alike. Presidents Sarmiento and Irigoyen intervened as much, proportionally, as did Perón. As in the United States Constitution, there are many articles dedicated to abrogating economic, political, and legal barriers among the several Argentine provinces which hitherto had jealously guarded their unilateral controls. Argentine citizens are guaranteed the rights of travel, work, association, speech and writing without censorship, rest from work each week, a minimum wage, free trade unionism, and the right to strike and to bargain collectively. The state is responsible for social security, retirement pay and pensions, full family protection under welfare, and decent housing.

Under "rights and guarantees" slavery is not recognized nor are the prerogatives of birth and blood thus assuring all individuals equal rights under the law. Property is held inviolable except for reasons of public utility. Article 18 assures all accused persons a series of guarantees all of which fall under due process of law. Article 23 provides the President with the right to declare a state of siege and to suspend constitutional guarantees. A subsequent article explicitly encourages European immigration especially in the areas of farming, industry, and the arts and sciences and places no restrictions or tax burdens of any kind upon their entry.

Thus we have briefly scanned important provisions of the constitutions of five of the major Latin American nations seeking clues to their political history as much as guidelines to their current political behavior. These documents are integral parts of a nation's political culture and are testimony to widely shared national experiences.

The five constitutions, like most constitutions, concentrate on what man cannot do as much as on what he is allowed to do. They are all amalgams of guarantees and proscriptions. The later the constitution the more emphasis placed on a whole catalog of guarantees, many of which are far removed from individual rights. Such was the case of the Mexican and Brazilian Constitutions. Eighteenth and nineteenth century constitutions like those of Argentina and the United States are simpler and more basic frameworks for a political system, and there is less emphasis upon enumerating every potential right of man in society. In Latin America restrictions on the central government have gradually weakened by the use of implied powers while individual guarantees have been encroached upon whenever social stability has been in doubt. It is important to keep in mind that the Argentine Constitution was written during its authoritative period, which accounts for its balanced formula for strong executive powers along with certain rights given the provinces. This Constitution is very concerned with the basic organization of a state and the kind of arrangements that will allow it to survive. The Chilean Constitution was written during the aggregative period of the country's development, thus much attention is paid to the problems of capitalization, labor, and the government's role in the social sphere in general. The Mexican and Brazilian Constitutions, written during the distributive period of each nation, demonstrate a great concern with social and labor guarantees and with the role of government as the great social and economic arbitrator and benefactor. These "distributive constitutions" are unashamedly nationalistic and propagandistic, which accounts for their vehemence, pomposity, and long-windedness. They are twentieth century documents concerned with the explicit espousal of their national character. The United States and Argentine Constitutions are rather soberly framed bodies of laws meant to depict and predict political relationships rather than to self-consciously ideologize or eulogize their nations.

Thus it is important to know the atmosphere in which a constitution is drawn up since it is a political document written by politicians who usually happen to be lawyers. These individuals, even the best of them, are prisoners of the time and circumstances in which they live. The authors of the Argentine Constitution were concerned with launching a viable and unified state; the Mexican in authorizing a veritable social revolution; the Peruvian in stabilizing society under a paternal and noncontroversial authority; the Chilean in strengthening executive powers vis-à-vis a hitherto dominant parliament which had been a roadblock to social legislation for three decades; and the Brazilian in reestablishing political stability after two decades of political turmoil while at the same time retaining the social and economic programs begun under Vargas and others. And so it goes, each document reflecting its political and historical ecology.

None of the constitutions studied represent a patient façade. These constitutions, unlike the Stalin Constitution of 1936 and the Perón Constitution of 1949, were not just so many words put forth by authoritarian governments in an effort to create an impression of democracy. The guarantees are not so outlandish and preposterous as to be inapplicable, nor are any limitations on the executive so stringent as to make their adherence a prelude to anarchy.

Within this context of political institutions and attitudes, the questions remain: Is there a real commitment to democracy in Latin America today? What are the current views of authority? What is politically legitimate?

In general, democratic institutions have as yet not taken root. There is, however, an ever greater acceptance of such institutions and the increased role of government as the public mediator of social inequalities. Democracy is possible mainly because the rigidities of a communistic system do not meet the psychological and social needs of most Latin Americans. The individualism observable in Latin American social organizations and personal relationships would seem to readily adapt to a democratic society were it not for the large degree of organization and discipline required of an efficient democratic system. The inculcation of democracy must await reform in many areas, such as law enforcement, governmental anonymity, educational commitment, and tax-assessment changes. Class preferences, social conventions, and prenational loyalties must also first be overcome. Democracy requires respect for institutions, acceptance of peaceful transitions of government, and an opposition which is loyal to the social fabric. Only a small number of Latin American societies have achieved these political conditions. A spirit of social engineering is still not possessed by those who seek power and office; however, the Latin American mentality is not "authoritarian" but "laissez-faire," which makes it quite prepared for at least the theory of democracy. Democratic institutions offer less of a monolithic threat to the Latin way of life than a minority caste dictatorship or class authoritarianism.

The phenomenon of Cuba perhaps best exemplifies the extent to which political pride preconditions and exposes political cultures to radical new governmental approaches. The extreme Yanquiphobia and heartfelt pride at escaping North American dominance decidedly undermined democratic pretensions and possibilities in Castro Cuba. Peronism in Argentina and several communist parties in Latin America all have catered to a sense of national pride which occasionally has acted at variance to democratic development.

Severe upheavals and dissension in Latin America are a constant reminder of the continuing commitment to democratic theory. This commitment is often so intense that energies are dissipated in activity against undemocratic regimes. The new democratic governing groups have been so exhausted that they are often unable to resolve animosities and elicit support from the society as a whole.

The meaning and relevance of authority in Latin America is extremely complex. In its most rudimentary pattern it is likely to be very rarely delegated and, even less, shared. Parliamentary experiences, for example, have been confused and unsuccessful. The dilution of presidential authority appears to be incompatible with Latin American conceptions of political responsibility, which has sometimes led to cruel and wanton dictatorships.

Few, however, have had the temerity to foster totalitarian systems. The Latin American political culture opposes the stultification of personal alternatives yet tolerates strength, the active pursuit of power, and dynamic leadership.

From another perspective, however, this conception of authority mitigates an organic, integrative, democratic system that requires a rather high degree of public-mindedness, intergroup cooperation, and a certain amount of abnegation of individualism. The authority concept in Latin American political culture then has not only by and large prevented rampant totalitarianism, but it has confronted public policy with cultural propensities that often cripple democratic, responsible behavior. Thus authority and its continual breakdown have competed with peaceful transition, quiet elections, and delegation of responsibility expected of mature democracies, the result of which has often meant the preeminence of extenuating circumstances over legal continuity.

The desire for liberty combined with the need for excessive authority reaches back into the history of Latin America, to the passive and accepting indigenous peoples, and the virulent self-assertive and spirited Spanish and Portuguese. Perhaps the major cause for this confusion is the mistaken identification of liberty with complete freedom and uninhibited self-assertiveness.

Though the assumption of authority in Latin America has not always been restrained by constitutional guidelines, neither has the naked employment of power been exercised with consistent disregard for the ideological and ethical constraints of the constitutions. Power has been used in many ways, but the right of most governments over the years to rule on behalf of the people has been generally recognized as legitimate. Of course, as Max Weber first indicated, legitimacy has been claimed by all governments, revolutionary or traditional. A moderate test of legitimacy is whether opposition groups accept the government as the duly constituted authority. This usually necessitates agreement as to the basic rules of procedures by which both aggregates of the majority and aggregates of the minority can live.

Legitimacy is a socially binding force between the rulers, who have most of the power, and the ruled, in whom rest the ultimate power to grant authority. Such legitimized cooperation is strengthened when the governments in power perform the major tasks of political development outlined in Part I. These include demonstrating strength through longevity and viability, augmenting the people's trust by showing compassion, and acting with justice and fairness among competing social claims. Legitimation of power also requires a supportive political culture. Authority is then established by a mixture of rational, charismatic, and traditional underpinnings.

Since the majority of Latin American countries are dominated by the executive, it is often difficult to determine which are the forces for change and which the forces for the status quo. The preponderant position of central governmental bureaucracies covers up the pushes and pulls that affect the social and political evolution of the country. The stresses and strains upon the system are much more difficult to discern when an administration has developed a full head of steam than when democratic processes require it to submit itself for public approval. It is, for the most part, only during periods of political transition, whether electoral or revolutionary, that conflicting concepts of government are distinguishable. It is usually toward the end of a particular administration's life that these products of dissent are unleashed. During these periods, which occur quite regularly in democratic systems and under dictatorial *continuismo*, one has the opportunity to test the legitimacy of the government, because the constitution, which is always democratically conceived, forces dictatorial and democratic regimes to hold either fraudulent or honest elections.

At such times it is also possible to observe the influence of political minorities and opposition groups. One is able to determine whether these groups are loyal, whether they have been coopted by the majority party, or whether they have become a visible opponent. Where political opposition is little more than farcical, it is during these periods of transition that the naked power of the government is best revealed. Similarly, the amount of respect for political alternatives also becomes clear. A dictatorship is likely to be at its weakest prior to an election, which is contradictory to its very dictatorial rule. Submitting to an election may even be construed as a sign of weakness or, at least, of throwing a bone to constitutional government. An ostensible democratic regime is also severely put to the test at election time.

Coups, revolutions, and other extralegal means of shifting the locus of power also serve the purpose of baring forces which previously were insidious and unidentifiable.[8] A dictatorial regime that is not sustained by a popular following is most likely to buckle when its mandate is scheduled to come under consideration. Legitimate democracies, as history has amply demonstrated, are more capable of surviving such popular tests of approval and thus are more apt to represent stability which is real rather than apparent. A pseudodemocratic regime is most likely to show its true colors when faced with the prospect of electoral defeat and may show its teeth near the eve of the event.

Governmental succession is also likely to demonstrate the absence of a definable elite which has been accepted by the majority of political participants. This type of deep-rooted institutional disagreement is most effectively channeled into opposition during periods of political transition. A postcharismatic leadership dilemma over naming a successor also gives a major oppor-

[8] The research of Harry Eckstein, using the *New York Times Index*, makes it clear, however, that the basic pattern of violence in Latin America is represented, not by coups, revolution, and mass terrorism, but by sporadic rioting not dissimilar from civil rights protests in the United States.

tunity to study rival leadership struggles and ideological patterns. Latin America, as most developing parts of the world, does not always demonstrate a continuous process of political change. Many political shifts are brought about by methods not usually considered legitimate or democratic by outsiders and generally not by a majority of the system's own participants. Such changes are at times considered necessary when the government does not provide legal means for and does not accept the idea of any loyal opposition.[9] Where there is no agreed upon ideology of development, political transition may result in instability. Again, when a government is directionless and has maintained its power merely through threats of violence, peaceful or violent change may bring on an unstable situation.

By and large elections are the most common means of affecting political transition today and the majority of Latin American nations rely on this essentially democratic mechanism. However, in many cases, including Brazil and Chile, though voting is obligatory, literacy requirements severely limit political participation. Of the five nations considered, only Argentina has an electorate of close to half of the total population. Thus elections are often symbolic of what only some of the population wants. Since literacy is below 50 per cent in much of Latin America, this electoral requirement often disenfranchises politically informed but uneducated groups of people. The monopoly of the communications media by the governing party tends to make impossible a genuine confrontation among several competing parties. Occasional electoral fraud and widespread electoral restrictions upon specifically determined political groups further tend to limit popular decision.

Nonelectoral changes of government are usually confined to coups and revolutions and a large variety of forceful alterations that can be categorized under these two general headings. Coups usually represent shifts of governing personnel without the accompanying institutional change, though this is by no means an iron law. In fact, one cannot prejudge the long range effects of a coup, since it is a *mechanism* of takeover that may later develop policies which are quite revolutionary.[10] The usual difference from a revolution as a means of change is that the coup leaders, once secure in victory, institute a revolution from above and are usually not committed to vast sectors of the population, as they would be had they ridden into power on

[9] William Kornhauser has suggested that certain rebellious forces may even contribute positively to the process of political development by limiting arbitrary power and/or extending civic rights. "Rebellion and Political Development," in Harry Eckstein (ed.), *Internal War: Problems and Approaches* (New York: Free Press, 1964), pp. 142–156.

[10] The problem of defining a coup d'etat is exemplified by David C. Rapoport in Carl J. Friedrich (ed.), *Revolution* (New York: Atherton, 1966), pp. 53–74. Rapoport supports the view that though most coups are very different from revolutions, some perform similar functions depending upon their ultimate accomplishments.

the basis of a widescale popular uprising. A revolution as a method of gaining power must be distinguished from revolutionary programs of government. The former is usually violent, while the latter is merely radical. However, the use of revolutionary means of attaining power usually results in a government that will undertake profound and long-range reforms.

There may be very little hint on the horizon of an impending coup, whereas the rumblings of revolutionary discontent are usually felt by labor strikes, peasant seizure of land, or isolated acts of revenge against the government long before the actual outbreak.[11] A coup usually emanates from the direction of part of the military and from a point inside the institutions of governmental authority. Thus it usually has the merit of being bloodless, since it is close to the control of power in the first place. A revolutionary situation is usually convulsive because it is a seizure of power by an organized group who usually have a popular following, who have hitherto not shared in the process of political control and leadership, and must now use violent means to attain the levers of power.

Most changes in Latin American governments have neither been violent nor, concomitantly it seems, profound. Though individual acts of bloodshed abound, the general coup d'etat is usually moderate. Though coups have for a long time been the most common means for governmental transition, contemporary governments of Latin America show signs of undertaking peaceful policy revolutions. Thus revolutionary minority groups, extremists of one persuasion or another, must use increasingly violent methods to topple basically representative governments. This phenomenon might be called the "minority revolution" in that though it is revolutionary in its desire to transform society, it does not receive mass support, and should it achieve political control, it might be an unpopular administration which must use force to keep its position of command.

Mexican transitions have been peaceful though limited to one party. From the Calles until the Echeverría administration, each President has filled out his six-year term of office without any major extra-party aberration. There has been some change within the PRI, but it has been primarily concerned with the nominating function rather than with any truly competitive electoral pattern. Political transitions have been institutionalized, and nowhere in Latin America is political succession carried on more smoothly.

Peru has been a rather closed political system, as in a sense is Mexico's, without the virtue of Mexico's stability. The military has been in command by means of coups for almost half of the period, from 1930 to 1970. Included

[11] Chalmers Johnson, *Revolutionary Change* (Boston: Little, Brown, 1966), p. 106, depicts, by means of a flow chart, several disequilibrating functional failures that may cause a revolution: (1) incoherent socialization, (2) inappropriate ensemble of roles (of elites), (3) dissension on goals, and (4) failure to resolve conflicts peacefully.

within the period of forceful control of power was an eight-year interlude under the directorship of Manuel Odría. Until the accession to the Presidency of Belaunde Terry of the Acción Popular, Peru had a limited government allowing only the Conservative party to alternate with the military. The Aprista party, until 1963 the most popular party, has never been accepted by the military as having a legitimate option for governmental control. In several elections beginning in 1931 and ending in 1962, the Apristas scored electoral victories only to be denied the office by the military. Thus succession in Peru has neither been peaceful nor democratic.

Brazil has had three parties which have participated in governing, which testifies, when compared to Mexico and Peru, to a looser and more pluralistic accession to political power. With the fall of the Vargas regime in 1945 the PSD served as governing party for five years. The PTB returned for five years until 1955 when the PSD reestablished control and later gave it away to the UDN in 1960. In 1961 with the resignation of Jañio Quadros, the PTB again acceded to power. There has been a sharing of power and considerable party "turnover."[12] Brazil until the military coup of 1964, presented a more positive picture of participation than the single-party system of Mexico or the electoral restrictiveness of Peru.

By far the best example of the use of democratic procedures combined with stable political transition has been Chile. It is the only nation in the whole of Latin America in which essentially "opposition" parties (Socialists, Communists) shared political power for a number of years. There have been numerous parties—Conservatives, Liberals, Socialists, Communists, inter-party alliances, Christian Democrats—all of which at one time or another have shared political power. There have been few constitutional crises since 1930, and minority representation has been for the most part safeguarded.

In Argentina, like Brazil, a combined military, dictatorial, and party government route has been followed. For 33 out of the last 40 years, dictatorial apparatuses and restrictive electoral provisions have been in existence, even though ostensibly free elections were carried out in the 1930s and during the Perón era. Distinct from Chile and Brazil, opposition parties have not competed equitably, and military coups have been the transitional means par excellence.

[12] This is largely because the Brazilian leadership has been rather successful at co-opting societal groups before they could assume militant stances. James Rowe, for example, cites the fact that Brazil had labor legislation before it had much experience with industrial life and trade unions before it developed a self-conscious labor force. "The Revolution and the System: Notes on Brazilian Politics," *American University Field Staff Reports,* East Coast South American Series, vol. 12, no. 4 (July 1966), pp. 1–2.

CHAPTER 9 Ideologies and Political Culture

As the ancient Greek city-states had an intellectual fiber and rational scepticism that made theirs the "age of philosophy" and as the middle ages, with its dogmatism and serene conceptions of reality, has been described as the "age of belief," so by the eighteenth century one sees the approaching age of ideology. Though the Latin American nations were not national entities during the ages of philosophy and belief, the ideas of these periods managed to compete until very recently with ideological conceptions of the world.

Though the Latin American nations took the cue for their independence movements from imported European ideologies, the nineteenth century represented a struggle between the forces of eighteenth century rationality, upon which their national independence movements were predicated, and the forces of previous centuries of human thought. Ideology as a modern phenomenon only began to make its imprint upon Latin America by the end of the nineteenth century. Socialism, communism, nationalism, liberalism, conservatism, fascism, and Christian Democracy—all basically political ideologies—were influential in Europe before their absorption or development in Latin America.

The American, French, and Industrial Revolutions were viewed from the Latin American angle with interest, but their ideologies were merely used as backdrops and trappings to events which bore little relation to these major events in North America and Western Europe. This is only too well documented by the paucity of deep-seated social and political change during the greater part of the nineteenth century.

With the beginning of the twentieth century, one sees the first instance of ideology related to political movements. Perhaps nationalism was the single most effective political ideology, with socialism being the next. The use of political ideology for widespread popular acceptance of a particular mode of organizing society was not common in Latin America until the Mexican Revolution of 1910. Until then, in the majority of Latin American countries political ideology was the private preserve of the leading elites. Through the Mexican Revolution derivations of socialism finally began to seep down to the masses and gain popular currency. Other quasi-socialistic movements arose like the Aprista movement in Peru and Peronista movement of Argentina. The former was tinged with a special concern for the indigenous peoples of Latin America, following as it did, the Mexican Revolution. The latter was a highly nationalistic version of socialism, which borrowed from the Mussolini experiment in Italy.

The real impetus in Latin America toward a widespread employment of political ideology was finally given by economic and social frustrations. It was hoped that institutional-governmental changes might quickly effect socio-economic transformations.

Thus one can really only begin speaking about widespread national political ideology in Latin America by the first quarter of this century. Previously, ideology had first been a private affair of the ruling families reflecting their views of nineteenth century economic liberalism and, later, the belief system of a small elite in each of the Latin American countries.

To study ideology as one aspect of political culture implies that the ideology has been generally accepted by the public and is an important influence on social and political development. As such, nationalism has been the overriding national political ideology in Latin America. Though nationalism is not unique to Latin America, it did find a very trenchant and continuous influence there. It has had far more universal application and has been able to cross religious, class, and party lines, something which the ideologies of socialism, fascism, and communism (or, for that matter, democracy) have never managed to accomplish. It can be said that nationalism is easy to inculcate because it reaches down to the lowest common denominator and that its application requires the least amount of comprehension and effort.

Next to nationalism as a subsidiary ideology one hesitatingly places democracy, which, though it is supposedly a goal of many isms, is a concern in many Latin American nations today, particularly as it bears relationship to the underlying attractions of individuality and liberty in the Latin American political culture.

Indeed, the overconcern with individual freedom and personal dignity retards the growth of the kind of nationalism that is a prerequisite for economic growth and political maturity.

Though it has been for the most part isolated from the cross currents of European ideological conflict in the nineteenth and twentieth centuries, each view of social and political life has found some response in Latin America. Though nationalism has found the best conditions for development and growth, each ideology has left its mark on twentieth century Latin America.

Conservatism, widely accepted by Latin American leaders in the nineteenth century, is today generally an outmoded doctrine of government. Its tenets are anathema to the speed at which these nations wish to develop economically. The Conservative political ideology of acceptance of a hierarchical division of power and of creeping evolutionary shifts in society has proven much too slow for impatient Latin American leaders of the twentieth century. The last several decades have proven to the elites in Latin America that the inherent proposition of conservatism which states that thorough changes of governmental policy are ill-considered is not necessarily true and that they may, to the contrary, redound to the benefit of the majority of the people. Conservatism serves a nonvolatile, insulated nation with little frustration and a high degree of creature comforts, but Latin America with its tremendous population growth rate, unemployment crises, and educational deficiencies cannot readily accept or afford a conservative expression of political life without forsaking most of its population. To adopt a conservative ideology would mean to remain subservient to other nations and without the power or economic vitality of a mobilized nation. Maintenance of the social order, one of the cardinal principles of conservatism, is a luxury that these development-conscious leaders cannot afford, especially since conservatism has been rejected by the developed nations of the West—including England, the home of nineteenth century conservatism.

The requirements of industrialization are not met by a conservative ideology which would maintain the developing countries of Latin America as raw material suppliers for the industrial nations, a relationship which most Latin American leaders hope to break. According to the conservative view, any tampering with normal economic and social processes is inappropriate and may disrupt basic and normal human relationships. In general the matter in which the Latin American nations have been increasingly experimenting has not been compatible with the conservative tradition.

The propositions of liberalism, once so favored by the forward-looking intellectuals of the nineteenth century, are as discredited as those of conservatism. As an opposing view to Spanish mercantilism and trade restrictions, liberalism found widespread currency throughout Latin America in the early nineteenth century. It was a pragmatic philosophy useful for the development of Latin America's trading potential. With the modern need for incipient industrial growth and the creation of larger Latin American markets, which may call for protectionism and import substitution policies, free-trade liberalism is no longer sufficient. As a democratically oriented middle-class philosophy, it achieved its greatest following in the latter half of the nineteenth century and was used as an ideological weapon to strike at the church's predominant position in society and to permit a slow refocusing of the emphasis from rural landowners to urban commercial classes. The latter were considered to be the bulwark of prosperity and national power. However, when liberalism failed to close the gap of poverty between their own and the developed nations, it too lost favor among the ruling elites. Liberalism had no major weapon in its ideological arsenal to combat poverty, illiteracy, and other social disequilibriums; rather it assumed the state to be no more than a "night-watchman." Incompatible with the social orientation of many developed countries, liberalism contributed little to Latin American plans for social change. Liberal revolutions, such as the American and French, were not immediately imitated in Latin America, and when Latin America finally was able to make its own antiaristocratic insurgence one hundred years later, these revolutionary examples were no longer very meaningful.

Liberal emphasis on political equality, free elections, and civil rights were compatible with twentieth century Latin American developments; but they essentially excluded economic and social goals. Thus today there is no Latin American government that adheres to either the conservative or liberal principle as a guideline for making domestic and foreign policy. Conservative and liberal parties exist in almost every country, but they have lost support everywhere, and their following is diminishing.

Socialism made its first imprint on early twentieth century Latin America through the movements of international socialism and the famed ideological disputes carried on in Europe between the various shades of Marxists. Latin American proletariat groups did not appear to take strong sides at first between the Marxists of Socialist and Communist orientation; however governmental suppression of communism coupled with the more compromising views of socialism after World War I left the Socialists in a stronger position to organize the workers into the first syndicalist movements of Latin America. Thus Socialism, willing to work within existing liberal systems for a more distant social evolution rather than clandestinely battle for the immediate and violent takeover of power, was permitted to develop roots in Latin America. Socialism developed in Latin America, as elsewhere, because liberalism was unable to meet the demands of the socially and economically impoverished sectors of society. The first attempt to organize the working man for political and economic objectives was carried out by socialists. However, in time, its international orientation, its appeal to intellectuals, its heavy emphasis on study, discussion, and literary circles, and its neglect of the peasant and other "prenational" groups began to limit its following and left it open to the imprecations of being incompatible with patriotism and of adjusting its thinking to European rather than to national ideology. To many culture-bound Latin Americans, the verbal conflicts concerning dialectical materialism, revisionism, utopian socialism, and economic determinism all had little meaning and appeared as some foreign debate about alien concerns removed from the Latin American reality.

Christian Democracy amalgamates ideological suppositions of recent socially-conscious papal encyclicals and traditional democratic theory. Economic theory among Christian Democrats represents an interlocking admixture of socialism and capitalism. In this confluence of political and economic theory, Christian Democracy appears as that set of ideological commitments most in conformity with the pervasive overtures of nationalism so prevalent among political elites in Latin America. Despite Christian Democracy's overseas origins and international, or at least Inter-American, tenor, the movement as a main force in contemporary Latin America seems predominantly concerned with overriding national issues. It is making its appeal in the nationalist vernacular and has more multiclass adherence than the Socialist movement.

Christian Democracy slowly developed in the pre-World War II years, but it was not until the mid-1950s that it flourished as a significant contemporary ideology and political alternative. Its most meaningful and imposing impact has been felt in Chilean and Venezuelan politics. There Christian Democracy has managed to fill an ideological vacuum between the class-conscious socialist movements and the traditional conservative and old-fashioned liberal philosophies. The movement now competes with other democratically oriented reformist groups who oppose the Christian Democratic links to Catholic pronouncements.

To countervail this categorization as a clerical movement, the Christian Democrats have espoused national programs of welfare legislation, mixed state-capitalist enterprises, land distribution and reform, and community development—all concerns that are crucial for Latin American economic development and meaningful to large political constituencies.

The Communist Revolution of 1917 was understood by all classes, and it became widely popular among the lower classes throughout the world, including Latin America. However, the subversive nature of postrevolutionary activities in Latin America plus the split with the Democratic Socialists weakened the Communist movement in Latin America. The interminable Communist party shifts in relation to the war in Europe also discredited the party in the eyes of the nationally oriented leaders of the Americas. Soviet imperial designs in the post-war period added to the growing uncertainty with which the Latin American nations viewed the Communist revolution.

Fascism and Nazism had a short-lived popularity at the beginning of World War II in several of the Latin American nations. This sympathy was somewhat a reaction to Anglo-American dominance, and they had no wish to fall under the aegis of new forces from the European continent. The Latin American tradition of neutralism vis-à-vis extra-continental conflicts guided the foreign policy of the Latin American nations, especially the larger, more independent ones. Here was the beginning of what was to become a tendency among many smaller nations in the world to remain unaligned vis-à-vis the major powers. However, the threats of Nazi totalitarianism combined with United States victories as well as economic and psychological pressures committed most of the Latin American countries to the allied cause by mid-1943.

Underlying the development of socialism, Christain democracy, communism, and national socialism was the much more important ideology of nationalism.[1] In analyzing this most subtle of all ideologies, one must go back to the roots of national consciousness in Latin America.

Nationalism can be defined as the geographical, cultural, and historical

[1] Rupert Emerson sees nationalism as the single most important force in the revolutionary movements of Asia and Africa; revolutionary in the sense that legitimacy is increasingly defined in terms of the people's aspirations. "Nationalism and Political Development," *Journal of Politics*, vol. 22, no. 1 (February 1960), pp. 1–28.

identity that amalgamates peoples within a particular time and space.[2] This is nationalism described in its simplest and most general formulation—one that does not consider the various implications and suppositions associated with nationalism as a political ideology or political force.[3] Nationalism implies a wide ranging loyalty beyond one's immediate physical experience to an authoritative arbiter. Such subordination is usually consonant with political cultural values understood by the people and the leaders. Though associated with urbanization, modernization, universal education, and industrialization, a sense of national identification is necessary before the achievement of such development phenomena. In its earlier stages nationalism develops upon political rather than upon economic or social objectives. It is primarily a mood, an inclination, and a desire to certify pride in national autonomy. The use of such nationalism is an effective and self-conscious political mechanism to achieve national cohesion.

The independence movements in Latin America were essentially nationalist acts as people born in the Americas strove to implant their political control on territories dominated by people whose principal loyalties were to overseas nations. Thus local loyalty replaced one that had seemed more and more incompatible with local identities and interests. A sort of loosely allied empire was eventually replaced by over a dozen struggling national units, each of which was faced with overwhelming problems of integrating their populations into a nation-state. Thus the independence leaders shared several identifiable and mutual traditions. They all were loyal to the new lands in the Western Hemisphere, they all rebelled against the tyranny (economic and political) of the Spanish monarchs, and they all held similar aristocratic conceptions of the formulation of a new society.

The development of anticlericalism in many of the Latin American nations by mid-nineteenth century was an assertion of nationalism. The anticlerics were not against the theories and principles of the church per se, but against dogmas and doctrines which originated overseas. In Uruguay, Brazil, Mexico, and Chile the church-state struggle was particularly invigorating for the development of national consciousness. Another test of nationalism in the nineteenth century was the amount of energy spent on subduing local and regional caudillos. In every case these internal battles helped to foster a spirit of national unity. The subjugation of local to national interests was prerequisite to the development of national constitutions which supplied the framework for the incorporation of diverse geographical units within the

[2] See Carleton Hayes' formulations of the various aspects of nationalism, interpretations that have influenced each subsequent writer on the subject. *Essays on Nationalism* (New York: Macmillan, 1928).

[3] Hans Kohn gives a comprehensive survey of the historical significance of nationalism as a powerful moving force. *Nationalism: Its Meaning and History* (Princeton: Van Nostrand, 1965), pp. 9–91.

nation's jurisdiction. Constitutions in Latin America prior to the consolidation of national territories were more formal creations. The more lasting constitutions in Latin America came on the eve or on the following morn of national movements of unification. A change in the type of leaders was also evident. From Iturbide to Juárez, from Pedro I to Pedro II, from Rivadavia to Rosas, there was a noticeable reorientation in leadership conceptualization. These new breeds of men no longer had any European loyalties and were bent on establishing strong and sovereign nations. They sought to use original instead of foreign methods to accomplish similar tasks. None saw any alternative to the creation of nationalism as a basic and inevitable ingredient of their new states, and each had an essential pride in national undertakings.

Occasional victories, diplomatic and military (although these were not common on the American scene), increased the resolve to apply national solutions to domestic problems. Mexican nationalism was particularly bolstered by Mexico's victory over the French in the 1860s, by their hapless but nevertheless romantic defense of Mexican soil against the United States invasions in the 1840s, and again the invasion in 1914 during the Wilson administration. Brazil's national prowess was stimulated by her overwhelming victory in the Paraguayan War of 1865–1870. Chilean nationalism might be traced to Chile's military victories over the Peruvians and Bolivians in the War of the Pacific from 1879–1883, and by the same token, Peruvian and Bolivian nationalism was heightened by their defeat in this same significant war. Latin American self-determination was most eloquently espoused by the Argentines and the Mexicans throughout the early twentieth century. Though Latin America as a whole was a relatively peaceful continent in terms of internation warfare and diplomatic intrigue during the nineteenth century, there were enough confrontations to engender nation-state self-respect at national accomplishments.

However, the greatest impetus to nationalism in Latin America, as elsewhere in the world, awaited the development of a small but nationally minded middle class. It is under their banners and through their formulations that nationalism developed and became a cohesive movement.

Today Latin America has many of the requirements of so-called "cultural" nationalism: It has a common racial amalgamation, a common religious orientation, a common language for the most part, a European-conceived intellectul foundation, and a general, if loosely defined, commitment to democracy. These are basic and long-run strong points for the development of nationalism as a political force. In a sense they even have had common historical and contemporary enemies—first Spain, then the United States with the possibility of the Soviet Union in the near future. The common memories, shared experiences, and coincidental historical records coexist today with the common goals of industrialization, modernization, and the betterment of social standards. Latin American leadership has accepted the access of the mass of people to the sharing of national resources, and governments have accepted the responsibility of making citizens and political participators out of parochial peasant nonparticipants as well. All this need not imply any serious humanitarian commitment on the part of the leadership but an enlightened self-interest approach to national development and political power. There is an attempt being made to harness not only natural but human resources.

Thus nationalism today is striving to create a basis for national integrity and interest. Nationalism is no longer confined to a mere distaste for the foreigner and his ideas or his influence, but rather it has developed into a positive force for national consolidation and political integrity. Effective, modern nationalism, despite the fact that it is often undertaken for diverse reasons, implies the democratization of society. It means the incorporation of more and more people into a better and fuller mode of existence. The state begins to satisfy the rising expectations that it has originally created.[4]

How successful has nationalism as a development ideology been in contemporary Latin America, and what problems remain unresolved in the drive for modernization?

Though Latin American independence is over a century and a half old, problems of internal consolidation still exist. However, this problem of political integration does not necessarily dampen antiforeign chauvinism in times of national crises, but it does hamper the development of the economic community. From an institutional, legal, and geopolitical point of view a general sense of nationality is assured in each of the Latin American nations and the few attempts by Europe and North America at invasion and intervention were eventually repulsed or were withdrawn voluntarily. The "balkanization" of the Latin American states was not brought about by any foreign power but was the result of patriotism in early nineteenth century Latin America. The breakup of Gran Colombia, La Plata, and Central America came more as a result of nationalist demands rather than foreign plans to "divide and conquer." Despite this early awakening of Latin American nations, they have met with overwhelming obstacles to the development of national cohesion, something much harder to implant and less dependent on romance or heroics. The problem has been to consolidate in the absence of any external threat to national sovereignty.

Once these external dangers are minimized, a process of internal integration may be initiated. It is in the twentieth century during the distributive period of their national development that Latin American governments have begun to perceive the immense challenge that this integration of its peoples implies. They now fully realize that a common tongue, common religion, com-

[4] This thesis is advanced by Rupert Emerson, "Nationalism and Political Development," and K. H. Silvert (ed.), *Expectant Peoples: Nationalism and Development* (New York: Random House, 1963), pp. 3–38.

mon social mores, common national and racial background, and common historical symbols are not automatic assurances of political and economic development, and of themselves, they cannot provide national power and prestige.

National development then is a broad process which must include bringing into active social life hitherto isolated and compartmentalized groups who are only existing within the nation. It is in the success of this process that one can distinguish the developed from the developing countries.

There is a correlation between the numbers of people a nation has mobilized into the national political community and the economic market place and the nation's ability to develop its economy and pluralize her social functions.[5] Increasing industrialization has developed Latin America's infrastructure. Again by stimulating intercommunications, contact among citizens, class mobility, and a general accession to cultural programs and educational media, the nations of Latin America now have a more refined tool for unification. Expanding technology is having an appreciable influence on the speed at which a developing nation's peoples are being transferred from parochial to participant status. This is a meaningful change, since a participant member of society not only earns income and pays taxes but belongs to social groups, votes, reads, and interprets public policy. The parochial member of society is isolated from most if not all of these functions and therefore does little to contribute to the nation's economy, information resources, and educational level. He also does little to reveal his material necessities or his political tendencies. It is essential that the government be able to interpret social requirements in the process of political and economic development. Almond's "input" factors of political socialization, interest articulation and aggregation, and political communication are essential requirements of modern nationalism because they offer the necessary feedback from public to government. Without intercommunication a government may be working in a vacuum which might foster political instability.

It therefore becomes paramount for a developing nation to "universalize" nationalism to all corners of its territory. Governments of developing countries are in the process, then, of eroding traditional cultures on their way to establishing modern, "national" cultures. It involves the concept of the "utilization" of hitherto "underutilized" peoples living within but not contributing to the state entity.

Most Latin American societies are now fully in the process of establishing a national community, and in the immense drive toward this goal many middle-range problems must be faced. A major challenge exists in the process of urbanization. City life is capable of breaking up feudal economic structures and autocratic family structure. However, during the transitional period or the

[5] This thesis is attributed to Karl Deutsch's *Nationalism and Social Communication* (Cambridge: MIT Press, 1953).

period in which the so-called "traditional" men are becoming acquainted with modern forms, a break-down often occurs which affects newly arrived migrant's immediate capacity to function effectively. At the same time the national government is not always prepared to educate, feed, employ, and protect such individuals. Almost every urban area in Latin America is now in the midst of this critical stage in the formation of a modern nation-state. The new elements in the cities often become a source of political pressure because of their growing sophistication in manipulating authority.[6] Put crudely, many governments have unleashed national forces which they have not been able to totally control. The willingness and ability of contemporary Latin American governments to respond to these masses of hitherto unintegrated people is one of the essential factors for political stability.

Mexico

Though the alienation of the individual Mexican from the national community still exists as a large-scale problem, in general an integrating nationalism is replacing the more primitive nationalism in Mexico.

First of all, the Mexicans have adjusted to ideas and realities that once were a major source of national frustration and inhibition. Mexican nationalism has come of age by way of a slow maturation achieved through domestic political experience and international relations. The Mexican Revolution was launched against an upper-class structure which was subsequently discredited and today is no longer a threat to the governing elites or to the goals of contemporary Mexican ideology. The former rural elite of prerevolutionary times has been defeated, bringing harmony to the political environment and assuring a consensus among most political activists. Secondly, the church, once an ideologically bifurcating institution, was relegated to a secondary position in the national political community after being defeated in open combat between 1917–1930. Later accommodations to the church were made not because of a negotiated truce between equal combatants but because of the state's desire to accommodate a potentially alienated institution. Thirdly, the expropriation of foreign oil companies in 1938 under the presidency of Cárdenas fostered an increasing nationalism. For Mexico this was an especially significant victory over foreign capital since national identity was preserved.

These significant governmental stances against the landowning classes, the clergy, and foreign capital inspired Mexican confidence in the validity of her national postures. Such victories have been rare in nineteenth century

[6] See William Mangin, "Latin American Squatter Settlements: A Problem and a Solution," *Latin American Research Review*, vol. 2, no. 3 (Summer 1967), pp. 65–92.

Mexico when the latifundios reigned, when the church lost a battle to Juarez but won the war under Díaz, when foreign capital investments were given free reign, and foreign armies under the leadership of Texans, North Americans, and Frenchmen occupied and annexed vast portions of Mexican soil.

World War II and its aftermath has seen a growing self-confidence in Mexican solutions to Mexico's developmental problems. The basic problem remaining today is that of whether to capitalize rapidly, and thereby sacrifice another generation of the poorer elements in society, or whether to distribute immediately, and thereby possibly stultify rapid economic growth. This ambivalence and uncertainty can be traced to deeply ingrained national mores and to the psyche of the Mexican. The seeds of the dilemma may be found in the original relationship between conquering Spaniard and defending Indian. The struggle between the two resulted in the victory of the Spaniard over the Indian; however, the physical victory was complicated by the social and moral claims of the Indians. In the centuries following the conquest of Mexico, the conflict and the guilt-ridden shame remained. There has been a ceaseless preoccupation over the debased social and economic position of the Indian.

As Mexico slowly became racially amalgamated (an Indian majority absorbing a Spanish minority) into an essentially Mestizo Nation, the problem has gradually diminished. However, the blatant and obvious defense of the Mestizo culture may perhaps be hiding a continuing insecurity as to the meaning of national character in modern Mexico. The Mexican political culture has inherited a distrust of the rapacious white European and an empathy and loyalty toward the exploited Indian. It is enough to say that Cuauhtemoc is respected in the Mexican history while Cortés is portrayed as a villain.[7] *Malanchismo* means the betrayal of Mexican nationalism to a foreigner and refers to Cortés's mistress who was used by the Spaniards as interpreter, spy, and general guide to the Aztec empire. This ambivalence has led to the infusion of psychological aberrations into the political culture even in contemporary times. While the Mexican, seeking to modernize, wishes to use all the elements at his disposal provided by the developed world (of which the conquering Spaniard is symbolic), he is reluctant to adopt foreign solutions for domestic problems (of which the Mexican Indian is symbolic). This duality was much stronger while Mexico was asserting its patriotic variety of nationalism. Today compromise is being worked out.

The Spanish-Indian duality becomes apparent in the "machismo" complex among the Mexican male by the way he ruthlessly subjugates the women in his life, of which the submissive and enduring Mexican Indian is again symbolic. Thus he carries on the tradition of his Spanish forefathers. This ambivalence that every Mexican shares, to be rational, hard-headed, and

[7] Frederick C. Turner, *The Dynamic of Mexican Nationalism* (Chapel Hill: University of North Carolina Press, 1968), p. 175.

realistic, on one hand, and considerate, socially aware, and moral on the other, has found its way into contemporary political and economic views of society and is the source of the growing Mexican debate concerning which way to approach economic development and whether another generation of the lower classes must be sacrificed for developmental purposes. Few want to sacrifice the Indian on the altar of modernization, yet the developmental choice may lead to this and thus kindle the feeling of guilt among Mexicans.

Thus what we have to juxtapose is the older variety of Mexican nationalism with its wary view of foreigners, the status of the Indian, and the rigors of economic development which require modern nationalism. Because of its Indian population, there is no doubt that the leaders of Mexico would like to pursue economic development and social adjustment with equal vigor and dispatch. But this may prove impossible, and thus the stated objectives of the Mexican Revolution, which are continually espoused by Mexican leadership, may not always be followed by acts designed to provide the Indian and marginal mestizo classes with the amenities of life.

In any case, Mexican nationalism today is related to industrialization and a mixed system of government and private ownership. Xenophobia has been successfully relegated to the more realistic control over rather than escape from foreign capital. There is also a growing concern with modernization of the agricultural sector which would free the rural worker for urban employment in mass-producing units. Indeed, this is one of the areas in which the revolutionary ideology of uplifting the indigenous sectors of society conforms with national development criteria.

Another important area of convergence in recent years has been the success of Mexico's ruling groups in making their interpretations of constitutional traditions at different periods of development compatible with Mexican aspirations. President Lopez Mateos's 1961 state of the union address, for example, held that his government was "left within the constitution," while President Echeverría, during the 1970 electoral campaign, promised that his government would "not move to the left nor to the right but up. . . ."

The PRI has attempted to democratize the political system as far as is compatible with Mexican nationalism and the continuation of political stability and economic growth. This has resulted in minority parties receiving representation in Congress for percentages of over 2.5 per cent of the vote, up to 20 total deputies for each party.

Lastly, Mexican national ideology is compatible with its military nonalignment, its support of nonintervention and national self-determination, and its refusal to break diplomatically with Cuba. Pride in the viability of the Mexican Revolution gives Mexico the national cohesion which allows her to regard the Cuban Revolution as unnecessary for a nation that has already achieved a successful social transformation. This plus the utter weakness of

Mexican communism gives the Mexican leadership a good deal of self-confidence that they can avoid any dangers of Castro subversion. Recognition of the Castro government not only emphasizes Mexican political stability but reinforces Mexican nationalism.

Peru

Peruvian national identity as compared to Mexican was very slow in developing. Though Peru won her national independence at approximately the same time as Mexico, it neither underwent the important internal changes or the foreign penetrations that served to foster nineteenth century Mexican nationalism. The Peruvian nineteenth century political experience was unidimensional, and few internal or external developments were powerful enough to leave an imprint. The loss of much of Peru's territory to Chile in the War of the Pacific had some effect in terms of a reassessment of its national strength and the resolve to restore lost national pride.

Geographic isolation, class divisions, and a feudalistic economy combined to stultify a modern sense of nationalism in Peru. These socioeconomic relationships kept the vast majority of the people illiterate, out of the money economy, industrially unorganized, and commercially and socially unable to communicate.

The beginnings of nationalist mentality in Peru came on the heels of an intellectual revolution rather than the more practical social revolution as in Mexico. Despite the great impact of a new popular doctrine—Aprismo—it is closely identified with several individuals, the most noted being Victor Raúl Haya de la Torre. Aprismo developed as a political ideology and had developed some force by the mid-1920's. It is a self-conscious political idea that seeks to adapt European socialism, Mexican "indigenismo," and aspects of Marxism to the South American environment. Haya de la Torre, as promulgator of this movement, was exiled in 1923 and spent the next seven years traveling throughout Latin America and Europe. This long hegira to the "Meccas" of social revolution and ideological ferment greatly bolstered Haya's own original synthesis of modern socialist thought translated into the nationalist terminology of Peru and other countries of the Americas. Aprismo and its national promulgation in Peru became the most powerful ideological force for more than a generation, and by a revamping of Peruvian problems and prospects it marked the beginning of a modern conception of nationalism. It was not antiforeign nor overly chauvinistic, but represented a reassessment of Peruvian domestic problems and a turn inward upon itself rather than an act of aggression against the external world.

In Haya's many trips during his exile and during his periodic imprisonment, he gradually developed his political philosophy, much as Nehru had evolved his political and economic thought which he eventually promulgated against British dominance. As Nehru gleaned much from his frequent visits to London, so Haya made ample use of his sojourns to Mexico. The work of Vasconcelos, "Raza Cosmica," particularly impressed Haya and became one of the underlying motifs of Aprismo. Vasconcelos's theory revolved around the idea of amalgamating the Indian and European cultures and peoples into an original race never known before, a fusion of the three racial prototypes.

This became the underlying principle of Aprismo, which developed many other more practical formulations built on this basic "indigenista"-European cultural and racial synthesis. It was anti-imperialist in its formulation but differed essentially from the Leninism which saw imperialism as an inevitable outgrowth of an advanced stage of expanding capitalism. The Aprista view merely suggested a rigorous control of foreign capital while it recognized the necessity of foreign capital for development and the universality of the profit motive.

Aprismo sought the inter-Americanization of the Panama Canal not for military or demagogic reasons, but rather as a first step in the development of inter-American cooperation. Haya's view was that having worked collectively in a massive common venture, this experience could be enlarged upon to encompass a whole gamut of cooperative undertakings in the areas of political and economic organization. He hoped that such a small beginning would make clear to the Latin American nations their common needs and the necessity for working toward political and economic union. The Apristas felt that common cultural characteristics would assist in such a large joint endeavor. They also entertained, as early as the mid-twenties, the idea that each of the Latin American nations must eventually specialize in certain products because the great majority of them did not have a sufficiently large domestic market. Only Brazil was considered large enough to provide a market for its own internal production.

The Apristas feared that a confluence of productive undertakings would lead to severe competition which, according to Lenin's thinking, might lead to fratricidal warfare. The Apristas also supported nationalization of essential industries and the parcelization and distribution of land. In general, many of the ideas which the Apristas put forth four decades ago are now accepted economic and social alternatives promulgated by a variety of national governments, by the Alliance for Progress technical teams, and by the inter-American banking and financial community.

Paradoxically, though the Apristas have never succeeded in attaining power, many of their political and economic perceptions have now found response in the present Velasco military government, which may represent a feasible alternative to traditional Peruvian ideological positions.

Brazil

Brazil has not produced an indigenous ideology. Brazilian nationalism has been largely economic and is geared to the requirements of post-World War II economic development. There are historical reasons for the particular type of Brazilian nationalism or lack thereof. The monarchy of Pedro II was markedly international and cosmopolitan in direction. Brazil had no declared enemies and her boundaries were relatively secure. Pedro's personal predispositions favored looking toward Europe and the United States. He welcomed foreign innovation, traveled a great deal himself, and sought whenever possible to tie his realm to the republic of the United States and to the cosmopolitan constitutional monarchies of Western Europe. Universal appeal surpassed national appeal during most of Brazil's nineteenth century development.

The Republican government established a system of sectional politics which replaced the universalism of the Pedro II regime but did not itself establish any national myth or ethos. This dominance of state over national ideology continued until the dictatorship of Getulio Vargas, which broadened the sphere of political participation and heightened feelings of Brazilianism.

However, even today Brazilian nationalism is less strident and more moderate than the ideological nationalism of some of the other Latin American nations. Brazilian nationalist commitments rely little on national patriotism, despite the fact that there is tremendous pride in Brazil's achievements and stature. Brazilians have long taken sustenance from a nonideological view of political life which has permitted them to "muddle-through" difficulties by compromise solutions. They have elevated pragmatism to a social art, and this has often saved the Brazilian nation from bloody revolutions, political violence, and military fratricide.

The Brazilians are also proud of their historical capacity to integrate the races, and they feel that theirs is a unique experiment in the amalgamation of the cultures of the African and American continents. Brazilian leaders have reiterated at length that their role has been as mediator among the African and Western states. Brazil, they state, has a special contribution to make in this field. This ability at amalgamation has strengthened Brazilian aspirations of being one of the foremost leaders of the so-called independent bloc of nations.

Brazilians have been relatively successful in halting inflation, developing industry, and integrating Brazil's domestic economy. Since the Vargas administration and through every succeeding government, economic ventures have been the principal focus of Brazilian nationalism, including the founding of the Brazilian Petroleum Corporation (Petrobras), Kubitschek's development of the internal capital of Brasilia, Quadros' independent foreign policy and his rigorous attempts to rationalize the overly politicized Brazilian bureaucracy, Goulart's various measures to distribute land and his sanction of the nationalization of foreign-owned utilities in several Brazilian states, notably in Rio Grande do Sul, and the three post-1964 military governments' austere anti-inflationary development policies.

United States unilateral criteria for intervention and recognition have found little favor among Brazilian governments prior to 1964. Contemporary relations with the United States are exceptionally close but are more symbolic of Brazil's tremendous need for United States capital assistance than of any long-range shift in attitude. In any case, the military governments from Castelo Branco to Garrastazú Médici are completely aware of the great economic development obligations of Brazil, and in this Brazilian nationalism is still bound to economic determinants.

Chile

Chile's modern nationalism has had much to build upon: a fairly literate society, a large middle class, a sophisticated urban proletariat, and a long tradition of national identity. However, Chile has been advancing slowly in its quest for a thoroughly national and popular government. Modern nationalism in Chile is closely identified with the early twentieth century struggles of socialism and communism. Both the Communist and Socialist parties in Chile represented the first really popular, urban, mass-based, and worker-supported parties. They are much more powerful and represent larger segments of the population than anywhere else in Latin America. This is perhaps due to the wide range of ideology that was contained within the scope of these two parties throughout the thirties, forties, and fifties and the many factional disputes and public debates throughout these decades. However, until the victory of the Christian Democrats in 1964, Chilean nationalism was not a governmental development policy but an oppositionist force, mainly of Socialists and Communists. Until the contemporary period, twentieth century nationalist development met with many failures.

One might divide Chile's modern nationalist development into four phases. The first phase came in 1931 on the heels of a nationalist uprising led by a Socialist military officer, Marmaduke Grove, against the dictatorship of Carlos Ibañez. The first Socialist Republic in the Americas was established. It lasted but twelve days, however, and was destroyed by countercoups that eventually prepared the way for the reascendancy of Arturo Alessandri in 1932. Grove and the Socialists were anxious to experiment with a national policy of integrating the workers into all levels of government and, at the same time, of greatly strengthening their rights of organization.

The second phase of nationalist development occurred in 1937 with the founding of the Popular Front among the Communists, the Socialists, and to provide the necessary margin of victory over the traditional parties on the conservative side of the political spectrum, the Radicals. As already discussed, the Popular Front was a reasonable facsimile of the European Popular Fronts, but, as was so common in Europe, it was not created as a political mechanism with which to oppose Nazi-Fascism, never a real threat to Chile. Rather it was part of a nationalist struggle against the monopoly of political power by the Liberals and Conservatives. World events merely provided a convenient set of circumstances for hitherto antagonistic parties to bury past resentment and meet on common ground for a common political goal. This goal was political power through the ballot boxes, and in the 1938 presidential elections the Popular Front emerged the victor. Again, however, national criteria were sidetracked as the Radicals used the Front to become Chile's most powerful party. They proceeded during the middle of World War II to wreck the front and win the elections of 1942 and 1946 on their own. Radical policy then developed along the same traditional lines which had been espoused by the Conservative and Liberal parties. The Socialists broke with the Radicals by the early forties, while the more opportunistic Communists hung on until they were expelled from the governing cabinet and outlawed in 1948 by Radical president Gonzalez Videla. The two nationally oriented parties who had been able to integrate working class votes into the Popular Front column were eliminated. Because of this in all probability, the Radicals from then on gradually lost their popular base.

The third phase of nationalist development arose out of the extra-party coalitions struck up under the personalist movement of former dictator Carlos Ibañez. Ibañez said he stood for ruling without the discredited Chilean parties, and though he did not seek the active support of any political organization, his own personal machine was devoted to his apolitical appeal. Factions of the Socialists and the entire Communist party supported his candidature. Ibañez appealed to these nationalist parties as a symbolic figure that could rule above the petty corruption of party politics, particularly that of the Radical party between 1938 and 1952. Ibañez's close personal relations with Juan Perón of Argentina strengthened his ties with the laboring classes, and he easily won the presidential election of 1952. Argentine nationalism, so sensational at this height of its power, greatly impressed both the Communist and Socialist parties of Chile. These political groups came to feel that Ibañez would be the only man who could supersede the class conflicts between the upper, middle, and lower classes which had become so prevalent since the Popular Front days. As it turned out, Ibañez's regime developed into a standstill, vacillating government which played off one political group against another and which performed very poorly in important economic areas. Support for Ibañez dropped off so that by 1958 his regime was thoroughly unpopular. It did, however, remain essentially democratic, and before the end of his term in 1958, Ibañez legalized the Communist party.

The fourth phase in nationalist development shows promise of being the only one that will have any long-range effects on Chilean political society. In 1964 Eduardo Frei became Chile's president by an overwhelming vote of close to 60 per cent, the first such margin ever received by a single party. This was also the first time that a party in power had ties with all classes and was totally committed to national development. The success of the Christian Democrats resulted in the weakening of the Radical, Conservative, and Liberal parties, which left only FRAP, another highly nationalist-minded political party, as the major opposition group and the subsequent successor to political power.

Argentina

Argentina has had its difficulties in defining with any sense of unanimity its national interests. There are still important divergences of opinion about the virtues or contributions of many of Argentina's national figures like Rosas, Sarmiento, Irigoyen, Alvear, Perón, and Frondizi. There is no national consensus as to the social values espoused by any of these individuals, and all have their detractors. Lack of agreement in the world of ideas can be fruitful, but it also can become harmful when it makes political compromise difficult or impossible. In Argentina there has been no national focus or general agreement as to the goals of political and economic development. The main problem can be traced to agrarian versus the industrial values in the society. Few regimes in recent Argentine history have been able to satisfy both these economic and social sectors. Perhaps the Frondizi experiment provided the closest approximation to a national development policy which attempted to reach at least minimum political consensus between hitherto antagonistic groups.

This ambivalence is complemented by geo-political distinctions between the urban immigrant and the rural Argentine. This essentially unitarian-federalist struggle has persisted as an obstacle to national cohesion. The urban people provide the mainstay of the industrial interests, and the agricultural interests are represented by the rural people. Each division thereby reinforces the other. What was a regional confrontation has in many cases become an ideological conflict.

The Perón experiment in authoritarian government has led to a further societal disagreement. High consumption standards of labor, politicized labor unions, and a militant Peronista governing party incited opposition groups who desire a weak labor movement, a small labor share in consumption, and a thoroughly weakened Peronista party. The present military hierarchy is the largest group which opposes the Peronistas, and an accommodation between these two influential groups may go a long way in providing modern Argentina with the key to economic development and national unity and cohesion.

Modern nationalism in Argentina, as represented by a government, can be traced to 1943 when a chauvinistic military junta took power. The junta was eventually replaced by the personalist-populist dictatorship of Juan Perón. The Perón regime, however, also performed several valuable services in the development of a national integration policy. The working sector was brought into the national community. The peasants, for the first time in Argentine history, were given some national protection against private exploitation. The government became responsible for economic decision making in such areas as railways, foreign trade, and grain and beef exports. These changes undertaken by Perón were far more important than his highly aggressive foreign policy and his rabble-rousing class-baiting, which served mainly to heighten class division. However, Perón's ability to identify the workers with national concerns was an important contribution to Argentina's quest for a sense of total nationhood.

Today Argentina still lacks a nationally-oriented middle class which could assume responsibility for a policy of economic development. Frondizi's government might have turned Argentina in this direction, but his administration could not survive the tremendous cross-pressures from the Peronistas and the military. These two leading political groups viewed the national interest in distinct ways, and Frondizi could not manage the difficult job of mediation. He succumbed under the Peronista drive for political recognition and the military demand for labor subordination and industrial development.

Since 1930 military interventionism has served to undermine general public confidence in peaceful political transition. There is no majority consensus evident, and Ongania's government was an imposed one. The nation had overwhelmingly elected Frondizi president in 1958 yet discarded him without much ado four years later. Government by decree has become commonplace, and has helped to foster disrespect for any predictable political continuity. Argentina has been living under crisis government for four decades. Since the military coup of 1930, the country has been subjected to military governments, military-controlled civil governments, revolutionary regimes, dictatorial governments, and provisional governments.

Much of the resentment, mutual recriminations, and state of near rebellion is based on the fact that the Peronistas are still not integrated into the political fabric. Under the circumstances it becomes increasingly difficult to effectively use social suasion and moderate leadership. Once Peronismo can fill a nonauthoritarian place in political society, national cohesion may then be a reasonable goal.

Summary

Nationalism is thus the most influential ideology or, at least, a series of understood national values and attitudes, in Latin America, and it is being used increasingly to develop industrial power. At the same time, nationalism may be serving the purpose of undermining traditional conceptions of ideology as a political force. Nationalism has become so pervasive a social value and so much the means of political integration and economic development that it has led both leaders and the masses away from the world of ideals and ideas, away from ideology as doctrine, dogma, or prescription. Ideology no longer has the force and impetus it once had in Latin America. It was important when societies were less complex and when simple formulas were put forth as sure cures for society's ills. The masses of the people were ignorant of national and world trends and had to be initiated into political life by a set of simple axioms. The elite was able to use ideology as an effective means to manipulate and control society. There was general confidence in the power of ideas and small groups of aristocrats, who had no intellectual competition, were able to set the standards and guidelines for moral and social behavior. Ideology was instrumental in defining the goals of society.

As the political revolutions of the nation-states were followed by industrial revolutions and national unification drives, ideology met its first overt competition. Modernizing elites were not terribly interested in the moral tenets of most ideological thought. In the twentieth century the ideologies of Nazism, Communism, and Fascism have all been either discredited or tremendously reduced in acceptability.[8] All have given way to the more pragmatic considerations of the social and political community.

Today new requirements are downgrading ideology as an effective tool to deal with the growing demands upon governing elites. In earlier periods ideology was used to set class against class, nation against nation, or religion against religion. These conflicts are not particularly meaningful in the modern age. Ideologies that foster dissent and division are now usually thought to be counterproductive and/or antinational. The emphasis today is on smoothing down regional and class differences and seeking the lowest common denominators rather than heightening divisions which often develop into physical warfare. Fanaticism and political passion are considered wasteful. The modernized nation-state or the state striving for modernity has little patience with those monolithic ideologies that seek to place all problems into one tidy package and then apply some preprocessed solution. Pure democracy, the perfectibility of man, classless societies, and equal opportunity are no longer considered within easy reach. The emphasis is now on developing the potential of the peoples of each nation and working for immediate and obtainable goals.

Economic productivity requires no patterned ideological commitment but rather the broad commitment to national power.[9] Growing technology

[8] This view particularly took shape in the immediate aftermath of the Second World War. See, for example, E. H. Carr, *Nationalism and After* (New York: Macmillan, 1945).

[9] Zbigniew Brezezinski and Samuel Huntington have found, though some altogether understandable differences exist, that the United States and USSR

and communications in Latin America are increasing the size of the middle class which is the least ideologically conscious. Seemingly wherever this class becomes influential, ideology loses force. Communist, Socialist, and Capitalist societies all appear to have similar developmental goals, and all tend to use any means, regardless of its ideological consistency, to achieve these generally shared goals. Thus distinctive ideologies are harder and harder to define.

As societies grow more sophisticated, pragmatism and the scientific method of trial and error and experimentation gain broader acceptance over ideologies which are often based on untested truths. We are in a sense in the age of cynicism. The cure-alls of the total views of society and the unalterable plans for the future are no longer trusted. Perhaps the "demonstration effect," already common parlance in the economic world, will be the new political "ideology." Whatever is experimented with in one country and observed to work will be adopted by other countries regardless of other concerns. Today some developing countries are choosing Communism, others Capitalism, and the majority a mixed system of Welfare Capitalism because of what they see. Everywhere ideologies are under attack from the technocrats, the scientists, and the scholars. It is probably a question of time when the empirical spirit will inundate the present political leaders of the emerging nations.

---

face similar domestic and international problems, pursue comparable political goals, and (despite the authors' resistance) have more in common today than 50 years ago. See their study, *Political Power: USA/USSR* (New York: Viking Press, 1963).

PART V
Political Forces

The amalgam of the Latin American tradition of the indivisibility of power with the requirements of welfare legislation and administration during the distributive period have combined to strengthen the institution of the Latin American executive at the expense of all other sources of political power. The basis for executive preeminence was laid during the authoritative phase following independence from Spain, and the aggregative phase saw this branch of government widen its sphere of influence because of its own predilections and because of the legislative, judicial, and public sectors' inability to broaden their political control. This process gradually resulted in an absorption of legislative, judicial, and regulatory functions by the central government's executive branch.

With the growing mechanization of distributive society, responsibility for fast-moving legislation has more and more devolved on the executive. The central government has shown that it is willing to carry out more complicated social functions and that it has the technical wherewithal to carry out the necessary programs.[1] Modern means of communication have strengthened the executive's ability to respond quickly to disaster, conflict, and controversy as it has assumed the role of arbitrator on questions of social discrepancy. The ubiquity of the executive office has earned it fame, popularity, and growing national dimension in Latin America. Whether it receives approval or disapproval, it is the sole focus of continual public attention.

Crises, whether on the domestic or international scene, tend to temporarily enhance the powers of the executive. When normality is reestablished, often much of the accumulated powers remain with the executive, or

[1] Charles Anderson discusses the limiting effects of corruption, patronage, and nepotism upon administrative competence but affirms the overwhelming preponderance of executive dominance. *Politics and Economic Change in Latin America* (Princeton: Van Nostrand, 1967), Ch. 6. David H. Bayley has discussed certain beneficial development consequences arising out of graft, bribes and other publicly practiced improbities. "The Effects of Corruption in a Developing Nation," *The Western Political Quarterly*, vol. 14, no. 4 (December 1966), pp. 719–732.

at least the predisposition to use such powers has been strengthened. The people have become accustomed to, and the executive has become adept in, the employment of greater power. In developing nations crises are not necessarily related to foreign adventures or domestic violence but to the staggering problems of rapid development which confront these societies daily. Crisis becomes a perpetual social phenomenon and, given a permanent "war" on poverty, underdevelopment and undereducation, the areas of responsibility of the executive are tremendously extended.

CHAPTER 10

Executive Power and Administrative Dominance

With government as the major economic planner, the principal production manager, and the major corporation shareholder, it is not surprising to find the executive simultaneously acting out many functions that, in more developed nations, would be more widely dispersed.[1] This concentration of economic and political power within the executive branch of Latin American governments has resulted in several associated political problems.

When political power becomes absolute and overwhelming, it becomes a prize well worth the capturing. With the private sector controlled by a relatively small percentage of the population and the public sector in control of industry, foreign trade, and the utilities, it is not surprising that the control of government becomes not only a political goal but an economic one as well. Thus the very monopoly of executive power makes its position unstable. Political struggles take on a vital meaning when to be in opposition may mean to suffer economic eclipse. In most developing countries it makes a difference, especially to those in opposition, who governs. To be in opposition may mean to lack political legitimacy, social status, and economic security. Thus the drive to executive power is quite important in a society still lacking in widely-diversified interest groups, sizable private industry, and a decentralized political framework. Those groups holding power are much more reluctant to give it up and return to careers in the private sector, for often the choice is quite meager. Thus holding political power becomes very important and all means are used to either keep or capture it. This may be one of the underlying factors of the institutional instability in many Latin American nations.[2]

Both the one-party and multiparty systems tend to further reinforce the powers of the executive in a developing nation. Where only one party has control, there is little distinction between politics and administration, housed as they are under the same roof. The president is not only head of the government but usually de facto leader of his party. Both the party and the govern-

[1] Frank Brandenburg has compiled statistics for the larger Latin American countries that show that in the major half-a-dozen or so enterprises, the government maintains majority if not total ownership. *The Development of Latin American Private Enterprise* (Washington, D. C., National Planning Association, 1964), pp. 52–66.

[2] See the suggestive article written over a decade ago by Merle Kling, "Toward a Theory of Power and Political Instability in Latin America," *Western Political Quarterly*, vol. 9, no. 1 (March 1956). Peter Calvert also suggests that concentration of power in few hands favors the use of force. "The Typical Latin American Revolution," *International Affairs*, vol. 43, no. 1 (January 1967), pp. 88–89.

ment feed on one another and sustain each other's commitment to the power structure. While in the Soviet Union it is the party's national secretariat which is the predominant partner in state power, in Latin America's one party arrangements, it appears to be the bureaucracy associated with the executive that assumes the major share of responsibility and power. Here the party has become a device to generate new turnover within the governing elites, to assist in the essential tasks of political communication, and to aggregate moral support for the government between elections and actual support for it at election time.[3]

Within a multiparty framework the executive's power also may become quite formidable. In Latin America, it is because of the absence of a formally organized, responsible and alternative opposition which could, as in a viable two-party system, assume political power without undue social upheaval. The Latin American governments which are under a multiparty arrangement often owe their political success to other parties but have not always been very prone to invite these parties to join the government, as so often happened in France's Fourth Republic. If such an arrangement has occasionally been necessary, minor party governmental officials have usually been co-opted by the ruling party bureaucracy. Parliamentary power is generally very limited in Latin America, but a multiparty distribution of seats in the national congress makes the executive even more disposed to bypass the legislative branch of government where there might be some opposition to its programs. Both the Fifth Republic of France and the majority of Latin American nations have emphasized the role of the executive as the principal "rule maker" and patently downgraded parliament's law-making powers by sheer disuse, by employment of emergency executive powers, or by decreeing administrative changes that would normally require legislative acts.

Whether power is in the hands of a duly elected civil president, a government military junta which came to power through a coup, a dictator who has perpetuated himself in power, or of a one-party governing directorate, a general centralization of power in the hands of the executive has been widespread. Each of the five nations fits the patterns in its own distinctive way.

Mexico

The official party bureaucracy in Mexico has as little competition for power as that in many far more dictatorial regimes. The focal point of this power lies in the office of the presidency, in his immediate cabinet, and in the

[3] See Frank Brandenburg's study of Mexico's controlling "Revolutionary Family," *The Making of Modern Mexico* (Englewood Cliffs: Prentice-Hall, 1964), Ch. 1.

directors and advisors to the government's principal economic and industrial corporations and enterprises.[4] This rather small nucleus is further supported by a vast network provided by the PRI's massive political organization which has its roots in every institution of the country.

The Mexican PRI is a governing party which rules undeterred and unfettered by any other major political force. The administration is free to undertake programs that are worked out within the governmental hierarchy that are in no danger of immediate political reprisal. The executive is aware of pressures from the business communities and various sectors within its own party apparatus, but these pressures are best described as "interfamiliar" and can be dealt with without any consequent loss of political force. The Mexican government has been blessed with almost four decades of administrative experience, which allows it to rule from a position of omniscience and acquired grounding in all phases of government. There is no other governing party in Latin America's distributive period that has been so consistently responsible for the destinies of its country as has the PRI in Mexico. The tradition of government gives the executive the advantage of having it generally assumed that it alone can do the job of governing properly and adequately. It tends to make the populace wary of entrusting the reins of government to an untried political party. Thus the status quo is perpetuated and a party like the PRI becomes more entrenched as the only feasible administrator.

The present Mexican government is a legitimate political group that has earned respect and need not prove itself from day to day. It is the recognized elite of the country.[5] There are no doubts as to its right to rule and even its most outspoken opponents do not question its legitimacy. Unlike a newly established dictator, military junta, or untried political party, the PRI need not rationalize about its legal right to promulgate laws or institute policies. The PRI government has been extremely effective in wrapping its policies in the most cherished traditions of Mexican political mythology and history. Mexican development under a single, dominant party government has perpetuated a unifying ideology that makes no distinction between the PRI, the Mexican Revolution, and Mexican institutions. The PRI executive branch is closely identified with and is considered the best interpreter of Mexico's national interests, both on the domestic and international scene.

[4] See William Glade and Charles Anderson, *The Political Economy of Mexico* (Madison: University of Wisconsin Press, 1963).

[5] James D. Cochrane, in "Mexico's New Cientificos: The Díaz Ordaz Cabinet," *Inter-American Economic Affairs*, vol. 21, no. 1 (Summer 1967), pp. 63–68, showed that the twenty-two Mexican cabinet members were, in the main, university graduates with law or engineering their principal fields, with government service their initial professional experience and their career position at the time of nomination to the cabinet. When nominated, thirteen of twenty-two occupied posts in the national executive branch and 10 of twenty-two held some public office.

As Mexico's largest single employer, the government is able to increase its prestige and importance in the economic and social spheres. In this capacity alone it can increase the devotion of its partisans, stir the loyalty of uncertain sectors, and even make some political opponents "available" for governmental employment. With permanent control over a significant sector of the political economy, the executive branch of government can entrench its influence among the most powerful and outspoken elements of Mexican society. The far-flung bureaucracy, the so-called Popular Sector, is the most important part of the PRI party, and from its ranks come the greatest number of presidents, governors, and legislators. The bureaucracy's close control over basic industries, public utilities, and the nation's financial institutions gives it further leverage over the economic lives of the great majority of Mexican citizens. The power to withhold credit from one employer and give it to another, the power to grant an import license to one industrialist and not another, to give a crucial loan to a steel executive in the midst of expansion and the denial of this to a struggling aluminum factory owner, to declare a tax exemption for an incipient auto manufacturing plant and not for a textile concern, to set a price ceiling here or approve a wage rise there—all entrench governmental power within the general Mexican community.

Peru

Peru has a similarly influential executive-administrative branch of government, but here its power is tempered by the presence of a powerful opposition party that has demonstrated a long run predisposition toward political power. The Aprista party, often allied with the Odriista party, is a feasible alternative, though its assumption of executive control remains unlikely under current conditions while the military maintains its controlling role in Peru. But as in Mexico, all the fruits to be won go to those in control of executive power. The Aprista party in opposition, first to conservative governments and recently to the military government, has continued to be Peru's largest party, yet it has not become the predominant party for the exclusive reason, it seems, that it has never led a government or ruled from a position of strength. Similarly, one might guess that the Acción Popular of Belaunde Terry, though it was in a minority position in both the Chamber of Deputies and Senate, would grow in popularity and strength merely by having been the presidential party. As the party in command, it had a monopoly on job distribution, government contracts, and other economic levers.[6]

[6] The Acción Popular has succeeded in changing the traditional Peruvian pattern of elite recruitment. See Arnold Payne, "Peru: Latin America's Silent Revolution," *Inter-American Economic Affairs*, vol. 20, no. 3 (Winter 1966), pp. 70–71. For example, 43 per cent of Prado's (1956–1962) cabinet ministers had landowning interests, none of Belaunde's. Nineteen per cent had been recruited

Acción Popular, new to political ascendancy, did not, of course, develop the certain and ubiquitous position of the PRI, but it did have the leverage to spread its gospel and machinery. With the implied protection that the AP received from the armed forces, its relative longevity seemed assured, even though it was to continually find disfavor in the eyes of the Aprista party, which, itself, is not yet considered legitimate by the military, at least not as an executive in government. The AP meanwhile had shown a desire to spread its governing coalition and had invited the Apristas to join the governing cabinet. Since the military forces, however, now occupy the executive position alone, the Apristas and AP have been reduced to political eclipse.

Thus the great powers of the administration in Peru must be, in a real sense, shared with the military hierarchy, something that in Mexico has long ago been done away with. The necessity to share power with the military along with the fact that there is a definite opposition lessen the total power of the civilian executive in Peru. Lastly in distinction to Mexico, Peru has a less stable social system in which no definitive pattern of political development is yet discernible. Elections are still nullified, dictators, both civil and military, are still able to gain immediate rapport with the public, and civil and personal guarantees are still subject to momentary withdrawal. The political aggressiveness of the labor movement[7] and the swelling peasant discontent over agrarian reform[8] also help to keep the society unstable and susceptible to social revolutions and political warfare.

The fact that during its administrative tenure the AP had to curtail and adopt some policies because of the prevalent military opinion or institute some programs because of Aprista agitation made it difficult to resolve all policy decisions within the confines of its own inner circle as the PRI can in Mexico. Political bargaining becomes extragovernmental in Peru, whereas in Mexico it is largely a matter of intraparty developments.

Brazil

The Brazilian executive, since the inception of the Republic, has been the center of the struggle for political power. Brazil's tradition of state oriented politics was kept intact by a system of political bargaining among

---

from the diplomatic service under Prado, only one in Belaunde's. Thirty-eight per cent of Belaunde's cabinet members are technical-developmental specialists, 13 per cent in Prado's. Regional representation in the cabinet has also shifted away from Lima (73 per cent to 42 per cent) toward other coastal cities, the Andes and Jungle regions (27 per cent to 58 per cent).

[7] As discussed in James L. Payne, *Labor and Politics in Peru* (New Haven: Yale University Press, 1965).

[8] See Anibal Quijano Obregon, "Contemporary Peasant Movements," in Lipset and Solari, *Elites in Latin America* (New York: Oxford University Press, 1967), Ch. 9.

the stronger states who sought the executive mandate. Pedro II's emphasis on administration relegated political movements to a secondary status, and this largely continued up to Brazil's republican days. The major concern of those few involved in politics was the effectiveness and efficacy of administration, though in order to run a massive country like Brazil, there was occasionally some political bargaining. Vargas's emphases on cross-regional and multiclass movements helped, after his own political demise, to initiate the development of political parties. However, only since 1945 has politics, in the sense of party campaigning, party platforms, and party recruitment, become a factor in the management and control of the executive branch. The three major Brazilian parties who shared the control of public administration all brought somewhat different conceptions of the rule of good government. This brought the executive branch for the first time within the realm of political controversy and discussion. The aloofness and apolitical attitude displayed by the executive branch has, though the executive is still very powerful, been replaced by a willingness to conform to the political requirements of other important power centers in Brazil—political, economic, and military.

This "politization," as it were, of the executive has in no way weakened the role of the Brazilian president. Rather it has made the capture of the presidency the principal preoccupation of identifiable political groups rather than the sometime ambition of the members of Brazil's oldest families. As the experiment with parliamentary government seems to indicate, the most influential and vocal sectors of Brazilian society generally accept the idea of a strong executive. The military forces share this view and have imposed their own representative for that vaunted post and prescribed the type of individual and the kind of party that may assume the awesome responsibility. It is the armed forces that have since 1966 shown no hesitation in providing, for example, the da Costa y Silva and Garrastazú Médici regimes with extensive decree powers which will, no doubt, have a permanent effect on strengthening an already powerful public administration.

The weakness of strong, differentiated interest groups and the void left by a generally unorganized and unparticipating public sector have left the executive as the fulcrum for public petitions and group solicitations.[9] The National Congress in Brazil, with its history of party affiliates and with the loose structure of its party program, had been largely diverted from its potential role as the representative and delegate of the people. At present the most powerful sources of pressure on public policy emanate from the executive branch—namely from the middle-level bureaucrats and the military. The bureaucrats perform the task of primary legislators while they simultaneously represent organized and specialized political views that have great effect on

[9] Nathaniel Leff has discussed the autonomy with which bureaucrats make public policy. *Economic Policy-Making and Development in Brazil, 1947–1964* (New York: John Wiley, 1968).

the President. The great numbers within Brazil's public bureaucracy function as a sophisticated, literate, politicized, and eloquent minority in a country where political apathy is not unknown. They know well what they want and are able to communicate these wants to the decision makers. The military are responsible for the institutionalization of a powerful, politically preeminent chief executive. Their demands are directly funneled into the executive branch, and when the army and navy present a unified front, they are far more powerful than any other pressure group. They share closely in policy making and initiate most institutional reforms.

Chile

The Chilean political community, since the reform of the Constitution in 1925, has been in basic agreement that a strong executive branch is an essential barrier to the dominance of a divided parliament. The executive branch has gradually amassed more and more power, especially under the administrations of Arturo Alessandri, Aguirre Cerda, Gonzalez Videla, and Eduardo Frei. Probably this trend will continue under the administration of Salvador Allende. Frei's Christian Democrats, as Belaunde Terry's Acción Popular, undertook a quiet revolution, not only in the policy sphere but in the public administration sphere. Both these parties no doubt did much to broaden the prestige, efficiency, and power of the executive branch of government.

As Executive of a free society, the Chilean President holds a very prestigious position among Latin American chief executives. Of the five nations studied here, his is least encumbered by the restrictions on public liberties and the overt or more subtle forms of military interference into civil affairs. The Chilean President represents a society that has given free play to competing political ideologies. He can be an individual rather than a symbol, and he can appear in public without the usual entourage. The presidency is a lofty position, resplendent in its immunity from detrimental institutional and social factors of many Latin American societies. The Christian Democratic party itself was not able to solidify its power. However, since the peasants remain an unorganized, class-conscious group and labor remains an important group but nonrevolutionary in its outlook, there was much leeway for Frei to broaden his authority. Until 1969–1970, election trends emphasized the fact that there was little organized public, which was continuously ideologically antagonistic to the Christian Democratic political programs.

The Chilean executive, in the person of its President, is closer to the public-at-large than other Latin American executives, and perhaps only the political leaders of Cuba, Costa Rica, and Uruguay come close. There is no formal gap between the President and his constituents. There is less pomp and circumstance surrounding the chief executive than in Brazil, less of an authoritarian aura than in Mexico. Chile's relatively open society is reflected in the office of her President.

Control of the public administration apparatus has become more and more essential with the growth of Chile's bipolarized political community. Two welfare-oriented groups—the Christian Democrats and the Unidad Popular (Popular Union)—consistently share approximately two-thirds of the electorate, which gives Chile something close to a two-party orientation. It is still difficult to predict how permanent this situation will be, but both groups appear to be administratively oriented, and both seek to initiate fundamental changes in Chilean society rather than perpetuate a restricted ruling elite or preserve minority privileges.

Argentina

Argentine Presidents have been the center of public power since the very establishment of the national government, from the important first administrations of Mitri and Sarmiento to the twentieth century governments of Irigoyen and Perón. In recent times when the military has supported a strong executive, there has been a dictatorship as were the Perón, Aramburu, and Onganía governments. When the military has fallen out with a government, it has meant the weakening and eventual demise of that government, such as was the case with Irigoyen's second administration and the Frondizi and Illia administrations. Thus a strong, radically conceived government must receive military acceptance in order to survive, though a moderate or conservative administration, such as the former Illia government, may continue on the basis of military sufferance.

The presence of Peronismo as a continuing political force has given further reason to maintain a strong executive one which can either eradicate the Peronista threat or quickly institute programs which will counter the propaganda effects of the Peronistas on the less fortunate sectors of the society. Thus when the Illia government was finally overthrown by the armed forces, it was not because it was usurping the powers of other branches of government but rather because the Illia administration had been ineffective and thus had not appreciably lessened the threat of resurgent Peronista popularity.

Ever since the Perón administration, the executive has become tremendously strengthened in relation to the legislative branch. The process has continued regardless of the political tenor or complexion of various administrations. In numerous ways, by its political autocracy, economic "liberalism," and societal puritanism, the Argentine military government under Lieutenant General Juan Onganía resembled the Brazilian. The governmental functions were heavily centralized in two newly created agencies, The National Security Council and the National Development Council—the first heavily staffed by the military hierarchy and the second by technicians and economists. These agencies work apart from the regular cabinet offices staffed at the inception of the 1966 revolution. The military government intent on making profound changes in the economy have taken vigorous steps to coordinate all governmental corporations within prescribed production quotas while assessing "guidelines" for private enterprise. Thus executive dominance in Argentina is at its zenith, and effective countervailing pressures from labor, agricultural interests, the universities, political parties, and legislatures are conspicuously impotent. What is more, there seems to be a growing popular acceptance that some of these major economic reforms can only be undertaken by a superordinate, unfettered administration.

Thus, particularly since World War II, the legislatures, rather than being legislative organs, have tended to act more like assemblies or parliaments of debate where major issues and causes are aired. When, in the past, legislatures have had more members of the opposition than of the governing party, such as in the Chamber of Deputies of Peru, Chile, and Argentina, the likelihood that there will be this type of outlet for criticism and ideological debate is greater. In these nations, however, the congress is incapable of either delimiting or toppling an administration. In Mexico, on the other hand, the national legislature is rather like an arm of the administration through which, for the benefit of the public, ideas and viewpoints may be floated as trial balloons. If later there should be some misgivings about a certain item, the PRI administration, without loss of face, may disassociate itself from the legislative position. On the other hand, the Argentine Chamber of Deputies before the military intervention of 1966 resolved, commemorated, decorated, dedicated, and generally kept active though its legislative role was inferior to that of the Chilean or pre-1968 Peruvian legislatures. At the moment, the Brazilian legislature is very much on the defensive in relation to the military regime in power. This is not to say that the national legislatures are not places of exciting public debates and scenes of real political confrontation. In these off-the-cuff parliamentary battles the observer is able to gain a perspective of the issue orientations and political attitudes of the various parties.

The size of the Senate and Chambers of Deputies has ranged from 45 and 147 in Chile to 66 and 409 in Brazil. All theoretically meet regularly and at constitutionally set times. With the exception of Mexico, all seated a considerable proportion of members of opposition parties. In Peru until the military coup of 1968, the Aprista and Ordriista parties made up a majority in opposition in both the Chamber and Senate. Before the disbanding of parties in Brazil in late 1965, the UDN and PSD parties had a majority as they did under the PTB government of João Goulart. In Chile the Christian Democrats have had an absolute majority in the Chamber of Deputies until

1969[10] but have never had that margin in the Senate where they had to pick up votes from the Radicals or Socialists, depending on the issue. Argentina until the 1966 military coup had the most varied representation of the five nations studied. The governing Radicals made up only 70 of the 192-member Chamber of Deputies and about half of the Senate membership. They had to solicit support from various minority and provincial parties, such as the Conservatives, the Intransigent Radicals, and the Federation of Provincial Parties.

Private member bills are a rarity in these congresses. Most of the policy decisions are made within the party outside of congress and then passed on to the congressmen who represent that party. Important measures are invariably introduced by the executive and then formally proposed by the chairman (a member usually of the governing party) of an appropriate committee. The proportional representation list system, that is used everywhere but Mexico, also helps to develop party deputies rather than men committed to their state, province, or municipality. The goal of a legislator is to receive or maintain a high position on the list at each election, and this is determined by his party, either on a provincial level alone or occasionally in conjunction with the national party directorate. Thus he must please the party rather than the electorate to remain in office. This helps to keep a congressman obedient to the party hierarchy and to influential party bureaucrats. There is a vacuum between the Latin American congressman and his constituency, and this is reflected by campaign methodology which emphasizes even at the local level only national issues and prestigious leadership. What is at stake is always the whole party list.

The legislative branch is further weakened by the fact that interest groups also tend to concentrate on executive branch administrators and upon ruling party leadership rather than upon individual congressmen. Had legislators an independent source of campaign funds, for example, they might be able, once in congress, to demonstrate greater independence.

Though legislators are peripheral members of the ruling elite, they do perform the function of publicizing important issues.[11] Their debates are published in the newspapers and thus serve as a source of education. Sometimes a legislator may act as intermediary for an individual in his attempt for example, to gain a post with a governmental department or receive a pension, scholarship, or public assistance. In fact, much of a congressman's time is filled with carrying out these personal requests. He is a public mes-

[10] For a breakdown of the post-1969 Chilean congress, see George W. Grayson, "The Frei Administration and the 1969 Parliamentary Election," *Inter-American Economic Affairs,* vol. 23, no. 2 (Autumn 1969), p. 62.

[11] Robert Scott assesses the influence of "politicos" as less than their public role would indicate. "Political Elites and Political Modernization," in Lipset and Solari, *Elites in Latin America,* p. 120.

senger, a representative of friends, associates, and acquaintances rather than a legislator for the general public.

As in the United States, the majority of the Latin American republics maintain an overlapping and staggered judiciary system with courts on the state and national level as well as a full complement of specialized courts in the fields of administration and civil law. In many areas of personal grievances and the adjudication of property, wills, and other civil matters, these various courts serve somewhat similar functions. However, it is in the area of judicial review where there is the most distinction.

The Supreme Court stands at the apex of the Latin American judicial branch, and its decisions are final and binding. It has trod a very cautious road and has avoided taking an "activist" role in the area of federal legislation, rarely if ever striking down either an executive order or a legislative act.[12] It has performed the role of arbiter for private suits rather than as counterpoise to executive-legislative action. In no country has it attempted to brake the increasing rule-making function of the executive. It has avoided controversy and generally upheld the status quo as interpreted by the executive branch of government.

Since the Latin American court systems work under the Continental codification system of laws, they don't have the built-in self-renovating mechanism which exists in the case of the Anglo-Saxon legal tradition. Thus, especially in the areas of public powers and social legislation, the Supreme Court has not been able to renovate itself as quickly and effectively as have the other branches of the national government. Such is the state of the supreme court in Latin America that there are no "cause celebres" with which we can identify its development in the twentieth century.[13] They have not led in the adjustment of social inequalities and economic injustice, though they have not opposed such measures when initiated by the executive. Again since the executive so clearly dominates the legislature, the supreme court need not act as the bar of last resort or the mediator between the two branches, as is the case in the United States.[14] Since a viable federalism does

[12] In fact, as William Pierson and Federico Gil have pointed out, the courts have usually accepted the legitimacy of new governments who came to power by way of a coup as long as they gave lip service to the existing constitution (which they might later abolish or revise). *Governments of Latin America* (New York: McGraw-Hill, 1957), pp. 152–158.

[13] This is distinguished from the U. S. Supreme Court's defense and expansion of basic societal freedoms. See for example Henry J. Abraham, *The Judiciary: The Supreme Court in the Governmental Process* (Boston: Allyn and Bacon, 1965), Ch. 2; and, for a less sanguine view, Robert A. Dahl, *Pluralist Democracy in the United States: Conflict and Consent* (Chicago: Rand McNally, 1957), pp. 163–170.

[14] Robert C. Fried writes that the "courts are less vulnerable to executive attack and domination than Latin American legislatures." He cites their relatively

not exist, there is also no need for the court to settle disputes between the national and state governments. The quarrels are between member states and are usually less important, therefore, the Supreme Court is unable to derive any great prestige when it intervenes. Nor has the Supreme Court acted as the defender of the constitution, since the constitutions, though strictly conceived, rarely demand compliance with the letter of the law.

The court system has also done little in the defense of voting rights, political rights of opposition, and basic freedoms of speech, assembly, and petition. Nor has there been any concern, until the very recent period, with the equitable division of the land and with tax structures.

Summary

Given the crisis atmosphere surrounding the press for rapid economic development, which is particularly evident during a nation's distributive period of national development, the executive branch of government invariably provides most of the policies, plans, and ideas by which to achieve this national objective. More than other public or private agencies or associations, it tends to have a monopoly of technology, skills, and financial wherewithal. Growth of the nation in Latin American political culture has tended to strengthen the image and prestige of the national executive and his administration as they represent the most visible part of the bureaucratic iceberg. Even regular coups, military interventions, and civil-military squabbles do not lessen the dominance of the executive over legislatures, courts, political parties, associational interests, and public opinion. The very ease with which the executive can be identified augments its claims on political legitimacy and assures its authority despite any changes in its personnel.

Thus the executive branch has occupied a dominant position in public policy making in Latin America; yet the executives over the years have shown a consistent predisposition not to monopolize all political power or abrogate lesser sources of public or private responsibility. It is this seeming paradox that has maintained most of Latin America as plurally-disposed open societies rather than closed, authoritarian ones. Though they have been clearly subordinate powers during the distributive period, pressure groups, political parties, information media, the legislatures, the courts, and public opinion do not seem to be in any danger of extinction.

---

higher moral legitimacy. *Comparative Political Institutions* (New York: Macmillan, 1966), p. 45.

CHAPTER 11 Political Parties

Important changes have taken place since World War II that appear to have altered aspects of political party competition in Latin America. The growth of middle sectors, urbanization, industrialization, greater literacy have had impacts upon Latin American society in general and political parties in particular.[1]

It may be too early to speak of a newly acquired accommodating attitude in politics, but it is apparent that there has been some shift in public sentiment, political activity, and governmental concerns. The important issues of the day are distinct from those of the pre-World War II years, as in the general mood of the political participants. It is difficult to pinpoint the change, but it becomes noticeable when we approach political party activities in the past decade.[2]

For the most part, it seems that the more dynamic, larger, more powerful, wealthier Latin American nations are meeting the challenges of modernization in the distributive phase. They have generally overcome severe internal crises and have lived through deep disturbances to their societal fabric. Latin American economic growth, partially evident from modernization indices,[3] has engendered a spirit of political incrementalism—that is, of not going too far afield from tried formulas, not deprecating casually, or violating abruptly that which has been achieved.

It appears that vast sectors of Latin America's politically socialized groups have reached a level of cooperative and mutual political bargaining regarding some of the hitherto deeply divisive social issues.[4] There are few institutional groups in Latin America that would opt for implanting a dictatorially conceived totalitarian political structure. Bonapartist populism

[1] Parts of this chapter appeared originally as an article entitled, "A Two-Dimensional Typology of Latin American Political Parties," *Journal of Politics*, vol. 30, no. 3 (August 1968), pp. 798–832.

[2] Survey research conducted with mass publics, responding to questions about their views on political issues, is largely untapped in Latin America. One exception to this is Gabriel Almond and Sidney Verba's *The Civic Culture* (Boston: Little, Brown, 1965), a cross-national study, which includes a survey of Mexican attitudes regarding their level of political cognition, their sense of competence, and the impact of government on their lives.

[3] See Chapter 1.

[4] It is difficult to say just who makes up these groups but there are some helpful statistics: voter turnout figures are given in the volumes of *Statistical Abstract of Latin America* (Los Angeles), and there are various country electoral analyses by the *Institute for the Comparative Study of Political Systems* (Washington, D.C.); urbanization indices are provided by the *United Nations Demographic Yearbook* (New York); figures for total work force in the industrial sector are included in *United Nations Statistical Yearbook* (New York). There are many economic

of the Perón variety has been generally discredited, as has the harshness and dislocations of the Castro-led experiment. The nineteenth century version of unencumbered capitalism is as out of style with Latin America's political culture as is an all-controlling state supervision over every aspect of the domestic market. To completely disengage from United States investments and political interests is as unrealistic today as the acceptance of a completely unchecked flow of United States investments and assistance. The church-state issue has been reasonably interred. The church is recognized symbolically as part of the nation's official personality and accepted as an influential partner in political socialization within essentially private sectors of political life, but its public force has been relegated to a negligible role. This is no better exemplified than by the positions taken by Christian Democratic parties, both in and out of power.

Centralism versus decentralism, the federal-unitary struggles that so long immersed many Latin American nations in tragic internal conflicts, has also been resolved. The acknowledged winner in every case has been the central government which has acted moderately and reasonably enough to avoid secessionist movements or extreme domestic discontent. Certainly in the federal systems of Mexico, Brazil, and Argentina, a bargain among unequal powers has been formed which has not deterred the increasing control and competence exercised by national governments. Advocates of complete parcelization of land are as infrequent as those who would leave the nation's natural resources in the control of unproductive hands. The military's institutional role in society has generally been accepted as a possible force for good, despite its inveterate backsliding into learned reflexes of intervention. "Welfare socialism," or a "regulated capitalism" is the most popular image of the future economy. Domestic procedures liberally sprinkled with guided governmental authority are generally the expected political system.

The social systems of these Latin American countries have all sustained and supported competitive political parties. There are no powerful social institutions or political mechanisms for inhibiting a fairly open exchange of political information. Despite current military predominance in three of the five countries, interaction among political groupings does go on. Even where parties cannot formally participate in the political process, repressive measures have been taken, not against the presence of parties in the political system as such, but rather temporarily against the leadership and programs of these parties, which represent a different bias in terms of the overall political culture. Parties in these countries, whether or not they are actually in a position to wield power, or whether or not they represent significant portions of the population, are visible and functioning political units. They offer the public a variety of political perspectives.

---

indices surveys published regularly by the *Economic Commission for Latin America* (New York).

This portrayal of Latin American political culture is by no means meant to discount certain alienated sectors in almost every Latin American society. However, the chances of integrating these disaffected segments of people is a challenge that the majority of Latin American nations have begun to meet.

Within the context of party politics in our five-country perspective, there is an evident development during the distributive phase of development both in the types of parties evolving and their concomitant political behavior. Initially, one is made aware of the plethora of parties and of the mixed nature of these parties in terms of origin and age. Actually few of the major and significant parties have their beginnings in the nineteenth century. This alone may account for some of the changes that have occurred in party activity.

In Mexico the two most influential parties are creations of the twentieth century. The governing PRI party had its beginnings in the 1920s, though its formalization must be placed during the period of President Calles's dominance or 1928–1934. The major opposition party PAN arose in the late 1930s. In Brazil the major, though now defunct, political parties all developed into fullfledged parties during and since World War II. In Peru, the former, governing party, Acción Popular is less than a decade old, as was its coalition partner, the Christian Democrats and the Odriista Party of General and former dictator Manuel Odría. The fourth party, the Apristas, had its origin in the 1920s and represents the only "mature" party.

In the more "mixed" political party systems of Argentina and Chile, there exist side-by-side both nineteenth and twentieth century parties. Of the two major political groupings in Argentina, the Radicals and the Peronistas, the first is a late nineteenth century development and the second is an immediate post-World War II incipient. In regard to the Conservative and Socialist party sectors, the former group can trace its development to the formation of the Argentine Union (1860s) and the latter to the birth of international socialism shortly before the turn of the twentieth century. Factions which split off the parent Radical Party are of very recent vintage (1957–1963) and represented additional young parties in the political spectrum. Chile tends toward a similar melange. Three of its parties have nineteenth century roots—the Conservatives (1830s), the Liberals (1820s), and the Radicals (1860s). The most influential, the Christian Democrats, are a development of a decade ago, though it has its antecedents in the pre-World War II period. The other major party grouping is the Popular Union (UP), an association of Socialist, Communist and lesser parties which can be traced to the early 1930s, though their amalgamation was conceived on an on-again, off-again basis by 1937.

This exercise in chronology alone makes sufficiently clear the need for reevaluation of parties in Latin America, merely from the standpoint of analyzing the overwhelming number of political party newcomers to power and to principal opposition categories. As parties which have recently developed in response to new conditions, they have in turn had a vast influence on Latin American political systems.

Latin America as a whole can be best described in general terms as having essentially a multiparty political pattern.[5] Since much of the past instability of the Latin American political systems has occurred because of the activities of institutional interest groups (for example, the military), it does not seem overly optimistic to label the majority of Latin American party systems as essentially working multiparty systems. Based on the supercession of old issues, on contemporary socioeconomic indicators, and on the growing homogeneity of the Latin American political culture, the Latin American party system may be profitably viewed in the light of their increasing success at making multiparty systems work.[6]

Left-right classifications are no longer particularly useful. For instance, some parties which are benign in their relationship with the church are vigorous prosecutors of profound land reforms; some who are friendly to United States private investments demand nationalization of basic industries; some who favor the legalization of the Communist party opposed the basic tenet of the progressive tax reforms proposed by the Alliance for Progress, and so on, indefinitely. Who is to say then which is left and which is right? It is also not very meaningful to merely cite a party's social identification (for example, workers—socialists, land-owners—conservatives, church—Christian Democrats, trade unionists—Peronistas, and so on) or to solely refer to "economic" groupings, such as "statists" versus "free enterprisers" or ideological groupings, such as Marxists versus Democrats. Such party pigeonholing may obscure the cooperation which appears to have been reached as to the apolitical role of the church, on the avoidance of the totalitarian forms of institutional controls, and on the requirements of a mixed economic partnership.

More recent typologies have neglected many pertinent factors which may be considered in the assessment of Latin American political parties. The

[5] See John D. Martz, "Dilemma in the Study of Latin American Political Parties," *Journal of Politics*, vol. 26, no. 1 (August 1964), p. 517.

[6] This phrase used by Dankwart A. Rustow, "Scandinavia: Working Multiparty Systems" in Sigmund Neumann (ed.), *Modern Political Parties* (Chicago: University of Chicago Press, 1956), has come to mean that certain political systems with a minimal amount of societal consensus and no major political cleavages can make multiparty systems function effectively. The chapters by Hans Daalder, "Parties, Elites, and Political Developments in Western Europe," and Giovanni Sartori, "European Political Parties: The Case of Polarized Pluralism," in Joseph LaPalombara and Myron Weiner (eds.), *Political Parties and Political Development* (Princeton: Princeton University Press, 1966), both caution against the tendency of Anglo-American scholars to write off working multiparty systems as some sort of aberration of more authentic two party systems. Also see Gabriel A. Almond, "Introduction," p. 42 in Gabriel A. Almond and James S. Coleman, *The Politics of Developing Areas* (Princeton, N.J.: Princeton University Press, 1960), for Scandinavian version of the multi-party system.

typologies are usually rather static, though often sophisticated analyses of party systems and party functions. These typologies have tended to place the burden on Latin American scholars to either demonstrate exceptions to the rule or confidently place Latin American parties into the dictatorial one-party or unstable multiparty systems. The latter approach has found much favor in Latin American political party analyses.[7]

In the typology of political parties suggested here, the concepts of *party mobility* and *party perception* are used. By political parties it is meant those identifiable, autonomous organizations with known values and beliefs which they propose to promulgate upon achieving political office. Though the selection is for the most part composed of important national parties that consistently compete in elections, it also includes parties which, from time to time, have been politically restricted though their political organization remains intact. Party mobility refers to the likelihood with which a party tends to ally with another party or parties. It describes the means and methods considered legitimate in a party's attempts to attain power and influence. It refers to self-imposed rules governing party activity vis-à-vis other organized seekers of authority. Party perception refers to the manner in which a party views societal problems and their solution. It implies something about the values adhered to by a party and the general nature of its commitment to political and social change and the degree of certainty with which it creates definite and prescribed goals for the whole society.

Under the *party mobility* category, there are three groupings which encompass all parties acting within the confines of any particular political system: (1) Aggregator party, (2) Resistor party, and (3) Isolator party.

Under party perception, we similarly list three groupings: (1) Perservator party, (2) Innovator party, and (3) Rejector party.

An *Aggregator party* is extremely flexible and infinitely adaptive. It finds itself comfortable in wide-ranging and loosely conceived party alliances. In its relationship to other parties, it is both purposeful and ambiguous and is anxious to maximize the possibilities of "other-party" cooperation. It recognizes the importance of combining political groupings until a sufficient plurality of political support has been amassed. It is preoccupied with constructing enough cooperation among other parties to allow it to possess a minimum amount of political power.

A *Resistor Party* is highly competitive and finds the resources for its policies and actions mainly from carefully prescribed internal formulations. It

[7] A typical classification, for example, divides ". . . political parties into those which are traditional, that is, which came down from the earliest years of these countries' independence; those which are of European inspiration, the national revolutionary parties; and those which can be classified as totalitarian." Robert J. Alexander, *Latin American Politics and Government* (New York: Harper & Row, 1965), p. 49.

derives strength from acting in an autonomous manner and usually refuses the commitments that it fears are inherent in multiparty arrangements. It looks upon interparty arrangements as weakening its capacity to achieve power alone. It finds it difficult to adapt its means of competing for power to those of other political parties. It opposes the "conventions" of interparty agreements.

An *Isolator Party* represents a relative "outsider" in the political arena, both from necessity and choice. Its assessment of political life makes it incompatible with its political competitors. It eschews the mediation required for party agreements and dislikes the features of political compromise and political bargaining. Preferring to act in opposition, it is most amenable to refutation and confrontation.

In the category of *perception:* The *Preservator Party* resists any deep-seated alterations of society and identifies its political life with the existing socioeconomic relationships. It distrusts any basic readjustment of societal patterns of development. Committed to the continuation of present patterns of social stratification, it is likely to support the trend of contemporary allocations of goods and services.

The *Innovator Party* demonstrates an essentially empirical approach to socioeconomic problems. It is willing to experiment with various political formulas and does not overly commit itself to an absolute view of society. It will bend to the political exigencies of the moment in order to resolve political impasses or economic obstacles. It seeks to accommodate the largest possible sources of interest.

The *Rejector Party* does not accept the basic suppositions of other parties and sees contemporary societal adjustments and adaptations as poor substitutes for a profound restructuring of society's institutions. Suspicious of incremental reformist approaches to economic and social problems, it prefers seeking solutions through measures not easily accepted by most societal interests.

The perception categories should not be confused with traditional typologies of left-right-center. These categories do not describe the relative extremism or moderation in party pronouncements or party dogma but rather the capacity and/or willingness of parties to react flexibly and nondoctrinally to changing socioeconomic conditions affecting the political system.

Any given party that has been classified within the traditional left-right-center can be placed into any one of these perception categories. For example, a left-wing party by the same token can be an innovator or a preservator. A right-wing party may be a rejector. In addition, both may be any one of the three mobility categories, as well, depending on their degree of isolation from the mainstream of political party interaction.

Our use of the word aggregator is confined to the aggregation in some kind of bargain, alliance, or coalition with other parties and *not* necessarily to the act of incorporating social strata and interest sectors into political participation by means of political parties. It is an interparty definition, not a sociopolitical concept.

In the usual Latin American multiparty system, it is easier to win an election in aggregation with other parties. Since it is probable that all parties want to mobilize more and more of the public as adherents of its party's formulas, to aggregate with other parties presents a shortcut to aggregating social sectors, because it is assumed that the party with which one aggregates also has its constituents. Thus to aggregate with parties can result in aggregation in the broader societal sense. This seems to be particularly true in a multiparty system. If one party does not make such a move to initiate party aggregation, then other parties will, striving as they are (most of the time) to preserve or gain influence in governmental decision making—a *sine qua non* of party politics.

No distinctions are made between enduring alliances and temporary electoral "fronts." Electoral alliances are the specific factors that are considered, though coalition governments are treated since they are significant indicators of a similar aggregative predisposition. Parliamentary alliances and joint voting behavior are *not* considered because of the repetition of such agreements by all parties in a multiparty system. Voting in common in the legislature is not indicative of party mobility or perception. Parties often vote with others simply because with only a positive, abstention or negative vote and more than two parties participating, there are few voting alternatives for the legislator.

An attempt is made to arrive at a two-dimensional typology of Latin American political parties—that is, in the sense used here, a method of defining parties in light of the added dimension of motion within the political party system. Such observable party characteristics as mobility and perception may then be the working concepts in predicting power and stability within a political system.

With greater agreement present in Latin America over issues and ideology, there is now a discernible movement to comply with a developing electorate's predisposition for the pragmatically resolvable issue rather than the ideologically bifurcating issue.[8] The major parties are competing for what they feel is the aggregator-innovator position where the bulk of the votes are likely to be found both now and in the future. The tendency to merge toward this "center" of the political arena appears just as strong in a multiparty system as in a two-party system. As the landed classes are slowly weakened and as the urban and rural workers increasingly, albeit slowly, move up economically, it is from the growing middle sectors that support must be increasingly gained.

[8] See Charles W. Anderson, "Central American Political Parties: A Functional Approach," *Western Political Quarterly*, vol. 15, no. 1 (March 1962), p. 136.

It is, therefore, interesting to note how parties have changed in their mobility/perception orientation and how they are changing and probably will change. It appears that political power will be increasingly fought out in relation to the parties' mobility and perception potential and that the aggregator-innovator party has the best chance of achieving lasting political influence. Parties which move toward this aggregator-innovator position face the possibilities of either assuming power, developing into a principal opposition party, or facing the possible absorption by a larger or more effective aggregator-innovator party within the same category.

There seems to be a relationship between the capacity to achieve and hold power and the success at reaching an aggregator-innovator outlook. It appears that once a party becomes an aggregator in terms of its mobility, it usually follows that this party is bound to shift to a more innovative perception view by way of its close interchange with other political parties. This proposition also holds for a party which becomes innovative first, leading it to accept extraparty commitments with much more ease and developing thereby an aggregative view.

Once a party makes a bid for power, it appears it must first become an aggregator or an innovator. Other positions such as a resistor-preservator or an isolator-rejector are much further removed from power and will probably have to undergo important mobility-perception shifts to challenge the parties in power. Parties may, however, survive for long periods in these weaker positions, but once they make a bid for power, it seems they must move toward some form of either aggregation or innovation. This initial move seems to be followed by a complementary change in the other dynamic function of aggregation or innovation.

On the other hand parties that maintain preservator or rejector perceptions, that do not adapt their perceptions toward an innovative view of society, usually remain in the nonaggregative mobility categories of resistors and isolators. If their mobility factor would allow them to aggregate then it would probably be necessary to make a perception move toward innovation. Similarly, a party that alters its perception first to one of innovation will normally be available to extra-party alliances forecasting a mobility shift on the part of that party.

As parties aggregate and innovate, they tend to reinforce habits of compromise and accommodation. This increases the amount of interparty consensus and lessens the need for confrontation. Distinct from that of the aggregator-preservator and of the aggregator-rejector, the alliance of aggregator-innovators is grounded on a continual expansion of the points of ideological contact. This alliance breeds majoritarian aspirations. The other two are content with holding some power through a significant minority. The continuing search for consensus subjects aggregator-innovator parties to inner stresses and strains. This internal dimension is one of adaptation to the political ecology as varyingly interpreted by its leaders. Given such a party's unwillingness to abort experimentation, these conflicts and internal dissensions will continue. Should aggregative-innovative coalitions break up, it is predictable that the parties concerned will have gained valuable experience from the partnership in terms of having a new taste for power, acquiring more tolerance for political compromise and developing sensible programs grounded in reality.

Minor parties within the isolator-rejector and isolator-preservator categories continue to persist not only because of their consistent interpretation of society but also because they provide status, jobs, and psychological gratification for their permanent membership. This sustains their dedication to a uniformity of perception.

Mexico

Mexico has essentially a one-party dominated political system, though, as in other Latin American examples, the roots are present for a potential extension of that system to include another party or, less likely, two more parties. The existence of Mexico's single-member electoral mechanism leaves room for the development of a second major political party in opposition.

Mexico, though it has as yet not established viable alternative governing parties, has a stable political system, and PRI can be classified as an aggregator-innovator. PAN has not, until very recently, demonstrated any willingness to either aggregate or innovate and has, for the most part, remained in the resistor-preservator category.[9] However, PRI has been increasingly sensitive to the accusations of "one-party dictatorship" and has appeared to be making overtures to the PAN party as evidenced by the awarding of governmental jobs and by the electoral provisions giving PAN representation of up to twenty seats in the Chamber of Deputies for votes over 2.5 per cent of the total cast (which alone usually cannot assure PAN victory in any single-member district). In return PRI would hope that on PAN's side the party would respond by recognizing basic democratic features of Mexican institutions. PAN may face the dilemma of absorption, an apparent risk of aggregation-innovation. Presently a resistor-preservator, PAN is being increasingly invited to aggregate (in terms of receiving governmental posts). This will

[9] PAN supporters include ". . . old established families . . ., certain *nouveaux riches* . . ., many of the upwardly mobile middle class . . ., and an uncertain base of peasants and artisans whose susceptibility to clerical propaganda has placed them within the PAN ranks." Kenneth F. Johnson, "Ideological Correlates of Right Wing Political Alienation in Mexico," *American Political Science Review*, vol. 59, no. 3 (September 1965), p. 659.

mean a move toward the aggregator-preservator category from where, if PAN adjusts itself to the goals of the "Mexican Revolution," it stands to be absorbed by the PRI party. PAN has shown evidence of resisting this move and has generally remained a resistor-preservator. As such it is safe but powerless. On the other hand, PAN may choose to first innovate its policy views. Once having shown the predisposition to innovate, it will then be in a position to more easily come to terms with PRI. At this point the party may be able to challenge PRI effectively *or* be absorbed as a distinct political party.

PRI's dilemma is that while searching for a "loyal opposition" party it threatens to either absorb PAN or maintain it as a resistor-preservator, which means it will have no real opposition and again will be susceptible to cries of "dictatorship." In the past rather than PAN, the Union Nacional Sinarquista (UNS) has acted as the leading representative of alienated isolator-rejector politics in Mexico. PAN, on the other hand, has shown of late a perception response toward a more innovative view and acceptance of parts of the PRI program it hitherto rejected. Its problem consists of having a desire to innovate without finding itself in a potentially fatal aggregation with PRI.

The Partido Popular Socialista (PPS) continues to have a small following among the Mexican electorate. In the last three presidential contests it did not advance its own candidate but rather supported the PRI candidate while it ran its own members for legislative races. It has shown an increasing tendency to support PRI domestic and international policies. As an aggregator-rejector, the PPS has often allied with other rejector parties who have negligible followings and have been highly critical of the government. For the PPS there are two unpleasant alternatives. From their aggregator-rejector position they may move toward innovation and likely absorption by the PRI or toward the resistor-rejector position where they are unlikely to play an important role in the political system.[10] Their absorption by the PRI is the more likely alternative given former party president Lombardo Toledano's increasing tendency to identify with PRI policies. Since 1961 factions of the PPS dissatisfied with the growing accommodation between the PPS and the PRI abandoned their party to form other small rejector groups.[11]

[10] Lombardo Toledano spoke out often and unequivocally about the successes of the Mexican Revolution and the continuing socioeconomic achievements of the PRI. As Robert P. Millon points out, "The PPS places its greatest emphasis upon realizing a program of concrete reforms in alliance with the progressive elements of the PRI." *Mexican Marxist: Vicente Lombardo Toledano* (Chapel Hill: The University of North Carolina Press, 1966), p. 192.

[11] See L. Vincent Padgett's, *The Mexican Political System* (Boston: Houghton Mifflin, 1966), pp. 75–78, and Bo Anderson and James D. Cockroft, "Control and Cooptation in Mexican Politics," *Journal of Comparative Sociology*, vol. 7, no. 1–2 (March 1966), pp. 11–28. The latter study is particularly helpful in depicting the relationship to the PRI party of radical urban and rural groups (e.g.,

Peru

Peru has seen the emergence of the Acción Popular (AP) as an aggregator-innovator party. The Prado government, represented by the Movimiento Democrático Peruano (MDP), was an aggregator-preservator. The Aprista Party (APRA), occasionally collaborating with the government, maintained an aggregator-rejector position. The aggregation between the MDP and the Apristas did not endure, as neither party made lasting innovative concessions. This was probably because of the fairly inflexible nature of Prado and the MDP's political perception, since it appeared that the Apristas, after years of unbending opposition, were ready to aggregate with a truly innovative political party.

The contemporary situation has, of course, been superseded by the military intervention. The AP and the Christian Democrats had developed a governing alliance with a growing coincidence between themselves and the Apristas on the major Peruvian economic problems: oil, land reform, and taxation questions. The Apristas, understandably cynical about the possibilities of gaining power on their own, had shown a predilection for this type of collaboration.

The fourth important party, the Unión Nacional Odriista (UNO), was an aggregator-preservator. It had been allied with the Apristas since the election of Belaúnde Terry in 1963. However, as the Apristas moved toward closer ties with the AP and Christian Democrats, the Odriistas were forced into a resistor-preservator position. Odriista intransigence may be responsible for the fact that the post-1963 Aprista-Odriista alliance had not been based on a really conciliatory attitude. The Apristas have evolved toward an aggregator-innovator position. Haya de la Torre no longer speaks of the necessity of a social revolution in Peru but rather sees potential for social change from above. Among Aprista leaders the immediate distribution of wealth is receiving secondary emphasis in favor of the need for concomitant capital accumulation and investment.[12]

As for the AP it appeared aggregative and innovative enough to mediate any outstanding difference with the Apristas. Whether a concordance between

---

the MLN, the Movement of National Liberation, and the CCI, the Independent Peasants Association). The leader of the MLN, Lázaro Cardenas, eventually supported Díaz Ordaz's candidacy in 1964. By making certain concessions to the CCI, the PRI leadership forced a split in the peasant movement, the core group returning to the PRI fold by mid-1965.

[12] See Frederick B. Pike, "The Old and the New APRA in Peru: Myth and Reality," *Inter-American Economic Affairs*, vol. 18, no. 2 (Autumn 1964), pp. 30–45. For the most comprehensive account of Peruvian party politics since 1963 the reader is advised to consult Carlos Astiz, *Pressure Groups and Power Elites in Peruvian Politics* (Ithaca, N.Y.: Cornell University Press, 1969), Ch. 6.

the two most powerful Peruvian parties is ever established or whether the Apristas remain to become again the leading opposition force depend, to a great extent, on the predisposition of the Peruvian military to reinstitute democratic participation through the existing political party system.

Brazil

Brazil's present political affairs are in a period of institutional flux. However, historically, none of Brazil's major three parties has permanently maintained a position as aggregator-innovator. With Brazil's formerly employed multimember, preferential list voting districts, a proliferation of splinter parties and sectional coalitions all but completely blurred party responsibility and cohesiveness. This made it almost impossible to win over 50 per cent of the vote in any national or state election without resorting to the formation of coalitions.[13]

The Kubitschek PSD government was essentially aggregative-innovative, allying both electorally and administratively with the PTB, from whose ranks Vice President João Goulart arose. However, both the UDN personalist government of Jañio Quadros and Goulart's PTB administration after Quadros's resignation, though each began as an aggregator-innovator, became aggregator-rejectors.[14] One ventures a conjecture that Quadros would have been destined for military overthrow had it not been for the existence of the even more rejector-like perceptions of his vice-president.[15] By the advent of the Goulart government of 1961, both the UDN and PSD were aggregator-preservators, though they did not formulate policies with any consistent mutuality.

Recent Brazilian political party history has brought to light the dilemma of a charismatic, personalist leadership, followed by parties that do not provide a cohesive organization ready to act in consonance with the leadership. The presidencies of Quadros and Goulart, particularly, pointed out the essential isolation within which the administration operated. This may offer a clue to the lack of party response to the resignation of Quadros and the ouster of Goulart. As both administrations turned to a rejector-type of political percep-

[13] Phyllis Peterson, "Brazil: Institutionalized Confusion," in Martin Needler (ed.), *Political Systems of Latin America* (Princeton: Van Nostrand, 1964), p. 483.

[14] Helio Jaguaribe describes the rejector policies of Quadros. See *The Brazilian Structural Crisis,* Seminar Report no. 1 (Riverside: University of California, 1966), pp. 12–14.

[15] James Rowe sees the groups who supported Quadros as a coalition of irreconcilable antisystem extremists of all political colorations. James Rowe, "The Revolution and the System: Notes on Brazilian Politics," *American University Field Staff Reports,* p. 14. (First cited in Ch. 6.)

tion, their intra- and inter-party aggregative alliances melted away, allowing the two decapitated parties to be eclipsed by the military.[16] With the political suspension of former President Kubitschek of the PSD, the cycle was completed.

The newly formed, military-sponsored political parties of Arena (Aliança Renovadora Nacional) and Modeb (Movimento Democrático Brasileiro) are a military-imposed response to the Brazilian party power vacuum. However, without a mass-based party organization and with negligible public participation, these creatures of the state may founder in a preservator-type of perception that may maintain the Brazilian political community without a mass-based innovator party.

Chile

The Christian Democrats of Chile are an aggregator-innovator party with solidly based mass support and political monopoly of the center of Chile's party politics. They have moved toward the center of the political spectrum for a decade now and appeared to be firmly entrenched, even more so than the aggregator-innovator Acción Democrática of Venezuela and the Acción Popular of Peru. The Christian Democrats moved from resistor-preservator in the mid-1950's to a resistor-innovator position under the Alessandri administration. By 1964 they had evolved toward an aggregator-innovator position from whence they made their successful bid for power.[17]

The original aggregator party *par excellence*, the Radicals, in the 1964 presidential election shifted to a preservator perception while in 1970 they sought aggregation with other major political parties.

[16] "The ideological confrontation of Left-wing and Right-wing blocks, expressing the radical polarization of the big cities, powerfully contributed to the sliding of the Goulart government from its initial (and viable) Center-left position to its later (and non-viable) Radical-left posture. This confrontation also exerted a similar effect on the army, as the most representative and effective political agent of the middle class." Helio Jaguaribe, *Political Strategies of National Development in Brazil*, Studies in Comparative International Development, vol. 3, no. 2, 1967–8 (New Brunswick, N.J.: Rutgers University Press), p. 40.

[17] The aggregative-innovative strain among the Christian Democrats has become somewhat clearer by the visible internal factions among its membership. This can be seen best in the party's controversial refusal to censure former Socialist Senator Salvador Allende (now President of Chile) for participating in the Havana-led Latin American Solidarity Organization meetings, held in August 1967, which was predicated on promoting guerrilla warfare throughout the hemisphere. For an examination of internal party splits on major issues among the Christian Democrats between 1964 and 1968, see George W. Grayson, "Chile's Christian Democratic Party: Power Factions and Ideology," *Review of Politics*, vol. 31, no. 2 (April 1969), pp. 147–171.

The Liberals and Conservatives, traditionally aggregator-preservators, have since 1964 shown indications of accepting a *modus vivendi* with the Christian Democrats. Having been thoroughly weakened by recent electoral trends, they supported the Christian Democratic presidential candidate Eduardo Frei in the 1964 election. Their accommodating move may mean absorption in return for governmental jobs and a slight innovative policy shift by the Christian Democrats, of which the latter are perfectly capable. The early 1966 organizational fusion (National Party) of the Liberals and Conservatives (punctuated by their relative success in the 1969 congressional elections) demonstrated their resistance to this eventuality.

The UP (a popular front of Socialists and Communists) has generally acted as an aggregator-rejector, but the conditions of the 1970 presidential campaign of Salvador Allende forced an innovative perception move.[18] The Christian Democratic electoral process has left the UP as the governing coalition. This factor could enhance the development of a responsible two-party system, with either group acting as an aggregator-innovator governing party.

The Christian Democrats have occupied the vacuum left by Radical lack of innovation. The Radicals for years aggregated easily but found it difficult to maintain their original policy of innovation initiated with Socialists and Communists in 1937. The three-way aggregator-preservator alliance among the Radicals, Liberals, and Conservatives (Frente Democratico) of 1961 indubitably diverted Radicalism from any innovative perception it may have contemplated and left the Christian Democrats a free field as an innovative party mobilizing toward aggregation.[19]

In the post-1969 period, all the major parties have been attempting to readjust policies and assuage internal dissatisfactions. The fluidity and flexibility of the Chilean party system has never been more apparent. Indeed a formidable alliance developed to challenge the aggregator-innovator position of the Christian Democrats. Despite occasional interparty difficulties, the Socialists and Communists will probably continue to govern under moderate Socialist and Communist leadership and are consciously attempting to in-

[18] As among the Christian Democrats, certain growing pains within the UP are observable. Herbert S. Dinerstein, "Soviet Policy in Latin America," *American Political Science Review*, vol. 61, no. 1 (March 1967), p. 88, notes that the Communists have been closer to a position in support of President Frei. The Socialists have shown the greater resistance (see Ernest Halperin). It is also noteworthy that the Communist party (and not the Socialists) condemned the Havana solidarity conference.

[19] Federico G. Gil and Charles J. Parrish, *The Chilean Presidential Election of September 4, 1964: An Analysis* (Washington: Institute for the Comparative Study of Political Systems, 1965), p. 19. Anibal Pinto states that the Radical Party refused to consider important fiscal and land reforms in the post-war period and became more and more the prisoner of its traditional wing and its commitment to the largest landowners. This eventually undermined the Popular Front. *Chile: una economia dificil* (Mexico: Fondo de Cultura Económica, 1964), pp. 172–177.

novate their perceptions. The Radical party, despite its aggregative tradition, still retains a preservator mentality that appears likely to restrict it in any long-term innovative alliance whether with the government or preservator groups.

Argentina

The Radicals (UCRP) of Argentina were a minority governing party. The main concern of the UCRP was to develop a working majority party. The UCRP faced the dilemma of either aggregating, something which has been traditionally distasteful to them, or facing political eclipse at the hands of the Peronistas who were split momentarily between factions favoring innovation and others supporting rejection. Events since the March 1965 election indicated that the Peronistas as a massive, consolidated block were more likely to innovate than the resistor-conscious UCRP were apt to aggregate.

The Peronista-UCRI (and other smaller parties) alliance in 1958 and the Peronista-UCRI-Christian Democratic (and other smaller parties) alliance of 1963 have amply demonstrated Peronista propensity toward aggregation. The Peronistas had moved toward aggregation and were innovating toward respectability and thereby the possible assumption of power. A certain amount of Peronista innovation was already apparent in Peronista moderation both before and after their March 1965 Congressional victory. Peronistas, as in the past, were receiving support and aggregative feelers from the UCRI, the MID of Arturo Frondizi, and the Christian Democrats.[20]

The governing Radicals hitherto had been unable to aggregate, though it appeared an internal party struggle over this issue was about to commence before the 1966 military coup. They found themselves more and more isolated in their resistance and forced to aggregate with the Conservative party, forming a resistor-preservator alliance.

Of several minor parties within the Argentine party system, the more important MID, UCRI, and Christian Democrats were all essentially aggregator-innovators, which demonstrates the relatively high potential for consensus among many of the Argentine political parties. The remainder of the smaller parties were resistor-preservators and isolator-rejectors.

In summary, among the dominant parties, the Peronistas, in line with their immediate aspirations and holding military political activity constant, appeared to be in the most advantageous political position. It would have taken quite a mobility shift within the ranks of the Radicals to maintain

[20] Peter Ranis, " Peronismo Without Perón: Ten Years After the Fall (1955–1965)," *Journal of Inter-American Studies*, vol. 8, no. 1 (January 1966), pp. 122–128.

themselves as a viable and preponderant governing party. Meanwhile, their resistor-innovator views promoted a generally unsettled atmosphere in Argentine society. The continued UCRP resistance to aggregation resulted in a lack of innovation among the party leadership and organization. Their highly restricted party government prevented the entry of new technical personnel and new development ideas. The incapacity of the Radical administration to resolve Argentina's outstanding inflationary and, in general, socioeconomic problems, coupled with their insulation from other parties, heightened tensions in Argentina and augmented the vulnerability of the Illia government to military intervention. In the months prior to the military coup, the Radical governing party appeared willing only to develop alignment possibilities with the Conservatives, which was not a serious alternative to fully aggregating with parties of various perceptions.

Summary

We have been attempting to describe political parties in Latin America by means of a two-dimensional typology based on party mobility and party perception. The typology has been applied to political systems in flux.[21] The aggregator-innovator position seems to represent the large, basically unvarying field of power. It is as if there were a continual gravitational attraction emanating from this political power center which accounts for party coalitions as parties vie for power within a multipartism situation. Parties give indication of moving toward the center as they seek to approach political influence and enjoy greater expectation of being awarded power. The more influential parties tend not to be very narrowly based, ideology appears to be playing an ever-declining role, and parties are sharply aware of the political facts of life.[22]

Because of the essential flux of Latin American party systems, what bears particular observation is the direction in which parties move vis-à-vis other parties. Ideological classifications are not true indicators of the ability of a party to compromise. Some examples are in order: In Argentina the Peronistas were willing to compromise and the Socialists were not, yet within ideological typologies both might be lumped as leftists. In Chile the UP

[21] Another method of comparing political systems cross-nationally is provided in the typology formulated by Joseph LaPalombara and Myron Weiner, *Political Parties and Political Development* (Princeton: Princeton University Press, 1966), pp. 33–42. It pertains not only to the relative competitiveness of a political system (hegemonic as against turnover systems) but to a second characteristic classifying either type of system along an ideological-pragmatic continuum.

[22] Some of these country examples may put in question Lipset's estimation about the importance of ideology in developing countries. Seymour M. Lipset, *Political Man* (New York: Doubleday, 1963), pp. 454–456.

is defined as "left-wing," yet it has moved toward innovation, an ingredient much less visible under an ideological categorization. In Peru, the Apristas are momentarily undergoing doctrinal change; thus an understanding of where the party has been and where it is going is needed. It is necessary to distinguish among parties hitherto often banded together because of a similar "ideology."

What has been discussed is the degree to which certain parties are able to weaken ideological rigidity, freeing them thereby for greater mobility and interaction with other parties. The first is essential for the second and the second impossible without the first. Said another way, the more strongly the "nondoctrinal element" in the party emerges to the forefront, the greater the possibility that the party will be able to aggregate and innovate.[23]

All types of parties want to win votes, and thus all act pragmatically to a degree in appealing to the voters. However, the acid test of true pragmatism seems to be the willingness of a party to aggregate with other parties, thereby giving up some of its own doctrinal concepts. The narrowness or broadness of a party is a function of whether it is truly aggregative and innovative. If a party is just personalistic or develops a following on just one issue, then that party undoubtedly will not withstand the test of time that a truly aggregative-innovative party will.

By the application of this typology of parties, the following political characteristics appear to be true. Firstly, there is nothing *de facto* in a multipartism situation that will prevent party coalitions or even rule out the eventual formation of a bipartism party system.[24] Secondly, party perceptions are both a substantial basis for party action and tools toward gaining governmental control. This is the case in Latin America as elsewhere in politicized national communities.[25] Thirdly, those Latin American parties in which ideology plays a smaller role will remain powerful or emerge victorious in the near future, and those in which ideology assumes a dominant role will fall to or remain on the peripheries of power.[26] Fourthly, in a multiparty system, there is usually a necessity to coalesce or ally with other parties either before

[23] Neil A. McDonald, *The Study of Political Parties* (New York: Random House, 1955), p. 32.

[24] One of Maurice Duverger's key exceptions to his general rule is that multiparty systems do not preclude the development of one- or two-party dominance and the possible stabilization implied in such a party system. *Political Parties* (New York: John Wiley, 1963), pp. 314–315.

[25] In *An Economic Theory of Democracy* (New York: Harper and Row, 1957), pp. 96–102, Anthony Downs hypothesizes that political parties are interested in gaining office per se, not in promoting a better or ideal society. These parties employ varying ideologies in order to maximize their vote potential.

[26] Downs, *An Economic Theory of Democracy*, pp. 111–113, agreeing with Neil McDonald, explains that the attempt within parties to "modernize" will cause a conflict between those adherents to former ideological dictates and those members whose prime concern is to win elections.

or after elections. With electoral victory as a rational and reasonable party goal, electoral coalitions present a flexible and normal mechanism for its achievement.[27] Thus there is a meaningful correlation between the propinquity to political power and the propensity to form alliances and coalitions. Fifthly, the process of aggregating and innovating serves the double stabilizing function of either providing a second innovating party that will loyally oppose a similar party or of absorbing smaller aggregating parties which do not have a sufficiently identifiable policy or have too small a popular base of support.

From our triangular diagram, we can conceivably calculate the relative strength and weaknesses of a given political system. It could be determined which parties are far from power and which potentially close. The Figure might indicate the degree of political consensus present which, in turn, may offer a clue to potential political development. All nine boxes could logically be filled with the type of party that would fit that mobility-perception category. Thus a corresponding number of boxes could be filled in for any political party eventuality. It might then be possible to predict party changes within a political system and perhaps anticipate any broad recasting of the political culture.

This two-dimensional typology has been devised in order to complement other approaches to the study of parties within the political development process. This method of viewing political parties has not been directly concerned with a party's organization, its leadership, or the degree of its grass-roots support. Rather it has been assumed that the more institutionalized, broader-based parties will gradually come from the aggregator-innovator categories. Parties with these mobility-perception attitudes are likely to attain longevity and gain or retain popular-mass support through organized interest groups and the general participating electorate.

The aggregator-innovator parties of Mexico, Peru, Chile, and Argentina, not to mention several in Venezuela, Costa Rica, and Uruguay, appear to have had the perceptiveness to ameliorate and mollify the evident dissensus among major political and economic interests in Latin America. As governing entities or major opposition groups they seem closer to combining the political ideals of strength, compassion, and justice than parties of rejector and preservator perceptions. Secondly, they are most in tune with the conflicting and often contradictory demands of distributive politics. Thirdly, the aggregator-innovator parties best mirror the attributes, conditions, and restraints built into the Latin American political culture.

In terms of criteria of political development, aggregator-innovator parties can elicit broader popular support by reason of their rational predisposition to political power. Once in office these parties rarely overpower major societal

[27] William Riker spells this out in detail in his stimulating treatise on political coalitions. *The Theory of Political Coalitions* (New Haven: Yale University Press, 1962), pp. 21, 184–186.

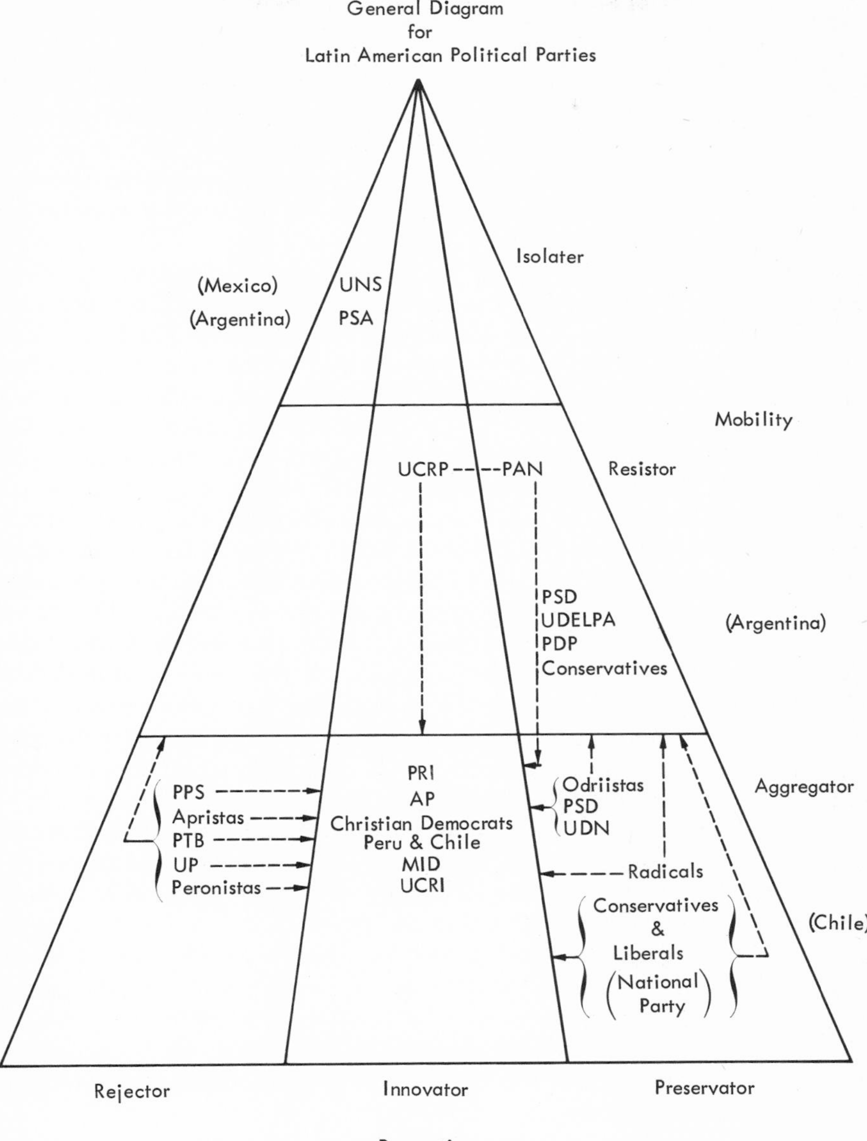
General Diagram
for
Latin American Political Parties
(Mexico)
(Argentina)
UNS
PSA
Isolater
Mobility
UCRP -- --PAN
Resistor
PSD
UDELPA
PDP
Conservatives
(Argentina)
PRI
AP
Christian Democrats
Peru & Chile
MID
UCRI
PPS
Apristas
PTB
UP
Peronistas
Odriistas
PSD
UDN
Aggregator
Radicals
Conservatives
&
Liberals
(National
Party)
(Chile)
Rejector
Innovator
Preservator
Perception

interests and thus help promote the climate of a stable political administration. A peaceful political transfer of power is more predictable under these conditions because of the aggregator-innovator party's essentially nonideological approach to political responsibility. They are therefore more likely to conform to the rules of the game as they compete for power. They are not prepared to restructure society totally in conformance with a preconceived set of ideological hypotheses. Therefore they will more readily adapt to the slowly evolving patterns of political legitimacy. Thus it becomes less and less in the interests of organized sectors of the populace to confront such political parties and more and more in their interests to make these parties even more responsive and representative.

Because they are rarely committed to more than one societal interest, their electoral and political pretensions consist of satisfying a consistent majority of social interests. The continual construction and rebuilding of such majorities tends to have important public payoffs. The political community *en todo* is more likely to see the aggregator-innovator party as a fair and just arbiter because they do not identify the party with any one set of antagonistic interests. Further, given this rather dynamic relationship between government party and various national constituencies, the aggregator-innovator party is least likely among all the parties to fear the growth and further mobilization of newly participant political sectors.

Distributive phase politics requires a balanced relationship between governmental intervention on behalf of minimizing societal differences and fomenting industrial development as an antecedent for further social equalization. Because of the aggregator-innovator party's healthy respect for combining many minority interests in its construction of a majority, it is best able to intervene on behalf of distributive policies without laying waste the social plurality structure or succumbing passively to a single organized interest group. Under this set of circumstances such major groups as the military, church, bureaucrats, labor, industry, commerce, and students may find incremental change preferable to winning or losing all.

Lastly, aggregator-innovator parties, by their natural acceptance of dissent and opposition, tend to foster a participatory political culture. Their autoperception precludes the absorption of all societal functions, and they thus perceive the prerequisites of societal autonomy. The innovative perception simply does not permit the adoption of such messianic, chiliastic measures. They see themselves as a creation of the society's political culture rather than as *the* representative of some new order or the protector of one or several special views of how society ought to remain.

CHAPTER 12 Nonparty Political Groups

Almost all of Latin America, and certainly the five countries under study here, can be best described as transitional societies fully committed to economic and political development. In this type of environment, unorganized as well as organized interests are bound to have substantial effect. These interests compete with each other in the development process in order to attain what they consider their share of the goods that governments intend to distribute. Particularly in those societies in which political growth is progressing at a faster rate than economic growth there will be a proliferation of interests which challenge the political system in order to divide limited economic resources. These interests are working within a political framework which is still not entirely mature and so seek to establish a *modus vivendi* that will assure them at least modest compensation. Once public and private relationships are established, interest groups usually settle down to more limited and specific functions, but until such time in Latin America, nonparty political groups continue to play disproportionally important roles in the political arena.

All interest groups either seek to change or to preserve contemporary social patterns. All, given the right combination of circumstances, will enter the political sphere in order to make their influence felt. The degree of success with which any particular political group operates is contingent upon its degree of organization, its size, its prestige, its wealth, and the means and tactics it employs to reach the political elites.

Since, in general, Latin America is not as stable as Western Europe and the United States, interest groups often resort to more overt forms of political intervention, the more extreme forms of which portend social revolution. Unable to secure a certain modicum of economic benefits, many political groups launch themselves openly into competition with political parties and the governing administration. Interest groups occasionally seek power rather than influence. Instead of working by and through the existing system, they oppose the system and often move outside of the normal avenues of political pressure.

In Latin America interest groups focus mainly on the administration and the political executive who heads the governing agencies. However, some influence is exerted at the legislative and party level and is proportional to the openness of the society and to the division of formal powers and the degree of differentiation between a majority party and the government. If the political system is rigid, then there is little interest activity on the party and legislative level. All is generally focused on the administrative level.

It is in this area of political penetration that one may meaningfully categorize political groups in Latin America. In the larger sense it is possible to speak of two types of interest groups: the institutional and the noninstitutional. The former refers to those groups such as the military,[1] the various bureaucratic sectors, the public agencies (for example, petroleum corporations and national development institutes), and the church—all of which are considered part of the establishment in Latin America. The church, however, is slowly being relegated to a less formal position in the public structure. Noninstitutional interests are those groups within the private sector of society that elicit support from and wield pressure upon agents of the public sector. These are groups representing labor, agriculture, business, and students as well as lesser groups—those which don't usually maintain a permanent organization, such as political action societies, academic associations, and women's groups.[2]

Within each of these two categories, it is possible to further divide the interests into three headings: latent, channeled, and direct pressures upon the government. Latent pressure refers to that applied by groups who have a potential for organization but, for one reason or another, remain on the periphery of political action. Individuals within these groups share many common beliefs and viewpoints but do not organize effectively. Channeled pressure emanates from those groups who, upon organization, are able to make use of the means of political communication and make contact within the political system. They can make their wishes known through the existing instruments available to social and political groups. Channeled pressures work through public and party organizations and have a continuous effect upon public policy and decision making. Direct pressures arise from those groups who maintain that they are underrepresented or who deeply disagree with the pattern of political and economic development. These groups openly confront the political system through such mechanisms as demonstrations, strikes, terrorism, coups, and revolution in order to assert the political goals which they feel are being suppressed. Direct pressure is exerted by those who are openly opposed to the criteria for value and goods allocations and who therefore reject the normal processes for channeling interests.

A latent interest may develop into a channeled pressure which may later assume the proportions of a direct pressure. Political groups may move along a scale of activity from latent to direct. The more stable a society and the

[1] A very commendable survey of the growing literature on the military in Latin America is L. N. McAlister's, "Recent Research and Writings on the Role of the Military in Latin America," *Latin American Research Review*, vol. 2, no. 1 (Fall 1966), pp. 5–36.

[2] A dichotomy between "institutional" and "functional" pressure groups has been made before in the literature. For example see S. W. Eisenstadt's chapter "Bureaucracy and Political Development," in Joseph LaPalombara (ed.), *Bureaucracy and Political Development*, pp. 118–119.

more organized and representative its institutions, the more likely will the vast majority of interests seek to exert channeled pressures. Traditional societies, those which have barely achieved national political organization, have a preponderance of latent interests which, in a more developed environment, will become channeled or direct.

Because of the transitional nature of Latin American society, interest groups are preponderantly channeled or direct-pressure groups. A great number are within the institutional category because of the tendency in Latin America to absorb leading pressure groups within the governmental structure. Many of these political groups in more institutionalized societies would fall under noninstitutionalized categories. Given the strength of executive dominance in Latin America, interests must readily avail themselves of any feasible approach to the locus of power which is the public administration.

As elsewhere, the more influential interest groups represent labor, agriculture, and business. Other groups, such as the military, church, and students, while not directly and continually concerned with wages and prices, are peripherally involved in these and also in deepseated societal questions. With the public corporations so widespread in Latin America, many of the most powerful pressure groups are part of the governmental structure and can channel their interests through to the policy makers. This inhibits their independence and often results in their capture by the party in power. This is especially true in nations in which there has been a predominant party in power over a series of years. Elsewhere major political parties represent one important interest and are a marriage between political power and economic support. Here the interest group does not shop around for support from other political parties. Often labor, the church, or landowners' associations give their support for long periods of time to the same political party. Business groups, professional associations, students, and other associations identified with the middle sectors tend to be more pragmatic in their choice which they base upon a continual reassessment of sociopolitical conditions.

The spontaneous, short-lived interest group appears to be both rare and unimportant in Latin America. This is no doubt a function of the limited complexity and nondifferentiated nature of the social structure. These short-range, one-issue interest groups are usually unheeded, absorbed by a major interest structure, or forced to apply direct pressure which jeopardizes governmental institutions or results in the suppression of that group.

Interest groups are, however, on the increase as governmental regulation and supervision extend to more and more sectors of the society and the economy. This development is necessitating an increasing participation in public affairs by the various groups, who seek to influence legislation and regulations affecting their special interests. The government, as principal employer, financier, investor, and rule- and law-maker, is the center of a vast empire that must be given attention if the interests which comprise it are to continue to function under the growing state regulation of private sectors of society. In such a situation political activity is as essential as economic activity to the private interests concerned.

One reason that the activities of interest groups are centered on the executive branch of government is the weakness of Latin American legislatures and the discipline wielded by party leaders of the executive branch over party people who sit as legislators. The general weakness of the federalist structure in Mexico, Brazil, and Argentina also contributes to the absence of interest group activity on the regional and local level in those countries, since most of the largess is distributed at the national level. In their quest to obtain benefits or protect their interests, pressure groups in Latin America often perform the function of representation quite apart from the population or regional representation afforded constituents in elections. Especially because of the weakness of the legislative branch of government, the large parties and important interest groups do much to represent basic interests in society. Though this aggregation of interests is an important input function, it does, because it is so highly polarized, result in largescale, organized conflicts. Interest groups thus perform a type of functional representation. However, the growth of aggregator-innovator parties may tend to alleviate the problem of group confrontation. Party aggregation of interests on the other hand is made difficult by the apparent capacity in developing societies for monolithic and single-minded interest groups to mobilize so completely. Because most Latin American countries do not have completely open societies yet, there is little overlap of interest-group membership, which tends to soften the effects of pressure tactics. With the lack of a full-fledged pluralism, citizens tend to join but one organization to which they give undivided attention, financial support, and complete loyalty. This factor helps to bifurcate Latin American society at a time when there appears to be enough group cooperation present to resolve political and economic development problems.[3]

[3] The study of organized group interests and particularly identifiable subcultures does not abound in the social science literature on Latin America. Several studies, however, merit mention here along with some of the other citations of this chapter. On urban interests (such as the industrialists, labor, students), the church and peasantry see Seymour Martin Lipset and Aldo Solari (eds.), *Elites in Latin America* (New York: Oxford University Press, 1967); and John J. Johnson, *Continuity and Change in Latin America* (Stanford: Stanford University Press, 1964); Particularly on the church, see W. V. D'Antonio and F. B. Pike, *Religion, Revolution and Reform* (New York: Praeger, 1964); and F. Houtart and E. Pin, *The Church and the Latin American Revolution* (New York: Sheed and Ward, 1965); On labor, *Labor Relations in Argentina, Brazil and Chile* (New York: McGraw-Hill, 1962); On students, L. R. Scheman, "The Brazilian Law Student: Background, Habits, Attitude," *Journal of Inter-American Studies*, vol. 5, no. 3 (July, 1963); Frank Bonilla, "The Student Federation of Chile—50 Years of Political Action," *Journal of Inter-American Studies*, vol. 2, no. 3 (July 1960), and Kenneth Walker, "Family and University Influences on the Political Socializa-

Interest groups in Latin America, since they are either absorbed into the institutional structure of the government or integrated into a particular party, do not perform research, consultation, education, and other functions that assist legislators in modern nations. By the same token legislators and administrators do not look upon them as very reliable sources of information or as necessarily representing vast sectors of the population. There is the further problem of the apparent inability of interest groups to represent one particular interest at a time. Rather these associations often present packages which have little chance of being accepted or sometimes even considered.

Interest groups, because of the social situation, are often forced to use direct methods of action which further weaken the social stiuation. A vicious cycle commences which heightens distrust between the government and opposition pressure groups. Direct action by pressure groups is an indication of the lack of channels available to reach the government.

Mexico

The Mexican situation demonstrates the effectiveness of channeling not only interest groups into a predominant political party but in absorbing major socioeconomic groups into the governmental structure. The Mexican leaders have made an effort over the years to make sure that disaffected groups did not habitually turn to direct action against the government. Also of importance to the continuing success of the PRI is its capacity to organize latent interest even before they turn to unchanneled means of political expression.

The leading interest group in Mexico is the upper administrative class which fills most of the important executive positions and which maintains nominal representation within the popular sector of the PRI party giving that sector the most important role in the party hierarchy.[4] It is these administrators, along with the top leadership of the PRI party, which are the most important policy makers in Mexico. Since the most influential group in Mexico is an integral part of the governing hierarchy, it is better able to channel interests or manipulate policy.[5] The other two important interest

tion of Colombian and Uruguayan University Students" (Paper delivered at 1967 Annual Meeting of the American Political Science Association, September 5–9, 1967).

[4] Distinct from minority parties, the PRI administration can offer the bureaucratic interests all kinds of opportunities, services, spoils, and other incentives that give this pressure group great cohesiveness. On this general situation see Fred W. Riggs, "Bureaucrats and Political Development: A Paradoxical View," in Joseph LaPalombara (ed.), *Bureaucracy and Political Development* (Princeton: Princeton University Press, 1963), p. 130 ff.

[5] In addition, such a functional overlap between politics and administration serves to ensure some sort of social and political stability. See Robert E. Scott,

groups which channel their pressure through the PRI party are the labor and peasant sectors. Though currently not as important as the public managers, these two groups maintain party liaison with the party rank and file and are instrumental in mobilizing the support for the party among the organized workers and peasants.

The military is not a separate entity within the PRI organization but rather a part of the popular sector. Thus it is able to channel its views both through the political leadership and through the popular sector of the PRI. Many other eloquent and influential interests, such as professional teachers of secondary schools, intellectuals, and middle class businessmen, have been for the most part, integrated into the governing party structure.

In contemporary Mexico, only the church, the largest landowners, some elements of corporate business, and certain factions among the students have not been entirely absorbed into the party structure. The Mexican Revolution was launched against the first three groups, and thus ideological considerations make their complete incorporation difficult. Certainly the PAN party is successfully competing in many sections of Mexico for the support of these groups. The PRI party has by no means accepted the idea that it cannot integrate these groups, but feels rather that it has other political policy priorities. The PRI view of economic development by way of a mixed capitalist-socialist system is flexible enough to circumvent permanent obstacles. In the meantime PRI has been careful not to completely alienate these groups. For instance, large acreage property still exists in private hands, and there is little thought among Mexico's leaders of launching any total collectivization. The church continues to be allowed full religious freedom, and nothing has been done by the government to perpetrate a national mystique that would view Catholicism as an antinational phenomenon, as is the case in Eastern Europe, the USSR, and Cuba. Restrictions upon the church include only delimiting its activities in the political and commercial sphere and prohibiting its organizing for any nonreligious purpose. So-called "big business" is showing an increasingly ambivalent attitude toward the PRI and, given the Mexican government's solicitude for the private foreign and domestic sector, appears to be rapidly moving toward an accommodation with the government.

Students, however, often feel themselves alienated from the bureaucratic ubiquity of the PRI and continue to agitate on foreign policy issues, increasing participation of workers in industry, the autonomy of the university, and on other areas where they feel that the Mexican government has betrayed its revolutionary promise.

The PRI, as a national political organization, maintains liaison with

---

"The Government Bureaucrats and Political Change," *Journal of International Affairs*, vol. 20, no. 2 (1966), p. 307.

interest groups all over the country, using those interest groups that best represent a particular economic interest in a particular region. By this type of specialization the PRI has managed to avoid overt interest group confrontation.[6] Aside from this effective division of functional representation, the PRI has managed to organize interests not on an ad hoc but rather on a permanent basis, as a result of which the interests feel continually able to communicate their wants before the party. Once an interest group has been identified, the PRI gives it a sense of belonging to the decision-making process and supports it by the various means at the disposal of the Mexican government. The result is that most interests are channeled through controllable bureaucratic institutions.[7]

Peru

In Peru the leading interest group is the military. It is an institutional pressure group which has exerted a predominant role in politics throughout most of Peru's history, the latest example of which was the overt military intervention in 1968. Today their channeled pressure affects almost all civil and military decision-making policies.[8] The landowners and their associations, various business groups, labor, and students all exert pressures that vary between direct and channeled. In the last decade, and to some extent since the post-World War II period, it has been labor that has acted in the most

[6] For an interesting case study of how the PRI maintains itself responsive to sectional, intra-party interest group demands, see William Tuohy and David Ronfeld, "Political Control and the Recruitment of Middle Level Elites in Mexico: An Example from Agrarian Politics," *Western Political Quarterly*, vol. 22, no. 2 (June 1969), pp. 365–374.

[7] As Fred W. Riggs, *Bureaucrats and Political Development*, pp. 140–141, has pointed out, the creation of some interest groups follows a bureaucratic initiative. Riggs goes on: "They are not a spontaneous product of citizen demand in response to felt needs. The groups extend the reach of the bureaucracy, providing it with transmission belts through which total mobilization can, potentially, be achieved. Hence, the growth of state sponsored interest groups augments bureaucratic control, without necessarily strengthening any centers of autonomous political power capable of bringing bureaucratic machines under popular control. In other words, this process leads to political development in the sense of politicization, but not democratization. Quite the reverse, for here we see how accelerated economic and social development contributes to bureaucratic power. . . ."

[8] Particularly so because the Peruvian military increasingly sees itself as a potential modernizing agent with definite views of development criteria. Liisa North came to this conclusion in light of her review of the official journal of the army, *Revista Militar*, in the years 1949–1951 and then again—1962–1964. *Civil-Military Relations in Argentina, Chile and Peru* (Berkeley: Institute of International Studies, 1966), pp. 52–57. Also see Rudolph Gomez, *The Peruvian Administrative State* (Boulder: University of Colorado, 1969), pp. 17–20.

direct manner.[9] The other noninstitutional pressures, because of the bias of the Odría administration in favor of the landed and business interests, have generally been channeled. The church, as part of the total institutional picture, exerts important channeled pressures and is a leading public opinion maker.[10] The peasants of the Peruvian highlands are the only latent interests, as most of them are generally unorganized and the various Indian villages are not coordinated.

The Acción Popular as well as the subsequent Velasco military governments have begun steps in the direction of channeling Indian interests through community development and land reform and parcelization schemes. And as an aggregator-innovator party, AP began the lessening of tensions between the labor and business representatives of the urban middle sectors.

Brazil

In Brazil the channeled institutional pressure of the military has been converted into the direct assumption of power. Though the military has not usually acted as a monolithic and unanimous bloc, they have been the predominant organized interest to affect governmental activity. Since 1930, by commission or omission they have prevented certain civil governments from acting while they have sustained the activities of others.[11] In 1945 they were instrumental in the overthrow of the Vargas government which was replaced by a regime headed by a military man. Military pressures by the predominant faction allowed President Kubitschek to assume his presidential office in 1955. After the Quadros resignation in 1961, the military forced through the constitutional change from a presidential to a parliamentary system. The return by plebiscite to a presidential system under Goulart was interrupted by open intervention and the seizure of the national administration.

The military has acted as the principal policy maker since early 1964, and the likelihood is that they will remain on the forefront of the political scene for many years.[12] The da Costa y Silva government received support

[9] See James L. Payne, *Labor and Politics in Peru* (New Haven: Yale University Press, 1965).

[10] Ivan Vallier assesses the institutionalized church elites in Peru as "politicians." By this he refers to religious leaders who maintain connections with the political sphere and depend on their capacity to manipulate both power groups and public opinion. See Vallier's "Religious Elites: Differentiations and Developments in Roman Catholicism," in Lipset and Solari, *Elites in Latin America*, pp. 190–226. An excellent anatomical survey of the church in a most valuable book on Latin America.

[11] For a comprehensive study of the military in Brazil during the last several decades see J. J. Johnson, *The Military and Society in Latin America* (Stanford: Stanford University Press, 1964), pp. 202ff.

[12] President Artur da Costa y Silva reaffirmed this trend by naming military

from many sectors of the society, including the middle classes, the large landed interests, and some sectors of the intelligentsia. More than ever before during a period of military intervention the armed forces appeared to see themselves not solely as constitutional caretakers but as the agency responsible for economic development.[13] Since assuming power in Brazil, the military has virtually acted by decree. Political parties have been disbanded and ordered to reorganize, individuals have been deprived of their civil and political rights, and legislation has been by fiat in most sectors of the economy. The military government has been careful to maintain normal relations with other representatives of the middle sectors, and many of its appointees to the public administration are civilians who were opposed to the economic and political policies of the Goulart government.

TABLE 12-1 Military Expenditures

Country	*Percentage of National Budget*	*Percentage of GNP*
Brazil	16.1	3.4
Argentina	15.0	2.3
Peru	13.1	3.4
Chile	8.8	1.8
Mexico	8.2	.7

Source: Inter-American Economic Affairs, vol. 20, no. 4 (Spring 1967), p. 93.

The various governmental agencies, ministries, and autonomous corporations exert continuous pressures. The military regime has strengthened the bureaucracy while it has weakened political parties, the national legislature, and noninstitutional pressure groups, such as labor, business, and agriculture. The church, never as powerful here as in the northern Latin American nations, is not exerting important pressure in areas of public policy.

---

officers to half of his eighteen-member cabinet. The Armed Forces were awarded such major posts as Ministers of Labor, Interior, Industry and Commerce, Mines, and Energy and Transport. It is not insignificant that Brazil leads the other Latin American countries in their military expenditures ($940 million).

[13] The Brazilian situation (mirrored in Argentina and in Peru) demonstrates the importance of viewing the military as an intricate group within the decision-making sphere of economic and political development. The military is increasingly recognized by social scientists as a complex institution that merits profound analysis in terms of its continuing role as a modernizing elite group. Past interpretations of just a few years ago already seem dated because they are overly normative in character and thus overvalued certain democratizing characteristics and discounted developmental criteria. For example, see Victor Alba, "The Stages of Militarism in Latin America," in J. J. Johnson, *The Role of the Military in Underdeveloped Countries* (Princeton, N.J.: Princeton University Press, 1962), pp. 165–183.

Chile

Chile's relatively open society allows for interest groups to channel their wishes at various levels of the government. With the legislative and judiciary branches to a greater degree separated from the executive, interest groups have more areas of penetration than in Mexico, Brazil, or Peru. In Chile, the usual institutional pressure groups—the church and the military—are generally apolitical, though they act as staunch defenders of their associational interests.[14] It has been rare in the last several decades for either of these groups to take any consistent public position on issues not directly related to their interests. The ubiquitous, far-flung bureaucracy is the most powerful institutional interest, though all the autonomous agencies, ministries, and nationalized industry and utility commissions do not take any unified position.

Among the noninstitutional groups, the labor and student sectors are the most vocal and the most likely to resort to direct pressures upon the government.[15] The copper miners, though the aristocracy of Chile's labor force, exert the most militant pressure for economic and social reform.

The Christian Democrats were the first party in recent Chilean history that gave hope of representing enough of a cross section of business, agriculture, and labor as to be able to assure at least minimum satisfaction to these interest groups as they channel their demands into the political system.

[14] Liisa North, *Civil-Military Relations in Argentina, Chile, and Peru,* pp. 26–31, attributes the professional character of the Chilean military as due to the unwillingness of civilians to use the army as an instrument for the attainment of political ends. This is contrasted to the high politization of the Argentine military by various political parties. As far as the church is concerned Ivan Vallier sees Chile as the stronghold of the "pastor-pluralist" tendencies within the church: the former group emphasizing congregation-oriented themes to better weld the societal community to the Catholic liturgy and sacraments; the "pluralists" representing clerical groups who seek to assist any enterprise, religious or otherwise, in social and economic amelioration. Lipset and Solari, *Elites in Latin America,* pp. 203–226. For a comparison of the social concerns of the Catholic Church of Peru and Chile see Frederick B. Pike, "The Catholic Church and Modernization in Peru and Chile," *Journal of International Affairs,* vol. 20, no. 2 (1966), pp. 272–288.

[15] Militant student power has increased markedly within the national Chilean Student Federation (FECH) since 1968 and reached its height during violent student protests in the hectic presidential campaign of 1970 in which the government established martial law in several departments. See George W. Grayson, "Chile's Christian Democratic Party: Power, Factions, and Ideology," *Review of Politics,* vol. 31, no. 2 (April 1969), p. 168. On the other hand, relatively little cohesive, organized pressure emanates from the largely fragmented Chilean industrial sector. See Dale L. Johnson, *The National and Progressive Bourgeoisie in Chile* (New Brunswick, New Jersey: Rutgers University Studies in Comparative International Development, vol. 4, no. 4 (1968–69), p. 78.

Argentina

Post-Perón Argentina, including the recent Radical government, has witnessed a deep-seated struggle between a channeled institutional pressure—the military—and the often direct-action oriented General Confederation of Labor which represents the vast majority of Argentine urban organized labor. The Argentine military, as the most powerful pressure group, has, within the last forty years, often reverted to direct intervention and has during more than half of that period been in physical control of the executive branch and the principal support of dependent governments during the other half.[16] Since 1930 the military has been in a continually stronger position with no threat of any rival pressure except possibly labor, which became institutionalized under the Perón regime. This threat was overcome with the military overthrow of Perón, and there has been none since. However, following the military intervention into the CGT in 1956, labor reorganized by 1961, under the presidency of Arturo Frondizi, redeveloped a central organization, and once again became a leading pressure association. The basic rivalry between labor and military interests far exceeds in importance the activities of any other noninstitutional pressure group. Party politics in Argentina is very much dependent upon and subordinate to this profound conflict.[17]

The largest agricultural interests are represented by the Sociedad Rural which exerts channelled pressure and is the agent of some of Argentina's most affluent and powerful cattle ranchers. The Argentine Chamber of Commerce, ACIEL (Association for Free Enterprise) and the Unión Industrial all have varying degrees of influence upon the public sector. Organized bureaucratic workers of government agencies also exert channeled pressures upon the executive. Governmental monopolies, as semi-independent corporations, are within this category. In this latter category, the Argentine Petroleum

[16] José Nun sees the military as a political force being employed increasingly by the middle class for its own economic and political ends. This would account for the recent increase in military coups in Latin America. See his "A Latin American Phenomenon: The Middle Class Military Coup," in *Trends in Social Science Research in Latin America* (Berkeley: Institute of International Studies, 1965), pp. 55–91. A different interpretation is offered by Marvin Goldwert, "Dichotomies of Militarism in Argentina," *Orbis*, vol. 10, no. 3 (Fall 1966), pp. 930–939. Goldwert states that the military in Latin America have assumed the role of the guardians of ordered change (reconciling economic modernization with political order) because of the failure of military men to find adequate and competent civilian vehicles for these goals.

[17] For an analysis of the various party and interest configurations that revolve about a basically bipolarized political community see Peter Ranis, "The Background to the 1965 Argentine Elections," *The World Today* (May 1965); "Peronismo Without Peron: Ten Years After the Fall," *Journal of Inter-American Studies*, vol. 8, no. 1 (January 1966).

Corporation (YPF) and Argentine Airline and Iron-steel industrial concerns (SOMISA) wield important influence. Finally, the church as part of the Argentine public arena continues to exert a channelled pressure, but only in matters pertaining to church-state relations, marriage and divorce laws, educational problems, and legislation that might be construed as infringing on the church's established position in Argentina.

Many Argentine interest groups have had close and obvious relations with one or another of the political parties. The military, though it tried to remain aloof from direct party warfare, has usually been identified with the conservative party or, given weak conservative public support, with groups of similar political propensities. This confluence of interests is not necessarily based on socioeconomic factors. As a whole, the military is a middle class group, while the groups which support the conservative parties in most provinces are usually affluent landowners and other traditionally upper class segments of Argentine agrarian society. Business interests in the urban centers tended to support Radical and other moderate parties, such as MID.

The labor unions electorally, financially, and ideologically support the Peronista party.[18] Though the party still receives its principal political support from labor, other groups have in the recent past begun to look more favorably on the Peronista movement as the only viable alternative to the ill-advised and noninnovating Radical party. Before the 1966 coup, government bureaucrats were generally inclined toward support for the Radicals and the Peronistas, with a small minority identifying with the various Socialist parties. The Catholic Church remains ambivalent and appears to be willing to work with almost any aggregator party which poses no threat to the church's preeminent social position. In this connection, only the Socialist and Communist parties have taken an overt stand for weakening the church in areas of education and social mores (in other words, legalizing divorce, separating church and state, and so on). The continuing weakness of the Christian Democratic party has not made it necessary for the church to take a public stand on this party, but it appears the church is not overly impressed with the rather radical stand of the Christian Democrats on land reform, tax reforms, and the nationalization of important industries. In relation to the two leading parties, the church appears prepared to work with either. Direct military intervention has been favorable to the church's interests.

[18] Apparently only 40 per cent of the rank and file laboring class are *consistent* supporters of Perón and Peronism. The remainder are distributed over a wide political spectrum, including Peronism. See Jeane Jordan Kirkpatrick, *Peronist Politics in Argentina: Composition, Expectations, and Demands of the Mass Base* (Columbia University, Doctoral Dissertation, 1968), p. 217.

Labor in Argentina: A Case Study of a Direct Pressure Group

As Perón and the Peronista movement were a principal issue in the precipitation of military intervention, so this grouping had an important impact upon the precedents and intricacies of the Argentine labor movement. Perón, the founder of the Peronista political party and a general in the Argentine army, was also Secretary of Labor between 1943 and 1946, the year he was elected to the presidency. His socioeconomic ties were threefold: political, military, and laborial. In this case study the political role of the General Confederation of Labor (CGT) will be briefly spelled out.

Though the CGT suffered several splits since its amalgamation of the Argentine Syndicalist Union and the Confederation of Argentine Workers in 1930, it has remained as an identifiable, substantially cohesive bloc representing the great majority of organized workers in Argentina.[19] There is substantial evidence to support the claim that the CGT is the most powerful and active labor force in Latin America. The peak of its power was achieved under the dictatorial leadership of Juan Perón. After the overthrow of Perón, the CGT suffered the military's intervention into union affairs from November, 1955, to March, 1961. Any chance to retrieve the unions from their close associational ties with Peronism was largely dissipated by the harsh nature of their treatment under the military provisional government. Thus the workers in a nonadaptive spirit have feared the post-Perón regimes, have not been very cooperative or adept at bargaining, and continue to cling to the memories of the Perón era where they attained goals by decree[20] and received socioeconomic gains without seeing these ameliorations in terms of the larger society.

Though the CGT is not necessarily synonymous with Peronism per se, it is generally accepted that its leadership has been largely drawn from Peronista ranks and its following is highly susceptible to Peronista aims. The CGT represents political unionism *par excellence*. The Confederation is distinguished by its high degree of politization. Its sociopolitical position is consistent with the main criteria of a political oriented labor movement.[21]

[19] Robert J. Alexander in Walter Galenson, *Labor in Developing Economies* (Berkeley: University of California Press, 1962), p. 163.

[20] See Tomás R. Fillol, *Social Factors in Economic Development: The Argentine Case* (Cambridge: MIT Press, 1961), p. 91.

[21] Bruce H. Millen, *The Political Role of Labor in Developing Countries* (Washington, D.C.: The Brookings Institution, 1963), p. 9, typifies several essential criteria: (1) The frequent use of direct mass action in support of nonindustrial objectives, and a propensity for tailoring the performance of economic functions to serve political ends; (2) A minimal of ideological conformity among the leadership; (3) Trade unionism alone is considered an inadequate instrument with which to attain the political, economic, and social reforms.

Under the Aramburu military government the labor movement received its worst setbacks. The unions were intervened, many labor leaders were jailed on conspiratorial charges, collective bargaining agreements were rescinded, and the Ministry of Labor was disbanded in all but its title. Under the Frondizi and Illia administrations, labor again assumed a more preponderant role. However, the Aramburu years placed the CGT "in opposition," from which it has not emerged. The labor movement, with the only real exception being the first few months of the Frondizi administration, has not supported any post-Perón Argentine government's policies. All parties have continued to compete for labor's support, but only the Peronista groups have been successful in receiving the majority of the CGT's backing. A full-fledged labor party has not developed, and labor continues to be "unrepresented" politically. In fact, the labor sector has been politically wooed more often than it has been economically satisfied.

The CGT has never pretended to represent an apolitical point-of-view.[22] It assumes a far more extensive attitude than typical craft unionism. The labor movement has not only provided individual Peronista candidates for high political office, but it is illustrative of a large societal pressure group before which no issue is too far reaching, no interest too minute.[23] However, it is incorrect to categorize the CGT as a monolithic superstructure. In contradistinction to the basic suppositions agreed upon within the military structure, workers have not, since the fall of Perón, been able to work in concert in the pursuit of their goals.[24]

During the period when the CGT was under government control (1955–1961), internal splits (not unaided by the Ministry of Labor) divided it into four major blocs: (1) the "62" Peronista unions which constituted the largest bloc, (2) the "32" or "democratic" unions, (3) the "independent" unions, including dissidents from both the "62" and "32" blocs, and (4) the "19" MUCS (the Unified and Coordinated Labor Movement) made up of Com-

[22] A recent study "The Labor Elite—Is it Revolutionary?" approaches the subject differently. Henry Landsberger's discussion of politically oriented unions is so restrictive that it makes its application less than useful in analyzing labor movements in Latin America. Furthermore, he tends to append political goals to a necessarily revolutionary ideological approach. One is the articulation of interests and the other, certain implied values and perceptions. See his article in Lipset and Solari, *Elites in Latin America*, pp. 256–300.

[23] As the head of the Argentine Textile Workers once put it: ". . . national unionism must affirm with facts, with doctrine and with words, its absolute opposition to apolitical syndicalism, because it is the best means for the subjection of the workers. And understand well that we are saying "political" and not "partisan," which are two distinct things. It is a stupidity and an injustice to ask a member to which party he belongs. Correspondingly the labor syndicates have clear and concrete political objectives and national and social interests." *La Nacion*, May 8, 1961.

[24] Fillol, *Social Factors in Economic Development: The Argentine Case*, p. 92.

munist-affiliated unions.[25] The actual numbers refer to the original groupings after the initial disagreements and do not correspond exactly to contemporary divisions of strength. It was in the August 1957 Congress of the CGT that the "32" and "19" unions withdrew, leaving the "62" as the major faction. The division was further aggravated by the refusal of the "32" unions to join the "62" in a forty-eight-hour strike called for October 23, 1957, protesting the government's wage-freeze policies.[26] By 1959 the "62" and the "19" were basically in agreement on most issues with the "32" still opposed. The "62" and "19" eventually formed the short-lived Unified Workers Movement, pledging themselves to oppose governmental austerity programs.[27]

The area of accord among all the unions was the return of the CGT to the workers themselves. In 1959, with a population of twenty million, Argentina contained eight million employable men and women. Of these, about three and one-half million were organized in national and local unions.[28] As a prerequisite for governmental recognition, the unions created a provisional federal committee of the CGT. It included "20" unions with half from the "62" and the rest divided between the "independent" and the "32" unions. This committee was to coordinate and direct the CGT with one voice. The government's view remained that the committee must preserve a basically nonpolitical posture. With the reactivation of the Law of Professional Association,[29] the CGT hoped to be able to speak with one voice as in the days of Perón. The differences that had developed since Perón's ouster were much more deep seated and consequential than the labor leaders dared admit during this sudden burst of unity.

Within the committee of "20," a compromise on the voting procedure was reached. Major matters such as calling strikes would require a two-thirds majority vote. All other matters required a simple majority. The secretariat to the committee was limited to eight members, four from the "62"—two each from the "32" and the "independents." Here, as within the political party system, the communists ("19") were frozen out. According to the Law of Professional Association, in the CGT Congress each union receives one representative if its membership is between 501 and 2,000; two representatives for a membership of 2,001–5,000, and five representatives for a 5,001–15,000 membership. For each union with a greater number than 15,000, one more representative will be granted for each 3,000 adherents. Within this framework it was estimated that the "62" could count on 500 out of the total delegate strength of about 900,[30] thus giving it a majoritarian control over the 2,500,000 strong CGT.

[25] *Hispanic American Report*, vol. 17, no. 2 (April 1964), pp. 164–165.
[26] *Buenos Aires Herald*, October 23, 1957.
[27] *La Nación*, January 23, 1961.
[28] Ibid., January 2, 1961.
[29] One union representing each industry.
[30] Ibid., March 12, 1962, p. 3.

Under the new machinery, CGT elections were held in February, 1963. José Alonso, former Peronista deputy and head of the Garment Workers Union, was elected General Secretary. The number two position as CGT Interior Secretary went to another Peronista, Avelino Fernandez.[31] The eight positions of the Secretariat were made up of five members from the "62" unions and three from the "independent" and "32" unions. On the larger twenty-man committee the "62" could count on twelve out of twenty of the members. Peronistas are particularly powerful within the textile, metallurgical, meat-packing, lumber, and other industrial unions. Radical and other party influences are strongest within the railway brotherhood, bank clerks, commercial employees, municipal employees, maritime workers, and other service unions. The Communist influence is basically confined to the construction and chemical workers' unions.[32]

The on again-off again marriage of the "independents" and the "62" unions, since the recovery of their autonomy in March, 1961, has been a difficult attempt at compromise and compatibility. The former base their responsibility upon achieving purely advantageous economic and security goals for the laboring force. Theirs is a membership of about 800,000 affiliates. The "62," with 1,700,000 followers, meanwhile find themselves willingly involved with a wide range of political and social issues. They continue to cooperate for fear of further weakening the labor movement. Both tendencies know that a single CGT gives them substantial bargaining powers regardless of their family squabbles.[33] Though the member unions have nominally remained as part of the CGT, 1964 brought deeper conflicts within the Confederation. The "independent" groups of unions, in protest against the "62's" leadership in the development of the "Battle Plan" (discussed below), resigned their three positions of leadership within the Secretariat of the CGT. By August of 1964 the Secretariat was controlled by Peronistas only.[34] Thus the labor movement was strictly under the control of Peronista party members and sympathizers, and the post-1964 period has seen an increasing confluence of Peronista-CGT political and economic goal orientations.

Now let us confine ourselves to the scale of labor goals in the political, economic and social fields and the parallel governmental attitudes and responses. There is little doubt that the labor unions represented a public

[31] Ibid., February 2, 1963, p. 4.

[32] A decree-law issued in August, 1967, qualifies Communist leadership in the CGT as illegal. Executive posts may not be filled by those so judged as Communist. See *La Nación*, August 26, 1967, p. 1.

[33] "Dos lineas sindicales," *Comentarios*, vol. 1, no. 15 (April 29, 1964), p. 4.

[34] Alonso (Garment Workers), Donaires (Paper Workers), Racchini (Soda Water Workers), Bustamente (Meat Packers), A. Fernandez (Metallurgical Workers), Elias (Textile Workers), Angeleri (Light and Power Workers), and Widmann (Insurance Employees). Bustamente was later replaced by L. Fernandez (Maritime Workers).

sector large enough to demand not only a hearing but a large degree of acceptance.

With the inauguration of President Arturo Frondizi, the labor movement breathed more deeply, blossomed under its newly found freedoms, and proceeded to initiate a substantive and aggressive labor program on all fronts. The first substantial conflict between government and labor arose in November, 1958. Frondizi had announced the contracts with foreign oil companies for the exploration and development of Argentine oil resources. The CGT sought to repudiate the contracts and requested their revision. On November 9 the labor leadership issued a series of demands culminating in an ultimatum which promised a series of gradually prolonged strikes until the whole petroleum industry was paralyzed.[35] However, the oil workers continued to delay the strike, apparently fearing the imposition of martial law which Frondizi had threatened to implement. When the petroleum workers finally did go on strike, it was met with a state-of-siege and the wholesale arrest of many strikers. Frequent government promises to hear out the laborers' views of the oil contracts, the high cost-of-living, and the right-to-strike were largely ignored as the strikes were met with force. Sympathetic railway strikers were forcibly mobilized on a military footing, and the most adamant were arrested.

This was one of the many instances of labor's inability to bargain peacefully or strike effectively. The failure of the petroleum strikes and the sustainment of the oil contracts permanently placed the CGT in opposition to Frondizi, though they continued on occasion to work with him. As has been noted, their victories under Frondizi were confined to the organizational unity and independence of the labor movement as compared with that under Aramburu's administration, rather than any effective solution to labor's economic and social claims. In fact, it is more in the recuperation of certain organizational rights, achieved under Perón, that the labor movement made its most pronounced strides.

In its economic proposals the CGT was often much less successful. The labor leadership has continually, since 1958, issued detailed statements of purpose. In the 1963 election year they advocated raising wage levels to match the rising cost of living, shortening the duration of labor contracts, setting maximum prices on basic goods, the stabilization of prices in accordance with strictly controlled production costs, and the limitation of profit. They recommended that full employment be attained by prohibiting the importation of domestically produced goods, rehiring of workers dismissed due to labor disputes, reducing taxes on Argentine-produced goods, and increasing bank credit to indigenous enterprises. The CGT, furthermore, urged the payment of all overdue wages and pensions, the elimination of huge military budgets, and the imposition of higher taxes on luxuries.[36]

In further petitions after the election of President Arturo Illia the CGT

[35] *Buenos Aires Herald*, November 9, 1958, p. 8.
[36] *Hispanic American Report*, vol. 16, no. 3 (May 1963), p. 293.

recommended higher old-age pensions and a sliding minimum wage. The failure of the administrations to meet most of these labor demands caused the CGT to launch its "Battle Plan" in the spring of 1964. In a series of maneuvers, workers would "occupy" various factories for twenty-four hours, create a temporary work stoppage, expel the employers and foremen, and after the appointed time lapse, return the factories to their owners. The relative nonviolent manner in which these occupations were carried out resulted in reciprocal governmental action, also couched in self-conscious moderation. These simultaneous seizures had great romantic and historical appeal and served notice of labor's organizational capacities. In May, 1964, within a period of twelve hours, 150,000 CGT members occupied more than 490 factories and businesses.

There is no question that the CGT's most important post-Perón organizational successes came under Frondizi's administration. By May, 1961, military intervention in the trade unions was ended, and the Law of Professional Association was reinstated. Internal dissensions kept the CGT from developing their own regulatory mechanisms until January, 1963. Thus, the 1955–1966 period has given the laborer fewer immediate benefits than the preceding Perón decade though certainly the CGT was not free under Perón in the sense of free trade unionism. In fact the post-Perón military interventions in the unions even had precedents under Perón. Though this paternalism has been previously made clear, it is important to reaffirm the workers' unfamiliarity with real autonomy. In the post-Perón period, it was not until 1961 that the CGT received an autonomy, unknown to it in the dictatorial decade.

The pronounced decrease in institutional tensions with the election of President Illia, again, as in early 1958, provided a period in which government-labor relations could be mollified and adjusted. The consequent easing of formerly inflexible attitudes also substantially cleared the air. The 1963 Illia annulment of the oil contracts negotiated by Frondizi assuaged the leadership of the CGT. In February, 1964, the labor sector supported Illia's success at having seen the legislature pass his controversial "Supply law." The law provided for a means to confront speculation and the repression of normal supply outlets. As its objective the law attempted to regulate the supply and production of essential commodities and maintain them at reasonable prices to the consumer. The law also provided for prison terms of from three to ten years for ". . . crimes against the national economy." Under emergency conditions, it gave the executive powers to determine rates of production, prices, and the rights of inspection and approval.

Although the military government's takeover under Juan Carlos Ongania caused great consternation among the CGT labor leaders, it also failed to unify the various factions of the labor confederation. The military government subsequently greatly weakened the confederation by intervening two of the largest, best endowed labor unions, the railway and dockworkers unions, thus depriving the CGT treasury of a large source of its revenue. By 1968, the CGT again made new but unsuccessful efforts to unify its various factions. This first of several so-called "normalization congresses" gave birth to a series of new labor divisions that continue to the present time. The labor movement was now divided among the "62" unions headed originally by Raimundo Ongaro, the "dialoguistas" formerly headed by Agusto Vandor, and a smaller faction of "participacionistas." Though the leadership of these divisions has frequently changed, the three positions, vis-à-vis the military governments of 1966–70, have continued to mark meaningful differences.

The "62" unions have represented militant confrontations based on a whole series of structural and socioeconomic critiques of the unrepresentative and unresponsive nature of the military governments. The "dialoguistas" advocate a permanent issue-oriented opposition to particular errors of economic policy committed by the government, while the "participacionistas" offer collaboration and support in return for the resolution of labor's outstanding bread and butter demands.

Though labor, as the most self-conscious pressure group in the country, went along with the Peronistas in the political sector into full opposition to the Radical government, the antagonisms were not as overt and flagrant as they were in the latter Frondizi years.[37] This semi-coexistence was temporary, a result of the UCRP's ambitious attempts to distribute income through cyclical wage increases while neglecting the fundamental needs of diversified production, foreign and private investments, and a general plan for heavy industry. The CGT as it became more long term developmentally directed rather than short term consumer oriented began manifesting greater impatience with the lack of Radical governmental initiative. As the Peronistas have turned toward an ever greater innovative-aggregative political approach, so the CGT has proven itself since the fall of Frondizi (who today would have received more understanding from labor leaders, if not from the rank and file), to be ever more motivated by functional problems than ideological attachments.

One of the principal concerns of labor in the contemporary is in the area of structural changes. It is becoming generally more aware of the problems of economic development. One very well-known CGT document stated:

> It seems that the country has continued its process of modernization but has not had the capacity to bring about the necessary transformations which, at the appropriate moment, should have and could have converted us not only into a modern nation but a developed one. This is one of the principal causes of our crisis.[38]

[37] José Luís de Imaz, *Los que mandan* (Buenos Aires: Editorial Universitaria de Buenos Aires, 1964), p. 211.

[38] The CGT's *Hacia el cambio de estructuras* (Buenos Aires: Confederación General de Trabajo, 1965), p. 9.

The same study goes on to delimit the essential stumbling blocks to consistent development as: (1) the rapid, voluminous, and premature growth of the middle class, largely as a result of overstaffed public bureaucracies and enterprises, a phenomenon similar to more developed countries that can more readily absorb and afford them; (2) the rapid raising of the workers' standard of living despite the absence of the economic infrastructure of developed countries; and (3) the coalition of national and international groups interested in maintaining Argentina's traditional economic structure.[39] All these factors, along with the problem of extreme consumer pressures and traditional modes of production and distribution, continue to militate against rapid economic development.

Though the eloquence and the perspicacity of the trade unions seem to be on the upswing, their power as an effective interest group is still limited by their own lack of technical preparation vis-à-vis bureaucratic, business, and agricultural groups. Also, together with the existing conflicts among the Peronista "62" and the "Independents," the organizational incapacities of the Communist "19", and the practical inoperativeness of the democratic "32",[40] there has been a general decline in membership over recent years and a growing rank and file disinterest in internal union affairs.[41]

Thus, though the CGT has an automatic political weight advantage over the majority of the parties combined, it is by no means a necessarily monolithic, Peronista-controlled organization.[42] Rather it is the CGT which, in its rank and file majority, fully support Peronismo and, given present societal conditions and the policies of the military government, will continue to do so. The CGT has suffered military interventions and deprivations after a period of relative ascendancy under Perón and thus is likely to uphold Peronismo until the realization of those social conditions which would make such a commitment one of diminishing returns.

Summary

Because of Latin America's transitional stage between traditional and modern political culture, demands from nonparty political groups remain subordinate in their impact to demands often manufactured and stimulated by bureaucracies within the government and special agencies within the ad-

[39] Ibid., pp. 18–19.

[40] Leonardo Dímase, *La situación gremial Argentina* (Buenos Aires: Ediciones Libera, 1964), pp. 29–33.

[41] José Luís de Imaz, *Los que mandan*, p. 233.

[42] In fact, since mid-1965, there have been growing political differences between the neo-Peronist labor leaders allied with Agusto Vandor and the more militant, fundamentalist leaders led by José Alonso (both leaders met violent deaths between 1968–70).

ministration. Most secondary groups among noninstitutional interests of the channeled variety do not yet have the substantial means to significantly affect public policy except when there is strong and viable accommodation among several of them.

Except for labor unions and student groups, most channeled noninstitutional interests tend to work through a small leadership personnel rather than by massive turnouts of members who are committed to one or another position. Thus though there are more groups who are willing to channel pressure, their ability to reconcile membership needs with the requirements established by public policy priorities puts many of them into the predicament of creating greater direct pressures. This, coupled with the built-in intelligence, financial, and communications advantage of institutional interests, has created a certain gap between social aspirations and governmental compliance.

Not only are many channeled interests largely unrepresentative but a certain inbreeding exists among many of Latin America's leaders in government who have attended the same faculties of law, economics, commerce, and engineering at national universities in the various capitals. These bureaucrats are similarly linked to the leadership of leading institutional groups.

However, interests continue to proliferate in every category and the patterns of political culture in Latin America lend merit and meaning to organizing around some interests. Though demands and information do not flow with any predictable freedom and consistency, long-range governmental inhibition of developing interests is not seriously espoused by any responsible political leader.

PART VI

Politics, Economics, and the Social System

The five countries under discussion are still developing countries, even though certain social, economic, and political sectors in each of them strongly resemble much more advanced nations. However, the carryover of some of these more urban institutions to the agrarian realm is much more tenuous. Stable relationships and symbiotic partnerships between social, economic, and political institutions are much rarer than in more developed polities. The concluding part of the book will examine the basic relationships and discuss some of the key problems that affect the connections between various institutional structures.

This section will explore in many ways very tentative though essential concepts. In the very nature of politics the importance of economic systems and social structure is of a crucial impact. Though it is hard to typify these patterns of contact, it is meaningful to try to relate these nonpolitical structures to contemporary political behavior. In turn a partial examination of social and economic systems assists in broadening the understanding of politics.

For example, if one were to adhere strictly to an investigation of Latin American political systems, it might be possible to be overly optimistic about the level of national development that has already been achieved. Levels of modernity are clearly above average in terms of the world polities, though certain pervasive social and economic factors act as obstacles to sustained and even political development. If one observes the modern urban setting with its confluence of services, commerce, and public and private bureaucracies, one comes away with a different picture than if one investigates, let us say, the productive capacity of either the industrial complex or the agrarian sector. Since political scientists tend to concentrate more on urban administrative structures than on either urban or rural productive enterprises, it is with caution that one can speak of levels of modernization and degrees of political stability. Thus to gain a more complete picture of Latin American politics, it is necessary to study not only questions of modernity and political development but also the ramifications of the economic and social developments.

We will conclude with an examination of the levels of and challenges to economic development, the impact of economic development on politics and public administrative decisions, the nature of the Latin American urban/rural dichotomy, the special concerns of the urban and agrarian sectors, the role of economic and political leadership and elites, and the social structure and its effects on political development.

CHAPTER 13 A General Statement on Modernization

Modernization is a criterion generally accepted by Latin American political leadership. It is sought both for the material goods it can bring and for values it can impart to a society. However, the process of modernization, while it cannot of itself perform industrial miracles overnight, often disrupts traditional institutions. Many of the larger Latin American nations as they enter the 70's are in this transitional stage.

Demonstration effects create demands that essentially nonindustrialized nations cannot immediately meet. The gap between desire and fulfillment forms the backdrop to the current dramas being acted out by most Latin American governments. Though the desire to achieve is essential for development, it tests the limits of institutional capacity. As often as not, there is a decline in social cohesion and political stability because of the tremendous explosion of human wants, which are perceived but still far from being satisfied. Modernization becomes a goal before the machinery has been developed to bring about its achievement.

The achievement of modernity requires a commitment to pluralism, democracy, and rationally conceived social objectives. These values, however, require the increasing amelioration of social discontent. It is as if, to invert Marx, the realm of commitment to these values is forcing important societal changes. This phenomenon is further stimulated by the easily accessible communications of more developed social systems from which come a veritable stream of information often creating ideational changes. The modernization impulse is thus a source of inspiration for economic development and, at the same time, the creator of a whole series of problems that complicate and irritate social interaction.

Competing with these impulses toward modernization certain inefficient economic practices, past privileges, and static interclass relationships remain. For example, prestige is still associated with certain nontechnical professions, the leisurely life is still a fairly pervasive goal, and many lower sectors of Latin American society are still immobile. These factors have resulted in many bottlenecks to economic development and, in general, are the cause of poor use of the land and the underutilization of almost all natural resources. There is general underemployment and a very inequitable consumption rate in which the upper stratas of society far outconsume the total population and divert valuable capital into conspicuous consumer goods and foreign bank holdings. The result is a depreciation of potential government revenue. Social and economic factors tend to reinforce each other in maintaining the status quo, and then it becomes important for the government to take the lead in breaking the self-perpetuating cycle. The crux of the problem appears to be to further loosen the grip the nonenergetic elements of society maintain over the bulk of investable capital. One method applied is the governmental manipulation of tax structures and investment opportunities for the wealthy and occasional use of firm moral suasion by the government. In conjunction with this, more people are given a stake in the operative commercial economy.

A major problem is the agricultural sector. Though important reforms have taken place in several of the Latin American countries, notably Mexico, the farms still do not produce enough to feed the growing industrial sectors. Social conditions in the rural area, for the most part, lack many of the rudimentary physical and commercial facilities needed for improved production and distribution. The apparent inability to mechanize the agricultural base can be traced to the present land-tenure pattern, poor technification, and the lack of a continuous investment flow. The landholdings system is burdened by the twin phenomena of the minifundios and latifundios, very small parcels of land or extremely vast landholdings. The minifundios, often the results of national agrarian reform programs, can be as unproductive as the latifundios. A very small piece of the land is often only large enough to feed the family that runs it. However, the minifundios serve a stabilizing psychological and social function by integrating the family into the national community and giving it a feeling of usefulness. Nevertheless these small holdings are usually too small to commercialize efficiently and too poor to make their influence felt on the domestic market. On the other hand, the latifundios are often labor intensive and undercapitalized ventures that usually underproduce and often have no pretensions of increasing productivity or conforming either to the consumptive need of the country or to the requirements of the export-trading sector. They are often economic enclaves which are self-sufficient because of the vast amount of cheap labor available and whose owners are content to raise a single crop, netting them a sufficient income.

Neither of these two landowners appears very interested in or committed to technification—the former because he lacks the wherewithal, the latter because he does sufficiently well without the introduction of scientific management. The possible policy implication consists of convincing the large landowner of the feasibility of commercializing his agricultural holding and of combining small farmers into various forms of mechanized cooperatives. This would, however, free labor for the industrial sector which must be able to absorb it. This leads to the second major problem—that of insufficient employment opportunities in the urban areas to which excess labor usually migrates. This unemployed labor, plus the high birth rate in Latin America, deepens the frustrations of urban life for the millions of Latin Americans who are partially employed or hold no steady position at all. The problem is aggravated by the fact that many of the newly established industries are capital intensive and need less labor than otherwise.[1] The labor they do hire usually comes from the ranks of the skilled, which again leaves the unskilled, recently migrated labor unabsorbed.

Thus small-scale rural industry becomes a seeming priority if the large cities are not to be overpopulated with people in search of immediate employment. Concomitantly, large industries could be established in the larger metropolises. The burden upon Latin America's largest cities is overwhelming as its mounting population continually outstrips the physical capacity of the city to absorb new groups.

A type of "brain drain" has developed in the Latin American countryside, as the most competent and professionally trained seek the opportunities of the larger cities. Again, this points to the importance of creating rural industries, of diversifying existing bank structures, of expanding enterprises of every kind, and even of redefining the responsibility and duties of local government, a rather sad entity today in most of Latin America.[2]

There is the further problem of establishing or relocating industry in the nation's interior. Few corporations or smaller companies want to settle in areas far from domestic markets where there is no water power, electricity, telephones or communication system, and little skilled labor. This dilemma is perhaps the most difficult to overcome and requires joint public-private cooperation. One of the groups which could provide immense assistance in developing the nation's interior is the military. This institutionalized interest, receiving as it does usually twenty-five per cent of the national budget, could perform the valuable and meaningful function of putting their leisure and their skills to work for the general betterment of society. This would not only make use of an otherwise underemployed armed forces but might increase the contact and mutual understanding between the military and civilian populations. It has often been the lack of understanding between these two groups that has heightened rivalry and tension. In several countries, again notably Mexico, the armed forces have been willing and able to put their resources, skills, and prestige to work in developing the hinterland. Not only has rural development been a result, but the military is indirectly contributing (apart from their income) to the GNP by laying the foundation for the further extension and proliferation of industry.

The urban-rural imbalance in Latin America is one further result of inequitable modernization. The imbalance occurs not only in income, capital investment, and skilled management and labor, but in cultural and educa-

[1] This problem of capital intensive industry is discussed in detail for the Brazilian case by Glaucio Ary Dillon Soares, "The New Industrialization and the Brazilian Political System," in J. Petras and M. Zeitlin, *Latin America: Reform or Revolution* (Greenwich, Connecticut, Fawcett Publications, 1968).

[2] In the Brazilian case, Frank P. Sherwood discusses the policy constraints on municipal governments as well as the lack of national financing. *Institutionalizing the Grass Roots in Brazil* (San Francisco: Chandler, 1967).

tional advantages, something that in the United States, despite its advanced stage of modernity and economic development, has not as yet happened. In the United States there are scores of cities having under one-hundred thousand inhabitants where people do not feel culturally or educationally deprived.

The Latin American situation calls for painful public policy choices geared to a total national development scheme rather than to the development of enclaves of comfort and opportunity within a nation of poor and disadvantaged people. Total development may require legislation that asks medical students to settle in the interior after receiving several years of state-supported medical training, the formation of more domestic development corps (similar to Chile's and Peru's), the creation of more and better equipped rural universities, governmental incentives to business which relocates in secondary cities, the relocating of military bases to some of the poorest and least populated regions for purposes of stimulating local economies by both physical assistance and the creation of more money in the community, government sponsored hydroelectric projects in order to build the infrastructure and provide jobs, and possibly, as Brazil and Venezuela have done, the creation from scratch of whole new cities which would take some of the pressure off the major cities and at the same time contribute to an expanding economy.

The difficult problem of educating an ever-increasing proportion of people under twenty years of age must be solved if sound economic development is to be achieved. Many countries find that their educational system is not geared to the society's technical needs and that the output of universities and secondary schools is not put to use once the education has ceased. The arts, literature, philosophy, history, while completely legitimate forms of endeavor, cannot be easily converted into the tangible skills required by a society in the process of modernization.

Finally, many Latin American countries are saddled with a foreign-trade pattern that is difficult to alter. The inelastic demand for Latin American primary goods exports places her economies at the mercy of small fluctuations in the international market price. Yet it is these same food and raw material exports that make up the vast bulk of Latin America's revenue which is needed to industrialize, break the monopoly of one or two exports, and end the cycle of overwhelming reliance on external economies.

With these very real obstacles to economic and social development, the way will be difficult and require profound reassessments of the traditional patterns of life for millions of people. Many of the resolutions concerned with Latin American underdevelopment may focus on a multilateral approach in the 1970's. Certainly the development of the Latin American Free Trade Agreements and the Central American Common Market have partially shifted thinking away from the nation as the only instrument for economic development. A population of 250 million is enough reason to think in terms of a larger production potential and, more important, a greater consumer market. Certainly some form of national planning is necessary in the Latin American nations if jobs, income, and social security is to be made available for a continent where only Argentina has *less* than 33 per cent of her population under fifteen years of age and where most countries have between 40 and 50 per cent under fifteen years of age. Should the facilities become available, Latin America can count on a great number of people who will be able to contribute to an increasing economic growth rate.

Central governments may have to make quick and forceful decisions which will raise the revenue necessary for industrial expansion so that the increasing employable population can be profitably absorbed. Better prices for her raw materials in Western European and United States markets may not be enough, nor will expanded trade with the Eastern Bloc and uncommitted countries resolve the pressure. The solutions lie more with the increasing capacity of Latin American governments to motivate private investment, heavily tax unused land, mechanize it wherever possible, and relate the requirements of industrialization to the educational system.

Inter-American trade may be able to lessen the dependence which now exists upon a few exportable items, such as petroleum, coffee, sugar, and cotton. Together, these make up about three-fifths of the value of all Latin American exports. Inter-American cooperation may result in specialization by each country in the manufacture of industrial goods which, in the main, will be exported to one another. Tourism is already a commodity which certain Latin American countries, for example, Mexico and Uruguay, are beginning to exploit and one which eventually promises to place second to petroleum as the biggest foreign-exchange earner. Most Latin American nations are physically situated well enough to develop their Acapulcos or Punta del Estes. Latin American governments have lately been demonstrating that they do not intend to ever again overemphasize one commodity for export merely because the international demand for it is great at a given moment. This mistake was made at the end of World War II and resulted in extended hardships in the fifties as prices went up and down with mercurial speed. Not only were the Latin American economies affected, but their social structure was unbalanced resulting in the toppling of otherwise legitimate governments.[3]

[3] A recent paper raises this problem as meriting much future research. Gilbert W. Merkx states: "Commodity markets were strongly affected during the 1930–1965 period by six events: the Depression, the 2nd W.W., the recessions of 1936, 1948, and 1954 and by the terms of trade decline of the early 1960's." An inspection (of these events) shows that the number of illegal changes coincides with economic events. "Legality, Political Shift, and Social Impact in the Changes of Latin American Presidents, 1930–1965" (Paper presented at Annual Meeting of American Sociological Association, San Francisco, August 1967), p. 14.

CHAPTER 14 The Obstacles to Economic Development

In assessing the data that indicate levels of economic productivity and Gross National Product and its distribution per capita, the labor force working in industry as opposed to agriculture all are closely related to each other. The higher their absolute levels of growth patterns the more likely a healthy and thriving economy. When these indices are relatively high, investment patterns in the economy and capabilities in the formation of capital and the development of economic infrastructures will also gain impetus.

Latin American GNP rates have shown several years of sustained growth: 1964—6.3 per cent, 1965—5.3 per cent, 1968—5.7 per cent, 1969—5.9 per cent (with dips in 1966—3.7 per cent, and 1967—4.3 per cent). Comparing the five Latin American countries to our cross-national sample for several consecutive years in terms of capital formation levels, the Peruvian performance stands out well above many more developed nations.

TABLE 14-1 Gross Domestic Capital Formation as Per Cent of GNP

Ranking Among 77 Nations	*Country*	*Per Cent*	*Years*
6	Japan	29.2	1950–1959
11	*Peru*	26.2	1950–1959
21	West Germany	23.8	1950–1959
29	Italy	20.9	1950–1959
35	*Argentina*	19.3	1950–1959
40	United States	17.8	1950–1959
47	*Mexico*	16.6	1952–1958
51	*Brazil*	15.5	1950–1958
68	India	10.8	1950–1956
71	*Chile*	10.1	1950–1959
73	Nigeria	9.4	1950–1956

Source: Bruce M. Russett, et al., *World Handbook of Political and Social Indicators* (New Haven: Yale University Press, 1964), pp. 168–169.

For a recent year the five Latin American countries managed to show respectable economic growth, in most cases maintaining a level of development above world growth averages.

The rather positive growth achievements must be examined in conjunction with the distributive impact on the public. The intervening variable that is important here is the large population increase annually which ab-

TABLE 14-2

Country	*Per Cent Increase of GNP for 1968*
Mexico	7.0
Brazil	6.9
Argentina	4.8
Peru	3.5
Chile	2.7
United States (1967)	2.5

Source: Social Progress Trust Fund, Ninth Annual Report (Washington, D.C., Inter-American Development Bank, 1970.

sorbs so much of economic growth rate. The following table demonstrates the disjunction between absolute and per capita growth rate.

TABLE 14-3 Growth Rate of Total and Per Capita Product at Constant Prices (1958 = 100)

Country	*Total*	*1965 Per Capita*
Mexico	149	117
Peru	149	125
Brazil	142	114
United States	136	123
Chile	129	110
Argentina	120	107

Source: Statistical Abstract of Latin America (Los Angeles: University of California at Los Angeles Press, 1967), p. 162.

These index numbers make very clear that the high growth figures for Mexico, Peru, and Brazil were not sustained on a per capita basis because of the rate of population growth. The index number was diminished by 32, 24, and 28 respectively. The lower birth rate of Chile caused the index number to decline by only nineteen, while low population growth rates for United States and Argentina showed up in a much smaller decline of thirteen for each.

Some interesting recent data compiled by the Inter-American Development Bank allows a comparison of these five countries under several important categories related to economic development. The data have been adapted and rearranged so as to be presented in a comparative table (14-4).

Two factors mitigate further developmental gains in industrial and agricultural productivity. The first and more important is inflation, and the second is the weak export sector. These often reinforce each other. Inflation has been a particularly acute problem for Argentina, Brazil, and Chile.

Inflation is usually the result of cyclical economic pressures that are

TABLE 14-4

Item	*Argentina*	*Chile*	*Mexico*	*Peru*	*Brazil*
Population (1967)	23m.	9m.	46m.	12m.	86m.
Per cent urban	74	68	51	47	46
Gross Domestic Product (1967) per capita	$635	$385	$455	$300	$225
Central Govt. tax revenue as per cent of GDP (1967)	9.4	20.2	7.0	12.3	8.4
Manufacturing sector as per cent of GDP	32	26	26	19	28
Agricultural sector as per cent of GDP	15	10	17	18	28

Source: Social Progress Trust Fund, Eighth Annual Report (Washington, D.C., Inter-American Development Bank, 1969).

TABLE 14-5 Inflationary Rates in Per Cent

Year	*Argentina*	*Brazil*	*Chile*	*Mexico*	*Peru*
1964	22	87	47	4	—
1965	29	45	26	2	18
1966	32	41	17	3	9
1967	29	25	22	—	20
1968	16	23	27	3	8
1969	10	16	30	—	—

Source: Ibid., *Ninth Annual Report,* 1970 (figures gleaned from various sections).

structurally embedded in the rigidity of the export sector and the difficulty in planning on a certain foreign income per annum. Most Latin American countries are dependent on one or two agricultural or natural-resource products for more than half their yearly foreign exchange. This rigidity and overdependence of the export sector leads to a more weakened import sector which, for lack of capital, finds it difficult to import necessary equipment and other capital goods essential for industrialization. The economic effects at this point in the cycle became more widespread and tend to undercut levels of industrial investment and levels of productivity. Further important social overhead and infrastructure capital is not available. Curtailed productivity levels then force up prices according to economic price/pull theories. The national government must then undertake deficit financing in order to take up the slack of a slowed-down private sector.

Reaction to incipient inflation and low productivity (which stimulated more unemployment) often forces the government to take an additional step-devaluation of the currency. This is undertaken to increase exports and foreign earnings. Certainly one of the intermediary results of devaluation is to foster more domestic inflation which, in turn, weakens the purchasing power of the working and middle sectors. In Argentina, for example, using 1956 as a base year with an index number of 100 representing the inflationary rate, by mid-1967 the index figure had reached 2,154 or a rise of twenty-one-fold. Between 1960 and 1967 inflation brought about a cost of living increase of approximately 26 per cent per annum. Inflation, as it usually does, has taken a larger toll on the laboring classes than on the middle classes. In Argentina the workers' share of national income has diminished from a high of 47 per cent in the years 1952–1955 to 43 per cent average since 1960. According to the Argentine General Labor Confederate, worker productivity was meanwhile increasing from an index of 100 in 1956 to 217 in 1966.[1]

In Brazil the effects of inflation have been no less startling. The Brazilian exchange rate was seventy-seven cruzeiros to the dollar in 1954 and 1,850 by 1964, a twenty-four-fold increase. Meanwhile in the same period the money supply was expanded nearly twenty-seven times, from 151 to 4,035. The cost of living index moved from 122 to 2,889, a twenty-four-fold increase which closely paralleled the exchange rate devaluations vis-à-vis the dollar. However, during the same period productivity doubled, and gains in iron ore and manufactures increased by five to seven times. According to one account, between 1947 and 1961 the average annual rate of growth of the GNP was 5.8 per cent, one of the highest rates in the world.[2] Again the general Latin American phenomenon is repeated in Brazil. Inflation is pervasive because of a number of successive and reinforcing developments. A decline in export stimulus serves to dampen agricultural production. The government attempts to take up the general productivity slack by resort to subsidies. This results in deficit spending, often a prelude for further devaluation of the currency.

Weakness in the export sector is clearly a factor in the other major Latin American countries as well. Globally, the Latin American share of world trade has decreased in the period 1956 to 1965. During this period the Latin American annual growth of trade was 3 per cent compared to 11 per cent for Africa and 15 per cent for Asia. On the other hand, domestic growth rates are comparatively much better in terms of worldwide comparisons.

[1] "Elementos para un analisis de las condiciones economicas y sociales de los trabajadores" Departmento de Estudios e Investigaciones Economicas y Sociales, Confederación General de Trabajadores (Buenos Aires: 1967), p. 63.

According to Ivor Coffin, "The Argentine Coup and its Aftermath" (Paper presented at University of London, April, 1967), p. 9. "The most important single cause of inflation in Argentina is the extremely low productivity of labor. In the private sector this is one of the main causes of high prices; in the public sector, and especially in the state-owned public service, it is the main cause of large operating losses, which are a charge on the National Treasury and over many years have accounted for large proportions of the annual Treasury deficits."

[2] John Brooks, "Brazil: Growth and Inflation, 1954–1964" (Paper presented at the University of London, April, 1967), pp. 2–5.

According to the Alliance for Progress sources, thirteen out of a total of twenty-five developing nations which increased their GNP figures from 5 per cent to 10 per cent in 1966, were Latin American nations.[3] Thus it is important for Latin American economic development that the availability and fruits of expanding and dependable foreign markets be applied to the domestic industrial sector that shows increasingly such positive signs as investment levels, the mobility of private sources, and governmental commitment to economic reform.

In the domestic economic sector two other problems are associated with a continuing high level of productivity: (1) the disequilibrium in investment and output between the agricultural and industrial sectors of the economy and (2) the stratification of manpower and human resources.

Many Latin American economists see underinvestment in the domestic economy as one of the main barriers to development. Raul Prebisch, for many years the chief spokesman for the Economic Commission for Latin America, has written:

> Among these upper strata (5 per cent of the population), which account for about three-tenths of Latin America's total consumption, average consumption per household is fifteen times greater than that of the lower strata (50 per cent of the population). If this ratio were reduced to 11:1 by the restriction of consumption in favor of increased investment, the annual rate of growth of per capita income could rise from 1 per cent to 3 per cent.[4]

This disproportionate investment power of the conspicuous consumer in Latin America is made clear even when class-income distribution in Mexico is compared with several non-Latin American sample countries (Table 14-6). It should be remembered that Mexico was the only one of the five countries studied to undergo a structural revolution, which might allow for better income distribution. No data was available for other Latin American nations.

Disequilibrium in investment patterns also manifests itself in the vast distinctions between productivity outputs in agriculture and industry. Though it is difficult to document, there is some evidence from landholding concentrations to point to the fact that the high-consumer, low-investor upper strata, whose income is largely generated by their ownership of large estates, are in

[3] *Alliance for Progress Newsletter*, December 18, 1967, pp. 2–3.

[4] Raul Prebisch, *Towards a Dynamic Development Policy for Latin America* (New York: United Nations, 1963), p. 6. See also David Felix, "Economic Development: Take-Offs Into Unsustained Growth" *Social Research*, vol. 36, no. 2 (Summer 1969), pp. 267–293. Felix corroborates Prebisch's testimony by showing, among other negative factors in development, that the top 5 percent of Latin America's income groups buys 74 percent of the consumer *durables*, while the next 45 percent consumes 26 percent, and the lowest 50 percent less than 1 percent of total purchases.

TABLE 14-6 Income Distribution Before Taxes: Gini Index of Inequality

Ranking Among 20 Countries	*Country*	*Gini Index*	*Year*
1	Mexico	.540	1957*
2	West Germany	.473	1950
10	Italy	.403	1948
13	United States	.397	1956
17	India	.365	1956

Source: Russett et al., *World Handbook of Political and Social Indicators,* p. 245.

* No Mexican data after taxation.

large measure responsible for the low productivity of the rural sector vis-à-vis the urban sector and concomitantly, and directly related, the much slower growth of agriculture than industry. A couple of samples should suffice to make this pattern, so universal in Latin America, quite clear.

TABLE 14-7 Percentage Annual Change of Mexican GNP by Sectors

Year	*GNP*	*Agriculture*	*Industry*
1960	5.7	0.4	8.6
1961	3.5	3.0	3.5
1962	4.8	5.3	6.4
1963	6.3	1.5	9.2
1964	10.0	8.1	14.2
1965	5.1	3.0	7.0

Source: Pablo González Casanova, *La democracia en Mexico* (Mexico: Ediciones ERA, 1965), p. 247.

Another breakdown by James Wilkie over greater time intervals points to the same disequilibrium.

TABLE 14-8 Representative Indices of Economic Growth in Mexico (1940 = 100)

Sector	*1940*	*1950*	*1960*
Volume of manufacturing	100	217	465
Volume of steel production	100	262	1,034
Volume of agriculture prod.	100	177	318

Source: James W. Wilkie, *The Mexican Revolution: Federal Expenditure and Social Change Since 1910* (Berkeley: University of California Press, 1967), p. 196.

He further breaks down GNP by percentage contribution by sector of origin

TABLE 14-9 GNP by Sectors of Origin in Mexico: 1940–1960

Sector	*1940*	*1950*	*1960*
Primary (agriculture, hunting and fishing, ranching)	21	24	23
Secondary (mining, construction, petroleum, manufacturing)	25	33	36
Tertiary (public and private services)	55	44	41
	101	101	100 (individual percentages rounded off)

Source: James W. Wilkie, *The Mexican Revolution,* p. 202.

Although it is clear from the previous tables that Mexican agriculture has continued to progress in productive capacity, its contribution to national income has remained static when compared to the much more dynamic industrial sector.

A similar pattern prevailed in Brazil during the fifties at a time when it is acknowledged that Brazil's growth rate was very high. Again the major contributor to this climb was the industrial sector and not the agricultural sector.

TABLE 14-10 Industrial and Agricultural Output in Brazil (1953 = 100)

Year	*Industrial Production*	*Agricultural Production*
1947	60	79
1948	67	85
1949	74	90
1950	82	94
1951	88	94
1952	92	98
1953	100	100
1954	109	108
1955	120	117
1956	128	114
1957	136	125
1958	158	128
1959	178	133
1960	197	138
1961	219	149

Source: Werner Baer, *Industrialization and Economic Development in Brazil* (Homewood Ill. Richard Irwin, 1965), p. 151.

The figures for both Mexico and Brazil indicate that economic development is chiefly dependent upon industrial productivity, though this is by no means a unique experience to Latin America. Elsewhere in the developed and semideveloped countries agriculture is contributing less and less to the Gross National Product. Many times this is not so much because of a very apparent productive lag on the farms but because of simply astounding advances made in industrial management, techniques, and the availability of more knowledgeable and skilled labor. In Latin America, the gap between the two sectors is also widening but for the more *negative* reason that the agricultural sector has not been able to maintain the type of accelerated growth rate needed for economic development. On a cross-national basis Latin America falls between the high-productivity industrial nations and the labor intensive agricultural economies of most developing countries.

TABLE 14-11 Percentage of GNP Originating in Agriculture

Ranking Among 75 Nations	*Country*	*Percentage*	*Year*
1	Nigeria	63	1957
8	India	48	1960
33	*Brazil*	27	1961
39	Peru	25	1959
49	*Argentina*	20	1961
51	Italy	17	1961
53	Japan	15	1960
55	*Chile*	14	1960
72	West Germany	6	1961
75	United States	4	1961

Source: Russett et al., *World Handbook of Political and Social Indicators*, pp. 173–174.

The availability of manpower and the existence of social stratification contributes substantially to existing deficiencies in investment and capitalization patterns. This can be seen by the distribution of labor within the economic system in terms of physical location as well as availability of work and technical preparation of the work force. In addition the biological age structure of the population is extremely pyramidal, which further strains the efficiency of the economy. Thus though the contribution of the agricultural sector to the GNP is usually no more than one-fifth of the total, it has continued, with few exceptions, to absorb (albeit inefficiently) approximately one-half of the labor force. For Latin America as a whole one can speak generally in terms of 50 per cent of the work force producing but 20 per cent of the wealth.

The Russett survey, though it contains some rather out-of-date statistics, still remains useful for its comprehensive internation comparisons. One can see the general spectrum of agrarian underemployment in Latin America and elsewhere in developing nations.

TABLE 14-12 Percentage of Labor Force Employed in Agriculture

Ranking Among 98 Nations	*Country*	*Percentage*	*Year*
19	India	71	1961
38	*Brazil*	61	1950
40	*Peru*	60	1950
41	Nigeria	59	1950
44	*Mexico*	58	1958
68	Japan	40	1959
75	*Chile*	30	1952
76	Italy	29	1946
80	*Argentina*	25	1950
88	West Germany	14	1959
96	United States	10	1957

Source: Russett et al., *World Handbook of Political and Social Indicators*, pp. 177–179.

Except for India all of the above countries show a steady yearly decline in the agricultural labor force by about half-a-percent per annum, with Italy showing the most rapid decline. The Latin American ratio of manpower to productivity has improved, particularly in the manufacturing sectors. The farm-sector ratio appears slightly improved by the mid-1960s, not so much because productivity greatly increased but because much underemployed and surplus labor migrated to urban areas, thus shrinking the rural population while agricultural productivity was not adversely affected. The agricultural population migration to industrialized urban areas has been very marked and has had a major impact of inflating the work force in both the secondary and tertiary sectors of the economy, as the survey in Table 14-13 by the Inter-American Development Bank, taken mostly in 1966–67, demonstrates.

Several features of Table 14-13 are worth noting. Argentina has a strikingly high number of economically active people compared to the general Latin American average, though much of the impact on productivity is weakened by the large absorption of manpower by the tertiary sector of commercial and public and private services.[5] This is equally true of Chile, but

[5] Much of this expansion of the tertiary sector occurred under Perón. In 1945 the service sector represented 44 per cent of the labor force. In 1954 it had risen to 52 per cent of the labor force. Meanwhile the industrial sector increased only 1.7 per cent during the entire Perón period. Thus one must credit the Frondizi administration for much of the shift to industrial employment. On Perón's economic policies see Bertram Silverman, *Labor Ideology and Economic*

TABLE 14-13 Percentage Distribution of Economically Active Population

Country	*Economically Active*	*Agriculture*	*Industry (includes Mining)*	*Services and Commerce*
Argentina	38	22	34	44
Chile	27	32	24	44
Mexico	32	50	22	28
Peru	31	50	23	27
Brazil	28	54	13	33

Source: *Social Progress Trust Fund: Seventh Annual Report* (Washington, D.C.: Inter-American Development Bank, 1968). Data presented under the various country analyses. A very excellent industry by industry breakdown, too detailed for our purposes here, can be found in *Statistical Abstract of Latin America* (Los Angeles: University of California Press, 1967), pp. 86–87.

having a much lower rate of total mobilized labor it can less afford such a large service sector. Furthermore, as we have come to expect, given their modern sociopolitical environment, Argentina and Chile's population distribution and occupational stratification is both more urbanized and more associated with the activities of industry, government, finance, commerce, and trade. It remains now to determine which of the five countries most efficiently uses its manpower resources for economic productivity. We may for convenience call this a "utility ratio," that is a means of relating productivity to human resource availability. From figures cited earlier we can relate productivity of the agricultural and industrial sector with the above distribution of economically active people.

TABLE 14-14 A Comparative Industrial/Agricultural "Utility Ratio"

Country	*Indus. Sect. Per Cent of GNP*	*Indus. W.F. Per Cent of Eco. Active*	*Indus. Util. Ratio*	*Agri. Sect. Per Cent of GNP*	*Agri. W.F. Per Cent of Eco. Active*	*Agri. Util. Ratio*	*Combined Utility Ratio*
Brazil	28	13	2.15	28	54	.52	2.67
Argentina	32	34	.94	15	22	.68	1.62
Mexico	26	22	1.18	17	50	.34	1.52
Chile	26	24	1.08	10	32	.31	1.39
Peru	19	23	.83	18	50	.36	1.19
			6.18			2.21	

These figures indicate Brazil's capacity to combine productive techniques with human resources surpasses that of the other four Latin American coun-

---

Development in the Peronist Epoch (New Brunswick, New Jersey: Rutgers University Studies in Comparative International Development, vol. 4, no. 11 (1968–69), pp. 243–258.

tries in our survey. Her industrial sector, particularly, is most efficient when combining production with manpower. Argentina, with its vast "pampa", ideal for cattle grazing and wheat growing, has the most efficient agricultural sector. Peru has the most inefficient industrial sector in terms of productivity per units of manpower, while Chile's utilization of man and land in her agricultural sector is the lowest of the five countries investigated. The aggregate data for the five countries indicates that the industrial sector is almost three times as productive as the agricultural sector. The general economic drag of those active in the tertiary sector adds another dimension to general per capita productivity and will be discussed later.

Related to the problem of manpower distribution and efficiency is population age, sex, and occupational structure. Latin America's birth rate, which is higher than any continent in the world, has a strong influence on the population structure. The percentage of available people who are capable of producing enough and sustaining the unproductive members of society, essentially the very young and to a much lesser degree the very old, is lower than elsewhere. It is generally accepted by economists and sociologists that the most productive years in a human life, in terms of physical and technical competence, are those between twenty and sixty years of age. Below twenty expertise and experience are missing and after sixty biological decline is a factor.

TABLE 14-15 Percentage of Population Between Ages 20 and 60

Country	*Percentage*
Argentina	51.6
United States	47.2
Chile	42.7
Brazil	42.2
Peru	41.0
Mexico	39.7

Source: Statistical Abstract of Latin America (Los Angeles: University of California Press, 1967). Figures extrapolated from tables on pp. 71–72.

In each of these countries there is no more than half of the total population from which to tap the necessary manpower to produce enough for the other half. Of course, in the United States example, as it would be for any other developed, modern nation, the medical revolution is not made apparent by the figures. More and more people are remaining productive beyond the age of sixty. The Argentine figure is the result of two phenomena: a very low birth rate, which decreases the sharpness of the population pyramid, and above average sanitation and health conditions. The problem of a minority producing for a majority which only consumes continues to be aggravated as birth rates continue to be very high in Mexico, Brazil, Peru, and Chile. In addition, because the social structure is still not mobile enough, the Latin American female is not nearly as likely to work as a fully productive member of the society as in a fully industrialized nation.

TABLE 14-16 Females as Percentage of Economically Active Population

Country	*Females Per Cent*	*Year*
United States	34.0	1965
Argentina	22.6	1960
Chile	22.4	1960
Peru	21.7	1961
Mexico	18.0	1960
Brazil	17.9	1960

Source: Statistical Abstract of Latin America, p. 83.

Using slightly broader categories for economically active years, Russett provides us with comparative data for the eleven countries.

TABLE 14-17 Percentage of Population of Working Age (15–64)

Ranking Among 127 Nations	*Country*	*Percentage*
3	West Germany	68
7	Italy	66
15	*Argentina*	65
19	Japan	64
40	United States	60
46	India	59
51	*Chile*	58
83	*Brazil*	57
105	*Peru*	53
113	Nigeria	52
115	*Mexico*	52

Source: Russett et al., *World Handbook of Political and Social Indicators,* pp. 25–27.

As Russett reminds us it is important to keep in mind that working age population in no way refers to those actually employed and adding to the national income. Thus we find in our developing countries examples for Argentina and Chile, a vast hiatus between those who could work if there were work and those who do work because there is work.

TABLE 14-18 Wage and Salary Earners as Percentage of Working Age Population

Ranking Among 79 Nations	*Country*	*Percentage*	*Year*
7	West Germany	54	1959
10	United States	52	1960
26	*Argentina*	43	1947*
28	*Chile*	43	1952*
32	Italy	41	1960
45	Japan	35	1959
51	*Brazil*	30	1950*
52	*Mexico*	28	1958
54	*Peru*	27	1940*
66	India	19	1961
79	Nigeria	3	1959

Source: Russett et al., *World Handbook,* pp. 29–30.
* Note early date of these figures.

The data shows that even among the gainfully employed in Latin America there is a very high proportion of those who are unskilled or, at best, semiskilled who have negative repercussions on total economic productivity

TABLE 14-19 Percentages of Economically Active Population by Occupation

Occupations	*United States*	*Chile*	*Mexico*	*Peru*
Professional, Technical and Related	10.8	4.9	3.6	3.3
Administrative, Executive and Managerial; Clerical	20.8	8.8	7.0	5.8
Sales	7.4	7.0	9.0	7.2
Farmers, Fishermen, Hunters, Loggers and Related	6.1	27.5	53.5	49.1
Miners and Quarrymen	.5	2.3	1.0	1.1
Transportation and Communication	4.6	3.3	incl. below ( )	2.3
Craftsmen, Producers and Laborers	31.0	26.6	(18.9)	17.5
Service, Sport and Recreation	11.2	13.5	7.0	8.9
Workers not classified by occupation; members of armed forces	7.7	6.2	—	4.8
	100.1	100.1	100.0	100.0

Source: Statistical Abstract of Latin America (Los Angeles: UCLA Press), pp. 84–85. This data has been rearranged by the author from tables appearing in the Abstract.

regardless of levels of employment. The data in Table 14-19 (though none was available for Argentina and Brazil) illustrate this problem.

First, it is clear that in the United States approximately one-third of the labor force has attained a certain minimum of technical and managerial skills (this does not include skilled laborers and craftsmen), while in the Latin American countries this figure is only about one-tenth. Second, although agricultural productivity is much higher in the United States, agrarian occupations are only one-quarter to one-eighth the size as compared to the three Latin American countries. Third, Chile's figures include a dynamic copper mining industry and a sizeable tertiary sector.

Thus the five Latin American nations are in the midst of severe economic challenges to their institutional stability and longevity. In many ways the crisis is economic in its origin, but in numerous other ways it is political and sociological as well. In fact the institutional crisis in contemporary Latin America has been largely brought about by the capabilities of an advanced, pluralistically-oriented competitive political sector attempting to channel or invigorate a less developed and more tentative economic sector. Both sectors confront the least dynamic but extremely resilient social structure. The social structure, in turn, has continued to act as a structural decelerator to the more fluid and responsive political sector and the evolving and galvanized economic sector.

CHAPTER 15 Politics and the Development Process

The pressures upon Latin American political systems are magnified because the means available to produce fairly large-scale and deep-seated socioeconomic changes are still limited and because of the short time span in which change is expected to occur. The more tasks that must be performed in a short period of time the greater the likelihood that frustrations and conflicts will increase. Thus a political system, which has been evolving since the development of governmental "liberalism" almost a century and a half ago, is attempting to mobilize intelligently and carefully an economic sector which is just gaining an institutional foothold against a social structure of conformity to outdated concepts of economics and politics.

In many ways, then, there is a double challenge to the makers of public policy to harness the social system to a more dynamic economic system and to increase societal mobility and undercut archaic social mores that inhibit the development of a progressive economy. This requires the complex political management of both men and resources. Latin American governments have taken it upon themselves to provide the leadership needed for this task. It is, in most cases, the government which is providing the economic infrastructure and social-overhead capital.[1] It is significant that where governments have thrown their resources behind massive efforts at economic development, in terms of, for example, governmental expenditures, revenues, and government employment, economic indicators tend to sustain their efforts as worthwhile. Russett, for example, has found a striking correlation between size of government and economic development indices.[2] Economic development, or at least an incremental steady progress in that direction, tends to redound favorably for the maintenance of stable government and an open political system. Charles Wolf attributes this to the fact that it is easier to distribute *increases* in national income and wealth than to redistribute the existing income and wealth.[3]

When the economy is developing steadily there is less pressure upon the government to use authoritative rather than manipulative methods to achieve economic growth. A dynamic economy is one more likely to avoid serious distortions and eccentricities in the political sector. Compromise and concilia-

[1] Wendell C. Gordon, *The Political Economy of Latin America* (New York: Columbia University Press, 1965), p. 292.

[2] Russett et al., *World Handbook of Political and Social Indicators,* p. 288.

[3] Charles Wolf, "The Political Effects of Economic Programs: Some Implications from Latin America," *Economic Development and Cultural Change,* vol. 14, no. 1 (October 1965), p. 4.

tion are more compatible with a developing than with a stagnant economic environment. The challenge in the latter situation becomes more pronounced and the remedy more acute. The revolutionary alternative often arises from extreme frustration and impatience at having to secure consensus by means of elections and to mediate among the various interests of the society—both of which are clearly integral parts of the Latin American political system. The revolutionary view implies a Rousseauian conception of society in which political leadership "understand" what it is the people *really* need and interpret their "will" by ruling on their behalf.

The temptation to arbitrate on behalf of a hardly defined national interest is not necessarily confined to revolutionaries but comes from a deep anxiety about the nature and public spirit of the more powerful and better organized interest groups that have shared power for many generations.[4] It is undeniable that in most of Latin America certain economic interests are well organized and have definite views on the question of public policy and economic development. The imposition of certain development plans must find a minimum of favor at least with some of these interests. This does not mean that an administrator cannot, while he pursues certain policies, skillfully tread the path between limited opposition of some interests and outright confrontation by several opposed groups. It is more likely, as Charles Anderson has clearly spelled out, for the administration to avoid completely eliminating any "power contenders" if it means backtracking and beginning all over again toward a wholly new conception of not only the economic system but the political system.[5] Thus unless the political leadership wishes to take the more extreme road to industrialization, they must be content to employ "pump-priming politics" or the tactics that have been described earlier as indicative of an innovative perception of society.

All five of the Latin American countries examined here have chosen the less romantic road to economic development with unequal success but yet with encouraging signs of long-term political viability and economic strength. Three patterns of development emerge among the five countries. Only Mexico has utilized a revolutionary framework for carrying out economic reforms. The radical change in political control and economic power made it possible for the revolutionary leadership to initially impose the costs of industrialization on the large propertied class. However, in later stages of Mexican economic development much of the burden of industrialization was placed on working classes both in the urban and rural areas. A second pattern of in-

[4] For example, Argentina sociologist Jorge Graciarena states: ". . . the politics of development requires thinking in terms of what must be done for the national interest, not what can be done and for the interests best represented nationally." "Presiones internas, inestabilidad politica y desarollo económico en America Latina," *Revista Mexicana de Sociologia,* vol. 28, no. 2, p. 302.

[5] Charles W. Anderson, *Politics and Economic Change in Latin America* (Princeton: D. Van Nostrand Press, 1967).

dustrialization has occurred in Peru and Chile where the working classes bore most of the original sacrifice, and only now are the large agrarian interests sharing some of the burden. In Brazil and Argentina a still different arrangement has taken place where responsibility was placed mostly on the lower classes, then shifted to the upper classes, and again, with different emphasis, back to the working groups.

In none of the three paths to development was the middle class called upon to bear the major burden of industrialization. Governments appear to have recognized that it was from the middle economic sector that the entreprenurial leadership and technical expertise had to come. It is apparent that a more equalitarian pattern is now being developed, clearly aimed at having the upper and lower classes, and to a lesser degree the middle classes share the burdens and seeming deprivations of industrial development.

The commitment to economic growth, while not ignoring necessary social services, is extremely well documented.[6] A more equitable tax structure is being developed which allowed Chile, Mexico, Peru, and Argentina to increase their tax revenues by at least 40 per cent by the end of 1967 and Brazil to attain a 30 per cent increase in receipts. Some of this money will no doubt find its way to the crucial social expenditures, which are listed below for the year 1966.

TABLE 15-1 Percentage of Central Government Expenditures, 1968

Country	*Education*	*Public Health*	*Other Social Services (1964)*
Peru	26.2	5.2	17.6
Chile	18.7	7.9	10.0
Mexico	17.9	4.5	10.0
Argentina	13.8	6.4	9.6
Brazil	7.1	2.5	—

Sources: Social Progress Trust Fund: Seventh and *Ninth Annual Report* and *Statistical Abstract of Latin America,* pp. 163–165.

Frank Brandenburg has provided data on four of the five countries that corroborates the trend of increased public involvement in and penetration of the economy. This is particularly true in the central governments' control and management of such giant public corporations as the railroads, electrical companies, petroleum corporations, and financial institutions (Table 15-2).

This type of active government involvement has greatly inflated the governments' role as a principal creator of wealth, capital, and employment.

[6] See the excellent review of the role in development of the Latin American public sector in Charles W. Anderson, *Politics and Economic Change in Latin America.* His examples are mainly drawn from the administrative experiences of ten Andean (including Peru) and Central American republics.

TABLE 15-2 Extent of Public Control Over Latin American Corporations: (Top Ten Corporations)

Country	*Percentage Ownership*	*Corporations*
Mexico	100	Railroads, Electricity, Petroleum, Finance
Argentina	85	Petroleum, Railroads, Electricity, Steel, Banking, Paper, Finance, Consumer Durables
Brazil	78	Railroads, Petroleum, Finance, Electricity, Steel, Telephones
Chile (before Chileanization of copper)	49	Copper, Railroads, Electricity, Petroleum, Finance, Ports, Nitrates

Source: The Development of Latin American Private Enterprises (Washington, D.C.: National Planning Association, 1964), pp. 53–63.

The government is not only participating in national development but is involved in fiscal and monetary matters as well as in the manipulation of the import-export sector. The last major area of governmental involvement has tended to be the agrarian sector where it is moving to alter land ownership and technify, by various methods, existing farms.

CHAPTER 16 The Dual Nature of Latin American Society: "Agraria" and "Industria"

We already indicated that most Latin American nations maintain a fairly modern political sector with generally participant political groups along with a structurally underdeveloped social sector.[1] Most social scientists who have written on Latin America in the last decade have, from one or another perspective, discussed this phenomenon. The duality is accentuated by urban-rural social differences and the disparity in consumption customs and capabilities.[2] This structural duality often has been described as a type of "internal colonization" in which the modern sectors maintain an iron grip on the levers of political influence and economic power and keep the traditional sectors politically dependent and economically deprived. S. N. Eisenstadt sees a relationship between this pattern of privilege and the inefficient nature of the Latin American economy.

> Thus first in almost all these countries there took place a continuous expansion and swelling of the bureaucracies by new aspirants, the continuous giving in, by the rulers, to the growing demands of the holders of these positions for tenure of office and for increased . . . wages and emoluments. . . . Such squandering of resources took place often because of "symbolic" or ideological reasons and because of the search of the rulers for support. . . . At the same time, because of lack of any clear principles or regulation or priorities, they tended to exacerbate the level of conflict between various groups as the aspiration (sic) of them all rose while the total output of the economy remained static or even decreased.[3]

Under conditions of severe inflation (as in Brazil, Chile, or Argentina), it is probably easier to maintain the pattern of privilege because of the greater ability of certain interest groups to bargain for equalizing wage increases. The

[1] The terms *agraria* and *industria* have been borrowed from Fred Riggs to symbolize the fused, traditional society as opposed to the diffracted, modern society. See his *Administration in Developing Countries* (Boston: Houghton Mifflin, 1964).

[2] The Chilean economist, Anibal Pinto, hints broadly that the modern sectors are so known mainly for their consumption habits and not for their production norms. He remarks that ". . . we are civilized in consuming and primitive in production." *Chile: una economía deficil* (Mexico: Fondo de Cultura Economica, 1964), p. 165.

[3] S. N. Eisenstadt, "The Development of Socio-Political Centers at the Second Stage of Modernization," *International Journal of Comparative Sociology*, vol. 7, no. 1–2 (March 1966), pp. 127–128.

situation is often compounded by the political demands, for example, of certain service sectors, public bureaucracies, and skilled labor unions. Also, the more affluent individuals of the rural areas tend to consume not only economic goods but to want the cultural and educational amenities which the urban environment affords. Since they have easy access to modern urban facilities there is little compulsion for them to duplicate them in the rural communities from which they come.[4]

The imbalance between the modern and traditional sectors exists in all five countries. The symptoms of this imbalance are apparent in such areas as income and consumption.

TABLE 16-1 Illustrations of the Gap Between Availability and Actual Consumption of the Poorer Classes

Country	*Calories*	*Proteins (in grams)* *Total*	*Animal*
Brazil (1961) avail., average	2,790	65	18
1961 "very poor" consumers (sample)	1,522	41	20
1961 "poor consumers" (sample)	2,067	60	29
1961 "middle class" (sample)	2,177	68	31
Chile (1961) avail., average	2,420	77	28
1962 sample in Ñuble (province)	2,060	69	17
1962 sample in Santiago	2,670	84	23
Mexico (1961) avail. average	2,680	75	24
1958–59 samples: "very poor" rural	1,788	45	na
"very poor" urban	1,803	51	na
"middle class" rural	2,275	57	na
"middle class" urban	2,331	64	na
Peru (1961) avail., average	2,170	54	12
1951–58 samples:			
mountain area	1,754	47	na
coastal area	2,205	64	na
FAO Guideline, minimum consumption	2,550	71	25

Source: Agricultural Development in Latin America (Washington, D.C.: Inter-American Bank, April 1967), pp. 123–124.

This table clearly points out that despite the national average caloric intake, most poor people and particularly the rural poor, consume a good deal below the average figure. The Brazilian figures indicate an extremely high consuming upper class which is not represented in the table. The Chilean urban/rural caloric breakdown shows the best distribution level according to

[4] Solon Barraclough and Arthur Domike, "Agrarian Structure in Seven Latin American Countries," *Land Economics*, vol. 42, no. 4 (November 1966), p. 398.

the FAO Guidelines. Though no data is available for Argentina, it can be assumed that its consumption of calories among a cross section of the population much surpasses that of Chile's.

Income distribution shows similar regional and community inequities.

TABLE 16-2 Mexico: Percentage of Persons by Income in Urban and Rural Areas (1961–62)

Peso Income/Month	*Mexico*	*Urban*	*Rural*
0–300	23	7	40
301–500	23	19	28
501–1000	28	34	21
1001–3000	23	34	10
more than 3000	4	6	1
	101	100	100

Source: Gonzalez Casanova, *La democracia en Mexico,* p. 278.

TABLE 16-3 Brazil: Regional Disequilibrium (1960)

Region	*Population*	*Percentage of National Income*
North	3	2
Northeast	24	11
East (Rio etc.)	34	34
South (São Paulo etc.)	35	51
Middle West	4	2
	100%	100%

Source: Baer, *Industrialization and Economic Development in Brazil,* p. 169. Also see Stefan H. Robock, *Brazil's Developing Northeast: A Study in Regional Planning and Foreign Aid* (Washington, D.C.: Brookings Institution, 1963), p. 35.

TABLE 16-4 Peru: Distribution of Per Capita Income by Geographic Region (1959–60)

Region	*Percentage of Population*	*Percentage of Income*
Coast	33	62
Sierra (plateau)	53	34
jungle (eastern Peru)	14	5

Source: David Chaplin, "Industrialization and the Distribution of Wealth in Peru" (Paper published at Land Tenure Center, University of Wisconsin, July 1966), p. 14.

Similar patterns (though based more on stratification than region) exist in Chile, less so in Argentina. In Chile the large landowners consume over 60 per cent of their disposable income, 75 per cent of which goes for luxury items. Twenty-five per cent of this total consumption is expended for imported goods.[5] Regarding Argentina, H. S. Ferns has written about the proliferation of automobiles, smart retail stores, and the most recent entertainment media programs, all of which closely resemble their counterparts in the most modern western capitals. At the same time there is underproduction of such important items as tractors, rural electrification, and university buildings.[6] Even after payment of direct taxes, the top decile of Argentine families controlled 38 per cent of all disposable income.[7]

Part of the agraria-industria disjunction can be explained historically. The rise of cities in Latin America was more a result of political and sociocultural than economic and commercial factors. This often led to a population disequilibrium. Richard Morse discusses the patrimonial Spanish disposition to develop political structures.

> The key observation here is that the political structure preceded the economic. In the case of medieval Europe, of course, not every town nucleus was of commercial origin. Many were historic centers of defense, or of civil or ecclesiastical administration; there were even cases of agricultural villages which received their liberties. But the transformation of such nuclei into full-fledged towns, particularly during the 13th and 14th centuries, is frequently attributable to a reawakened commerce. They became natural points of crystallization for an immediate region and for far-reaching arteries of trade. Their expansion, as suggested by the faubourg theory of Henri Pirenne, was centripetal. That is the town's increments of population and of economic activity in some measure obeyed regional and commercial determinants that were external to itself. In light of European urban history the Latin American town appears "artificial", . . . in so far as it aspired to be something more than a military, administrative or missionary outpost. For a New World town was established in a vast continent where regional trade routes and regional economies were not to achieve permanent features for generations, even centuries.[8]

In most of Latin America the urbanization pattern raised obstacles to the development of interior towns that could serve as reservoirs of economic innovation and political self-reliance. The urban political structure also in-

[5] William C. Thiesenhusen, "Agrarian Reform and Economic Development in Chile," *Land Economics*, vol. 42, no. 3 (August 1966), p. 283.

[6] H. S. Ferns, "The Argentine Economy: 1955–1965" (Paper presented at the University of London, April 1967), p. 2. Argentine consumption functions are also a subject treated by Aldo Ferrer, *The Argentine Economy* (Berkeley: University of California Press, 1967), pp. 210–211.

[7] *Economic Development and Income Distribution in Argentina* (New York: United Nations, 1969), p. 259 ff.

[8] Richard M. Morse, "Some Characteristics of Latin American Urban History," *American Historical Review*, vol. 67, no. 2 (January 1962), p. 322.

hibited the growth of an independent though necessarily small class of farmers who could be capable of experimenting with labor-saving, capital-intensive devices and who, once they achieved a modicum of production, would seek the mechanisms and infrastructure services to market their products. Thus, as distinct from, for example, the British and United States pattern of development, efficient, small rural entrepreneurs did not become a major factor for economic and political stability. During the subsequent republican years it was difficult for European immigrants to penetrate the rural social structure because most of the land was tightly held by "hacendados." These large landowners held the land as a speculative device to hedge against inflation and to keep production limited and prices high. Much of the produce was geared to foreign markets with little concern given to developing a large-scale domestic consumer market.[9]

Small, independent rural communities might have avoided populist political movements and paternal traditional relationships in rural areas as well as the rapid move to the major cities at a time when these centers were not yet prepared to accommodate an influx of migrants. In the United States and Western Europe, when the farmers finally did move off the farms, in response to rapid industrialization, they brought with them skills, education and certain modern conceptions of investment and development.

The structural problem in "agraria" can be focused on the fact that some people have too much and others not enough. Both land and income distribution are uneconomic and "antisocial". They lead to attitudes inimical to an equalitarian and mobile society. For example, in Latin America as a whole there are 3.6 million farm units with less than five hectares each, that is almost half of all individual farms. According to one economist these units not only average less than two hectares each, but they have poor, infertile soil and limited capital and managerial know-how.[10] Thus the problem

TABLE 16-5 Land Use in Latin America

Country	*Percentage Cultivated*	*Year*
Brazil	42.3	1950
Chile	29.4	1965
Argentina	23.3	1960
Mexico	23.1	1960
Peru	22.7	1961

Source: Agricultural Development in Latin America (Washington, D.C.: Inter-American Development Bank, April 1967), p. 115.

[9] Raúl Prebisch has often spoken about the weakness of rural demand being caused by the total system of land tenure in the countryside.

[10] See Garland P. Wood, "Agriculture and Social Change," in William Forn and Albert Blum (eds.), *Industrial Relations and Social Change in Latin America* (Gainesville: University of Florida Press, 1965), p. 14.

in most Latin American countries is not only the *latifundia* (large land holdings) and the *minifundia* (tiny land holdings) but also the dearth of arable soil which greatly affects levels of land utilization.

The complementarity between large and small land holdings is explicitly spelled out in Table 16–6.

TABLE 16-6 Agricultural Land Holdings (number and area by size classification) (hectares)

<table>
<tr><th>Country</th><th>Under 1</th><th>1–5</th><th>5–10</th><th>10–20</th><th>20–50</th><th>50–100</th></tr>
<tr><td>U.S. (1959) No.</td><td colspan="2">6.5</td><td colspan="2">21.9</td><td>17.8</td><td>32.0</td></tr>
<tr><td>Area</td><td colspan="2">.1</td><td colspan="2">1.9</td><td>4.3</td><td>17.4</td></tr>
<tr><td>Brazil (1960) No.</td><td>4.2</td><td>26.7</td><td>13.9</td><td>16.3</td><td>20.1</td><td>8.2</td></tr>
<tr><td>Area</td><td>—</td><td>.9</td><td>1.3</td><td>2.9</td><td>7.9</td><td>7.2</td></tr>
<tr><td>Argentina (1960) No.</td><td colspan="2">15.7</td><td colspan="2">24.0</td><td colspan="2">27.9</td></tr>
<tr><td>Area</td><td colspan="2">.1</td><td colspan="2">.9</td><td colspan="2">4.4</td></tr>
<tr><td>Chile (1955) No.</td><td>18.7</td><td>18.2</td><td>13.1</td><td>12.7</td><td>14.7</td><td>8.2</td></tr>
<tr><td>Area</td><td>—</td><td>.3</td><td>.5</td><td>1.0</td><td>2.5</td><td>3.1</td></tr>
<tr><td>Mexico (1960) No.</td><td colspan="2">65.7</td><td>7.0</td><td>9.7</td><td>5.1</td><td>4.3</td></tr>
<tr><td>Area</td><td colspan="2">.8</td><td>.4</td><td>1.2</td><td>1.5</td><td>2.5</td></tr>
<tr><td>Peru (1961) No.</td><td>34.1</td><td>49.0</td><td>9.0</td><td>3.6</td><td>2.0</td><td>.8</td></tr>
<tr><td>Area</td><td>.7</td><td>5.0</td><td>2.6</td><td>2.1</td><td>2.7</td><td>2.5</td></tr>
</table>

<table>
<tr><th>Country</th><th>100–200</th><th>200–500</th><th>500–1000</th><th>1000–2500</th><th>more than 2500</th></tr>
<tr><td>U.S. No.</td><td>12.7</td><td>5.4</td><td colspan="3">3.7</td></tr>
<tr><td>Area</td><td>14.8</td><td>12.2</td><td colspan="3">49.2</td></tr>
<tr><td>Brazil No.</td><td>4.7</td><td>3.5</td><td>1.2</td><td>.6</td><td>.4</td></tr>
<tr><td>Area</td><td>8.2</td><td>13.6</td><td>10.7</td><td>9.6</td><td>37.8</td></tr>
<tr><td>Argentina No.</td><td>12.9</td><td>8.4</td><td>5.4</td><td>3.3</td><td>2.5</td></tr>
<tr><td>Area</td><td>5.0</td><td>6.2</td><td>8.9</td><td>14.7</td><td>59.7</td></tr>
<tr><td>Chile No.</td><td>5.6</td><td>4.5</td><td>2.0</td><td>1.0</td><td>1.1</td></tr>
<tr><td>Area</td><td>4.2</td><td>7.6</td><td>7.6</td><td>7.6</td><td>65.5</td></tr>
<tr><td>Mexico No.</td><td>3.1</td><td>2.2</td><td>1.1</td><td colspan="2">1.7</td></tr>
<tr><td>Area</td><td>3.5</td><td>5.6</td><td>6.2</td><td colspan="2">78.4</td></tr>
<tr><td>Peru No.</td><td>.5</td><td>.4</td><td>.2</td><td>.1</td><td>.1</td></tr>
<tr><td>Area</td><td>3.2</td><td>5.6</td><td>5.7</td><td>8.9</td><td>61.0</td></tr>
</table>

Source: *Statistical Abstract of Latin America* (Los Angeles: University of California Press, 1967), pp. 110–111.

The figures are impressive in that they show in all of the countries a few landholders have most of the available land. Only in the United States are there many commercial farms of the fifty to one hundred hectare size in addition to the huge estates. All of the Latin American country samples show a coexistence of minifundias and latifundias. The largest acreage is held by very few while thousands upon thousands of farm plots exist under five hectares each.

The minifundia problem is particularly acute in Peru and Mexico. In Peru it is a result of the small communal lands held by indigenous groups in the altiplano who have existed on these traditional plots for many centuries. Many till the soil on nearby haciendas. In Mexico the number of minifundias has increased under agrarian reform. The Mexican government has made the division of the land a closely-held tenet of public policy. The large numbers of Mexicans who hold between under one and five hectares is symptomatic of this policy. However, even more significant is the fact that two-thirds of all Mexican land holdings form less than 1 per cent of all agricultural land. The minifundia problem is more extreme in Peru where over four-fifths of all land holdings comprise little more than 1 per cent of the total area. Nowhere in the United States and in these Latin American countries do the smallest property owners hold more than about 1 per cent of all the existing land. Brazil, Argentina, and Chile, along with the United States, have more moderate sized, commercially feasible farms than Mexico and Peru. Only the United States and Argentina sustain very large, usually highly mechanized, and very profitable farms—those between 100 and 200 hectares.

Given the general agreement among land economists that the most efficient farms are the family farms employing between two and four people and the multifamily farms employing up to twelve people it is instructive to examine Table 16-7. It points to the extraordinary concentration of hectares under the control of the large haciendas, which invariably seem to produce less than one might expect given available land and manpower. At the other end of the spectrum one is made aware again of the large numbers of very small units that appear wholly uneconomic and, at best, grow only enough to sustain the immediate family.

It is instructive that the two countries, Argentina and Brazil, which have better "utility ratios" have higher percentages of acreage under cultivation on family and multifamily medium-sized farms. Argentina has almost 60 per cent of her agricultural area in this class and Brazil 40 per cent. Further efficiency size data is provided for five countries.

With an overpopulated, underproductive agraria it is not surprising that a high proportion of people in Latin America are moving toward urban industria. Despite the fact that the urban industrialization base is still not fully developed in Latin America, the environment, chances for livelihood, and civilizing paraphernalia of modernity associated with city life favor the continuation of such internal migration.

The urbanization trend may be of universal benefit. Conditions are usually not worse in the city than in the country for those groups of migrants who initiate the move. Though enough industrial jobs, homes, and food are

TABLE 16-7 Relative Number and Area of Farm Units by Size Groups (percentage of country total in each size class)

Countries	*Subfamily**	*Family†*	*Multifamily Medium‡*	*Multifamily Large§*	*Total*
Argentina					
Number of farm units	43.2	48.7	7.3	0.8	100.0
Area in farms	3.4	44.7	15.0	36.9	100.0
Brazil					
Number of farm units	22.5	39.1	33.7	4.7	100.0
Area in farms	0.5	6.0	34.0	59.5	100.0
Chile					
Number of farm units	36.9	40.0	16.2	6.9	100.0
Area in farms	0.2	7.1	11.4	81.3	100.0
Peru					
Number of farm units	88.0	8.5	2.4	1.1	100.0
Area in farms	7.4	4.5	5.7	82.4	100.0

Source: Solon Barraclough and Arthur Domike, "Agrarian Structure in Seven Latin American Countries," *Land Economics*, vol. 42, no. 4 (November 1966), p. 395.

* *Subfamily:* Farms large enough to provide employment for less than two people with the typical incomes, markets and levels of technology and capital now prevailing in each region.

† *Family:* Farms large enough to provide employment for 2 to 3.9 people on the assumption that most of the farm work is being carried out by members of the farm family.

‡ *Multifamily Medium:* Farms large enough to provide employment for 4 to 12 people.

§ *Multifamily Large:* Farms large enough to provide employment for over 12 people.

TABLE 16-8 Relationships Between Value of Agricultural Production, Land, and Woik Force by Farm Size/Classification in Argentina, Brazil, and Chile

Country and Size Groups	*Per Cent of Total in Each Country* Agri. Land	Agri. W.F.	Value of Production
Argentina (1960)			
subfamily	3	30	12
family	46	49	47
multifamily medium	15	15	26
multifamily large	36	6	15
Brazil (1950)			
subfamily	0	11	3
family	6	26	18
multifamily medium	34	42	43
multifamily large	60	21	36
Chile (1955)			
subfamily	0	13	4
family	8	28	16
multifamily medium	13	21	23
multifamily large	79	38	57

Source: Barraclough and Domike, "Agrarian Structure in Seven Latin American Countries," p. 402.

not guaranteed in the urban centers, industria is still more dynamic than agraria, and if these groups of people will eventually be employed, housed, and fed it will probably be in urban rather than rural environments. Those who leave the rural or small village communities are those faring least well. Those who choose to remain are probably the best integrated in the rural life and most likely to benefit from creeping mechanization. For these individuals industrial mechanization and innovation would not be a threat to their community roles.

Also not all rural communities are uninterested in modernization, and all are not ultratraditional. Many of the urban political, economic, and social relationships will eventually involve rural communities. As has been justifiably pointed out, political participation at the local level is often more significant to the individual than a more mythical participation in the national society or in some national, collective movement. Effective participation at the local level may be more meaningful for political development, at some point, than national participation.[11] Given innovative leadership, rural communities may skillfully adapt to change without necessarily adapting to explicit urban sociological patterns.

Urban migration and a cautious distribution and utilization of the land are two feasible alternatives to Latin America's agrarian problems. However, even the best-intentioned land reform is subject to negative repercussions. For example, Mexico's thorough dedication to the redistribution of the land has given rise to extreme forms of unproductive minifundia. Mexico in her acts of land distribution has no counterpart in the developing world. Between 1915 at the height of the Zapatista concern for dividing up the land as a tenet of the Mexican revolution and 1960, 52 per cent of Mexico's farm families acquired some land. The decline in land concentration was a major achievement.[12] It has been more difficult to achieve the infusion of such productive inputs as technical skills and agricultural management.[13]

[11] Silvia Sigal, "Participation y sociedad nacional: El caso de las comunidades rurales Latinoamericanas," *Revista Latinoamericana de Sociologia,* vol. 3, no. 1 (March 1967), pp. 4–40. In fact it has been discovered in the Brazilian situation that precisely those peasants who do not participate effectively in the rural sector search out other organizational structures to provide them with some participatory role. See J. C. Van Es and Robert L. Whittenbarger, "Farm Ownership, Political Participation, and Other Social Participation in Central Brazil" (Unpublished Paper, Madison, Wisconsin, Land Tenure Center, July 1968), pp. 1–19.

[12] See the study of Hung-chao Tai, "Land Reform in the Developing Countries: Tenure Defects and Political Response" (Cambridge: Center for International Affairs, August 1967. Delivered at the American Political Science Association meeting September, 1967), pp. 82–92.

[13] William C. Thiesenhusen, "Grassroots Economic Pressures in Chile: An Enigma for Development Planners" (Publication of The Land Tenure Center, University of Wisconsin, February, 1967), p. 17.

If no jobs or land or housing is provided in rural areas, urbanization probably will continue to gain momentum. Thus to the degree that agrarian reform includes the redistribution of income as well as land will the flow to industria be slowed. A positive relationship may exist between economic development and societal mobility. To bring about structural changes that would stimulate investments and savings may at some point require agrarian reform. An efficiently controlled land distribution and reform policy would satisfy a considerable percentage of the rural population. However, agrarian reform has essentially been politically motivated. Allotments have been small and have been made as part of a short-run measure in the total process of industrialization. Often measures have been undertaken merely to give the urban industrial base a little more time to mature before being called upon to absorb rural migrants. Economic agrarian reform would require a maximum effort in the mechanization and commercialization of the farms. Labor-saving devices would again free surplus labor for internal migration.

Thus urbanization continues with no meaningful countertrend and has reached rather high proportions.

TABLE 16-9 Rural to Urban Migration Between 1950 and 1960

Country	*Percentage of 1950 Rural Pop. Migrating to Urban Areas*
Chile	29
Argentina	25
Brazil	19
Peru	14

Source: Barraclough and Domike, "Agrarian Structure in Seven Latin American Countries," p. 408.

Recent research on urban migrants has undercovered a surprising degree of satisfaction with their move to industria. The study of William Mangin offers a particularly thoughtful appraisal of the urban poor.

> Despite their poverty in relation to that of poor people in the United States, the fantastic disparity in wealth and power between the squatters and their own upper and middle classes, and the ambivalent attitude to the national governments reflected in the violence of the army and the police toward the squatters coupled with half-hearted attempts to assist them with housing, they are not alienated, hopeless people caught in a vicious circle of poverty. For most of the adults their condition in the squatter settlements is the best of their lives and a marked improvement on their previous two or three houses.[14]

[14] William Mangin, "Latin American Squatter Settlements: A Problem and a Solution," *Latin American Research Review*, vol. 2, no. 3 (Summer 1967), p. 91.

According to Mangin, these newly arrived rural migrants contribute in several substantial ways to national development. In building their squatter settlements they provide housing near their places of work, houses that the government would probably have been unable to provide without long delay. Again, and often hidden in national employment figures, many part-time and unskilled jobs are filled by squatters. Capitalization and development of small enterprises in these settlements provide income, services, and employment. Also important for political development, these migrant groups often develop community spirit and neighborhood loyalties which Mangin views as important social capital for the nation.[15]

[15] Ibid., pp. 65–90. For virtually the same arguments for the Peruvian case, see Henry Dietz, "Urban Squatter Settlements in Peru: A Case History and Analysis," *Journal of Inter-American Studies*, vol. 2, no. 3 (July 1969), pp. 353–370. For the Brazilian case of the "favelados," see Anthony Leeds and Elizabeth Leeds, "Brazil and the Myth of Urban Rurality: Urban Experience, Work, and Values in Squatments of Rio de Janeiro and Lima" (Unpublished ms, n.d.), p. 14.

CHAPTER 17 The Social System and Political Development

Before discussing the impact of the social system upon the levels of economic development and the political system, it is important to refer briefly to the role of both economic and political leadership. We have noted that the distribution of power and influence has broadened considerably since 1930 and that changes in political administrations brought new groups to positions of power that now fully share in the making of domestic policy. Many of the more significant changes in the power structure took place during the distributive period. It was during this period that we have the Cárdenas administration in Mexico, the Vargas administration in Brazil, the Popular Front in Chile, and Perón's government in Argentina. The advent of new groups, as Anderson establishes, has rarely overturned the political system but rather has shifted policy concerns and redistributed power, influence, and even prestige. Major societal eruptions have been few partly because continuing urban development has allowed for the political accommodation of new groups and the minimal satisfaction of their economic demands.

Elites and Entrepreneurs

There is no longer an unchallenged upper class—"oligarchic," "aristocratic," or otherwise in any of the five countries. Groups which were in positions of dominance during the aggregative phase have had to increasingly give up their hold on decision making or at least share their political and economic advantages with the middle, and in some cases, the lower classes of the society. In Mexico the upper classes were under severe attack during the later phases of the Mexican revolution, which culminated in the direct weakening of their economic power under Cárdenas. New political groups of civil servants and other elements of the middle class, laborers, and peasants were recognized as bargaining groups within the political process and integrated into the new institutionalized governing party.[1] Symptomatic of the political involvement of nonlanded groups was the reorganization and strengthening under Cárdenas of businessmen and industrialists into the CONCANACO (National Federation of Chambers of Commerce) and CONCAMIN (Confederation of Industrial Chambers of Mexico).[2]

It is generally agreed that the decline of the landed classes in Peru

[1] James W. Wilkie, *The Mexican Revolution: Federal Expenditure and Social Changes Since 1910*, pp. 70 ff.

[2] Frank R. Brandenburg, *The Making of Modern Mexico* (Englewood Cliffs: Prentice-Hall, 1964), pp. 88–90.

began by World War I and that middle class leadership assumed power after World War II.[3] The division of the "military-oligarchic" alliance under the presidency of Manuel Odría was a direct result of decreasing power.[4] The breach widened even further in 1962–63 when the military command supported the middle class leadership of President Belaúnde Terry. A new developmental military ideology coupled with the broad appeal of an aggregator-innovator party, the Acción Popular, succeeded in challenging the power of the so-called ruling "forty families".[5]

The year 1930 is popularly believed to be a watershed in Brazilian political evolution. The Vargas-led coalition of hitherto underrepresented forces successfully competed for public office and ushered in the distributive phase of Brazil's national development. Elements of the middle class and large factions of the younger army officers came to the support of Rio Grande do Sul in its attempt to end the monopoly of power shared by the two largest Brazilian states, São Paulo and Minas Gerais.[6] The upper classes could no longer expect the faithful patronage of the armed forces. No previous administrations were as receptive to the organizational and ideological goals of the laboring and middle classes as that of Vargas.

"The reign of the oligarchy" in Chile was ended during the Alessandri Administration and later under the military-dominated regimes of the late 1920s. Three experts on Chile, Silvert, Gil, and Halperin, agree that it was in 1920 that the dominance of these restricted interests came to an end.[7] On the other hand, in Argentina there was a relatively open interplay among several economic interests since the dictatorship of Manuel Rosas. This led to a steady accretion of new forces into the political arena, though penetration by the middle and lower classes was most intense under Irigoyen and Perón respectively. With the advent of universal suffrage in 1912 new economic groups entered the political system. At the same time the Conservative party began to decline. From a 96 per cent vote total in 1910 the party's electoral

[3] Arthur P. Whitaker, *United States and South America: The Northern Republics* (Cambridge: Harvard University Press, 1948), pp. 31 ff.

[4] Harold E. Davis, *Government and Politics in Latin America* (New York: Ronald Press, 1958), p. 159.

[5] Liisa North, *Civil-Military Relations in Argentina, Chile and Peru* (Berkeley: Institute of International Studies, 1966), pp. 52–57. The same point is made by Francois Bourricaud, "Structure and Function of the Peruvian Oligarchy," *Studies in Comparative International Development* vol. 11, no. 2 (New Brunswick, N.J.: Rutgers University, 1966), p. 30.

[6] Thomas E. Skidmore, *Politics in Brazil, 1930–1964* (New York: Oxford University Press, 1967), pp. 3–21.

[7] K. H. Silvert, *Chile: Yesterday and Today* (New York: Holt, Rinehart and Winston, 1965); Federico G. Gil, *The Political System of Chile* (Boston: Houghton Mifflin, 1966); Ernst Halperin, *Nationalism and Communism in Chile* (Cambridge: MIT Press, 1965.

support dropped to 21 per cent by 1930.[8] During the intervening two decades the urban, immigrant, middle class interests increasingly shared power with conservative elites. A decade later the Perón government mobilized the laborers.[9]

Thus economic and political leadership substantially changed since 1930 and in some cases before. Both the industrial revolution, which brought on rising sociopolitical expectations, and the rapid development in technology significantly changed the context in which elites must operate. With a shift in their class background, there has been a meaningful change in the value orientation of the leadership groups. The dynamism of the middle class weakened the traditional commitment to a preservator view of society. To see Latin American leadership groups as simply attempting to maintain the conventional socioeconomic and political relationships is to ignore the dynamism of the middle class.[10]

There are several reasons for the shift in elite attitude. Large landowners are becoming increasingly receptive to technical change and renovation that do not diminish profits. Often, of course, the response is reinforced by governmental activity in the area of agrarian reform and the implied threat to unproductive landholders. The military and church elites are also beginning to realize that their interests are not incompatible with rapid industrialization and economic development.

There remains the problem of secondary and university training patterns which often still emphasize the traditional pursuits, such as philosophy and law, to the detriment of engineering, agronomy, and the exact sciences.[11] A major institutional reassessment is occurring in the educational field, although professional attitudes of students (as future members of the political and economic elite) still appear to lag as a dimension of economic development.

A second major problem is the relative absence of entreprenurial skills and, what is apparently more important, dispositions. It is instructive that a

[8] Dario Canton, "Universal Suffrage as an Agent of Mobilization" (Paper presented to World Congress of Sociology, Evian, France, September, 1966), p. 22.

[9] See Jose Luís de Imaz, *Los que mandan* (Buenos Aires: Editorial Universitaria de Buenos Aires, 1964), for data on the impact of new groups within the elite structure.

[10] See George K. Blanksten, "Transference of Social and Political Loyalties," in B. F. Hoselitz and W. E. Moore, *Industrialization and Society* (Mouton: UNESCO, 1963), p. 187.

[11] Readers interested in Latin American problems of education and training at the secondary and university levels are advised to look at certain portions of two books: Frederick H. Harbison and Charles A. Myers (eds.), *Manpower and Education: Country Studies in Economic Development* (New York: McGraw-Hill, 1965), chapters by Morris Horowitz, William F. Whyte, and Rudolph Blitz; S. M. Lipset and Aldo Solari (eds.), *Elites in Latin America* (New York: Oxford University Press, 1967), pp. 343–513.

high proportion of the more active middle class is foreign born. Many of the immigrant groups were able to penetrate positions of great economic power because of the void left by the uninterested agrarian classes. Their innovative capabilities are not on par with similar groups in many other Western nations because of the ease with which they were able to achieve a measure of economic power. Because of their European culture, educational background, and basic (though often quite minimal) skills they managed to quickly achieve economic importance and attain considerable wealth. Their mobility pattern was cross cultural and horizontal rather than intercultural and vertical. Thus as several analysts have observed, the ambition function for entrepreneurs in Latin America is possibly less developed than in North America. It then becomes an important factor in how successful Latin American societies are in consciously building a national sense of mobility and economic drive which would pervade large elements of the present lower classes. Everett E. Hagen states the case in no uncertain terms:

> These facts raise the question why technological progress in Latin America has been so late to appear, not why it appeared so soon. The answer is dual. On the one hand, their conquest of the indigenous peoples gave many of the Europeans who came to Latin America positions of income and power through exploitation of their dominance over conquered peoples without the necessity of solving the problems of technological progress. Further, until new streams of migration set in during the last half of the nineteenth century the Europeans in Latin America were predominantly from the societies of Spain and Portugal, which the virus of technological progress had infected only lightly. They were of only weakly innovating stock.[12]

Another explanation of the relative weakness of the middle sectors in Latin America may be traced to their dependence on the initiative of monarchs, republican presidents and governors, dictators and military chieftains, and now, in many instances, central economic planners and government technicians. This can weaken the spirit of enterprise and self-reliance which,

[12] Everett Hagen, *On the Theory of Social Change* (Homewood, Ill.: Dorsey Press, 1962), pp. 23–24. Hagen in assessing the foreign innovator in Colombia essentially agrees with Gino Germani's analyses of the tremendous importance of the European immigrant in founding new industries and productively managing others. See Germani's *Politica y sociedad en una epoca de transición* (Buenos Aires: Editorial Paidos, 1965), p. 172. Dale Johnson, for example, takes a pessimistic view of the indigenous Chilean entrepreneur. He writes " . . . Most American observers, unfortunately, continue to think and write as if these industrial entrepreneurs were ex-artisans or poor, wandering immigrants of social marginality." Thus he agrees with Hagen's assessment of the dearth of native economic dynamism. See Dale L. Johnson, *Industrialization, Social Mobility, and Class Formation in Chile* (New Brunswick, New Jersey: Rutgers University, Studies in Comparative International Development, vol. 3, no. 7, 1967–68), p. 137.

according to Schumpeter and many others, are necessary ingredients of the entrepreneur.

The Social System and Political Development

In Part I we spoke of several components of political development: a stable, viable government which assumes an ever more responsible role within society and which, in turn, can expect increasing individual political participation, the free and unfettered organization of a multitude of interests, and properly channelled discontent and opposition. The type of evolutionary development taking place during the distributive phase of national development in Latin America confronts not only the economic obstacles mentioned earlier but perhaps the even more difficult barriers within the social system.

Much of the capabilities of a political system depend on the type of social system in which it seeks to make its influence felt. It invariably must face the seeming inpenetrables of not only sheer physical environment but such cultural responses as values and attitudes. As Max Weber has made clear people come by these values and attitudes through their "class status." According to Weber a person's status is related to his share of the goods and services available in society, the general conditions of his life, and his own subjective satisfaction or frustration.[13] The rigidity of class status is determined by the class structure and will depend on who owns the sources of wealth and who has some chance of acquiring part of that wealth. In income distribution it is apparent that there is an unequal class stratification in Latin America. However, the opportunity for sharing in a growing economy is increasing. Thus people who have acquired similar class status may be said to belong to the same social classes within various social systems. The levels of economic development and the proliferation of "civilizing paraphernalia" or modernity features cloud the observers' ability to make judgments of great precision on the class structure in Latin America. The changing dimension of the Latin American society has the effect of multiplying the types of social relationships. This makes any delegation of individuals to a particular social class difficult. Thus depending on one's point of departure the Latin American social system may be looked at from various viewpoints. This is no more graphically represented than in a recent sociological treatise on power in society. In Table 17-1, Gerhard Lenski depicts four ways of looking at a mythical Latin American social system.

Depending on which approach we take concerning the class categories (which are as complete as any) we may arrive at different conclusions regarding the distance between and among classes, the size of different classes, the

[13] Max Weber, *The Theory of Social and Economic Organization* (ed.), by Talcott Parsons (New York: Oxford University Press, 1947), p. 424.

TABLE 17-1

Political Class	*Property Class*	*Occupational Class*	*Ethnic Class*
Elite	Wealthy	Large Landowners	Spaniards
Bureaucracy	Middle Class	Indep. Farmers Officials Merchants Artisans	Mestizos
Apolitical Class	The Poor	Peasants Beggars	
Suspected Enemies of the Regime	The Impoverished	Prostitutes and Unemployed	Indians

Source: Gerhard Lenski, *Power and Privilege* (New York: McGraw-Hill, 1966), p. 80.

degree of mobility, and even questions suggesting relative stability or instability in the social system. Obviously important here are self-image, reputation, and prestige factors as well as more quantifiable participation, poverty, and race indicators. The nonquantifiable criteria seem to bear particular watching in Latin America where sociologists have often called attention to such social variables as style of conduct, education and other equally weighty considerations. Thus each of the above Lenski categorizations pertains to a distinct typology of social stratification, and the exclusive study of any one may lead to erroneous conclusions.

The pattern of social mobilization is certainly not becoming more polarized in Latin America but rather class demarcations tend to be less and less rigid. The generally open and competitive nature of the Latin American political system is lending itself to a greater interplay among a variety of values and ideologies. Even interclass behavior (witness the multitude of styles and attitudes of factions within the middle class) is not readily predictable in Latin America. The concessionary behavior on the part of the upper class, during the last four decades in particular, is now apparent in the middle class toward certain sectors of the skilled working classes. The capacity of both groups to avoid serious institutional conflicts has widened the areas of political compromise and has further assuaged class antagonisms.

Limited class conflicts in Latin America exist in restricted areas. Inflexible confrontations, however, are not occurring with as much frequency as has often been proposed. There has been in fact a good deal of agreement among certain segments of the various classes. A good number of values and attitudes are shared by significant portions of several classes. One reason for this may be that since World War II not only has interclass mobility been on the increase, but the industrialization process has brought comparative gain within the various classes.[14]

[14] Howard F. Cline aptly demonstrated the changing class structure in this sense. Taking Mexico between 1940 and 1960 he calculates a tremendous increase

For example, technological innovations in the agraria sectors benefit not only the upper-landed class but also the industrial and commercial classes who seek to sell their machinery and buy more and cheaper farm products. This in turn strengthens the wage structure in both the rural and urban areas. Attitudes toward trade in foreign goods and services are often held in common among farm and city business communities. A developmentally oriented military corps of engineers might find a favorable response from many sectors of society.

There is, however, the problem of disequilibrium which results when rapid interclass mobilization is sufficiently underway. Marginal groups which assume new social roles must adapt and react to new values, norms, and symbols.[15] The extent of disequilibrium is dependent upon governmental programs to alleviate new socioeconomic tensions, upon political party understanding of mobilizationally induced frustration, and upon the willingness of nonparty political groups to mitigate ideological rigidity. It is often much more beneficial for members of the political elite to work through existing political channels, collectively bargaining for incremental socioeconomic and political gains, and for lower class sectors to respond to economic incentives rather than to confront the entire system of resource allocation.

Given this level of political development and modernity as well as their economic and social structure, the five Latin American countries appear to meet many of William Kornhauser's criteria for a mass society as opposed to a communal and totalitarian one, though they are not yet differentiated enough to qualify as pluralist. As Kornhauser says:

> The theory of mass society does not imply a low valuation of democracy, but merely claims that certain tendencies in modern society must be checked if democracy is to remain strong. These tendencies are the loss of autonomy on the part of elites and the loss of independent group life on the part of the non-elites.[16]

Kornhauser's breakdown into four types of societies is an excellent means for observing different systems within a broad framework. Kornhauser's concern with the degree to which elites are accessible and the society-at-large is available for mass behavior has great relevance for Latin America.

> Pluralist society requires accessible elites and unavailable non-elites if it is to sustain its freedom and diversity—as in certain liberal

in the size of the stable and marginal middle classes as well as the "transitional" class. *Mexico: Revolution to Evolution* (New York: Oxford University Press, 1963), pp. 116, 121, 124.

[15] Wilbert E. Moore, *Order and Change: Essays in Comparative Sociology* (New York: John Wiley, 1967), p. 3.

[16] William Kornhauser, *The Politics of Mass Society* (New York: Free Press, 1959), p. 15. This agrees with Gino Germani's concern with the problems of integrating newly mobilized societal groups. See Gino Germani, *Politica y sociedad en una epoca de transición*, pp. 150–151.

> democracies. Elites are accessible in that competition among independent groups opens many channels of communication and power. The population is unavailable in that people possess multiple commitments to diverse and autonomous groups. The mobilization of a population bound by multiple commitments would require breaking up of large numbers of independent organizations, as totalitarian movements have sought to do.
>
> Mass society requires both accessible elites and available nonelites if it is to exhibit a high rate of mass behavior. Elites are accessible and non-elites are available in that there is a paucity of independent groups between the state and the family to protect either elites or non-elites from manipulation and mobilization by the other. In the absence of social autonomy at all levels of society, large numbers of people are pushed and pulled toward activist modes of intervention in vital centers of society; and mass-oriented leaders have the opportunity to mobilize this activism for the capture of power. As a result, freedom is precarious in a mass society.
>
> Totalitarian society requires an inaccessible elite and an available population if it is to sustain a system of total control from above—as in certain modern dictatorships. . . . The elite is inaccessible in that elite elements are selected and fixed through co-optation, by virtue of a monopoly over the means of coercion and persuasion in the hands of those at the apex of the structure. The population is available in that its members lack all those independent social formations that could serve as a basis of resistance to the elite. Instead, the population is mobilized by the elite through multiple organizations taken over or created for that purpose.
>
> Communal society requires inaccessible elites and unavailable non-elites if it is to sustain its traditional structure—as in certain medieval communities. Elites are inaccessible in that elite elements and standards are selected and fixed by traditional ascription. Non-elites are unavailable in that people are firmly bound by kinship and community. Such a population is very difficult to mobilize unless powerful forces have eroded communal ties, as happened in the late middle ages when the incipient process of urbanization and industrialization began their destruction of the medieval community, thereby unloosing portions of the population for participation in the various millennial movements that flourished during this period.[17]

The five countries bear quite striking resemblances to those which Kornhauser has classified as having a mass-based and oriented society, though communal and pluralist structures do exist in each of them. Certainly the totalitarian model of society does not readily pertain though as Kornhauser makes clear mass-societies are in a dynamic sociological condition that can go in either the pluralist or totalitarian direction. Much of the

[17] Ibid., pp. 40–41.

emphasis of this book has been predicated on the view that these five countries are moving, albeit imperfectly, toward a pluralist society. The elites are accessible and the masses potentially available. The intermediary group structures are at this time not yet well enough defined to comfortably allow for a positive pluralist assessment, even though a large number of minorities are clearly no longer available to mass demagoguery or revolutionary slogans.

The accessibility of the elites, and, concomitantly, the failure of a single elite to close off continual penetration of other leadership groups, has also vitiated against mass arousal against a monolithic hierarchy. Since Latin American political structures do not appear to be evolving into inaccessible leadership patterns, for a certain time they will be vulnerable to mass pressure by mobilized publics. Thus it becomes of singular importance that institutional stability be maintained, that the pressures of counter-elites be channeled, and that socioeconomic improvements be rapidly embarked upon. The social systems are in a dynamic phase in which accessible elites must integrate newly mobilized masses by democratic methods. In this sense they are the most vulnerable of the four societies. For a successful resolution of this transitional phase of development the primary task of the five countries is to create what Charles Anderson has called a ". . . society of responsible demands."[18]

These five Latin American countries are playing the game of the ". . . politics of catching up." Mass pressures mount on the political structure at the same time that governments are seeking developmental solutions. In this situation leadership may be less than completely tolerant of deviant directions that such pressures might take. Yet the public authorities generally do not seem to feel that government must completely dominate society or even that all demands must be squelched. Conditions do not warrant the often-made prediction that only a revolutionary response is possible. Though there certainly exists certain fertile ground for revolution, most of Latin America (certainly those nations more developed in manpower and resource potential) appears to be moving toward an instrumental redistribution of power under the auspices of increasingly modern and progressive leadership. As Charles Anderson has pointed out, in many cases the nonrevolutionary method is the cheaper, more efficient one. It is often cheaper to modernize the military, clergy, and the landowners than to destroy them as economic and human resources. It is cheaper to collectively bargain with labor and management than to suppress them. An incrementally-oriented political process appears at least as endowed as a revolutionary process in creating resources, if not in distributing them. Perhaps there is a growing realization that what apparently is the more difficult road is very often in reality the shorter road.

[18] Charles W. Anderson, *Politics and Economic Change in Latin America*, Ch. 12.

INDEX

A

Aggregative phase of political growth, 65, 91–109, 146 *t.*, 161

Agraria in Latin America, 308–311; agricultural land holdings, by area and size, 309 *t.*, 310; cultivated land, as percent of total land, 308 *t.*; *latifundios*, 282, 309; *minifundios*, 282, 309, 310, 312

Agriculture: percentage of GNP originating in, 293 *t.*; percentage of labor force employed in, 294, 294 *t.*

Aguirre Cerda, Pedro, 102, 128, 231

Alamán, Lucás, 69

Alberdi, Juan Bautista, 86

Alem, Leandro, 87–88

Alemán, Miguel, 113, 115, 116

Alessandri, Arturo, 100, 101, 128, 162, 217, 231, 316

Alessandri, Jorge, 129, 130

Allende, Salvador, 129–30, 193, 249 *n.*, 250

Alonso, José, 272

Alvear, Marcelo Torcuato de, 104–105

Anticlericalism, 207

Aramburu, Pedro, 138, 141, 142, 232

Argentina, 55, 61, 68, 77, 79, 89, 90, 100, 108; absence of established cultures during settlement of, 158–59; agricultural statistics for, 308, 309, 311; Catholic Church in, 135, 194, 268; Communist infiltration in, 107; Constitution of 1853, 86: content of, 193–94; constitutional system of, 179–80; during colonial period, 60, 61, 159–60; economic development in, 302; education in, 18–20, 23; establishment of YPF, 103; executive power in, 232–33; federalism in, 177, 178, 179, 182–83, 184, 238, 260, weakening of, 179, 182; immigration, 12, 164, 181; independence of, 83, 160; inflation in, 287, 288 *t.*, 289; interest groups in, 267–76; labor in (case study of a direct pressure group), 269–76; labor federations in, 106–107, COA, 107, CGT, 107, 137, 141, 267, 269–76, FORA, 106, 107, USA, 106, 107; legislature of, 233, 234; literacy rates in, 18; military (the) in, 268; modernity of, 44, 162, 163–64; nationalism in, 219–20; Perón, coup against, 138; Perón Constitution of 1949, 193, 195; Perón's military coup, 132–33; Perón's reforms, 135–38; Peronism, 106, 196, in post-Perón years, 138 *n.*, 139; political culture of, 158–66; political development of, 44, aggregative phase of, 103–107, 146 *t.*, authoritative phase of, 83–88, 146 *t.*, distributive phase of, 132–43, 146 *t.*; political instability in, 32, 33 *t.*, 142; political participation in, 161; political parties in, 39, 87–88, 103–107, 133–34, 138–40, 182, 201, 251–52, 254; Christian Democrats, 251, 268, Con-

Argentina (*cont.*)
servatives, 104, 105, 133, 162, 182, 234, 316, FORJA of Radical party, 105–106, MID, 182, 251, 268, Peronistas, 39, 134, 139, 140, 182, 219, 220, 232, 239, 251, 252, 268, 269–70, 272, 273, 275, Progressive Democrats, 88, 133, Socialists, 88, 107, 133, 162, UCRI, 138, 139, 182, 239, 251, UCRP, 138, 139, 182, 239, 251, 252, 275, Unión Cívica Radical, 87–88, 104, 105, 133, 138, 182; political succession in, 201; post-Perón politics in, 138–43; public control over corporations in, 303 *t.*; restrictions on the press in, 41–42; Sáenz Peña Law, 103; Sociedad Rural in, 267; Unión Industrial in, 267; Unitarians *vs.* Federalists, 160; universities in, 141; urbanization in, 9–12, 107; *see also* Frondizi, Arturo; International Statistics; Irigoyen, Hipólito; Perón, Juan; Rosas, Juan Manuel de
Authoritative phase of political growth, 64–65, 67–90, 146 *t.*, 150, 161
Automobiles in use, 27–28, 29 *t.*
Ávila Comacho, Manuel, 115, 116
Aztecs, the, 51, 52, 53, 54, 55, 159

B

Balbin, Ricardo, 138
Balmaceda, José, 81–82, 89
Belaúnde Terry, Fernando, 95, 117–18, 119, 201, 228, 247, 316
Benavides, Oscar, 74, 189
Black, C. E., 63 *n.*
Bolívar, Simón, 72, 178
Bolivia, 61, 72, 83; nationalism in, 208
Bolshevik Revolution, 162
Brasilia, 14, 122, 216
Brazil, 55, 83, 89, 100, 108, 316; absence of established cultures during settlement of, 158–59; agricultural statistics for, 308, 309, 311; Alliance for National Renovation (ARENA), 125, 126; Catholic Church in, 78; class distinction in, 165; Constitution of 1824, 75–76; Constitution of 1891, 96; Constitution of 1946, 121, 179; Constitution of 1967, 190–92; content of, 190–92; constitutional system of, 179–80; during colonial period, 58–59, 159–60; economic development in, 76–77, 97, 120, 122, 302; "Estado Novo" of Vargas, 120, 121; executive power in, 229–31; *fazenderios* of, 75, 76; federalsm in, 177, 178, 179, 183, 184, 238, 260, weakening of, 179, 183; immigration, 12, 181; independence of, 75; industrial and agricultural output in, 292, 292 *t.*, 293; industrialization in, 14; inflation in, 287, 288 *t.*, 289; Institutional Acts of, 124–25, 126; interest groups in, 264–65; legislature of, 233; military (the) in, 264–65; military coup in, 123–24; modernity of, 44; nationalism in, 216–17; political culture of, 158–66; political development of, 44, aggregative phase of, 96–98, 146 *t.*, authoritative phase of, 74–79, 146 *t.*, distributive phase of, 120–27, 146 *t.*, political instability in, 32, 33 *t.*, political parties in, 120–22, 125–26, 201, 248–49: Arena, 249, Modeb, 125, 126, 249, PSD, 121, 122, 201, 233, 248–49, PTB, 121, 122, 126, 201, 233, 248, reorganization of, 265, UDN, 121, 122, 201, 233, 248; political succession in, 201; population and national income of, by geographic region, 306 *t.*; public control over corporations in, 303 *t.*; regional relationship to economic and agricultural interests in, 183; restriction on the press in, 41–42; slavery in, 77–78, 89; United States and, 217; unwritten code of alternate succession to the presidency of, 98; Vargas coup, 97, 120; *see also* Goulart, João; International statistics; Kubitschek, Juscelino; Pedro II;

Quadros, Jañio; Vargas, Getúlio
Brazilian Empire, 75–79, 96
Brazilian Petroleum Corporation (Petrobras), 216
Buenos Aires, 10, 13, 14, 83–87, 107
Bulnes, Manuel, 80
Bustamente, José Luis, 95

C

Calles, Plutarco Elias, 112, 113, 116, 239
Campos, Roberto, 124
Capital formation, 286 *t.*
Cárdenas, Lázaro, 113–15, 116, 211, 247 *n.*, 315
Carranza, Venustiano, 112, 116
Castelo Branco, Humberto, 123, 217
Castillo, Ramón, 105, 133
Catholic church: in Argentina, 135, 194, 268; in Brazil, 78; in Chile, 80–81, 266, 266 *n.*; in Mexico, 68, 70, 93, 161, 164, 172, 188–89, 262; in Peru, 73, 164, 190, 264
Caudillos, local, 181, 182, 184
Central American Common Market, 284
Chile, 55, 72, 79, 88, 89, 108, 316; absence of established cultures during settlement of, 158–59; agricultural statistics for, 308, 309, 311; Catholic Church in, 80–81, 266, 266 *n.*; community-development program of, 34; Constitution of 1833, 80; Constitution of 1925, 100, 192, content of, 192–93; Corporación de Fomento (CORFO), 127–28; during colonial period, 59–60, 61, 159–60; economic development in, 302; executive power in, 231–32; freedom of assembly and speech in, 42, 128; freedom of press in, 41, 128; immigration, 164; independence of, 79, 160; inflation in, 287, 288 *t.*; interest groups in, 266; legislature of, 233–34; literacy rates in, 18; modernity of, 44, 162, 163–64; nationalism in, 208, 217–19; parliamentary government, period of, 98–100; "Pelucones" *vs.* "Pipiolos," 160; political culture of, 158–66; political development of, 43, aggregative phase of, 98–103, 146 *t.*, authoritative phase of, 79–83, 146 *t.*, distributive phase of, 127–32, 146 *t.*; political participation in, 161–62; political parties in, 39, 40, 80–81, 82, 99–102, 128–31, 201, 249–51, 254, Christian Democrats, 39, 129, 130, 131, 201, 206, 217, 219, 231, 232, 233, 239, 249, 250, 266, Communists (formerly Socialist Workers Party), 40, 99–100, 101, 128, 130, 201, 217, 218, Conservatives, 80, 99, 101, 102, 129, 131, 218, 219, 239, 250, Frente de Acción Popular (FRAP), 39 129, 130, 131, 219, Frente Democratico, 250, Liberals, 80, 81, 99, 100, 101, 128, 129, 131, 201, 218, 219, 239, 250, National Party, 81, 82, 250, Popular Union (UP), 232, 239, 250, 252–53, Radicals, 82, 99, 100, 102, 128, 130, 218, 219, 239, 249, 250, 251, Socialists, 101, 102, 217, 218, Unified Popular Action Movement (MAPU), 130, political stability in, 32–33; political succession in, 201; Popular Front in, 101–102, 106, 127, 128, 217–18, 250 *n.*, 315; public control over corporations in, 303 *t.*; Socialist Republic of (1932), 101; suppressed Nazi takeover in, 102; unitary type of government in, 178, 184; urbanization in, 9, 12; War of the Pacific, 73, 82, 89, 99, 162, 208, 214; *see also* Alessandri, Arturo; Frei, Eduardo; Ibañez, Carlos; International statistics
Chilean Student Federation (FECH), 266 *n.*
Christian Democracy, 205–206, 238
Class stratification in Latin America, 164–65, 319–23
Colombia, 61

Colonial period in Latin America, 57–62, 159–60
Communications: *see* Motion pictures; Newspaper circulation; Post office services; Radios; Telephones; Television
Communism, 206
Communist Party, 40, 99–100, 101, 107, 128
Conservatism, 203–204
Constitutions of Latin America, 185–95; Argentine, 86, 193–94; Brazilian, 75–76, 96, 121, 179, 190–92, 195; Chilean, 192–93, 195; Mexican, 69, 70–71, 112, 166, 179, 186–89, 195; Peruvian, 72, 73, 189–90, 195; principles in framing of, 186; *see also* listings under individual countries
Cortés, Hernán, 54, 212
Costa Rica, 231
Council of the Indies, 57, 61
Coups and revolutions, 198, 199–200
Cuba, 196, 231; Mexico and, 213–14

D

da Costa e Silva, Arthur, 125, 230, 264–65
Death rates, 14–16; *see also* International statistics: death(s)
Democracy, 203
Díaz, Felix, 111
Díaz, Porfirio, 72, 92–94, 111, 116
Díaz Ordáz, Gustavo, 115–16, 247 *n.*
Distributive phase of political growth, 65–66, 110–45, 146 *t.*, 163
Dutra, Eurico Gaspar, 98, 121

E

Echeverria Álvarez, Luis, 213
Economic development in Latin America, 300–303; patterns of, 301–302
Ecuador, 61
Education, 18–23; *see also* International statistics: education
Electoral process in Latin America, 35–37, 199
Encomienda system, 57, 60–61

F

Fascism, 206
Federalism, 183–84; defined, 178
Federalism in Latin America, 177–84; creation of, 178; weakening of, 184
Ferdinand VII, 67, 68
Fernandez, Avelino, 272
Frei, Eduardo, 129, 130, 131, 219, 231, 250
Frondizi, Arturo, 138–39, 219, 251, 267, 270, 273, 274

G

Garrastazú Médici, Emilio, 127, 217, 230
Germany, 102; *see also* West Germany
Gomes, Eduardo, 121
González Videla, Gabriel, 128, 218
Goulart, João, 122, 123, 125, 126, 217, 231, 233, 248, 264, 265
Gross national product, 286–87 *t.*, 290
Grove, Marmaduke, 101, 102, 217
Guerrero, Vicente, 68, 69

H

Hacienda system, 57 *n.*
Haya de la Torre, Victor Raúl, 74, 95
Hidalgo y Costilla, Miguel, 68, 160
Housing: number of persons per household, 18 *t.*
Huerta, Victoriano, 111

I

Ibañez, Carlos, 100–101, 102, 128–29, 217, 218
Ideologies, political: Christian democracy, 205–206; communism, 206; conservatism, 203–204; democracy, 203; fascism, 206; liberalism, 204–205; nationalism, 202, 203, 206–211; nazism, 206; socialism, 202, 205
Illia, Arturo, 139, 140, 270, 274
Immigration, 12, 163–64
Incas, the, 51–52, 53, 54, 55, 159
Independence movements, 160, 184–85, 207; *see also* listings for individual countries
India, 41, 178; *see also* International statistics
Industrial development, 13–14
Industrialization, 3, 163, 293–99; modernization and, 3–4, 283–85
Inflation, 287–88, 288 *t.*, 289
Interest groups in Latin America, 257–77; activities of, 259–60; channeled pressures of, 258, 259; direct pressures of, 258, 259; institutional, 258; latent pressures of, 258; noninstitutional, 258
International Petroleum Company, 118
International statistics (for individual countries): agriculture, 308, 309, 311, percentage of GNP originating in, 293, percentage of labor force employed in, 294; armed forces personnel, 38; automobiles in use, 29; central government expenditures for education, public health, and other social services, 302; death(s): per 1,000 population, 15, infant mortality rates, 15, from poliomyelitis, 16, from tuberculosis, 16; economically active population, distribution of, by industry, 295, females as percent of, 297, by occupation, 298; education: females as percent of total higher education enrollment, 23, literacy rates, 18, number of students in all educational institutions, by sex, 22, primary and secondary school pupils as percent of population, 19, public expenditures for, 34, student-teacher ratios, 20, students enrolled in higher education per 100,000 population, 19, universities, population in relation to, 21; electoral process: suffrage requirements, 35, voter participation, 37, votes for Communist Party, 40; Gini Index of inequality of income distribution before taxes, 291; gross domestic capital formation as percent of GNP, 286; gross national product, 286–87, per capita, 287; household(s), number of persons per, 18; immigrants per 1,000 population, 12; industrial/agricultural "utility ratio," 295; inflationary rates, 288; mail: domestic mail items per capita, 26, foreign mail items per capita, 31; medical care: inhabitants per hospital bed, 17, inhabitants per physician, 17; motion pictures: films produced, 28, per capita attendance, 27; national development in postindependence Latin America, 146; newspaper circulation, 24; nutrition consumption per person, 17; political stability and instability in Latin America, 35; population, 7–8, annual rate of increase in cities over 20,000 population, 11, between ages 20 and 60, 296, in cities over 100,000 population, 9, density of, 8, of largest city, as percent of total population, 10, percent of, of working age (15–64), 297, rate of increase, 9, in towns over 20,000 population, 100, in urban areas, by sex, 12; radios per 1,000 population, 25; rural to urban migration, 313; telephones, 26; television sets per 1,000 population, 28; union membership, 38; visitors from leading countries of origin, 30; wage and

International statistics (*cont.*)
salary earners as percent of working-age population, 298
Irigoyen, Hipólito, 88, 103–105, 106, 162, 179, 182, 316
Italy, 41; *see also* International statistics
Iturbide, Augustín de, 68, 69

J

Japan, 41; *see also* International statistics
João VI, King of Portugal, 75
Juárez, Benito, 70, 71, 92
Judiciary system in Latin America, 235–36; Continental codification system of law, 235
Justo, Agustín, 105
Justo, Juan B., 88, 107

K

Kubitschek, Juscelino, 122, 125, 248, 249, 264

L

Labor force in Latin America, 295–99
Lacerda, Carlos, 121, 122
Latifundios, 282, 309
Latin America: administrative dominance in, 225–33; *agraria* in (*see* Agraria in Latin America); class stratification in, 164–65, 319–23; colonial period in, 57–62, 159–60; communication in, 24–28; constitutions of, 185–95 (*see also* Constitutions of Latin America); coups in, 198, 199–200; during colonial period, 57–62, 159–60, changes under Bourbon dynasty, 60–61, 160, Council of the Indies, 57, 61, Ministry of Marine and Indies, 61; during indigenous period, 49–55, Spanish quest for riches, 49–50 (*see also* Aztecs; Incas; Mayas); early organizational conflicts in, 160–61; economic development in, 300–303; education in, 18–23, 171–72; electoral process in, 35–37, 199; federalism in, 177–84 (*see also* Federalism in Latin America); food consumption by the poorer classes in, 303, 305 *t.*; gross national product in, 286–87, 290; immigration to, 12, 163–64; independence movements in, 160, 184–85, 207 (*see also* listings for individual countries); industrial sector *vs.* agrarian sector, 163; inflation in, 287–89; institutional instability in, 225; interest groups in, 257–77; investment patterns in, 290; judiciary system in, 235–36; labor force in, 295–99; landholding system in, 282, 309–310; legislative branches in, 232–34; military's role in, 238; modernity in, 1–2, 162, indices of, 6–31; mortality rates in, 15; nonparty political groups in, 257–77; political culture of, 153–76 (*see also* Political culture of Latin America; political development in (*see* Political development in Latin America; Political development in postindependence Latin America); political ideologies in, 202–222 (*see also* Ideologies, political); political legitimacy in, 196–201; political parties in (*see* Political parties in Latin America); population of, 6–11; poverty in, 313–14; presidential authority in, 196 *ff.*, 225–33; public control of corporations in, 302, 303 *t.*; revolutions in, 198, 199–200; rise of middle class in, 315–19; social services in, expansion of, 34; social

system in, 164–65, 319–23; statistics for individual countries (*see* International statistics); tourism in, 29–30, 285; urban-rural imbalance in, 283; urbanization in, 9–14, 107, 310, 312–14; women in, 22–23, 36, 169, 170; world trade of, 284, 289; *see also* Argentina; Brazil; Chile; International statistics; Mexico; Peru
Latin American Free Trade Agreements, 284
Leadership during postindependence political development, 64–66; *see also* Presidential authority in Latin America
Leguía, Augusto, 73, 74
Levingston, Roberto Marcelo, 142
Liberalism, 204–205
Lima, Peru, 10, 13, 14
Literacy rates, 16, 18; voting and, 35–36
Lombardo Toledano, Vicente, 114, 116, 246
Lonardi, Eduardo, 138
López, Francisco Solano, 77
López Mateos, Adolfo, 115, 116, 213

M

Machismo complex, 170, 212
Madero, Francisco, 111, 116
Mauá, Baron, 75–77, 89
Maximilian, 71, 89
Mayas, the, 51, 52, 53, 54
Medical care: inhabitants per hospital bed, 17 *t.*; inhabitants per physician, 17 *t.*
Mestizo, the, 163, 167, 170, 175, 212
Mexican-American War, 69, 180–81
Mexican Revolution, 94, 111–12, 166, 181, 202, 211, 213, 262
Mexicanization legislation, 114–15, 116
Mexico, 79, 89, 100, 108, 122, 157, 285; agricultural sector of GNP, changes in, 291 *t.*, 292; agricultural statistics for, 308, 309; Catholic Church in, 68, 70, 93, 161, 164, 172, 188–89, 262; *cientificos* of, 94, 116; class distinction in, 165; Constitution of 1824, 69; Constitution of 1857, 70–71; Constitution of 1917, 112, 166, 179, 186, article defining government's inviolable ownership of lands, waters, and subsoil, 186, article referring to church and clergy, 188, as basis for later Latin American constitutions, 186, content of, 186–89, labor and social security articles of, 187–88; constitutional system of, 179–80; Cuba and, 213–14; cultural gap in, 175; dependence on the mother in, 170–71; "Dissolution Act" of, 175; distribution of persons by income, in urban and rural areas, 306 *t.*; during colonial period, 56–58, 61, 159–60, *encomienda* system, 57, 60–61; during indigenous period (*see* Aztecs); economic development and modernization of, 93–94, 301–302; economic growth in, 115–16, indices of, 291 *t.*; economic independence of women in, 169, 170; educational system in, 171–72, Universidad Nacional Autónoma, 171; effect of "mi tierra" on regionalism and centralization in, 181; executive power in, 226–28; expropriation of foreign oil companies in, 114, 211; federalism in, 177, 178, 179, 180–82, 184, 238, 260, effect of PRI on, 181, weakening of, 179, 180; Federalists *vs.* Centralists; foreign domination in important sectors of the economy, 92 *n.*, 93, 93–94 *n.*; freedom of press in, 41, 42; growth of middle class in, 169; immigration, 12, 181; independence of, 68–69, Plan of Iguala, 68, 160; industrial sector of GNP, changes in, 291 *t.*, 292; interest groups in, 261–63; Juárez Law, 70, 166; labor federations in, 113, 114, CROM, 113,

Mexico (*cont.*)
CTM, 114; land distribution in, 312; legislature of, 233; Lerdo Law, 70, 71, 92, 166; local *caudillos* of, 181, 182; *machismo* complex of males in, 170, 212; *mestizos* of, 163, 167, 170, 175, 212; modernity of, 44; National Financiera of, 113, 127; nationalism in, 208, 211–14; peasant organization (CNC) in, 39, 114; Plan of Ayutla, 70; political culture of, 158–66, case study of political communication, 167–76; political development of, 43, aggregative phase of, 92–94, 146 *t.*, authoritative phase of, 68–72, 146 *t.*, distributive phase of, 110–16, 146 *t.*; political participation in, 161; political parties in, 174, 200, 245–46, 254, CCI, 247 *n.*, MLN, 247 *n.*, PAN, 172, 181, 239, 245–46, 262, PPS, 246, PRI, 32, 39, 113, 114, 115, 116, 166, 172, 173, 174, 179, 181, 200, 213, 227–28, 239, 245–46, 261–63, UNS, 246; political stability in, 32–33; political succession in, 200; public control over corporations in, 303 *t.*; Reform Laws of 1859, 71, 93; role of the press in, 173–74; strengthening of businessmen and industrialists in, 315; structured social environment of, 158–59; United States and, 167–68, 180–81; *see also* Calles, Plutarco; Cárdenas, Lázaro; Díaz, Porfirio; International statistics; Juárez, Benito
Mexico City, 10, 13
Minifundios, 282, 309, 310, 312
Ministry of Marine and Indies, 61
Mitre, Bartolomé, 86, 87, 90
Modernity: industrialization and, 3–4; in Latin America, 1–2, 6–31, 162; level of, *vs.* processes of modernization, 4; use of term, 3
Modernization, 5, 281–85; process of, *vs.* level of modernity, 4; urbanization and, 12
Molotov–von Ribbentrop nonaggression pact, 102, 114
Montt, Manuel, 80, 81, 89, 161
Morelos, José María, 68
Motion pictures, 26–27; films produced, 28 *t.*; per capita attendance, 27 *t.*

N

Napoleon III, 71
Nationalism, 202, 203, 206–211; defined, 206–207; in Latin America, 207–211
Nazism, 102, 206
Newspaper circulation, 24–25
Nigeria, 41, 178; *see also* International statistics

O

Obregón, Álvaro, 111, 112, 116
Odría, Manuel, 95, 96, 201, 239, 316
O'Higgins, Bernardo, 79–80
Onganía, Juan Carlos, 140–42, 143, 220, 232, 274
Ongaro, Raimundo, 274
Ortiz, Roberto, 105

P

Panama Canal, 215
Paraguay, 61, 77, 83
Paraguayan War (War of the Triple Alliance), 77, 162, 208
Pedro I of Brazil, 75–76
Pedro II of Brazil, 76–79, 96, 161, 179, 216, 230
Perón, Juan, 85, 86, 104, 105–106, 132–38, 179, 218, 219, 220, 232, 269; "justicalism" of, 134; reforms of, 135–38

Peru, 79, 83, 88, 100, 108, 315–16; agricultural statistics for, 308, 309, 311; *Aprismo* in, 214–15; Catholic Church in, 73, 164, 190, 264; class distinction in, 165; community-development program of, 34; Constitution of 1828, 72; Constitution of 1920, 73; Constitution of 1933, 189, content of, 189–90; during colonial period, 58, 61, 159–60; during indigenous period (*see* Incas); economic development in, 302; executive power in, 228–29; independence of, 72; industrial law of July, 1970, 119; interest groups in, 263–64; legislature of, 233; military dominance in, 72, 73, 74, 95, 263; modernity of, 44; nationalism in, 208, 214–15; 1968 junta in, 118; political culture of, 158–66; political development of, 44, aggregative phase of, 95–96, 146 *t.*, authoritative phase of, 72–74, 146 *t.*, distributive phase of, 117–19, 146 *t.*; political instability in, 32, 33 *t.*; political parties in, 39, 95, 117–18, 200–201, 247–48, 254, Acción Popular (AP), 39, 95, 117, 118, 201, 228–29, 239, 247, 249, 264, 316, Apristas, 39, 74, 95, 96, 166, 189, 201, 202, 228–29, 233, 239, 247–48, 253, Christian Democrats, 117, 239, 247, MDP, 247, Odriistas (UNO), 233, 239, 247; political succession in, 200–201; population and income of, by geographic region, 306 *t.*; restriction on the press in, 42; seizure of IPC petroleum fields, 118; structured social environment of, 158–59; unitary type of government in, 178; War of the Pacific, 73, 82; *see also* Belaúnde Terry, Fernando; International statistics; Odría, Manuel
Pizarro, Francisco, 55
Political culture: defined, 149–51
Political culture of Latin America, 153–76; federalism and, 177–84; ideologies and, 202–222
Political development: components of, 4–5, 31
Political development in Latin America, 1–2, 31–46; absence or presence of freedom of the press, 41–42; assessments of political stability, 32–33; Communist Party, 40 (*see also* Communist Party); freedom of assembly and speech, 42; governmental responsibility, 34; interest groups, 41 (*see also* Interest groups); peasant organizations, 39; political parties, 39 (*see also* Political parties); union membership, 38–39, 106–107; voter participation, 34–37
Political development in postindependence Latin America, 63–143, 150; aggregative phase, 65, 91–109, 146 *t.*, 161; authoritative phase, 64–65, 67–90, 146 *t.*, 150, 161; distributive phase, 65–66, 110–45, 146 *t.*, 163; leadership during, 64–66
Political ideologies, 202–222; *see also* Ideologies, political
Political legitimacy in Latin America, 196–201
Political modernization, 4 *n.*; phases of, 63–64 *n.*
Political participation, 37, 161–62
Political parties: typology of, 241–45, 252
Political parties in Latin America, 39, 157–58, 237–56; development of, in twentieth century, 239; during aggregative phase, 92, 95–96, 99–102, 103–107; during authoritative phase, 74, 80–82, 87–88; during distributive phase, 112–15, 117–18, 120–22, 125–26, 128–31, 133–34, 138–40; *see also* listings under individual countries
Political socialization, 156
Political stability, 32–33
Population: *see* International statistics

Portales, Diego, 80, 89, 178
Prado, Manuel, 95, 247
Presidential authority in Latin America, 196 *ff*., 225–33
Prestes, Luis Carlos, 97
Prieto, Joaquín, 80

Q

Quadros, Jañio, 122–23, 125, 126, 127, 201, 216, 248, 264

R

Radios in use, 25
"Reformmongering," 157
Revolutions and coups, 198, 199–200
Reyes, Bernardo, 111
Rios, Juan Antonio, 128
Rivadavia, Bernardo, 84
Roca, Julio Argentino, 87, 88
Rosas, Juan Manuel de, 77, 84–86, 90, 92, 316
Ross, Gustavo, 102
Ruiz Cortines, Adolfo, 115, 116

S

Sáenz Peña, Luis, 87
Sáenz Peña, Roque, 103
San Martín, José de, 68, 72, 79, 178
Sánchez Cerro, Luis, 74
Santa Anna, Antonio López de, 69, 70
Santiago, Chile, 10, 13, 14
São Paulo, Brazil, 10, 14
Sarmiento, Domingo Faustino, 87, 90, 179
Siquieres, David, 175
Social services: expansion of, 34
Social system in Latin America, 319–23
Socialism, 202, 205
Socialization, political, 156
Soviet Union, 102, 178, 180
Stalin Constitution of 1936, 187, 195

T

Tables, statistical: *see* International statistics
Telephones in use, 26
Television sets, 27, 28 *t*.
Tomic, Radomiro, 130
Torre, Lisandro de la, 88

U

Union membership, 38–39, 106–107; *see also* Argentina: labor federations in
Unitary governments, 178, 183–84, 238
United States, 41, 180; Brazil and, 217; Mexico and, 167–68, 173, 180–81; *see also* International statistics
Urbanization, 9–14, 107; industrial development and, 13–14; trend in, 310, 312–14
Uriburu, José, 105, 106
Urquiza, Justo José de, 85, 86, 87
Uruguay, 20, 61, 77, 83, 113, 231, 254, 285

V

Vandor, Augusto, 275
Vargas, Getúlio, 98, 120–21, 179 183, 201, 216, 230, 264, 315, 316
Vasconcelos, José, 112, 215
Velasco Alvarado, Juan, 118, 215, 264
Venezuela, 61, 122, 254; Christian Democracy in, 206
Villa, Francisco "Pancho," 111, 112
Voter participation, 34–37

W

War of the Pacific, 73, 82, 89, 99, 162, 208, 214
War of the Triple Alliance, 77, 162
West Germany, 41, 178; *see also* International statistics
Women: economic independence of, in Mexico, 169, 170; position of, in Latin America, 22–23; suffrage for, 36

Z

Zapata, Emiliano, 111, 112